TRIAL PRACTICE LIBRARY: TRIAL TECHNIQUES FROM WILEY LAW PUBLICATIONS

CIVIL DISCOVERY AND DEPOSITIONS (SECOND EDITION)
Reagan Wm. Simpson

CIVIL JURY SELECTION (SECOND EDITION)
Arne Werchick

COURTROOM PSYCHOLOGY FOR TRIAL LAWYERS
Thomas Sannito and Peter J. McGovern

THE DEPOSITION HANDBOOK (SECOND EDITION)
Dennis R. Suplee and Diana S. Donaldson

DESTRUCTION OF EVIDENCE
Jamie S. Gorelick, Stephen Marzen, and Lawrence Solum

DOMBROFF ON UNFAIR TACTICS (SECOND EDITION)
Mark A. Dombroff

EVIDENCE IN CHILD ABUSE AND NEGLECT (SECOND EDITION)
John E.B. Myers

EXPERT WITNESSES: DIRECT AND CROSS-EXAMINATION
William G. Mulligan

FLORIDA TRIAL EVIDENCE
Hal P. Dekle and Don Beverly

JUDGMENT ENFORCEMENT PRACTICE AND LITIGATION
James J. Brown

JULIEN ON SUMMATION
Alfred S. Julien

LITIGATION FORMS AND CHECKLISTS
Nancy F. Schleifer

LITIGATION FORMS AND CHECKLISTS (DISK EDITION)
Nancy F. Schleifer

LITIGATING INSURANCE CLAIMS: COVERAGE, BAD FAITH AND BUSINESS DISPUTES
Guy O. Kornblum and William A. Cerillo

MAKING TRIAL OBJECTIONS
James F. McCarthy, Sr., Editor

MASTERS OF TRIAL PRACTICE: TECHNIQUES OF 22 NATIONALLY RECOGNIZED ADVOCATES
Janine Warsaw, Editor

THE PERSUASION EDGE
Richard J. Crawford

STRATEGIC USE OF SCIENTIFIC EVIDENCE
John A. Tarantino

TRIAL DIPLOMACY JOURNAL
John F. Romano and Rodney G. Romano, Editors

TRYING CASES TO WIN
Herbert J. Stern

TRYING CASES TO WIN: CROSS-EXAMINATION
Herbert J. Stern

TRYING CASES TO WIN: DIRECT EXAMINATION
Herbert J. Stern

THE WINNING EDGE: EFFECTIVE COMMUNICATION AND PERSUASION TECHNIQUES FOR LAWYERS
Richard H. Lucas and K. Byron McCoy

JUDGMENT ENFORCEMENT PRACTICE AND LITIGATION

SUBSCRIPTION NOTICE

This Wiley product is updated on a periodic basis with supplements to reflect important changes in the subject matter. If you purchased this product directly from John Wiley & Sons, Inc., we have already recorded your subscription for this update service.

If, however, you purchased this product from a bookstore and wish to receive (1) the current update at no additional charge, and (2) future updates and revised or related volumes billed separately with a 30-day examination review, please send your name, company name (if applicable), address, and the title of the product to:

Supplement Department
John Wiley & Sons, Inc.
One Wiley Drive
Somerset, NJ 08875
1-800-225-5945

For customers outside the United States, please contact the Wiley office nearest you:

Professional and Reference Division
John Wiley & Sons Canada, Ltd.
22 Worcester Road
Rexdale, Ontario M9W 1L1
CANADA
(416) 236-3580
Phone: 1-800-263-1590
Fax: 1-800-675-6599

John Wiley & Sons, Ltd.
Baffins Lane
Chichester
West Sussex, PO19 1UD
UNITED KINGDOM
Phone: (44) (243) 779777

Jacaranda Wiley Ltd.
PRT Division
P.O. Box 174
North Ryde, NSW 2113
AUSTRALIA
PHONE: (02) 805-1100
Fax: (02) 805-1597

John Wiley & Sons (SEA) Pte. Ltd.
37 Jalan Pemimpin
Block B # 05-04
Union Industrial Building
SINGAPORE 2057
Phone: (65) 258-1157

JUDGMENT ENFORCEMENT PRACTICE AND LITIGATION

JAMES J. BROWN

Columbia, Maryland

Wiley Law Publications

JOHN WILEY & SONS, INC.

New York • Chichester • Brisbane • Toronto • Singapore

This text is printed on acid-free paper.

Library of Congress Cataloging-in-Publication Data

ISBN 0-471-52838-2

Printed in the United States of America

10 9 8 7 6 5 4 3 2 1

To my wife, Alice, and my children,
Tod, Scott, Christine, and Danny.

PREFACE

Collecting and enforcing judgments is an important process in American jurisprudence. For many years of its history, the judgment enforcement process was shrouded in mystery, because the legal practice of collections was delegated to a very few specialized practitioners of the art and considered beneath the legal abilities of some professionals. However, in the last 20 years, judgment enforcement practice has come out of the closet and become a respected practice in even the major law firms in this country. The reason is that in hard economic times, clients need to have debts collected and judgments enforced. As many other forms of legal business have dried up, collections, judgment enforcement, and receiverships abound and become viable sources for law firm profits. In efficiently handling these legal matters, many professionals have found that there is money to be made in debt collection, judgment enforcement, and receivership practice. Because of the large number of substantial and complex cases being litigated, and the diversity of citizenship among creditor and debtor, federal courts are being used with more and more frequency.

Although I have litigated in this area for over 23 years, I have not found a comprehensive handbook written on this subject that is immediately useful as a desktop reference for lawyers, paralegals, law students, business persons, and other professionals needing information about the judgment enforcement process, in general, and federal judgment enforcement practice, in particular. This book is designed to be a definitive handbook that explains this subject in a simple, straightforward manner, with emphasis on this practice in federal courts. Naturally, because Federal Rule of Civil Procedure 69 incorporates state practice, there will be much discussion of how judgment enforcement practice works in the federal courts using particular state practices. However, it is not the purpose of this book to discuss how the practice works with every judgment enforcement matter in every state. That subject matter would be too detailed and too large to fit into a desk reference handbook. However, the discussion of federal rules and practice is useful, because many state procedural rules are now modeled on federal practice.

I believe that this book will be a valuable and essential handbook for every professional who wants an understanding of the judgment enforcement process, some details and explanation on its unique and unusual methodologies, and its practical application and strategies. Whether the professional using this book is experienced in the judgment enforcement and collection process, or whether this is the professional's first foray into this complex process, this book should serve as a useful and informative research and strategy tool on a number of important topics. To my knowledge this is the first book to address this topic in one, easy to use, handbook. The book is designed to give an overview of the general principles, the practice methods, the applicable rules, the important federal statutes (with particular emphasis on the application of the Federal Debt Collection Procedures Act of 1990)[1] (FDCPA), the leading federal case law, and some forms and strategy on this topic.

For example, the chapters in this book include particular discussion and explanation of the following matters:

1. The steps in the federal judgment enforcement process, including registering, preserving, and securing the judgment by maintaining the status quo during appeal and enforcement.
2. The steps in understanding the judgment debtor, obtaining basic information about the individual and corporate debtor, and understanding enforcement strategy for the small and large judgment enforcement case.
3. The steps in understanding the broad range of inquiry, the application of federal evidentiary privileges, and the basic evidence to establish in discovering and tracing the debtor's assets in federal court.
4. The steps in postjudgment discovery methods, including supplementary proceedings, interrogatories, requests for production of documents, informal discovery, targets of discovery, and methods for handling some unfair litigation tactics in such discovery.
5. The steps in handling the postjudgment execution process, including the specific execution process by the United States under the FDCPA, and the specific process necessary for such unique items as writs ne exeat republica, execution against airplanes, execution against state and local governments, execution against corporate stock, body execution, and search and seizure issues in the postjudgment process.
6. An analysis of some of the major theories of recovery in the postjudgment litigation process, including: (a) the fraudulent transfer claim; (b) the constuctive trust fund claim; (c) the piercing the corporate veil claim; and (d) the federal priority statute claim.[2]
7. Analysis of the process of using receivership as a collection device in federal court, including a discussion of the grounds for the appointment of a receiver, receivership in judgment enforcement and foreclosure and under the FDCPA, bar date for claims in a receivership, receivership

[1] Codified in 28 U.S.C. §§ 3001–3308.

[2] Codified in 31 U.S.C. § 3713.

jurisdiction and control over the property of the receivership estate, receivership stay orders, including the antibankruptcy injunction, and litigation by the receiver.

The idea of this book is that professionals will have a useful and informative handbook at their fingertips for easy access in approaching and attempting to solve the most important problems in the judgment enforcement process. It is my sincere hope that this book will save the professional time and energy in approaching this subject matter, and will be a new resource and armament in the library of lawyers, paralegals, law students, business persons, and other professionals.

The views expressed in this book are the views of the author and contributors, and do not represent the official positions of the Department of Justice.

Columbia, Maryland
February 1994

JAMES J. BROWN

ACKNOWLEDGMENTS

I would like to acknowledge the contribution of Eric S. Benderson, Esq., for the preparation of **Chapter 7** on "Receiverships as a Collection Device," and of Linda Samuel, Esq., for her sections of **Chapter 1** on foreign judgment enforcement matters. I also wish to acknowledge the use of some of the outline of Claude D. Brown in preparation of the materials in **Chapter 5.** I wish to acknowledge the assistance of Julie Ramirez, Dusty Strong, John Moore, Danita Lee, Karl Geercken, Mark Reene, and Rajiv Madden in research assistance on some of the research for this book. I also wish to acknowledge the assistance of Sharon Hardy in typing some of the forms for this book.

ABOUT THE AUTHOR

James J. Brown received his B.A. in History from the University of Texas (Austin) in 1968, and his J.D. from Boston College Law School in 1971. Prior to joining the Department of Justice (Department) as a trial attorney in March of 1976, Mr. Brown worked for almost five years as an attorney with Levy, Winer, a private law firm in Greenfield, Massachusetts. From 1976 until 1985, Mr. Brown was a trial attorney and later deputy chief of the Judgment Enforcement Unit of the Civil Division of the Department. During the period of July 1, 1985, to July 1, 1987, Mr. Brown worked as a senior associate in the bankruptcy and commercial litigation section of Weinberg and Green, a private law firm in Baltimore, Maryland. Upon his return to the Department in July of 1987, Mr. Brown worked as a trial attorney with the Environmental Enforcement Section of the Environmental and Natural Resources Division. On July 2, 1990, Mr. Brown became a trial attorney with the Asset Forfeiture Office of the Criminal Division of the Department.

Since 1977, Mr. Brown has been a frequent lecturer throughout the United States for U.S. attorney's conferences, government agency conferences, the private bar, and state and national associations. He has taught and written on various aspects of enforcing judgments, tracing assets and federal forfeiture law. Mr. Brown is also the author of eight legal articles and reviews published in various legal periodicals. Mr. Brown is the recipient of several awards from the Department of Justice, including Special Achievement, Distinguished Service, and numerous Outstanding Performance Awards, and has been selected to appear continuously since 1989 in Who's Who in American Law, based on his professional achievements.

ABOUT THE CONTRIBUTORS

Eric S. Benderson has practiced law for the last 25 years in Washington, D.C., where he has specialized in complex commercial litigation, particularly in the areas of bankruptcy and federal equity receiverships. He has contributed articles to a number of legal publications and is a frequent lecturer on various commercial litigation topics. At present he is Associate General counsel for Litigation at the U.S. Small Business Administration. He is an honors graduate of George Washington University School of Law and holds a Bachelor of Arts degree from Syracuse University and a Master of Arts degree from Columbia University.

Linda M. Samuels has served since 1990 as a Special Counsel for International Forfeiture Matters at the Asset Forfeiture Office, Criminal Division, United States Department of Justice in Washington, D.C. She spent six years before that as a Trial Attorney in the Commercial Litigation Branch of the Civil Division of the Department of Justice. Her educational background includes a B.S. degree from the Pennsylvania State University (1978), Law Degree from Catholic University Law School, Washington, D.C. (1981), and Master of Laws degree from Georgetown University Law School, Washington, D.C. (1986). She is a member of the bars of the District of Columbia, Pennsylvania, and the United States Claims Court.

SUMMARY CONTENTS

DETAILED CONTENTS

CHAPTER 1

BASIC ASPECTS OF JUDGMENT ENFORCEMENT*

* The author acknowledges the contribution of Linda M. Samuel in the preparation of §§ 1.12 and 1.13.

§ 1.1 Introduction

This book is designed to present practical information on judgment enforcement law and practice in a readable, straightforward method. In considering this practice, it is important to understand the judgment debtor, the methods of discovering her assets and the theories of recovery of assets from third parties in postjudgment practice. The techniques, methods and practice tips described and analyzed in this book are designed to assist attorneys, paralegals, law students, and other professionals in a better understanding of judgment enforcement law and application to everyday practice. The topic by topic analysis, case law and statutory research materials provided herein, are presented with the purpose of reducing the professional's time in approaching and applying judgment enforcement law and procedures. The materials apply generally to all judgment enforcement cases, but, of course, since state laws on judgment enforcement vary from state to state the attorney, or other professional, will have to apply particular state law where necessary to the particular case.

The emphasis in this book is on enforcing judgments in federal courts. As a result, the Federal Rules of Civil Procedure, as applicable to enforcing judgments, and cases thereunder, will be reviewed and explained. However, since Federal Rule of Civil Procedure 69(a) by its terms incorporates state practice and procedure on execution and supplementary proceedings, practice and procedure of certain states will be addressed in particular instances. Because many states have adopted rules of civil procedure which are based on the Federal Rules, the discussion of the Federal Rules and cases contained in this book will have practical application. Additionally, the overall concepts presented in the book which relate to such areas as:

1. the judgment debtor
2. discovery in aid of execution
3. the principle remedies of postjudgment enforcement
4. receiverships will serve as a handbook for attorneys engaged in collecting and litigating judgment enforcement cases.

One of the largest judgment creditors in this country, in terms of the volume and size of judgments, is the United States Government. Therefore, special emphasis in this book is placed on enforcing judgments of the United States and other creditors in federal court, and collection of such judgments. As such, this book includes treatment of postjudgment remedies of the United States promulgated as part of the Crime Control Act of 1990, in legislation popularly known as the "Federal Debt Collection Procedures Act of 1990," Pub. L. No. 101-647, 104 Stat. 4933 (codified at 28 U.S.C. §§ 3001 to 3308). This Act unifies the judgment enforcement remedies and procedures of the United States. Additionally, the text also includes discussion of many other federal statutes which are applicable to enforcing judgments in federal courts.

Among other things, the materials presented on the Federal Debt Collection Procedures Act and other federal statutes, are also designed to be an effective aid to Federal practitioners, to practitioners who handle one or more collection matters for an agency of the United States, and/or to practitioners who defend a client indebted to the United States.

This first chapter will include discussion of the basic rules of civil procedure applicable to enforcing judgments in federal courts; the process for registering judgments; preserving judgment rights; stays of proceedings to enforce judgments; various forms for judgment enforcement practice; and the Fair Debt Collection Practices Act, 15 U.S.C. § 1692a, et seq, as it applies to attorneys.

BASIC PRINCIPLES

§ 1.2 Basic Rules of Civil Procedure Applicable

In considering a judgment enforcement matter, it is appropriate to first consider Federal Rule of Civil Procedure 54 and the question of whether the judgment under consideration is indeed final. The term "judgment" is defined in Federal Rule of Civil Procedure 54(a) as "a decree and any order from which an appeal lies." This Rule is a starting place to determine whether you have a final judgment. A final judgment for enforcement purposes is one which ends the litigation on the merits and the court is left with nothing to do, but order execution on the judgment.[1]

If the case is one involving multiple claims or parties, the district court, pursuant to Federal Rule of Civil Procedure 54(b), "may direct the entry of a final judgment as to one or more but fewer than all of the claims or parties only upon an express determination that there is no just reason for delay and upon an express direction for entry of judgment." When ruling on multiple claims, the district court must determine that the judgment is final, in that it is "an ultimate disposition of an individual claim entered in the course of a multiple claims action.[2] A district court in applying Rule 54(b) should "consider such factors as whether the claims under review were separable from the others remaining to be adjudicated and whether the nature of the claims already determined was such that no appellate court would have to decide the same issue more than once even if there were subsequent appeals."[3]

Of course, a judgment is not final if it leaves open the question of additional damages.[4]

Next, in considering the basic rules applicable to your judgment, it is essential to review Federal Rule of Civil Procedure 58, and the question of whether the pleading are in the correct form. Rule 58 states: "Every judgment shall be set forth on a separate document." As stated in the comment to the Rule, this clarification to the Rule was added to eliminate any uncertainties as to when the judgment was entered, as distinguished from when the opinion or memorandum was entered by the court. The 1963 amendment to Rule 58 made it clear that a party need not file a notice of appeal until a separate judgment has been filed and entered.[5]

The separate-document requirement was intended to avoid the inequities that were inherent when a party appealed from a document or docket entry that appeared to be a final judgment of the district court only to have the

---

[1] Catlin v. United States, 324 U.S. 229, 233 (1945); International Controls Corp. v. Vesco, 535 F.2d 742, 747–748 (2d. Cir. 1976).

[2] Sears, Roebuck & Co. v. Mackey, 351 U.S. 427(1956); Curtis-Wright Corporation v. General Electric Company, 446 U.S. 1, 7 (1980).

[3] 446 U.S. at 8. (Supreme Court found no abuse of discretion by the District Court in granting petitioner's motion for certification under Rule 54(b).)

[4] International Controls Corp. v. Vesco, 535 F.2d 742, 748 (2d Cir. 1976); Aetna Casualty & Surety Co. v. Giesow, 412 F.2d 468, 470 (2d Cir. 1969); United States v. Burnett, 262 F.2d 55, 59 (9th Cir. 1958).

[5] Bankers Trust Company v. Mallis, 435 U.S. 381, (1978) (*per curiam*); Willhauck v. Halpin, 919 F.2d 788, 793-794 (1st Cir. 1990); McCalden v. California Library Association, 919 F.2d 538, 541-542 (9th Cir. 1990); *See,* United States v. Indrelunas, 411 U.S. 216, 220-222, (1973).

appellate court announce later that an earlier document or entry had been the judgment and dismiss the appeal as untimely.[6]

The separate-document rule must be "mechanically applied" in determining whether an appeal is timely.[7]

Federal Rule of Civil Procedure 58 states that a judgment is effectively final only "when set forth on a separate document" and "when entered as provided by Rule 79(a)." Rule 79(a) directs the clerk to enter, inter alia, "all appearances, orders, verdicts, and judgments" in chronological order in the civil docket, taking care that the entries "show the nature of each paper filed or writ issued and the substance of each order or judgment of the court."[8]

However, a combined opinion and order is valid if all parties waived the Rule, and except the judgment in that form.[9]

Certainly Rule 59 on amending a judgment or Rule 60 on relief from judgment, may be applicable to a judgment enforcement matter. Also, Rule 62 on stay of a proceedings to enforce a judgment, is one of the basic rules of civil procedure applicable in judgment enforcement. This Rule is discussed below, starting at **§ 1.20.** Importantly, Federal Rule of Civil Procedure 69 applies to the judgment enforcement process. Execution on a judgment is explained in detail in **Chapter 5.** The range of inquiry in discovery under Rule 69, and discovery proceedings using Rules 26–37, or state rules, including rules on supplementary proceeding, are discussed in detail in **Chapters 3** and **4** on post judgment discovery matters.

There may be other rules applicable in certain circumstances, but these are the rules you will most frequently use, and you must be familiar with their use and application to your postjudgment case.

§ 1.3 Application of the Federal Debt Collection Procedures Act

The Federal Debt Collection Procedures Act of 1990, Pub. L. No. 101-647, 104 Stat. 4933 (codified at 28 U.S.C. §§ 3001 to 3308) is applicable to judgments of the United States on a debt. 28 U.S.C. § 3001. The statute was effective on May 28, 1991, and is retroactive with respect to judgments of the United States entered after May 29, 1981.[10] The statute reads: "This chapter

---

[6] Bankers Trust Co. v. Mallis, 435 U.S. 381, 385 (1978) (*per curiam*).

[7] United States v. Indrelumas, 411 U.S. 216, 221–222 (1973); Bankers Trust Co. v. Mallis, 435 U.S. 381,91978); Willhauck v. Halpin, 919 F.2d 788, 793 (1st Cir. 1990); McCalden v. California Library Association, 919 F.2d 538, 542 (9th Cir. 1990).

[8] Willhauck v. Halpin, 919 F.2d 788, 793 (1st Cir. 1990).

[9] Bankers Trust Co. v. Mallis, 435 U.S. 381, 385 (1978).

[10] 28 U.S.C. § 3005; Pub. L. 101-647, Title XXXVI §§ 3611, 3631, Nov. 29, 1990, 104, 4937, 4966; *See,* United States v. Gelb, 783 F. Supp. 748 (E.D.N.Y. 1991).

shall not apply with respect to a judgment on a debt if such judgment is entered more than 10 years before the effective date of this chapter."[11] Emphasizing this fact in Congressional debates, Representative Brooks stated: "Similarly, the act makes clear that it does not apply to any court judgment entered more than 10 years before the act's effective date. The collection of debts based on these earlier judgments will continue to be governed by current law rather than by this act."[12]

The purpose of the Act is to provide uniformity in collection of debts by the United States. "The Federal Debt Collection Procedures Act of 1990, provides for nationwide procedural uniformity in the collection of sums owed to the United States."[13] The statute is the exclusive civil procedure for the United States to recover a judgment on a debt.[14] However, the Federal Debt Collection Act by its terms recognizes the procedures of other Federal laws for recovering on a judgment for a debt, to the extent that those procedures are not inconsistent with the Act.[15] In section 3003 of the Act, Congress placed limitations on the scope and effect of the Act.

The Act is not to be construed as limiting the rights of the United States:

1. To collect taxes
2. To collect any fine, penalty, assessment, restitution, or forfeiture arising in a criminal case
3. To seek the appointment of a receiver
4. To enforce a security agreement. 28 U.S.C. § 3003(b)(1)–(4)

Furthermore, the Act is not to be construed as superseding or modifying such other laws including:

1. Title 11 (Bankruptcy Code)
2. Admiralty law
3. The Federal Priority Statute, § 3713 of title 31 (31 U.S.C. § 3713)
4. Section 303 of the Consumer Credit Protection Act (15 U.S.C. § 1673)
5. A statute of limitation applicable to a criminal proceeding
6. The common law or statutory rights to set-off or recoupment
7. Any Federal law authorizing, or any inherent authority of a court to provide, injunctive relief
8. The authority of a court—

---

[11] 28 U.S.C. § 3005.

[12] 136 Cong. Rec. H13288 (daily ed. Oct. 27, 1990) (statement of Rep. Brooks).

[13] 136 Cong. Rec. H13293 (daily ed. Oct. 27, 1990) (statement of Rep. Fish).

[14] 28 U.S.C. § 3001(a)(1).

[15] 28 U.S.C. § 3001(b).

   A. to impose a sanction under the Federal Rules of Civil Procedure
   B. to appoint a receiver to effectuate its order
   C. to exercise the power of contempt under any Federal law

9. Any law authorizing the United States to obtain partition, or to recover possession, of property in which the United States holds title

10. Any provision of any other chapter of title 28, except to the extent such provision is inconsistent with the Act.[16]

The Act shall, moreover, preempt state law to the extent such law is inconsistent with the Act.[17] The Act does not limit the rights of the United States under foreign law, under a treaty of an international agreement, or otherwise under international law.[18] Excepted as provided otherwise in the Act, the Federal Rules of Civil Procedure apply to actions and proceedings under the Act.[19]

§ 1.4 Interest on Judgments

In federal courts, interest is allowed on money judgments in accordance with 28 U.S.C. § 1961. On October 1, 1982, the statute was amended. Under former § 1961, a civil money judgment earned interest at the rate allowed locally by state law. This amount was often an artificially low figure. The amendment substituted a uniform, but frequently changing, federal rate which is closely related to the current cost of money. Civil money judgments in Federal district courts now bear interest "calculated from the date of the entry of the judgment, at a rate equal to the coupon issue yield equivalent (as determined by the Secretary of the Treasury) of the average accepted auction price for the last auction of fifty-two week United States Treasury bill settled immediately prior to the date of the judgment."[20]

Recently, the Supreme Court of the United States made several important interpretations concerning this statute in the case of *Kaiser Aluminum & Chemical Corporation v. Bonjorno.*[21] In that case, Bonjorno, as respondents and the sole stockholders of a defunct aluminum pipe fabrication company, filed a Sherman Act case against petitioners (Kaiser), alleging monopolization of the aluminum pipe market. The original jury verdict for Bonjorno was entered on August 22, 1979. The District Court, finding the judgment was

---

16 28 U.S.C. § 3003(c).

17 28 U.S.C. § 3003(d).

18 28 U.S.C. § 3003(e).

19 28 U.S.C. § 3003(f).

20 28 U.S.C. § 1961(a).

21 494 U.S. 827 (1990).

not supported by the evidence, allowed a limited retrial on the issue of damages. On December 2, 1981, the jury awarded Bonjorno damages of $9,567,939. On December 4, 1981, the district court granted a partial judgment notwithstanding the verdict. Subsequently in 1986, the Third Circuit Court of Appeals vacated the latter judgment and reinstated and affirmed the December 4, 1981 judgment.[22]

At the time of Bonjorno's complaint, the prior version of 28 U.S.C. § 1961 was in effect which allowed calculation of interest from the date of entry of judgment, at the rate allowed by state law. In 1982, while the appeal was pending, § 1961 was amended to provide interest from the date of entry of judgment at the Treasury bill rate.

In *Bonjorno,* the Supreme Court considered and ruled on several important issues with respect to the Federal interest statute. First, with respect to the issue of whether the amendment to § 1961 was retroactive, the Court held that it was not.[23] "We conclude that the plain language of both the original and amended versions of § 1961 evidence clear congressional intent that amended § 1961 is not applicable to judgments entered before its effective date."[24] Second, Kaiser argued that interest should be calculated from the date of the entry of the later judgment, December 4, 1981, and not the date of the verdict, December 2, 1981. The Supreme Court concluded that "postjudgment interest properly runs from the date of the entry of the judgment."[25] Third, Bonjorno also asserted that the calculation of interest should run from the date of the first judgment entered on August 22, 1979, not the one in December 1981. However, the Supreme Court considered that neither party appealed the district court's determination that the jury's finding on damages was not supported by substantial evidence. Therefore, the damages were not "ascertained" on August 22, 1979, and the postjudgment interest should be calculated from December 4, 1981.[26]

In *H.J., Inc. v. Flygt Corporation,* the Eighth Circuit, in analyzing the application of the *Bonjorno* decision to the case before it, held that the calculation of interest ran from the date of the original judgment which ascertained H.J.'s damages.[27] In its prior decision in the case, the Eighth Circuit upheld the single damage award of $105,774.00 for attempted monopolization and as compensatory damages for tortious interference. "Our remand for retrial on punitive damages involved the tortious interference claim only and did not affect the portion of the damages award that was affirmed."[28] This

---

[22] 865 F.2d 566 (3rd Cir.), *cert. granted,* 491 U.S. 903 (1989).

[23] 494 U.S. 827 (1990).

[24] 494 U.S. 827 (1990).

[25] 494 U.S. 827 (1990).

[26] 494 U.S. 827 (1990).

[27] 925 F.2d 257, 262 (8th Cir. 1991).

[28] *Id.*

decision is based on the principle that where the "original judgment is upheld for the most part but modified on remand, postjudgment interest should accrue from the date of the first judgment.[29] But, in *McDevitt & Street Co. v. Marriott Corp.,* the District Court ruled that where a case is remanded and results in an increase in the judgment, postjudgment interest on the increase in the judgment resulting from the remand, would run from the date of the revised judgment rather than from the date of the original judgment.[30] In another postjudgment interest case, *Bernardi v. Yeutter,* the District Court indicated that the date of the judgment is not considered to be the date of a magistrate's recommendation, but only a final judgment order of the district court.[31]

In the instance of the United States, the general rule is that postjudgment interest is not awarded unless sovereign immunity has been expressly waived by statute.[32] Such a waiver has been passed by Congress under some statutes, including 28 U.S.C. § 2411 (in tax refund cases prejudgment and postjudgment interest are payable by the United States); 31 U.S.C. § 1304 (certain district court judgments where interest is permitted); and 26 U.S.C. § 1420(g) (where the Internal Revenue Service has filed a wrongful levy).[33] "The no-interest rule is to the effect that interest cannot be recovered in a suit against the Government in the absence of an express waiver of sovereign immunity from an award of interest."[34] However, it is clear that the no-interest rule simply means that a court cannot assess interest against the United States (whether prejudgment or postjudgment) unless sovereign immunity has been waived. Otherwise, the payment of interest by the United States without such a waiver of sovereign immunity would be like an unauthorized raid on the United States Treasury.

§ 1.5 Costs on Judgment

The federal statutes on taxation of costs and fees are 28 U.S.C. §§ 1911 through 1929, and Federal Rule of Civil Procedure 54(d). As a general rule,

---

29 Cordero v. De Jesus-Mendez, 922 F.2d 11, 17 (1st Cir. 1990).

30 754 F. Supp. 513, 516 (E.D. Va. 1991).

31 754 F. Supp. 743, 749 (N.D. Cal. 1990), *aff'd in part and rev'd in part,* 931 F.2d 59 (1991).

32 Library of Congress v. Shaw, 478 U.S. 310, 311 (1986); International Woodworkers of America, AFL-CIO Local 3-98 v. Donovan, 769 F.2d 1388, 1392 (9th Cir. 1985) (postjudgment interest not allowed against the United States unless specifically provided by statute); Thompson v. Kennickell, 797 F.2d 1015, 1017–1018 (D.C. Cir. 1986), *cert. denied,* 480 U.S. 905 (1987) (postjudgment interest not permitted unless waived by statute); Holly v. Chasen, 639 F.2d 795 (D.C. Cir.) (per curiam), *cert. denied,* 454 U.S. 822 (1981).

33 Library of Congress v. Shaw, 478 U.S. 310, 319 n.6 (1986).

34 478 U.S. at 311 (The Shaw case dealt with prejudgment interest.)

"costs shall be allowed as of course to the prevailing party unless the court otherwise directs" under Rule 54(d). "Taxation of cost is in the first instance performed by the Clerk of the Court and his decision is reviewable by the Court pursuant to Federal Rule of Civil Procedure 54(d)."[35]

Under Rule 54(d), the clerk may tax the costs on one day's notice. On a motion served within five days thereafter, the action of the clerk may be reviewed by the court. The Supreme Court of the United States indicates that the district judge has the "responsibility to decide the cost question himself" and that, in reviewing the Clerk's assessment of costs the district judge must exercise his own discretion.[36] Therefore, the matter of taxation of costs is largely a matter of trial court discretion.[37] The standards for what may be assessed generally are set forth in 28 U.S.C. § 1920. This statute provides:

A judge or clerk of any court of the United States may tax as costs the following:

1. Fees of the clerk and marshal
2. Fees of the court reporter for all or any part of the stenographic transcript necessarily obtained for use in the case
3. Fees and disbursements for printing and witnesses
4. Fees for exemplification and copies of papers necessarily obtained for use in the case
5. Docket fees under § 1923 of this title
6. Compensation of court appointed experts, compensation of interpreters, and salaries, fees, expenses, and costs of special interpretation services under § 1828 of this title

A bill of costs shall be filed in the case and, upon allowance, included in the judgment or decree.

Federal courts have considered a variety of cost items. A short recitation of some of those costs items is appropriate.

Daily Transcripts

The denial of costs for daily transcripts by the district court was affirmed by the Supreme Court in *Farmer v. Arabian American Oil Co.*[38] These costs were held to be convenient to counsel, made the task of the trial judges easier, but were not essential.

---

35 Castro v. United States, 104 F.R.D. 545, 548–549 (D.P.R. 1985).

36 Farmer v. Arabian American Oil Co., 379 U.S. 227, 233 (1964).

37 Castro v. United States, 104 F.R.D. 545, 549 (D.P.R. 1985).

38 379 U.S. 227, 234 (1964).

Transportation/Travel Expenses

The district court, may in the exercise of its discretion, refuse to tax as costs the actual transportation expenses of witnesses travelling from foreign countries, and limiting those costs to per diem costs fixed by law and expenses to travel to the long-standing 100-mile rule.[39] "Costs for witnesses travel are limited to 100 miles absent 'special circumstance.'"[40] However, costs of the government, amounting to $2,037.36 for transporting, feeding and housing an IRS case agent who was a witness in the case, are recoverable from the defendant in a tax evasion case.[41]

Also, the Supreme Court rejected a strict application of the 100 mile service-of-process limit in the *Farmer v. Arabian American Oil Co.* case.[42] Following the guidelines established in *Farmer v. Arabian American Oil Co.*, the District Court of Puerto Rico stated: "The relevance and necessity of the witnesses testimony are to be considered in determining whether to allow travel expenses beyond the 100-mile limit."[43] The witness in *Castro* was allowed the coach class fare, not the first class fare, from Washington, D.C. to Puerto Rico, for trial.[44] However, in *Hodge v. Seiler,* the Fifth Circuit upheld the discretion of the trial court in not allowing husband-wife plaintiff's air fare expenses of $750 for travel from California to New Orleans and return, in a civil rights housing discrimination case, after plaintiff-husband was transferred from Texas and later took a job in California.[45]

Transcripts

Fees for transcripts of a preliminary injunction hearing recoverable upon a proper showing that they were necessary to the case.[46] Daily transcripts for the convenience of the parties may not be allowed.[47]

---

39 379 U.S. 227, 234 (1964).

40 Goodwin Brothers Leasing, Inc. v. Citizens Bank, 587 F.2d 730, 734 (5th Cir. 1979; National Bancard Corporation v. Visa, U.S.A., Inc., 112 F.R.D. 62, 69 (S.D. Fla. 1986); Simmons v. McLean Trucking Co., 100 F.R.D. 61, 64 (N.D. Ga. 1983).

41 28 U.S.C. § 1920 and 26 U.S.C. § 7201 and § 7203; United States v. Dunkel, 900 F.2d 105, 108 (7th Cir. 1990), *vacated,* 111 S. Ct. 747 (1991).

42 379 U.S. 227, 233 (1964).

43 Castro v. United States, 104 F.R.D. 545, 551 (D.P.R. 1985).

44 *Id.,* at 550–551. *See, e.g.,* Simmons v. McLean Trucking Co., 100 F.R.D. 61 (N.D. Ga. 1983); Shevin v. Lederman, 92 F.R.D. 752 (D. Colo. 1981).

45 558 F.2d 284, 287 (5th Cir. 1977).

46 Castro v. United States, 104 F.R.D. 545, 549 1985; *See* Wahl v. Carrier Manufacturing Co., Inc., 511 F.2d 209, 217 (7th Cir. 1975).

47 Brumley Estate v. Iowa Beef Processors, Inc., 704 F.2d 1362, 1363–64 (5th Cir. 1983).

Depositions

Generally courts have held that § 1920(2) permits taxing as costs the costs of taking and transcribing depositions necessarily obtained for use in the case.[48] The costs of copying depositions which are introduced into evidence have also been allowed.[49]

Attorney Travel Expenses

The general rule is that attorney travel expenses are not among the items enumerated in 28 U.S.C. § 1920, and, therefore, are not recoverable as costs.[50]

Computerized Legal Research

Courts are split on whether computerized legal research costs are recoverable as costs under 28 U.S.C. § 1920. Several courts have held that computer-assisted research costs cannot be recovered through taxation of costs, and other courts allow such costs as a reasonable cost of litigation.[51]

Witnesses

Section 1920 of Title 28 provides the authority for fees paid to witnesses are recoverable as costs, and the § 1821 of Title 28 governs the attendance fees, mileage allowance and subsistence paid to witnesses who appear in court.[52]

---

[48] Allen v. United States Steel Corp., 665 F.2d 689, 697 (5th Cir. 1982); Sun Ship, Inc. v. Lehman, 655 F.2d 1311, 1318 n.48 (D.C. Cir. 1981); Economic Laboratory Inc. v. Donnolo, 612 F.2d 405, 411 (9th Cir. 1979); SCA Services, Inc. v. Lucky Stores, 599 F.2d 178, 181 (7th Cir. 1979); Keys v. School District No. 1, 439 F. Supp. 393, 417 (D. Colo. 1977); Action Alliance For Senior Citizens, Inc. v. Shapp, 74 F.R.D. 617, 619–620 (E.D. Pa. 1977) (depositions "reasonably necessary" for the defense of the case); *But cf.* Templeman v. Chris Craft Corporation, 770 F.2d 245, 249 (1st Cir.), *cert. denied,* 474 U.S. 1021 (1985); Copper Liquor, Inc. Adolph Coors Company, 684 F.2d 1087, 1099 (5th Cir. 1982, (costs of depositions are taxable only if they were either introduced in evidence or used during the trial of the case.)

[49] Templeman v. Chris Craft Corporation, 770 F.2d 245, 249 (1st Cir.), *cert. denied,* 474 U.S. 1021 (1985).

[50] Kiefel v. Las Vegas Hacienda, Inc., 404 F.2d 1163, 1170 (7th Cir. 1968), *cert. denied,* 395 U.S. 908 (1969); McHenry v. Joseph T. Ryerson Company, 104 F.R.D. 478, 480 (N.D. Ind. 1985).

[51] Ortega v. City of Kansas City, Kansas, 659 F. Supp. 1201, 1219 (D. Kan. 1987). *See also* Leftwich v. Harris-Stowe State College, 702 F.2d 686, 695 (8th Cir. 1983); Berkey Photo Inc. v. Eastman Kodak Co., 603 F.2d 263, 309 n. 75 (2d Cir. 1979), *cert. denied,* 444 U.S. 1093 (1980); Wehr v. Burroughs Corporation, 619 F.2d 276, 285 (3d Cir. 1980) (allowed computer-aided legal research as a reasonable cost of litigation.)

[52] 104 F.R.D. 545, 549–550 (D.P.R. 1985).

Experts

"Section 1920(3) contains the statutory provision for taxing witnesses' fees and costs. Section 1821 specifies the amount of such fees. The long-standing rule is that the 'federal statute governs'."[53] Additional amounts paid to expert witnesses as compensation, or fees, generally are not allowed to be taxed as costs.[54] Extraordinary expenses may be allowed in some circumstances if they have been specifically approved by the court prior to trial.[55]

Charts and Maps

If an attorney wants to have the reasonable costs of charts and maps taxed as costs against an opponent at trial, it is recommended that the attorney seek approval of these costs prior to trial at a pretrial planning conference under Federal Rule of Civil Procedure 16. The attorney should advise the court of the necessity for use of the charts or maps at trial, and have an estimate ready to discuss concerning the costs of preparation so as to prevent their disallowance later. These costs should be outlined, and approved by the court as part of the pretrial orders in the case. This procedure is necessary, because otherwise this cost may be disallowed.

For example, the cost of preparing charts, although the charts were stipulated into evidence and used by both parties at trial, was found not allowable as costs, where there was not an advance order allowing the incurrence of the expense.[56] In the case of *Johns-Manville Corp. v. Cement Asbestos Products Co.,* the Fifth Circuit explained the acceptable procedure of getting prior approval:

> Under Rule 16, F. R. Civ. P., the court may authorize prior to trial, the production of models and charts. This procedure avoids the possible abuse of incurring oppressive costs by one party, ex parte, which may be taxed to his opponent.

---

[53] Templeman v. Chris Craft Corporation, 770 F.2d 245, 249 (1st Cir.), *cert. denied,* 474 U.S. 1021 (1985), quoting from Henkel v. Chicago, St. Paul Minneapolis & Omaha Ry. Co. 284 U.S. 444, 448 (1932); Lock v. Jenkins 634 F. Supp. 615, 619 (N.D. Ind. 1986).

[54] Templeman v. Chris Craft Corporation, 770 F.2d 245, 250 (1st Cir.), *cert. denied,* 474 U.S. 1021 (1985); Pizarro-de-Ramirez v. Grecomar Shipping Aqency, 82 F.R.D. 327, 328 (D.P.R. 1976).

[55] Gradmann & Holler GMBH v. Continental Lines, S.A., 679 F.2d 272, 274 (1st Cir. 1982) (Attorneys travel to Europe, travel expenses for experts brought from Europe, telex communication charges, and investigation charges).

[56] Hiller v. Merrill Lynch, Pierce, Fenner & Smith. Inc., 60 F.R.D. 87, 90 (N.D. Ga. 1973). 428 F.2d 1381, 1385 (5th Cir. 1970); *But cf.* Mikel v. Kerr, 499 F.2d 1178, 1182–1183 (10th Cir. 1974); Advance Business Systems & Supply Co. v. SCM Corp., 287 F.Supp. 143 (D. Md. 1968), *aff'd and remanded on other grounds,* 415 F.2d 55 (4th Cir. 1969), *cert. denied,* 397 U.S. 920 1970). (where costs of maps, charts, graphs and other material approved without advanced court approval.

§ 1.6 Surcharge on a Debt of the United States

The Federal Debt Collection Procedures Act[57] authorizes a surcharge by the United States which is equivalent to 10 percent of the amount of the debt in connection with the recovery by the United States of the debt, to cover litigation and enforcement costs.[58] The 10 percent amount is intended to cover all costs other than those usually allowed to prevailing parties, such as the costs described in § **1.5** above. As indicated in the statute and in its legislative history, this surcharge may only be recovered in lawsuits which are brought under laws not providing some other amount to cover these costs and in which the United States does not receive an attorney's fee.[59]

§ 1.7 Nationwide Enforcement of Process by the United States

The Federal Debt Collection Procedures Act provides for nationwide enforcement by the United States of actions to collect debts and judgments.[60] Thus, under the Act, "any writ, order, judgment, or other process, including a summons and complaint, filed under this chapter may be served in any State . . . and . . . such writ, order or judgment may be enforced by the court issuing the writ, order, or process, regardless of where the person is served with the writ, order or process."[61] Nationwide enforcement has been upheld by the courts pursuant to other challenges of its constitutionality.[62] "This legislation—in the form we consider today—provides for nationwide enforcements of writs, orders, and judgments. . . . The new proposed statutory language will prove beneficial to the United States by simplifying and expediting many enforcement efforts. A provision for transferring the action or proceeding to the district of the debtor's residence—in response to a timely request of the debtor—safeguards debtor interests.[63] In this statement, Representative Fish is referring to 28 U.S.C. § 3004(b)(2), which provides a procedure for

---

57 28 U.S.C. § 3011; *see* Schueler v. Roman Asphalt Corp., 827 F. Supp. 247, 254–57 (S.D.N.Y. 1993).

58 *See* 136 Cong Rec. H13288–13289 (daily ed. October 27, 1990 (statement of Rep. Brooks); *see also* Schueler v. Roman Asphalt Corp., 827 F. Supp. 247, 255 (S.D.N.Y. 1993).

59 28 U.S.C. § 3004(b).

60 28 U.S.C. § 3004(b)(1)(A)(B).

61 Fitzsimmons v. Barton, 589 F.2d 330, 333 (7th Cir. 1979); *In Re* Outlet Company Stores Inc., 82 Bankr. 694, 699 (S.D.N.Y. 1988); *In Re* First Hartford Corp., 63 Bankr. 479, 486 (S.D.N.Y. 1986).

62 136 Cong Rec. H13289 (daily ed. October 27, 1990) (statement of Rep. Fish).

63 *But cf.* United States v. Palmer, 609 F. Supp. 544, 547 (E.D. Tenn. 1985).

the debtor, within 20 days after receiving notice of the action or proceeding, to request transfer of the action to the district court for the district in which the debtor resides.

Before passage of the Federal Debt Collection Procedures Act, the United States was authorized to issue long arm writs of execution nationwide pursuant to 28 U.S.C. § 2413.[64] This statute has been interpreted to include long arm garnishment and similar supplemental proceedings as well.[65]

Prior to the Federal Debt Collection Procedures Act becoming law, other than long arm execution, it was necessary for attorneys for the United States to register the judgment in another district pursuant to 28 U.S.C. § 1963, before taking enforcement action in the other district. Now, under the Act, it is not necessary for the United States to register its judgment in another district prior to taking enforcement action in that district.

Before exercising any postjudgment remedy, this subsection of the Federal Debt Collection Procedures Act incorporates the notice provisions of subsection 3202(b), which requires the United States to give notice to the judgment debtor or any person who has an interest in property to which the remedy is directed.[66] Under subsection 3004(c) of the Act, counsel for the United States can choose the time for service, but the time cannot be any later than the time the postjudgment remedy is put into effect.

§ 1.8 Recording the Judgment as a Lien

The Federal Lien Recordation Statute is codified in 28 U.S.C. § 1962. The statute provides:

> Every judgment rendered by a district court within a State shall be a lien on the property located in such State in the same manner, to the same extent and under the same conditions as a judgment of a court of general jurisdiction in such State, and shall cease to be a lien in the same manner and time. Whenever the law of any State requires a judgment of a State court to be registered, recorded, docketed or indexed, or any other act to be done, in a particular manner, or in a certain office or county or parish before such lien attaches, such requirements

64 United States v. Thornton, 672 F.2d 101 (D.C. Cir. 1982) (Section 2413 garnishment in Maryland on a District of Columbia statement pursuant to Fed. R. Civ. P. 69); United States *ex rel.* Marcus v. Lord Electric Co., 43 F.Supp. 12 (W.D. Pa. 1942) of Pennsylvania, permitting attachment execution of bank deposits, permitted execution of that kind in New York though New York law did not allow the relief). 28 U.S.C. § 2413 is not expressly repealed by the Act.

65 28 U.S.C. § 3004(c); 28 U.S.C. § 3202(b). [See the discussion of Notice of Enforcement By The United States and Judgment Debtor's Right to Hearing On The Notice in Chapter 5.]

66 Pub. L. No. 10-647, Title XXXVI § 3631, Nov. 29, 1990, 104 Stat. 4965, 4966.

> shall apply only if the law of such State authorizes the judgment of a court of the United States to be registered, recorded, docketed, indexed or otherwise conformed to rules and requirements relating to judgments of the court of the State. This section does not apply to judgments of the United States.

The last sentence in the statute was added as part of the amendments in the Act.[67] This sentence was added because the Federal Debt Collection Procedures Act provides a new method of recording judgment liens of the United States under subsection 3201 of the Act. Subsection 3201 requires the United States to file a certified copy of the abstract of judgment in the same manner as the notice of a tax lien would be filed under 26 U.S.C. § 6323(f)(1) and (2). The statutory language states that the lien created "is for the amount necessary to satisfy the judgment, including costs and interest."[68]

Beginning on May 28, 1991, a judgment of the United States, therefore, will no longer be filed in accordance with 28 U.S.C. § 1962, the Federal Lien Recording Statute. Instead, the procedures for filing and indexing a judgment of the United States to obtain a lien against real estate will follow the procedures for filing a notice of tax lien by the United States under 26 U.S.C. § 6323(f)(1)(A), (B), and (C).[69] This change should not affect current practice for the United States, however, because 26 U.S.C. § 6323(f)(1)(A) basically provides for filing against real estate as designated by state laws in the location where the property is situated. This procedure for the United States is similar to that previously required under 28 U.S.C. § 1962. However, the particular statutes should be examined to ensure the proper procedure is followed.

Once the filing requirements are met, docketing of a federal judgment in the office of the county clerk as provided in state law, creates a lien on the debtor's realty in that county.[70] A judgment lien so entered in the county land records will become a lien upon the judgment debtor's property, when the state law so provides, and the holder of the judgment lien on real estate will have a superior interest to a later purchaser of the property.[71] However, the judgment lien will be subordinate to prior recorded mortgages.[72] Ordinarily, a

---

[67] 28 U.S.C. §3201(a).

[68] 28 U.S.C. §3201(a).

[69] Knapp v. McFarland, 462 F.2d 935, 938 (2d. Cir. 1972) (New York law); United States v. Hodes, 355 F.2d 746, 748 (2d Cir. 1966), *cert. granted,* 384 U.S. 968 (1966), *cert. dismissed,* 386 U.S. 901 (1967) (New York law); United States v. Blakeman, 750 F.Supp. 216, 223 (N.D. Tex. 1990) (Texas law).

[70] Peralta v. Heights Medical Center Inc., 485 U.S. 80, 85 (1988) (So provided under Texas law, but U.S. Supreme Court reversed the judgment, holding that default judgment entered against debtor without notice violated due process rights.)

[71] United States v. Hodes, 355 F.2d 746, 748 (2d Cir. 1966), *cert. granted,* 384 U.S. 968 (1966), *cert. dismissed,* 386 U.S. 901 (1967).

[72] Encyclopedia Britannica v. Jones, 101 F. Supp. 521, 523 (D.D.C. 1951) (however, in this case, the court referred the creditor to rights against personal property rather than allow the sale of real estate to enforce a judgment of $98). (See Chapter 4 on Execution Process and Chapter 5 on Sale and Disposition Of the Debtor's Assets.)

creditor will be protected by the lien and will be entitled to have the debtor's real property sold for satisfaction of his judgment lien.[73]

In summary, then, recording a judgment is a ministerial act, so that a federal judgment can be filed and noticed in the county or city records as required by state law. The judgment becomes a lien on the debtor's property in the county where it is recorded.[74]

The procedures of nonfederal creditors to release a lien are provided in state law.[75] The procedures by the United States will also follow state law.[76] Of course, judgment liens should be renewed as provided by state or federal law.[77]

§ 1.9 —Checklist on Recording the Judgment

Recording the judgment is an essential element in the judgment enforcement process. There are a few steps that are necessary to appropriately record the judgment. Here is a short checklist.

____ 1. Obtain a certified abstract of the judgment for recording

____ 2. For a creditor, other than the United States, check the procedures in 28 U.S.C. § 1962, and file under the state recording statute requirements

____ 3. For the United States, check the procedures under 28 U.S.C. § 3201 and 26 U.S.C. § 6323(f), and file under the state recording statute requirements

____ 4. Obtain the required fee and make the check or checks payable to the proper recording agency

____ 5. Record the judgment or judgments in the proper state or county office

____ 6. Record the abstract in all locations where the debtor has property

____ 7. Recorded judgment becomes a lien on the debtor's property

____ 8. Recording the judgment is different from registering the judgment

____ 9. Once the judgment is satisfied, in whole or in part, a notice of release of lien should be filed by the judgment creditor in the same recording office. State law provides for the release of lien by nonfederal judgment creditors. 28 U.S.C. § 1962. The procedure for

---

[73] 28 U.S.C. § 1962; 28 U.S.C. § 3201.

[74] 28 U.S.C. § 1962.

[75] 28 U.S.C. § 3201(d); 26 U.S.C. § 6523(f).

[76] 28 U.S.C. § 3201(c). *Cf.* United States v. Kellum, 523 F.2d 1284, 1288–1289 (5th Cir. 1975); Matanuska Valley Lines, Inc. v. Molitor, 365 F.2d 358 (9th Cir. 1966), *cert. denied,* 386 U.S. 914 (1967); Stanford v. Utley, 341 F.2d 265 (8th Cir. 1965).

[77] For an explanation of the history of the statute, see Ohio Hoist Manufacturing Co. v. LiRocchi, 490 F.2d 105, 109 (6th Cir.), *cert. dismissed,* 417 U.S. 938 (1974).

the United States follows 28 U.S.C. § 3201(d), and, therefore, also incorporates state law for releases. 26 U.S.C. § 6323(f)

____ 10. Renew the lien as required by state or federal law. 28 U.S.C. § 3201(c)

REGISTERING JUDGMENTS

§ 1.10 Registration of the Judgment

The Federal Registration Statute is contained in 28 U.S.C. § 1963.[78] The registration of a judgment should not be confused with the recording of a judgment. As explained in § 1.8 above, recording the judgment is a ministerial act by which the judgment is filed in the county or city records according to state law. A certified abstract of the judgment is filed in the county or city land recorder's office, and the filing fee is paid. Recording the judgment is a ministerial act by which the judgment becomes a lien on the debtor's property in the location of the recordation.[79]

However, plaintiff's counsel may also want to encumber property of the debtor in another federal jurisdiction. Before the judgment can be recorded in another jurisdiction a different kind of action must be taken. The judgment must be registered or enrolled on the court docket in the other jurisdiction. This procedure is provided by 28 U.S.C. § 1963, the Federal Registration Statute. The Federal Registration Statute states:

> A judgment in an action for the recovery of money or property entered in any district court or in the Court of International Trade may be registered by filing a certified copy of such judgment in any other district or, with respect to the Court of International Trade, in any judicial district, when the judgment has become final by appeal or expiration of the time for appeal or when ordered by the court that entered the judgment for good cause shown. Such a judgment entered in favor of the United States may be so registered any time after judgment is entered. A judgment so registered shall have the same effect as a judgment of the district court of the district where registered and may be enforced in like manner.

A certified copy of the satisfaction of any judgment in whole or in part may be registered in like manner in any district in which the judgment is a lien.

---

[78] 28 U.S.C. § 1962 (for the non-federal judgment creditor); 26 U.S.C. § 6323(f) (for the United States.)

[79] Note, "Registration of Federal Judgments", 42 Iowa L. Rev. 285, 28–89 (1957). Air Transport Association of America v. Professional Air Traffic Controllers Organization (*In Re* Professional Air Traffic Controllers Organization) 699 F.2d 539, 544 (D.C. Cir. 1983).

Section 1963, therefore, is a registration statute, as distinguished from § 1962 of Title 28, which is a recording statute. Registration "is merely a matter of having the clerk of the court [in which the judgment is registered] enter the pertinent provisions of the . . . [sister court's] judgment on the judgment docket."[80] Using § 1963, a judgment can be registered in any district in which the debtor's property is located.[81]

The second sentence of the statute, concerning immediate registration by the United States even before expiration of appeal, was added in 1990, as part of the amendments made to other federal statutes in the legislation filed with the passage of the Federal Debt Collection Procedures Act.[82] This amendment enables the United States to register a judgment in another district even if that judgment is not final by expiration of all appellate rights. Also, under the terms of the statute in a 1988 amendment adding the language "or when ordered by the court that entered the judgment for good cause shown," the rendering court can allow immediate registration by a non-federal judgment creditor to prevent transfer of property by the debtor.[83]

Of course, when a judgment is registered in violation of the Federal Registration Statute, the registering court has authority to grant relief by annulling or vacating the registration, and any process issued thereunder, and restoring the status quo ante by returning assets seized or levied upon.[84] Wrongful registration may subject the judgment creditor to abuse of process claims.[85]

Prior to these recent amendments there were mixed decisions by the courts on whether one could register a judgment in another district when the judgment was not final on appeal.[86] That meant the debtor was free to transfer his property in the other district, if the judgment creditor could not register the

---

80 Pacific Reinsurance Management Corporation v. Fabe, 929 F.2d 1215, 1217–1219 (7th Cir. 1991).

81 28 U.S.C. § 1963.

82 Pacific Reinsurance Management Corporation v. Fabe, 929 F.2d 1215, 1218–1219 (7th Cir. 1991).

83 Ohio Hoist Manufacturing Co. v. LiRocchi, 490 F.2d 105, (6th Cir.), *cert. dismissed,* 417 U.S. 938, Goldsmith v. Midwest Energy Company, 249, 250 (N.D. Ohio 1980).

84 *Id.,* United Mine Workers of America v. Gibbs, 383 U.S. 715 (1966); Hurn v. Oursler, 289 U.S. 238 (1933).

85 Air Transport Association of America v. Professional Air Traffic Controllers Organization (*In Re* Professional Air Traffic Controllers Organization), 699 F.2d 539, 544 n. 19 (D.C. Cir. 1983); Urban Industries, Inc. v. Thevis, 670 F.2d 981, 984–985 (11th Cir. 1982); Stanford v. Utley, 341 F.2d 265 (8th Cir. 1965); Kelly v. Greer, 354 F.2d 209 (5th Cir. 1965); Hertzfeld v. Parker, 100 F.R.D. 770, 773 n.1 (D.Colo. 1984); Abegglen v. Burnham, 94 F. Supp. 484 (D. Utah 1950); Goldsmith v. Midwest Energy Company, 90 F.R.D. 249 (N.D. Ohio 1980); Dorey v. Dorey, 77 F.R.D. 721 (N.D. Ala. 1978).

86 Pacific Insurance Management, 929 F.2d 1215, at 1218–1219 (7th Cir. 1991).

judgment there, or otherwise restrain the transfer.[87] These amendments help both the federal and nonfederal judgment creditor. Of course, "an independent action on a judgment may be commenced in the face of a pending appeal. . . ."[88] An independent action, however, is time-consuming, expensive and much slower than the registration process.

Practice Tips

There may be concern about what is good cause which a nonfederal judgment creditor has to show under the 1988 amendment. An attorney for the judgment creditor must demonstrate that:

1. The debtor is about to transfer property in the other district
2. Or, alternatively, that the debtor has more property located in the other district, and has very little real property located where the original judgment was obtained
3. Based on these factors, the court should allow quick registration in the other district to prevent the transfer, and allow recording of the judgment, pursuant to 28 U.S.C. § 1962, in that second district, to prevent transfer or sale of the property by the judgment debtor.[89]
4. Check the state law and see whether it has adopted the Uniform Enforcement of Foreign Money-Judgments Act.[90]

Perhaps, if no supersedeas bond is filed under Federal Rule of Civil Procedure 62(d), it will be possible to use the Uniform Enforcement of Foreign Judgment Act, and enforce the judgment under state law pending appeal.[91]

When the judgment is registered in the new jurisdiction, it may be recorded there, because it has the same effect as a judgment of that district.[92] "The language of the statute is absolutely clear that once the judgment is registered in

---

[87] Air Transport Association of America v. Professional Air Traffic Controllers Organization (*In Re* Professional Air Traffic Controllers Organization), 699 F.2d 539, 544 (D.C. Cir. 1983).

[88] Pacific Reinsurance Management Corporation v. Fabe, 929 F.2d 1215, 1218-1219 (7th Cir. 1991).

[89] [See §§ 1.12 and 1.13.]

[90] *Cf.* Bechtel Corporation Western Contracting Corp., 414 N.W. 2d 130 (Iowa 1987) [See discussion of Uniform Enforcement Foreign Money-Judgments Recognition Act at **§ 1.12.]**

[91] Stanford v. Utley, 341 F.2d 265 (8th Cir. 1965); Federal Deposit Insurance Corporation v. British-American Corporation, 726 F.Supp. 622, 630 (E.D.N.C. 1989); United States v. Palmer, 609 F. Supp. 544 (E.D. Tenn. 1985).

[92] United States v. Palmer, 609 F. Supp. 544, 547 (E.D. Tenn. 1985).

the new district, it 'shall have the same effect as a judgment of the district where registered.' "[93] A judgment so registered is no longer considered as a "foreign judgment."[94]

Practice Tips

As a practical matter it is recommended that attorneys should use care here, because some court clerks may not understand that, once a judgment is registered, it is necessary to follow state law procedures for "foreign" judgments. If counsel has difficulty with a court clerk on this point, it is suggested that the matter be discussed with the chief clerk, and then walk the chief clerk through the pertinent cases and statutes, giving him copies of the cases for comfort.

The primary purposes of § 1963 are stated as follows:

> . . . to simplify and facilitate the enforcement of federal judgments, at least those for money, to eliminate the necessity and expense of a second lawsuit, and to avoid the impediments, such as diversity of citizenship, which new and distinct federal litigation might otherwise encounter. [Citations omitted.] If for enforcement purposes, registration were to be given a lessor status than a judgment on the judgment, some or all of these purposes are thwarted and the judgment creditor, in order fully to protect himself, must resort to the old and more formal procedure.[95]

Thus, the Federal Registration Statute is a fairly modern device to accelerate the enforcement of judgments from one federal district to another.[96] Once the judgment is registered, the judgment creditor has all rights as if the judgment was first filed there. "Following registration, a judgment creditor may secure a writ of execution from the registering court and deliver to the local Marshal for execution."[97] After the judgment is registered in the new district, execution procedures follow the law of the new district.[98] This procedure

---

93 *Id. See* Anderson v. Tucker, 68 F.R.D. 461 (D. Conn. 1975).

94 Stanford v. Utley, 341 F.2d 265, 270 (8th Cir. 1965). *Cf.* Dorey V. Dorey, 77 F.R.D. 721, 726 (N.D. Ala. 1978).

95 Air Transport Association of America v. Professional Air Traffic Controllers Organization (*In Re* Professional Air Traffic Controllers Organization), 699 F.2d 539, 544 (D.C. Cir. 1983).

96 United States v. Palmer, 609 F. Supp. 544, 549 (E.D. Tenn. 1985) (federal registration in 28 U.S.C. § 1963 compared to federal longarm execution in 28 U.S.C. § 2413).

97 Knapp v. McFarland, 462 F.2d 935, 940 (2d Cir. 1972). [For an explanation of the different kinds of execution available see Chapter 5].

98 Pacific Reinsurance Management Corporation v. Fabe, 929 F.2d 1215, 1219 (7th Cir. 1991); Fed. R. Civ. P. 69(a). ". . . [T]he law of the state in which the court of registration sits controls the proceedings. Thus, a District of Colombia judgment registered in Maryland would be executed according to Maryland law." United States v. Palmer, 609 F. Supp. 544, at 548. *See,* Juneau Spruce Corporation v. Longshoremen's Union, 128 F. Supp. 697, 705 (D. Hawaii 1955).

allows counsel for the judgment creditor to consider what location may enhance judgment enforcement rights. Counsel may be in a position to forum shop and execute against the debtor's assets in more than one Federal district.

Congress, therefore, provided in § 1963, a method for registering judgments in other districts where a debtor has property, without the necessity of filing a new lawsuit.[99] When the judgment is registered in each district, the attorney can request issuance writs of execution in each district until the judgment is satisfied.[100] However, the creditor's attorney may not execute against the debtor's assets beyond the amount of the judgment obtained. If the judgment is collected, the last sentence of 28 U.S.C. § 1963 provides that the satisfaction of judgment is to be registered "in like manner in any district where the judgment was registered as a lien."[101]

Territorial limits exist on the ability to enforce money judgments in the United States. The domestic approach for the enforcement of such judgments is based upon the following proposition: enforcement of judgments rendered by federal courts is governed by federal law and enforcement of judgments rendered by state courts is governed by state law. Moreover, the Full Faith and Credit Clause of Article IV of the United States Constitution requires courts of one state to recognize valid final judgments from courts of another state.[102] Thus, a judgment entered against an individual requiring the payment of money can be satisfied with whatever nonexempt assets that individual owns in the state in which the judgment was entered. When those assets are located in another state, various means are in place to enforce the judgment. Unfortunately, there is no national rule or nationwide system for giving effect to sister state judgments. Each state has crafted its own procedures. For instance, consistent with Article IV of the Constitution, the state in which the judgment is to be executed may permit the judgment to be registered and enforced or may require the filing of a new suit in order to effectuate the terms of the judgment.

---

99 United States v. Palmer, 609 F. Supp. 544, at 548 (E.D. Tenn. 1985).

100 Edmonston v. Sisk, 156 F.2d 300, 303–304 (10th Cir. 1946).

101 *Id.*, indicated in the last sentence of 28 U.S.C. § 1963, the satisfaction of judgment is to be registered "in like manner in any district where the judgment was registered as a lien."

102 U.S. Const. Art. IV, Sec. 1 provides that "[f]ull Faith and Credit shall be given in each State to the Public Acts; Records and judicial Proceedings of every other State. And the congress may by general laws prescribe the Manner in which such Acts, Records and Proceeding, shall be proved, and the Effect thereof."

§ 1.11 —Form for Registration of Judgment

AO 451 (Rev. 2/86) Certification of Judgment ⊕

United States District Court

______________________ DISTRICT OF ______________________

v.

CERTIFICATION OF JUDGMENT FOR REGISTRATION IN ANOTHER DISTRICT

Case Number:

I, ______________________, Clerk of this United States District Court certify that the attached judgment is a true and correct copy of the original judgment entered in this action on ______________________ *(Date)*, as it appears in the records of this court, and that

* ____

____

____

____

IN TESTIMONY WHEREOF, I sign my name and affix the seal of this Court on

______________________.
Date

____
Clerk

____
(By) Deputy Clerk

*Insert the appropriate language: . . . "no notice of appeal from this judgment has been filed, and no motion of any kind listed in Rule 4(a) of the Federal Rules of Appellate Procedure has been filed." . . . "no notice of appeal from this judgment has been filed, and any motions of the kinds listed in Rule 4(a) of the Federal Rules of Appellate Procedure [*] have been disposed of, the latest order disposing of such a motion having been entered on [date]." . . . "an appeal was taken from this judgment and the judgment was affirmed by mandate of the Court of Appeals issued on [date]." . . . "an appeal was taken from this judgment and the appeal was dismissed by order entered on [date]."

[*Note: The motions listed in Rule 4(a), Fed. R. App. P., are motions: for judgment notwithstanding the verdict; to amend or make additional findings of fact; to alter or amend the judgment; for a new trial; and for an extension of time for filing a notice of appeal.]

§ 1.12 Registration of Foreign Judgments

Unlike state court judgments, there is no constitutional obligation imposed to give full faith and credit effect to foreign money judgments.[103] Yet, contracts, import and export of goods, services and technology, credit transactions and the transfer of funds from one country to another is occurring with incredible frequency. Just as a purely domestic trade transaction can rupture and spawn litigation, so too can an international commercial transaction fall apart as a result of any number of factors, including fraud or misrepresentation, bankruptcy, late delivery, non-performance, and so forth. As economies globalize and international transactions become more commonplace, the parties to those transactions need certainty and stability in international commerce. And when problems arise, they want to avoid the expense of relitigating their claims against one another in multiple countries. However, unique problems exist for the commercial transaction in the international setting—such as where to seek relief, what law will be applied, and how the remedy will be enforced. It is this last problem that is of principle concern here.

Comity

Valid judgments of foreign courts are traditionally entitled to extraterritorial effect in the United States as a matter of comity. Comity has been defined as the:

> . . . recognition which one nation extends within its own territory to the legislative, executive, or judicial acts of another. It is not a rule of law, but one of practice, convenience, and expediency. Although more than mere courtesy and accommodation, comity does not achieve the force of an imperative or obligation. Rather, it is a nation's expression of understanding which demonstrates due regard both to international duty and convenience and to the rights of persons protected by its own laws. Comity should be withheld only when its acceptance would be contrary or prejudicial to the interest of the nation called upon to give it effect.[104]

The first case to set the comity standard for the recognition of foreign judgments was *Hilton v. Guyot,*[105] which addressed whether a French judgment requiring a New York resident doing business in France to take action required by a foreign judgment would not be enforceable in a United States federal court in view of the fact that under similar circumstances the French courts would not give conclusive effect to a United States court's judgment.

---

103 Andes v. Versant Corp., 878 F.2d 147 (4th Cir. 1989).

104 Somportex, Limited v. Philadelphia Chewing Gum Corp., 453 F.2d 435 (3d Cir. 1971) *cert. denied,* 405 U.S. 1017 (1972).

105 159 U.S. 113 (1895).

Although the court found this lack of reciprocity to be a legitimate ground for denying enforcement to the French judgment and ultimately refused to give effect to it, it nonetheless fashioned the general rule for when United States courts should enforce judgments of foreign courts:

> [W]here there has been opportunity for a full and fair trial abroad before a court of competent jurisdiction, conducting the trial upon regular proceedings, after due citation or voluntary appearance of the defendant, and under a system of jurisprudence likely to secure an impartial administration of justice between the citizens of its own country and those of other countries, and there is nothing to show either prejudice in the court, or in the system of laws under which it was sitting, or fraud in procuring the judgment, or any other special reason why the comity of this nation should not allow it full effect, the merits of the case should not, in an action brought in this country upon the judgment, be tried afresh, as on a new trial or an appeal, upon the mere assertion by the party that the judgment was erroneous in law or in fact.[106]

Thus, *Hilton v. Guyot* established a rule favoring the enforcement of foreign judgments as a means of upholding the policy of judicial finality.

The principles underlying this rule were preserved in the Restatement (Second) of Conflict of Laws § 98, which provides that "a valid judgment rendered in a foreign nation after a fair trial in a contested proceeding will be recognized in the United States." The same rationale for affording a *res judicata* effect to a domestic judgment applies with respect to a foreign judgment—namely, to avoid duplicative litigation and to bring a controversy to a final resolution. However, the Restatement does *not* require that every time a foreign national devotes substantial time, money, and energy to obtain a judgment in a foreign court against an American citizen, the foreign judgment will be automatically enforceable in the United States against the defendant's assets located here.

Applicability of State Law

As an initial matter, foreign judgments are not entitled to direct enforcement in the United States. They first must be recognized by having the United States court issue its own judgment based on the foreign decree. Moreover, as established by case law, recognition and enforcement of foreign judgments are determined by the law of the state in which execution is sought. *Erie Railroad Co. v. Tompkins,*[107] *Somportex, Limited v. Philadelphia Chewing Gum Corp.*[108]

---

106 159 U.S. at 203–03 (1895).

107 304 U.S. 64, 67 (1938). There, the Supreme Court held that in diversity of citizenship cases, federal courts are bound to apply state, rather than federal law in determining issues of substantive law, unless the matter in dispute is governed by the United States Constitution or by Acts of Congress.

108 453 F.2d at 435 (3d Cir. 1971), *cert. denied,* 405 U.S. 1017 (1972).

In *Somportex,* a foreign litigant brought a diversity action in federal court in Philadelphia to enforce a default judgment obtained in England. Somportex filed a breach of contract action against the defendant in an English court. The defendant was served, entered a conditional appearance to contest jurisdiction, changed strategies and attempted to withdraw its limited appearance. Upon its refusal to litigate the case, a default judgment was entered against the defendant. Relying on *Erie Railroad Co. v. Tompkins*, the court held that Pennsylvania law which looks to comity, not full faith and credit, determined whether the English money judgment was enforceable in the United States. In so doing, the court first examined whether the English court had jurisdiction to enter the judgment. In this regard, the court gave conclusive effect to the English court's findings that a litigant cannot choose to test jurisdiction, and that it was given an opportunity to present its case in England and waived it by not pursuing its motion to quash the writ. Accordingly, the United States court enforced the foreign judgment.

Defenses

When dealing with a foreign court judgment, a party opposing its recognition must determine the tactical alternatives and the consequences of their actions. For instance, had the American company not made a limited appearance in *Somportex,* under the law of Pennsylvania, it would not have been bound by the English judgment.

As suggested by the Restatement and pronounced in *Hilton,* a number of defenses exist in an action seeking to enforce a foreign judgment, which as stated above will be controlled by state law.[109] An American defendant seeking to prevent the enforcement of a foreign judgment against it in the United States can attack the validity of the foreign judgment. Among the defenses a litigant can raise are:

1. The Foreign Proceedings Were Unfair. This defense covers an assortment of challenges to demonstrate that the foreign tribunal did not

---

[109] The Supreme court held in *Hilton v. Guyot,* 159 U.S. at 205 that:

> [w]hen an action is brought in a court of this country by a citizen of a foreign country against one of our own citizens . . . and the foreign judgment appears to have been rendered by a competent court, having jurisdiction of the cause and of the parties and upon due allegations and proofs, and opportunity to defend against them, and its proceedings are according to the course of a civilized jurisprudence, and are stated in a clear and formal record, the judgment is prima facie evidence, at least, of the truth of the matter adjudged; and it should be held conclusive upon the merits tried in the foreign court, unless some special ground is shown for impeaching the judgment, as by showing that it was affected by fraud or prejudice, or that by the principles of international law, and by the comity of our own country, it should be given full credit and effect.

comport with basic notions of United States due process such as notice[110] and an opportunity to be heard. Note also *Julen v. Larsen*[111] in which a German judgment would not be enforced where service of process in German without an English translation did not provide United States defendant with adequate notice; *Banco Minero v. Ross*[112] in which a Texas court refused to enforce a money judgment rendered by a Mexican court upon no proof whatever and in which the defendant was denied a right to present a defense and denied the right to appeal on a frivolous ground.

2. The Foreign Court Lacked Personal or Subject Matter Jurisdiction. Whether a foreign court has jurisdiction over a foreign national is an issue that is frequently litigated. Most United States courts have reviewed the personal jurisdiction of foreign courts pursuant to the United States jurisdictional standards announced in such cases as *International Shoe Co. v. Washington*[113] which discussed whether a court has personal jurisdiction over an individual depends upon his minimum contacts with the forum including whether he invokes the benefits and protections of the forum state's laws, and the quality and nature of defendant's acts by which her purposefully avails himself of the privilege of conducting business within the forum state. *Koster v. Automark Industries, Inc.*[114] discusses a default judgment obtained in a Dutch court involving a contract executed in Italy for the production of goods in Switzerland which could not be enforced in the United States because the defendant did not have sufficient contacts with the Netherlands under the Illinois long arm statute.[115] Similarly, United States courts will not enforce judgments of foreign courts if they were not competent to render the judgment under their local law. In *Hunt v. BP Exploration Co. (Libya)*[116] an English court can have subject matter jurisdiction over a controversy, even if it must apply to Texas law.

3. Enforcement of the Foreign Judgment Would Violate Public Policy. This exception exists to provide United States courts with grounds for denying conclusive effect to those foreign judgments that penalize conduct that United States law may encourage. For instance, in *Ackermann v. Levine*[117] a

---

[110] Notice can be made in such a way that it satisfies the requirements of the Hague Service Convention or Rule 4 of the Federal Rules of Civil Procedure. Ackermann v. Levine, 788 F.2d 830 (2d Cir. 1986).

[111] 25 Cal.App.3d 325 (1972).

[112] 172 S.W. 711 (1915).

[113] 326 U.S. 310 (1965).

[114] 640 F.2d 77, 84 (7th Cir. 1981).

[115] *See also,* Restatement (Third) Foreign Relations Law of the United States § 482(1)(b) (1987).

[116] 492 F. Supp. 885 (N.D. Tex. 1980).

[117] 788 F.2d 830 (2d Cir. 1986).

New York court refused to enforce a default judgment rendered by a German court for attorney's fees as violative of that state's policy that an attorney seeking fees bears the burden of establishing that the fees are fair and reasonable and represent payment for actual work performed. Notably, the court indicated that the fact that a foreign plaintiff would not have been able to prevail if it had brought the original action in a United States court is not in itself sufficient grounds to prevent enforcement of the foreign judgment as contrary to public policy.

In contrast, the public policy defense was unsuccessfully raised in *Tahan v. Hodgson*[118] where an American doing business through a corporation in Israel was sued and served documents written in Hebrew which he did not understand. An Israeli Court entered a default judgment against the individual thereby piercing the corporate veil to impose liability. The plaintiff prevailed in his efforts to enforce the judgment in Washington, D.C., where the United States court held that service satisfied due process requirements and Israel's decision to pierce the corporate veil was not violative of United States public policy that there be "compelling justification" before doing so because Israel also had a similar policy and the action taken there was not done so lightly.

In the same vein, in *Toronto-Dominion Bank v. Hall*[119] a federal court enforced a judgment obtained by a Canadian bank against an Arkansas citizen despite his objection that enforcement would contravene Arkansas contract law and in so doing violate public policy. The court acknowledged that the bank had greater rights in Canada than it would received in Arkansas, but noted that the defendant freely entered into the contract and agreed to be bound by Canadian law. Failing to find any portion of the contract to be shocking, immoral, unconscionable, or unreasonably oppressive as required by Arkansas law, it allowed enforcement of the foreign judgment.

Time and time again, United States courts enforcing judgment have made clear that simply because the forum has a different rule of law will not automatically render the foreign judgment violative of the public policy of the forum. Indeed, it is unrealistic for the United States to insist that all foreign judicial systems mirror its system.[120] For instance, in *Somportex Ltd. v. Philadelphia Chewing Gum Co., Corp.*[121] the attorneys fees which were part of the English judgment that was enforced by a Pennsylvania court would not have been recoverable had the Pennsylvania court rendered the judgment. Rather than requiring litigants before a foreign tribunal to have received the full panoply of rights that they would have been accorded under the United States Constitution, we know from the Supreme Court's pronouncement as far

[118] 662 F.2d 862 (D.C. Cir. 1981).

[119] 367 F. Supp. 1009, 1015–16 (E.D. Ark. 1973).

[120] *See* Tahan v. Hodgson, 662 F.2d 862.

[121] 453 F.2d 435.

back as 1895 in *Hilton v. Guyot*[122] that United States courts should enforce foreign judgments so long as the defendant had, at a minimum, an opportunity to be heard before an impartial tribunal.

4. The Foreign Judgment Was Obtained by Fraud. This defense related to the manner in which the judgment was procured and not to those intrinsic matters that should have been raised before the foreign tribunal. Thus, it would be a defense to recognition if the evidence establishes that the defendant did not receive a fair trial by the foreign tribunal.[123] On the other hand, notwithstanding that the foreign judgment was based on forged documents, the defense would be unavailable since that is arguably something that could have been detected and asserted before the foreign court.

§ 1.13 Uniform Foreign Money-Judgments Recognition Act

States have acknowledged that it has become increasingly necessary for them to respect, register, and enforce the judgments of foreign courts, and have consequently enacted statutes to deal with these foreign judgments. The Uniform Foreign Money-Judgments Recognition Act (UFMJRA)[124] is a model law designed to have foreign money judgments be "enforceable in the same manner as the judgment of a sister state which is entitled to full faith and credit."

The Act creates a summary procedure in which a judgment creditor may file a suit in a United States Court[125] to enforce the foreign judgment. By distinguishing between those grounds in which United States courts must and may refuse recognition and enforcement of foreign judgments, the UFMJRA essentially codifies the common law described above in **§ 1.12.** In this regard, § 4, the most critical provision of the Act states that recognition of a foreign judgment will be disallowed where the foreign court lacked an impartial tribunal; due process; personal jurisdiction over the defendant, or subject matter jurisdiction. Additionally, while not mandatory, a foreign judgment need not be recognized if the defendant did not receive notice of the proceedings; the judgment was obtained by fraud; enforcement would violate the public policy of the state; the judgment conflicts with another final and conclusive judgment; the foreign court proceeding was contrary to

---

[122] 159 U.S. 113 (1895).

[123] 218 F. Supp. 164 (S.D. N.Y. 1963), *aff'd*, 333 F.2d 327 (2d Cir. 1964).

[124] *See* 13 ULA 417 (1986).

[125] Diversity Jurisdiction generally exists over such actions pursuant to 28 U.S.C. § 1332(a) to support filing the lawsuit in federal court. Federal courts sitting in diversity are bound to apply state law.

an agreement between the parties; or where jurisdiction is based only on personal service, the foreign court was a seriously inconvenient forum.

Consistent with the standards announced in *International Shoe Co. v. Washington*, § 5 of the Act allows the American court to assume that the foreign court has personal jurisdiction if certain conditions are met, for example, the defendant voluntarily appeared for the foreign proceedings; was served in the foreign state; conducted business or had its principal place of business in the foreign state.[126] For purposes of the UFMJRA adopted by California, personal jurisdiction existed over the defendant in the foreign forum when the defendant owned stock in a Canadian corporation, served as an officer and a director, and negotiated and executed a guaranty agreement in Canada with a Canadian bank. In addition, because the general rule in America is that the finality of a judgment is not disturbed by an appeal, § 6 of the UFMJRA permits a United States court to stay proceedings to enforce the judgment pending an appeal from the foreign court decree. For example, *Ingersoll Milling Machine Co. v. Granger*[127] in which a United States district court properly stayed further proceedings pending the outcome of Belgian appeal as a means to avoid duplication of effort and possible piecemeal litigation.

To date, 22 states have adopted the UFMJRA in its entirety or with slight modifications. Those states include: Alaska, California, Colorado, Connecticut, Georgia, Idaho, Illinois, Iowa, Maryland, Massachusetts, Michigan, Minnesota, Missouri, New Mexico, New York, Ohio, Oklahoma, Oregon, Pennsylvania, Texas, Virginia and Washington.[128]

PRESERVING JUDGMENT RIGHTS

§ 1.14 Maintaining the Status Quo

Once an attorney acquires a judgment for a client, counsel is immediately interested in preserving her client's judgment rights, and maintaining the status quo. In many cases, the attorney may be able to seek and obtain some prejudgment remedies, such as an attachment, receivership, garnishment,

---

126 Bank of Montreal v. Kough, 612 F.2d 467 (9th Cir. 1980).

127 833 F.2d 680 (7th Cir. 1987).

128 Volume 13 of the Uniform Laws Annotated 1992 Cumulative Annual Pocket Part at 47 provides a Table of Jurisdictions that have adopted the Uniform Foreign Money Judgment Recognition Act. (See **Table 1–1** at the end of this chapter.)

sequestration, preliminary injunction, freeze order or perhaps, a lis pendens, to prevent dissipation of the debtor's assets prior to judgment.[129] Traditionally prejudgment remedies have been more difficult to obtain, because a creditor's claim has not been reduced to judgment.

However, after the judgment is entered, rights of a creditor to maintain the status quo increase substantially because the amount of the creditor's judgment is fixed. When the judgment amount is certain, the court should be willing to maintain the status quo during postjudgment litigation matters, including appeals, so that the assets of the judgment debtor are not dissipated while counsel seeks to discover the location and kind of assets and prepares to execute against those assets. Therefore, it is suggested that counsel should consider some of the alternatives to preserving the status quo in the postjudgment phase of litigation.

Practice Tips

The alternatives available for preserving the status quo in postjudgment litigation, include:

1. Requiring a postjudgment bond or other security pending appeal. (See **§ 1.22,** on supersedeas bond and **§ 1.23,** on security conditions pending appeal.)
2. Recording the judgment as a lien against the debtor's real property wherever located. (See **§ 1.8** on recording the judgment and **§§ 1.10–1.13,** on registering the judgment.)
3. Obtaining preliminary injunction and freeze order. (See the forms in **§§ 1.15–1.17.**)
4. Filing a lis pendens in any new action to set aside fraudulent transfers of real estate, etc. (see **§ 1.18** on lis pendens, **§ 1.19** on a form of lis pendens)
5. Seeking the appointment of a receiver for the debtor's assets. (See **Chapter 7** on receiverships.)
6. Seeking restraining or turnover orders in supplementary proceedings. (See **Chapter 4.**)
7. Filing new suits against transferees of the debtor's assets to have them returned to the debtor. (See **Chapter 6** for some remedies of the creditor.)

---

[129] *See, e.g.,* 28 U.S.C. §§ 3101–3105; Fed R. Civ. P. 64, 65 and 66.

FORMS TO PRESERVE THE STATUS QUO

§ 1.15 —Freeze Orders and Injunctions

FREEZE ORDER FOR ASSETS OF CORPORATION/TRUSTS/INDIVIDUALS

UNITED STATES DISTRICT COURT
DISTRICT OF
[ ]

ORDER

______________________________, their agents, servants, employees and attorneys and all persons in active concert and participation with them, pending the final hearing and determination of this action from:

a) Removing, transferring, disposing of, wasting, liquidating, investing, conveying, encumbering in any fashion, or attempting to remove, conceal or in any way interfere with any real or personal property, assets effects or funds in ______________________________ Bank; any and all real or personal property of XYZ Corporation ____________________ ABC Corporation, ______________ Trust ________________ Trust ________________ or the individual assets and property of ______________, and ____________________, except for ordinary and necessary living expenses.

b) Removing, transferring, disposing of, wasting, liquidating, investing, conveying, encumbering in any fashion, or attempting to remove, conceal or in any way interfere with, any real or personal property, assets, effects or funds in the ____________________ Corporation, ____________________, Co., Inc.; except as the same may be necessary for the usual and normal day-to-day activities of the ongoing lawful business of the corporation, such as:

1) buying and selling of merchandise, supplies or other property in the normal course of business;

2) employing, discharging and fixing the compensation, salaries and wages of all employees, making sure none of the same are excessive;

3) purchasing or otherwise acquiring such materials, equipment, supplies, services or other property as the corporate management may deem necessary and advisable in connection with the operation of its business and the management, and preservation of the property of the corporation, and to pay for any such purchases;

4) entering into any contracts incidental to the normal and usual operation of said business, and the management and preservation of said property;

5) keeping the property of the corporation insured in such manner and to such extend as it may deem it necessary and advisable;

6) collecting and receiving all income, profits and all outstanding accounts, chosen in action, and credits due to become due to the corporation and holding and retaining all monies received to the end that the same may be applied under this or further or different orders of this Court;

7) paying and discharging out of any funds now or hereafter coming into the corporation's business all taxes and other charges lawfully incurred in the operation of the business and the preservation of the assets.

8) any real or personal property, or other assets of the defendant corporation, ______________________, a ________________ (state) corporation, with a usual place of business at ________________________.

And for its reasons and grounds for said Preliminary Injunction and Writ of Attachment, Plaintiff sets forth its reasons in the attached Affidavits and Memorandum of Points and Authorities.

Respectfully submitted:

Plaintiff,

§ 1.16 Lis Pendens

The federal statute concerning constructive notice of pending actions is found in 28 U.S.C. § 1964. This statute states:

> When the law of a state requires a notice of an action concerning real property pending in a court of the State to be registered, recorded, docketed, or indexed in a particular manner, or in a certain office or county or parish in order to give constructive notice of the action as it relates to the real property, and such law authorizes a notice of the action concerning real property pending in a United States district court to be registered, recorded, docketed, or indexed in the same manner, or in the same place, those requirements of the State law must be complied with in order to give constructive notice of such action pending in a United States district court as it relates to the real property in such State.

A Puerto Rico lis pendens provision applied to a federal court action, and once registered according to state law, the district court could deny a motion to expunge the filing of the notice.[130] However, the filing of a lis pendens does not create a lien, but may preserve an existing lien.[131]

---

130 Daniels v. Universal Investment Corp., 355 F. Supp. 693 (D.P.R. 1972).

131 Strom v. Palatine National Bank of Palatine, Illinois, 921 F.2d 836, 840 (8th Cir. 1991).

A notice of lis pendens can preserve a preexisting lien. A judgment creditor who has a lien on registered property can register a notice of lis pendens with the registrar and have the lis pendens noted on the title of the property. The lis pendens give notice of the lien to any subsequent purchaser and prevents that purchaser from being a bona fide purchaser who can avoid the lien.[132]

Constructive notice of a suit pending is necessary to tell the world that there is a dispute concerning the chain of title, or other matter where the title of the property is in dispute. A lis pendens notice is a warning of that dispute in the chain of title. The lis pendens places potential purchasers on notice of the litigation, and the fact that they may be bound by the result in that litigation.

§ 1.17 —Form of Lis Pendens

NOTICE OF LIS PENDENS

The above captioned action in which ________________ is plaintiff was filed in the United States District Court for the District of ____________ on ________________.

In that action the plaintiff seeks to enforce its $__________ judgment against defendant ______________ previously obtained on _________, 19___ in the United States District Court for the _________ District of _________, as Civil No. ___________, and registered in the United States District Court for the District of __________ as Civil No. ______________, pursuant to 28 U.S.C. § 1963.

In Civil No. _____________, the plaintiff lists causes of action for fraudulent transfer, alter ego and constructive trust claims, claiming among other things, and that all the corporate defendants are the alter egos of individual defendant, ________________.

Additionally in the action, the plaintiff seeks affirmative relief affecting title to real property owned by defendant [name of corporation and address.] The plaintiff claims the true owner of the property is the individual defendant ________________, since either the individual defendant ____________ is the true owner of the stock of [defendant corporation], or alternatively is the alter ego of [defendant corporation]. The plaintiff in the complaint seeks to have the real property sold to satisfy its judgment against the individual defendant.

The real property now owned by [defendant corporation] is described as:

---

132 921 F.2d 836, at 840.

[describe property as in deed, including address if known, and the book, page and date of recording of the deed.]

[Signature and notarization of document.]

FEDERAL RULE OF CIVIL PROCEDURE 62 AND APPELLATE RULE 8

§ 1.18 Automatic Stay of Proceedings to Enforce a Judgment

Under Federal Rule of Civil Procedure 62(a), there is an automatic stay for ten (10) days from the entry of a judgment, during which "no execution shall issue upon a judgment nor shall proceedings be taken for its enforcement. . . ." The failure to obtain a stay filing the expiration of the appeal may mean that the judgment can be executed after that time, and the judgment debtor will be powerless to defeat the execution.[133]

There are occasions where the judgment debtor will have to act quickly in obtaining a stay, because, under the exceptions in the rule, the automatic stay for 10 days is not applicable to "an action for an injunction or in a receivership action, or a judgment or order directing an accounting in an action for infringement of letters patent. . ."[134]

§ 1.19 Discretionary Stay of Enforcement Proceedings

Under Federal Rule of Civil Procedure 62(b), the district court "[i]n its discretion and on such conditions for the security of the adverse party as are proper . . . may stay the execution of or any proceedings to enforce a judgment pending the disposition of a motion for a new trial or to alter or amend a judgment. . . ." Although "a stay [under Rule 62(b)] pending disposition of a motion for judgment n.o.v. and/or a new trial will generally be resolved in

---

133 *Cf.* United States v. $2,490.00 In U.S. Currency, 825 F.2d 1419, 1420–1421 (9th Cir. 1987) (where forfeiture judgment was executed by depositing the currency forfeited into the United States Treasury after the expiration of the ten day period under Rule 62(a), and claimant failed to file a supersedeas bond pursuant to Rule 62(d) during that period, court lost jurisdiction over the res.)

134 *Cf.* In the Matter of Combined Metals Reduction Company, 557 F.2d 179, 192–193 (9th Cir. 1977) (court refused a stay of a bankruptcy sale, since the sale was made without the stay the court could not restore the status quo.).

far less time than the lengthy process of briefing, argument and disposition which an appeal entails," the district court should, nevertheless, provide adequate security for plaintiff's judgment pending resolution of the motions.[135]

Under Federal Rule of Civil Procedure 62(c), when the appeal is taken from an injunctive interlocutory or final judgment, the district court has discretion to "suspend, modify, restore, or grant an injunction during the pendency of the appeal upon such terms as to bond or otherwise as it considers proper for the security of the rights of the adverse party." In *Hawaii Housing Authority v. Midkiff*[136] Justice Rehnquist stated: "Whatever the current application of the so-called jurisdictional shift theory to modern appellate procedure, it is well settled that a court retains the power to grant injunctive relief to a party to preserve the status quo during the pendency of an appeal, even to this Court." Rule 62 permits the trial court to enter appropriate orders to preserve the status quo while the case is pending in an appellate court.[137]

In *McClatchy Newspapers v. Central Valley Typographical Union No. 46, International Typographical Union*[138] one of the issues reviewed by the Ninth Circuit was whether the district court had jurisdiction to enter an amended judgment while the appeal of its original judgment was pending. Originally the district court confirmed an arbitration award in favor of the Central Valley Typographical Union No. 46 (the Union). During the pending appeal process, the district court amended the judgment which reaffirmed the original decision and made additional directives. The publisher submitted that the district court was without jurisdiction to amend the judgment while the original judgment was on appeal. The Ninth Circuit agreed.[139] Noting that generally the filing of a notice of appeal divests the district court of jurisdiction over the matters appealed, the Circuit Court recognized certain exceptions apply. The Ninth Circuit stated:

Rule 62(c) is "merely expressive of a power inherent in the court to preserve the status quo where, in its sound discretion, the court deems the circumstances so justify."[140] It does not restore jurisdiction to the district court to adjudicate anew the merits of the case after either party has invoked its

---

[135] International Wood Processors v. Power Dry Inc., 102 F.R.D. 212, 215–216 (D.S.C. 1984) (district court required three of six defendants to post a $2.8 million supersedeas bond, which was the amount of their damage judgment, and three others, who were only liable for $70,000 in punitive damages, were required to give plaintiff written notice before material disposition of their assets, as a condition of the stay of execution.)

[136] 463 U.S. 1323, 1324 (1983).

[137] McClatchy Newspapers v. Central Valley Typographic Union No. 46, International Typographical Union, 686 F.2d 731 (9th Cir.), *cert. denied* 459 U.S. 1071 (1982); United States v. El-O-Pathic Pharmacy, 192 F.2d 62, 79 (9th Cir. 1951).

[138] 686 F.2d 731 (9th Cir. 1982) *cert. denied.*, 459 U.S. 1071 (1982).

[139] McClatchy Newspapers v. Central Valley Typographic Union No. 46. International Typoqraphical Union, 686 F.2d 731 (9th Cir.) *cert denied* 459 U.S. 1071 (1982); *cf. In Re* Federal Facilities Realty Trust, 227 F.2d 631, 654 (7th Cir. 1955).

[140] 7 J. Moore, Moore's Federal Practice § 62.05 at 62-19 to 20 (2d ed. 1979).

right to an appellate court. Rule 62(c) codifies the "long established" and narrowly limited right of a trial court "to make orders appropriate to preserve the status quo while the case is pending in [an] appellate court."[141]

§ 1.20 Mandatory Stay of Enforcement Proceedings by Posting of Supersedeas Bond

Under Rule 62(d), an appellant is usually required to give a supersedeas bond to obtain a stay of proceedings to enforce a judgment. However upon posting of the bond, the stay is granted as a matter of right. "A party taking an appeal from federal district court is entitled to a stay of money judgment as a matter of right if he posts bond in accordance with these rules."[142]

The purpose of Federal Rule of Civil Procedure 62(d) is to preserve the status quo by requiring an appellant to give a supersedeas bond in the unusual case to obtain a stay of proceedings to enforce a judgment.[143] Furthermore, some courts have expressed the purpose of requiring a supersedeas bond is to "secure an appellee from loss resulting from the stay of execution."[144] "If no bond is filed the status quo is not preserved and the judgment creditor may proceed to satisfy the judgment."[145]

Also, the stay should offer the judgment creditor some protection if the judgment debtor appeals. In *Geddes v. United Financial Group*[146] the Ninth Circuit held that the district court abused its discretion in imposing a stay of execution for one year based on the defendants abilities to pay the judgments. Such a time period was not covered by the Rules.[147]

---

141 McClathy Newspapers, 686 F.2d 731, 734 (9th Cir. 1982).

142 American Manufacturers Mutual Insurance Co. v. American Broadcasting-Paramount Theatres, Inc. (1966); United States v. Wylie, 730 F.2d 1401, 1402 N. 2 (11th Cir. 1984); Lamon v. City of Shawnee, Kansas, 758 F. Supp. 654, 655 (D. Kansas 1991).

143 International Telemeter Corporation v. Hamlin International Corporation, 754 F.2d 1492, 1495 (9th Cir. 1985); Poplar Grove Planting and Refining Co. v. Bache Halsey Stuart, Inc., 600 F.2d 1189, 1191 (5th Cir. 1979); Merrill, Lynch, Pierce, Fenner, & Smith, Inc. v. Goldman, 80 F.R.D. 70,71 (E.D. Mo. 1978), *aff'd sub. nom.*, United States ex rel. Goldman v. Meredith, 596 F.2d 1353 (8th Cir.), *cert. denied,* 444 U.S. 838 (1979); Redding & Company v. Russwine Construction Corporation, 417 F.2d 721, 727 D.C. Cir. 1969); Ascher v. Gutierrez, 66 F.R.D. 548, 549 D. D.C. 1975); Dorey v. Dorey, 77 F.R.R. 721, 722 (N.D. Ala. 1978).

144 Lamon v. City of Shawnee, Kansas, 758 F. Supp. 654, 655 (D. Kan. 1991); Miami International Realty Company v. Paynter, 807 F.2d 871, 873 (10th Cir. 1986).

145 Merrill, Lynch, Pierce, Fenner, & Smith, Inc. v. Goldman, 80 F.R.D. 70,71 (E.D. Mo. 1978), *aff'd sub. nom.,* United States *ex rel* Goldman v. Meredith, 596 F.2d 1353 (8th Cir.), *cert. denied,* 444 U.S. 838 (1979); Dorey v. Dorey, 77 F.R.D. 721, 722 (N.D. Ala. 1978).

146 559 F.2d 557, 561 (9th Cir. 1977).

147 559 F.2d, at 560.

§ 1.21 Alternate of Security Conditions Pending Appeal

The majority and modern view is that Rule 62(d) does not always require posting of a supersedeas bond to require a stay and permits a court's exercise of discretion in the matter.[148] The minority view is that posting of a supersedeas bond is required to obtain a stay.[149] To say that the district court does not have the discretion to require a stay with the posting of other security, or, in some cases, without security does not make good sense in view of the purpose of the Rule, to preserve the status quo. If the status quo can be preserved without requiring a bond, then the district court, just as the appellate court can under Federal Rule of Civil Procedure 8 (see **§ 1.27** below), has the discretion to enter the stay on such conditions as it deems suitable. Of course, in the normal situation, one appealing from a district court judgment can stay judgment enforcement proceedings by furnishing a supersedeas bond.[150] However, where an appellant seeks to prevent execution on a judgment and does not post a bond, it is within the court's discretion to permit other or lesser security or even an unsecured stay. In *Texaco, Inc. v. Pennzoil Company*[151] the court stated:

> A judgment creditor's primary concern when a judgment in his favor is stayed pending appeal is that he be "secure . . . from loss resulting from the stay of execution. . . ." In making that determination we look to general equitable principles. Accordingly, when setting supersedeas bonds courts seek to protect judgment creditors as fully as possible without irreparably injuring judgment debtors. . . . A full supersedeas bond may be required "where there is some reasonable

---

148 Townsend v. Holman Consulting Corporation, 929 F.2d 1358, 1367 (9th Cir. 1990); Miami International Realty Co. v. Paynter, 808 F.2d 871, 873 (10th Cir. 1986), Texaco, Inc. v. Pennzoil Company, 784 F.2d 1133, 1154, 1155 (2d Cir. 1986), *rev'd on other grounds,* 481 U.S. 1 (1987); Lightfoot v. Walker, 797 F.2d 505, 506 (7th Cir. 1986); Olympia Equipment Leasing Co. v. Western Union Telegraph Co., 786 F.2d 1492 (9th Cir. 1985); Federal Prescription Service Inc. v. American Pharmaceutical Association, 636 F. 2d 755, 757–758 (D.C. Cir. 1980); Poplar Grove Planting and Refining Co., Inc. v. Bache Halsey Stuart, Inc., 600 F.2d 1189, 1191 (5th Cir. 1979); United States v. Kurtz, 528 F. Supp. 1113, 1115 (E.D. Pa. 1981), *aff'd* 688 F.2d 827 (3rd Cir.), *cert. denied* 459 U.S. 991 (1982); Wunschel & Small, Inc. v. United States, 554 Suppp. 444, 445 (Cl. Ct. 1983). See, E. Carlson, *Supersedeas Bond Requirements—A Denial Process Rights?*, 39 Baylor L. Rev. 29 (1987).

149 Fidelity & Deposit Co. v. Davis, 127 F.2d 780 (4th Cir. 1942)(dictum) ("bond security payment of money judgment must be given, if . . . stay pending appeal is desired."); Markowitz & Co. v. Toledo Metropolitan Housing Authority, 74 F.R.D. 550, 551 (N.D. Ohio 1977) ("Fed. R. Civ. P. 62(d) requires posting of a supersedeas bond to stay execution of judgment); Slade v. Dickinson, 82 F. Supp. 416 (W.D. Mich. 1949).

150 American Manufactures Mutual Insurance Company v. American Broadcasting-Paramount Theaters, Inc., 385 U.S. 931 (1966).

151 784 F.2d 1133, 1154–1155 (2d Cir. 1986), *rev'd on other grounds,* 481 U.S. 1 (1987).

> likelihood of the judgment debtor's inability or unwillingness to satisfy the judgment in full upon ultimate disposition of the case and where posting adequate security is practicable", whereas no bond or reduced bond would suffice when the creditor's interest, due to unusual circumstances, would not be unduly endangered . . . .

For example, in *Miami International Realty v. Paynter*[152] following a $2,100,000 judgment for Miami, Paynter moved for a stay of execution and waiver of supersedeas bond or, in the alternative, approval by the court of a supersedeas bond for less than the full amount of the judgment. Paynter supported his motion with an affidavit in which he stated he did not have enough assets to post the necessary bond and that execution would cause him irreparable harm and place him in insolvency. To cover the judgment of $2,100,000, the bond would need to be in the amount of $1,600,000, because Paynter's malpractice insurance coverage was for $500,000. The district court, after allowing Paynter's Rule 69 examination to discover his financial position, determined that he did not have additional assets to be used for posting the full amount of Miami's judgment. The court ordered Paynter's malpractice insurance coverage to be placed in escrow pending the stay. It also issued a restraining order prohibiting Paynter from disposing of any assets he had, except those necessary to maintain his ordinary living and business expenses.[153]

A district court may not use unfettered discretion to stay execution without appropriate security, or sufficient reasons for a bond in an amount less than the judgment amount. This principle is expressed by the Fifth Circuit in *Poplar Grove Planting And Refining Co., Inc. v. Bache Halsey Stuart, Inc.*[154] In that case, Poplar Grove recovered a $270,000 judgment against Bache. Bache filed an ex parte motion to fix the amount of the supersedeas bond in order to stay enforcement of the judgment pending appeal. The court fixed a $10,000 bond as the total security. Bache filed the bond, and the court stayed the judgment.

Poplar Grove moved the district court to increase the amount of the bond. The district court denied the motion. Bache appealed the order, and, on the first trip to the appellate court, the case was remanded to the district court for the limited purpose of having the trial court explain its basis for limiting the bond. After the first remand, the district court did not fully explain its reasons for allowing a bond in less than the amount of the judgment. According to the Fifth Circuit, the record on appeal did not objectively determine that Bache was presently capable of responding to the judgment.[155] The Fifth

---

152 807 F.2d 871 (10th Cir. 1986).

153 807 F.2d 871 at 874, (1st Cir. 1986).

154 600 F.2d 1189 (5th Cir. 1979).

155 600 F.2d 1189 at 1191 (5th Cir. 1979).

Circuit again remanded with directions for the district court to promptly "establish some type of positive protection of the judgment creditor's right . . . or . . . to vacate its order approving a reduced supersedeas bond and require full bonded protection during the pendency of this appeal."[156] The Court of Appeals made it clear that the district court had discretion to require a lessor bond, or other security. Other courts have allowed other conditions for a stay pending appeal to preserve the status quo.[157]

§ 1.22 —Checklist for Security Pending Appeal

Checklist for Alternate Security

If a judgment creditor's attorney decides to negotiate for alternate security in lieu of a bond, these are some items to consider:

____ 1. Escrow of the corporate stock
____ 2. Escrow of individual's stock or bonds
____ 3. Pledge of dividends and interest on the escrowed security
____ 4. Pledge of cash security or partial bond
____ 5. Pledge of accounts receivable
____ 6. Security interest in certain personal property
____ 7. Mortgage [or deed of trust] in certain real property

Checklist for Conditions Regarding Security

If a judgment creditor's attorney decides to negotiate for conditions to be established by the court, these are some conditions to consider:

____ 1. Judgment debtors shall maintain the value of their assets and prevent a decrease in such value

---

[156] 600 F.2d, 1189 at 1191.

[157] Trans World Airlines, Inc. v. Hughes, 314 F. Supp. 94, at 96 (S.D.N.Y. 1970), *aff'd* 515 F.2d 173 (2d Cir. 1975), *cert. denied,* 424 U.S. 934 (1976) (Since posting a bond to cover a judgment of $161 million was "not practicable," court would exercise "inherent power in extraordinary circumstances to provide for form and amount for a stay pending appeal" and require a bond of only $75 million coupled with defendants's assurances that it would maintain a net worth treble the balance of the judgment); C. Albert Sauter Company, Inc. v. Richard S. Sauter Company, Inc., 368 F. Supp. 501 (E.D. Pa. 1973); *cf.* International Telemeter Corporation v. Hamlin International Corporation, 754 F.2d 1492, 1495 (9th Cir. 1985); Olympia Equipment Leasing Company v. Western Union Telegraph Company, 786 F.2d 794, 796–798 (7th Cir. 1986).

____ 2. Judgment debtor shall not pay any notes, debts, or other obligations to insiders or affiliates

____ 3. Judgment debtor shall make no financial commitments or expenditures for capital improvements or additions without prior court approval (or limit such expenditures to a certain amount and require court approval for such amounts greater than the set limit)

____ 4. Judgment creditor shall receive monthly profit and loss statements and balance sheets from the corporate judgment debtor, within set reasonable time limits from the end of the month

____ 5. Judgment debtor shall not pay any debts in whole or in part except in the ordinary course of business on debt obligations set forth in the financial statements

____ 6. Corporate judgment debtor shall have fixed salary and benefit limits for corporate officers and directors

____ 7. Judgment creditor shall obtain a conditional mortgage on any and all real and personal property owned by the judgment debtor

____ 8. Judgment creditor shall obtain a restraint on the business judgment debtor, its employees, agents, successors, or assigns from encumbering, conveying, transferring, selling, or assigning any or all of the debtor's property, real and personal, except in the ordinary course of business (or with regard to some assets, without court approval). The definition of ordinary course of business will include only the following:

  ____ a. purchase of supplies and equipment in an arm's length transaction

  ____ b. use of supplies and equipment in the performance of contracts which were executed and in effect at the time of the signing of this Order

  ____ c. payment of reasonable business salaries not to exceed ________ (approved limit set by court) per week for any of the judgment debtor's employees

  ____ d. payment pursuant to an arm's length transaction for the normal and average upkeep or maintenance of any real property, supplies, or equipment necessary for ordinary business operations

  ____ e. (here describe allowance of the ordinary and necessary business activities routinely performed)

  ____ f. payment of reasonable attorney's fees and expenses

____ 9. Judgment creditor shall obtain a restraint on the withdrawing of funds from the judgment debtor's savings and/or checking accounts, cashing time certificates of deposit, stocks, bonds or marketable securities; and removing the contents of any of debtor's safe deposit boxes

____ 10. Judgment creditor shall have the right to select an independent auditor to inspect any and all records of the judgment debtor to ascertain compliance with the Order of the court

____ 11. The judgment debtor shall prepare and execute all documents necessary to provide the conditions of security listed in the Order (or stipulation) within fifteen (15) [or other reasonable time] days of this Order. All escrow fees necessary for effectuating the conditions of security herein shall be paid for by the judgment debtor

____ 12. All filing fees necessary for the security conditions provided herein shall be paid for by the judgment creditor as a cost of this litigation

§ 1.23 Stay in Favor of the United States or Agency

Rule 62(e) provides: When an appeal is taken by the United States or an officer or agency thereof or by the direction of any department of the Government of the United States and the operation or enforcement of the judgment is stayed, no bond, obligation, or other security shall be required from the appellant.

Rule 62(e) was explained in the case of *Lightfoot v. Walker.*[158] The Seventh Circuit noted: Judgments against the United States, for example, are paid out of a general appropriation (the "Judgments Fund," as it is called) to the Treasury.[159] This makes Rule 62(e), which entitles the federal government (and its departments, agencies, and officers) to a stay of execution pending appeal, without its having to post a bond or other security, appropriate.

§ 1.24 Stay According to State Law

Under Rule 62(f), a judgment debtor is entitled to a stay as provided under the circumstances by state law. ". . . [A] motion seeking a stay of execution of a

[158] 797 F.2d 505 (7th Cir. 1986)

[159] *See* 28 U.S.C. §§ 2414, 2517 and 31 U.S.C. § 1304.

registered judgment under Rule 62(f) is addressed to the sound discretion of the district court in the same manner as motions seeking a stay of an original proceedings in a district court."[160] According to the plain meaning of the Rule, the district court must review the state law, and determine its applicability to the conditions under which the stay may be granted. In *Matthews v. CTI Container Transport International, Inc.,* the district court interpreting New York law stated: "a bond in the full amount of the judgment may be dispensed with 'only when the judgment creditor is afforded definite and certain recourse to some other means for the enforcement of his judgment.'"[161]

§ 1.25 Stay by the Appellate Court under Federal Rule 8

Ordinarily a request for a stay must be made in the first instance in the district court.[162] Rule 8(a) does permit a motion for stay in the court of appeals where such an application to the district court is not practicable, or where the district court had denied the application or has failed to afford the relief requested.[163] Rule 8 authorizes an appellate court to stay a district court judgment, and the requirement of posting a bond is discretionary.[164]

> Rule 8, which is based on the power conferred on federal courts and judges by the All Writs Act, 28 U.S.C. § 1651(a)[165] does indeed authorize this court to stay a judgment pending appeal, with or without bond; and if the basis of the application for such stay lay in events occurring after the district court had denied a similar application, we would make an independent judgment. But if as in the present case the application is in effect an appeal from the district judge's denial of the stay, we shall treat it as such and give the district judge's action appropriate deference.[166]

---

160 United States v. Home Indemnity Company, 549 F.2d 10, 14 (7th Cir. 1977).

161 Matthews v. Oil Container Transport International, Inc., 689 F. Supp. 348, 350 (S.D.N.Y. 1988).

162 Rakovich v. Wade, 834 F.2d 673 (7th Cir. 1987).

163 *Id.* at 675.

164 Lightfoot v. Walker, 797 F.2d 505, 507 (7th Cir. 1986); Federal Prescription Service, Inc. v. American Pharmaceutical Association, 636 F.2d 755, 760 (D.C. Cir. 1980); Perez v. United States, 578 F. Supp. 1318, 1320 (D.P.R. 1984).

165 See Note of Advisory Comm. to Rule 8.

166 Lightfoot v. Walker, 797 F.2d 505, 507.

§ 1.26 Collecting on a Bond or Other Security

A supersedeas bond is a contract, and interpretation of its terms are a matter of law.[167]

The interpretation of a bond agreement, however, is a unique task. While the parties' intent is controlling, much of the language in the bond is likely to be boilerplate, with portions dating back more than a century. Cases interpreting past bond agreements must be considered, for they almost certainly influenced the language the bonding company chose.[168]

The conditions which trigger a surety's obligation under a supersedeas bond are not defined in any federal statute, provision of the Federal Rules of Civil Procedure, or provision of the Federal Rules of Appellate Procedure.[169] The contract terms contained in the appeal bond determine the liability of the surety.[170]

Collecting on the bond, if the conditions of the bond are met, should be routine. If the judgment debtor loses the appeal, and the other conditions of the bond are satisfied, it is recommended that the judgment creditor's attorney send a letter to the bonding company requesting payment according to the bond's terms. The attorney should include in the letter attested or certified copies of the appellate judgment and any other documents necessary by the terms and conditions of the bond, so that the bonding company reviewing the letter will have all necessary documents to issue a check to the judgment creditor. Before sending the letter, it is suggested that a call be made to the bonding company's attorney to alert the company regarding the loss on appeal, and to check to see if all the conditions for payment of the bond have been met.

---

167 Beatrice Foods Co. v. New England Printing and Lithographing Company, 930 F.2d 1572, 1574 (Fed. Cir. 1991).

168 *Id.*

169 *Id.*, Tennessee Valley Authority v. Atlas Mach. & Iron Works, Inc., 803 F.2d 794, 798 (4th Cir. 1986); Moore v. Townsend, 577 F.2d 424, 426 n.5 (7th Cir. 1978).

170 Beatrice Foods Co., 930 F.2d 1572 at 1574; Aetna Casualty & Surety Company v. LaSalle Pump & Supply Co., Inc., 804 F.2d 315, 317 (5th Cir. 1986). The *Beatrice Foods* case is an excellent source for the discussion of particular bond interpretation and contains citations to the leading cases on the subject.

JURISDICTION OF THE FEDERAL COURT TO ENFORCE JUDGMENT

§ 1.27 Preserving Judgments of the Federal Courts

It has long been established that a federal district court has authority to enforce its judgments.[171]

"[T]he rule is universal, that if the power is conferred to render the judgment or enter the decree, it also includes the power to issue proper process to enforce such judgment or decree.

. . . [T]he jurisdiction of a court is not exhausted by the rendition of the judgment, but continues until that judgment shall be satisfied."[172]

Whenever a general rule as to property or personal rights, or injuries to either, is established by State legislation, its enforcement by a Federal court in a case between proper parties is a matter of course, and the jurisdiction of the court in such a case, is not subject to State limitation.[173]

A federal court, in order to effectuate its judicial power, may enforce its judgment and conduct proceedings to aid execution of its judgment through a writ of execution.[174] A federal court, in order to effectuate its own judgment may apply state law in the enforcement process.[175] "In the absence of controlling federal statutes, 'the district court has the same authority to aid judgment creditors . . . as that . . . provided to state courts under local law.' "[176]

In *Atlantic Purchasers, Inc. v. Aircraft Sales, Inc.*, the District court held that it had jurisdiction in enforcing the $46,000 judgment of Atlantic Purchasers, Inc. and other plaintiffs against Aircraft Sales, Inc. In the

---

171 Railway Co. v. Whitton's Administrator, 80 U.S. (13 Wall.) 270 (1871); Riggs v. Johnson County, 73 U.S. (6 Wall.) 166, 187 (1867); Argento v. Village of Melrose Park, 838 F.2d 1483, 1487 (7th Cir. 1988); McKee-Berger-Mansueto. Inc. v. Board of Education Of The City Of Chicago, 691 F.2d 828, 831 (7th Cir. 1982); Duchek v. Jacobi, 646 F.2d 415, 418–419 (9th Cir. 1981); United States *ex rel.* Goldman v. Meredith, 596 F.2d 1353, 1357 (8th Cir.) *cert. denied,* 444 U.S. 838 (1979); Kashi v. Gratsos, 712 F. Supp. 23, 25–26 (S.D.N.Y.) 1989); Atlantic Purchasers, Inc. v. Aircraft Sales, Inc., 101 F.R.D. 779, 781–782 (W.D.N.C. 1984).

172 Riggs v. Johnson County, 73 U.S. (6 Wall.) 166, 187 (1867).

173 Railway Co. v. Whitton's Administrator, 80 U.S. (13 Wall.) 270, 286 (1871).

174 Fed. R. Civ. P. 69(a); Hankins v. Finnel, 759 F. Supp. 569 (W.D. Mo. 1991).

175 Duchek v. Jacobi, 646 F.2d 415, 417 (9th Cir. 1981); United States *ex rel.* Goldman v. Meredith, 596 F.2d 1353, 1357 (8th Cir.) *cert. denied,* 444 U.S. 838 (1979); Atlantic Purchasers, Inc. v. Aircraft Sales, Inc., 101 F.R.D. 779, 782 (W.D.N.C. 1984).

176 Duchek v. Jacobi, 646 F.2d at 417.

enforcement process the court held that it was authorized to take several steps utilizing North Carolina law in the enforcement process. First, pursuant to North Carolina General Statutes § 1-352, et seq., the Court was authorized "to order discovery of defendant's assets, and to order sale by execution of defendants' property to the extent necessary to satisfy the judgment."[177] Next, pursuant to North Carolina General Statutes § 39-15, "both plaintiffs and the receiver are entitled under North Carolina law to institute actions based on fraudulent conveyance of defendants' property." The court was "satisfied that it may exercise ancillary subject matter jurisdiction over such claims, without regard to diversity of citizenship or amount in controversy." The district court, in the *Atlantic Purchasers* case, in assessing the possibility that defendants controlled a New York corporation from North Carolina, and may have transferred substantial corporate assets outside of the state, also considered that it had authority under North Carolina's long arm statute, North Carolina General Statutes § 1-75.4, and under general constitutional principles of due process, to bring the corporation within its jurisdiction. The court could also exercise in rem or quasi in rem jurisdiction to attach property located within the state pursuant to North Carolina General Statutes § 1-75.8, based on the fraudulent conveyance action.[178]

In fact, certain procedural law requirements of state law are not applicable to limit a federal district court's jurisdiction to enforce its judgment.[179] In *Duchek v. Jacobi,* a California procedural rule requiring a judgment creditor to file a petition with the county superior court to appraise a homestead and conduct an execution sale did not deprive the federal court of its jurisdiction to enforce its judgment.[180] Also, in *Kashi v. Gratos,* New York procedural law that required a judgment creditor to obtain permission of the Surrogate's Court prior to enforcing a judgment against the estate of a deceased judgment debtor did not limit a federal district court's jurisdiction to enforce its judgment. Of course, in *Kashi,* the court noted that state procedural law may impose some limits of the jurisdiction of a federal district court to enforce its judgments.[181] Among such state law limitations are those that determine "the type of property which can be subject to execution."[182] A federal district court's jurisdiction, however, is not limited by state procedural laws that, when read literally, indicate that only a specific state court may hold enforcement proceedings.[183]

---

[177] 101 F.R.D. at 782.

[178] 101 F.R.D. at 782–783.

[179] Duchek v. Jacobi, 646 F.2d 415, 417 (9th Cir. 1981); Kashi v. Gratsos, 712 F. Supp. 23, 26 (S.D.N.Y. 1989).

[180] Duchek v. Jacobi, 646 F.2d 415, 417.

[181] 712 F. Supp. at 25.

[182] Marshak v. Green, 746 F.2d 927, 930 (2d Cir. 1984).

[183] 712 F. Supp. at 25–26.

However, in *Eagerton v. Valuations, Inc.*, the Eleventh Circuit, in speaking of the use of ancillary jurisdiction to protect the judgment of a district court stated: "[a] distinction must be drawn between those acts which are necessary to enforce a judgment or order and those which are done merely for the sake of procedural convenience and bear no relationship to the court's earlier exercise of constitutional or statutory jurisdiction."[184]

§ 1.28 Stay of State Court Proceedings by Federal Courts

It is a settled principle of law that where a federal court has first acquired jurisdiction of the subject matter of a case, it may enjoin parties from proceeding in a state court action where the effect would be to defeat or impair the jurisdiction of the federal court.[185] A federal court, if it has fully and finally adjudicated a matter, may enjoin the relitigation of the matter in state court.[186]

In *Meridian Investing & Development Corporation v. Suncoast Highland Corporation,* when Suncoast failed to appeal a New York federal court judgment by Meridian, Meridian first registered the judgment in the United States for the Middle District of Florida pursuant to 28 U.S.C. § 1963. Next, Meridian started federal proceedings to collect the judgment. Suncoast obtained a restraining order against Meridian from the Pinellas County Circuit Court in Florida. Meridian, among other things, sought a preliminary and permanent injunction against Suncoast in the Middle District of Florida. The federal district court denied Meridian's motion. On appeal, the Fifth Circuit held that the district court should have granted Meridian's request for the dissolution of the Florida state court injunction.[187]

---

[184] 698 F.2d 1115, at 1119 (11th Cir. 1983). *See* National Westminster Bank U.S.A. v. W.S. Cheng, 751 F. Supp. 1158, 1160 (S.D.N.Y. 1990) ("Under the doctrine of ancillary jurisdiction, a federal district court is empowered to adjudicate ancillary claims involving state law without an independent basis of subject matter jurisdiction. . . . Ancillary jurisdiction may be exercised to protect a judgment of a court through enforcement.")

[185] Kline v. Burke Construction Company, 260 U.S. 226, 229 (1922).

[186] Meridian Investing & Development Corporation v. Suncoast Highland Corporation, 628 F.2d 370, 373 (5th Cir. Unit B 1980); International Association of Machinists & Aerospace Workers v. Nix, 512 F.2d 125, 130 (5th Cir. 1975). See generally Montana v. United States, 440 U.S. 147, 153–54 (1979).

[187] 628 F.2d 370, 372. *E.g.,* General Atomic Co. v. Felter, 434 U.S. 12 (1977); Donovan v. Dallas, 377 U.S. 408, 412–13 (1964).

FAIR DEBT COLLECTION PRACTICES ACT

§ 1.29 Attorneys Are Subject to the Fair Debt Collection Practices Act on Consumer Claims

Under the Fair Debt Collection Practices Act (Fair Debt Act) as originally drafted, the term "debt collector under 15 U.S.C. § 1692a(6)(F) exempted 'any attorney-at-law collecting or attempting to collect a debt as an attorney on behalf of and in the name of a client. . . .'"[188] This exemption from the Fair Debt Act for attorneys was deleted by the amendments to the Act.[189] "The statute as enacted on September 20, 1977, contained an exception for attorneys collecting debts on behalf of clients. . . . Congress deleted that exception, however, in 1986."[190] Thus, a lawyer is now subject to the Fair Debt Act if she ". . . regularly collects or attempts to collect, directly or indirectly, debts owed or due or asserted to be owed or due another" by a natural person, where the debt arises out of a consumer transaction, namely one primarily for personal, family or household purposes.[191] The Act's provisions for protecting consumers apply to lawyers who collect on an occasional basis and the small law firm which collects debts incidentally to the general practice of law.[192]

In *Crossley v. Lieberman* the regularity of Attorney Lieberman's debt collection practice was established by Lieberman's testimony on direct examination:

Q. Did you regularly conduct business on behalf of creditors at that period of time? Was that a principal part of your practice?
A. It's a part of it.
Q. Was it a principal part in September of 1986?
A. Yes.
Q. Did your practice for those creditors include and was it principally the collection of debt?
A. Yes.[193]

The statistics on Lieberman showed that he had filed 32 collection-type cases in the Court of Common Pleas during the relevant period, and had also filed

---

188 Pub.L.No. 90-321, Title VIII, § 803, as added Pub.L. No. 95-109, 91 Stat. 875(1977).

189 Pub.L.No. 99-361, 100 Stat.768(1986).

190 Crossley v. Lieberman, 868 F.2d 566, 569–70 (3d Cir. 1989).

191 15 U.S.C. §§ 1692a(3), 1692a(5), and 1692a(6).

192 Crossley v. Lieberman, 868 F.2d 566, 569 (3d Cir. 1989); Accord, Littles v. Lieberman, 90 B.R. 700 (Bankr. E.D. Pa. 1988); See R. Hobbs, *Attorneys Must Now Comply With Fair Debt Collection Law,* 46 Pa.J.L.Rptr., 3 (Nov. 21, 1987).

193 868 F.2d 566, 570.

175 mortgage foreclosures and collection suits for financial institutions.[194] However, in reviewing this decision, it is important to consider that only a portion of an attorney's practice has to be in the collection area, for collections to be considered a regular part of the practice and for the Fair Debt Act to be applicable. It is essential, therefore, for the practicing attorneys to comply with the Fair Debt Act in any consumer collection cases handled by their firm.

§ 1.30 Prohibited Practices under the Fair Debt Collection Practices Act

In the case of *Crossley v. Lieberman*[195] the Third Circuit explained that the Fair Debt Collection Practices Act "prohibits the use of abusive, deceptive and unfair debt collection practices by persons engaged in the debt collection industry."[196] The goal of the Fair Debt Act is to eliminate abusive debt collection practices, and the Act is applicable whether or not a valid debt exists.[197]

Practice Tips

In *Crossley,* the Court, quoting a Congressional Report on the matter listed the prohibited practices:

1. Late night telephone calls to consumers [15 U.S.C. § 1692c(a)(1)]
2. Calls to consumers' employers concerning the consumer's debts [15 U.S.C. § 1692c(a)(3)]
3. Frequent and repeated calls to consumers [15 U.S.C. § 1692d(5)]
4. Threats of legal action on small debts where there is little likelihood that legal action will be taken [15 U.S.C. § 1692c(2), (3); 15 U.S.C. § 1692d(1); 15 U.S.C. § 1692e(5); *Cf.* 15 U.S.C. § 1692f(6)]
5. Simulation of legal process [15 U.S.C. § 1692e(9), (13)]
6. Harassment [15 U.S.C. § 1692d]
7. Abuse [15 U.S.C. § 1692d]
8. Threats of seizure, and attachment and sale of property where there is little likelihood that such action will be taken [15 U.S.C. § 1692e(4), (5); Cf. 15 U.S.C. § 1692f(6)][198]

---

194 868 F.2d 566, 570 n.2.

195 868 F.2d 566 (3rd Cir. 1989),

196 868 F.2d at 570.

197 Baker v. G.C. Services Corp., 677 F.2d 775, 777 (9th Cir. 1982); Johnson v. Statewide Collections, Inc., 778 P.2d 93, 99 (Wyo. 1989).

198 H.R. Rep. No. 405, 99th Cong., 2d Sess. (1985), *reprinted in* 1986 U.S.C.C.A.N. 1752, 1755 (statutory references in brackets added.)

In *Crossley v. Lieberman,* Lieberman's actions which violated three provisions of Fair Debt Act § 1692e. First, he sent a letter in which threatened to take legal action within one week of the date of the letter, unless payment was made in full. The Pennsylvania foreclosure law did not allow suit within a week, and so, he had no intention of filing suit within the week. Second, his letter was misleading in that it failed to inform Crossley of her right under Pennsylvania law to cure the default and that a sheriff's sale was not imminent.[199] Third, Lieberman's letter was threatening in that he said, "I will be compelled to proceed with suit against you." Thus, the letter clearly implied that he would file suit within the week if payment was not received on behalf of his client.

It is clear that attorneys must now comply with all requirements of the Act. For example, if a consumer debtor requests verification of a debt within the meaning of § 1692g(b), the attorney has an obligation to provide the debtor with verification of the debt, or the name and address of the original creditor, or the information on the disputed debt. The Fair Debt Collection Practices Act, 15 U.S.C. § 1692g(a)(4), (5) and (b) provides that the debt collector shall send the consumer a written notice containing information on the validity of the debt, and the consumer's right to dispute the debt.

An attorney should specifically comply with those requirements. For example, if the consumer disputes the validity of the debt, as in the case of *Johnson v. Statewide Collection, Inc.*[200] the debt collector has a duty to comply with the statutory requirements, and send the consumer the validation information as stated in § 1692g(b). "It was CheckRite's duty, under the statute, to cease collection activities on the date it received the letter from Johnson's counsel until it sent Johnson, through his counsel, verification of the alleged debt." [201]

Also, the statute is clear and unambiguous that the verification required under § 1692g(b) must be in writing. "Application of that concept to this statute manifests an implicit requirement that verification furnished from the creditor must be in writing because the statute also requires that a copy of the verification be mailed to the consumer."[202] Such conduct by a law firm collecting a debt, would probably not be considered a technical violation.[203] In

---

199 Masuda v. Thomas Richards & Co., 759 F. Supp. 1456, 1460 C.D. Cal. 1991) (debt collector violated the FDCPA by sending consumer letters which purported to have been sent by an attorney).

200 778 P.2d 93 (Wyo. 1989)

201 778 P.2d at 100 (Wyo. 1989).

202 Johnson v. Statewide Collections, Inc., 778 P.2d 93, 100 (Wyo. 1989); *Accord,* Riveria v. MAB Collections, Inc., 682 F. Supp. 174, 177 (W.D.N.Y. 1988).

203 *Cf.* Pearce v. Rapid Check Collection, Inc., 738 F. Supp. 334, 338 (D.S.D. 1990) (court held there was a technical violation of the act when agency sent letter directly to debtor although debtor was represented by an attorney) with Johnson v. Statewide Collections, Inc., 778 P.2d 93, 102–03 (Wyo. 1989) (violation of Fair Debt Collection Practices Act)

fact, in *Pearce v. Rapid Check Collection, Inc.,* the district court for South Dakota noted the requirements of the Fair Debt Act which protects consumers, including the requirements of written validation of debts.[204]

Courts have consistently indicated that the Act is intended to be viewed from the least sophisticated consumer standard.[205] Thus, it is suggested that counsel should not consider one consumer, because of his occupation or education, to be more sophisticated than another consumer. On the application of this standard, all requirements of the Fair Debt Act should be met with all consumer debtors.

§ 1.31 Penalties Applicable to Attorneys Who Violate the Act

Civil liability for violating any provision of the Fair Debt Collection Practices Act is provided in 15 U.S.C. § 1692k. The statute provides:

> (a) Except as otherwise provided by this section, any debt collector who fails to comply with any provision of this sub chapter with respect to any person is liable to such person in an amount equal to the sum of—
>
> (1) any actual damage sustained by such person as a result of such failure;
>
> (2)(A) in the case of any action by an individual, such additional damages as the court may allow, but not exceeding $1,000; or
>
> (B) in the case of a class action, (i) such amount for each named plaintiff as could be recovered under subparagraph (A), and (ii) such amount as the court may allow for all other class members, without regard to a minimum individual recovery, not to exceed the lesser of $500,000 or 1 per centum of the net worth of the debt collector; and
>
> (3) in the case of any successful action to enforce the foregoing liability, the costs of the action, together with a reasonable attorney's fee as determined by the court. On a finding by the court that an action under this section was brought in bad faith and for the purpose of harassment, the court may award to the defendant attorney's fees reasonable in relation to the work expended and costs. . . .

---

by debt collector sending demand letter directly to debtor when collector had been advised that debtor was represented by an attorney).

204 738 F. Supp. at 337.

205 See Swanson v. Southern Oregon Credit Service, Inc., 869 F.2d 1222, 1227 (9th Cir. 1988) (applying the least sophisticated debtor standard to a claim that a debt collector made a "threat to take any action that cannot legally be taken" in violation of 15 U.S.C. § 1692e(5)); Jeter v. Credit Bureau, 760 F.2d 1168, 1172–73 (11th Cir. 1985) (applying the least sophisticated debtor standard to claim that debt collector used "false representation or deceptive means to collect or attempt to collect any debt" in violation of 15 U.S.C. § 1692e(10)); Baker v. G.C. Services, Inc., 677 F. 2d 775, 778 (9th Cir. 1982); Masuda v. Thomas Richards & Co., 759 F. Supp. 1456, 1460–62 (C.D. Cal. 1991); United States v. Central Adjustment Bureau, Inc., 667 F. Supp. 370, 375 (N.D. Tex. 1986).

For example, in *Crossley v. Lieberman*[206] the Bankruptcy Court awarded Mary Crossley, a Chapter 13 bankruptcy debtor, $500 based on violations of the Fair Debt Collection Practices Act by Arnold R. Lieberman, an attorney. The District Court modified the Bankruptcy Court findings of fact and conclusions of law, and increased the award to $2,000. Lieberman appealed. The Third Circuit Court of Appeals upheld the District Court finding that Lieberman violated the Fair Debt Act in several particulars. First, he threatened acceleration of Crossley's residential mortgage, violating § 1692e(5) and (10), by threatening legal action he could not then take and by falsely implying that Crossley's mortgage foreclosure case was already in litigation. Lieberman also threatened to take action "within one week" of the date of the letter unless Crossley paid $297.79 overdue to Fleet Consumers Discount Company. Additionally, the Third Circuit upheld the ruling that the letter was misleading because it failed to notify Crossley of her rights to cure the default and explain that a sheriff's sale was not imminent. Lastly, Lieberman's letter did not provide Crossley with a written validation notice as required by § 1692g. Based on an analysis of the liability factors under 15 U.S.C. § 1692(k), the Third Circuit found the award of actual damages of $1,000 proper, and also held proper the award of $1,000 additional damages under § 1692k(a)(2)(A).[207] Although there were multiple violations of the Act, the statutory liability for one plaintiff under section 1692k(a)(2)(A) were limited to $1,000.[208]

For example, although not involving attorneys as debt collectors, the Courts have been awarding statutory damages and attorney's fees for violations of the Act. In *Riveria v. MAB Collections, Inc.,* plaintiff made no claim for actual damages, but the Court awarded the plaintiff statutory damages of $1,000, plus costs and attorneys fees, in that it found MAB was intentionally circumventing the purpose of the Fair Debt Act by "hiding" the notice required under § 1692(g) on the reverse side of its form.[209] In another case, *Baker v. G.C. Services Corp.,*[210] the district court awarded statutory damages of $1,000, even though no proof of actual damages, and attorney's fees of $800 were upheld. The basic statutory damages of $1,000 were awarded by the District Court in *Masuda v. Thomas Richards & Co.*[211] A state appellate court upheld an award of attorneys fees and actual damages for violation of the Fair Debt Act in *Venes v. Professional Service Bureau, Inc.*[212]

---

206 868 F.2d 566 (3rd Cir. 1989).

207 868 F.2d 572–573.

208 868 F.2d, at 572; *Cf.* Harper v. Better Business Services, Inc. 768 F. Supp. 817, 819 (N.D. Ga. 1991) *aff'd* 961 F.2d 1561 (11th Cir. 1992); Harvey v. United Adjusters, 509 F. Supp. 1218, 1222 (D. Or. 1981).

209 682 F. Supp. 174, 179 (W.D.N.Y. 1988).

210 677 F.2d 775, 778 (9th Cir. 1982).

211 759 F. Supp. 1456, 1467 (C.D. Cal. 1991).

212 353 N.W. 2d 671, 675–76 (Minn. App. 1986).

Therefore, based on the analysis of some of the recent cases under the Fair Debt Collection Practices Act, it is a statute that now applies to practicing attorneys in consumer debt collection practice. Practitioners must comply with all provisions of the Fair Debt Act, or likely find themselves responsible for any actual damages the consumer incurs as a result of violations of the Act, plus statutory damages of up to $1,000 and attorney's fees. In any case of consequence, the consumer's attorney's fees could be quite considerable, and it is recommended that careful compliance with the Fair Debt Collection Practice Act is the best.

Table 1–1

Selected State Statutory Provisions

Alaska	1972, c. 68	8-16-1972	AS 09.30.100 to 09.30.180.
California	1967, c. 503	11-8-1967	West's Ann.Cal.C.C.P. §§ 1713 to 1713.8.
Colorado	1977, c. 197	7-1-1977	West's C.R.S.A. §§ 13-62-101 to 13-62-109.
Connecticut	1988, P.L. 88-39	4-13-1988*	C.G.S.A. §§ 52-610 to 52-618.
Georgia	1975, pp. 479–482		O.C.G.A. §§ 9-12-110 to 9-12-117.
Idaho	1990, C. 408		I.C. §§ 10-1401 to 10-1409.
Illinois	1963, p. 1506	7-15-1963*	S.H.A. ch. 110, ¶¶ 12-618 to 12-626.
Iowa	1989, S.F. 111	5-18-1989	I.C.A. §§ 626B.1 to 626.B.8.
Maryland	1963, c. 201	6-1-1963	Code, courts and Judicial Proceedings, §§ 10-701 to 10-709.
Massachusetts	1966, c. 638	9-3-1966*	M.G.L.A. c. 235, § 23A.
Michigan	1967, No. 191	11-2-1967	M.C.L.A. §§ 691.1151 to 691.1159.
Minnesota	1985, c. 218	5-23-1985*	M.S.A. § 548.35.
Missouri	1984, H.B. 957	6-21-1984*	V.A.M.S. §§ 511.770 to 511.787.
New Mexico	1991, c. 180	7-1-1991	NMSA 1978, §§ 39-4B-1 to 39-4B-9.
New York	1970, c. 981	9-1-1970	McKinney's CPLR 5301 to 5309
Ohio	1985, SB 19		R.C. §§ 2329.90 to 2329.94.
Oklahoma	1965, c. 448	6-30-1965*	12 Okl.St.Ann. §§ 710 to 718.
Oregon	1977, c. 61	10-4-1977	ORS 24.200 to 24.255
Pennsylvania	L. 1990, Act 139	12-21-1990*	42 P.S. §§ 22001 to 22009.
Texas	1981, c. 808	6-17-1981	V.T.C.A., Civil Practice and Remedies Code §§ 36.001 to 36.008
Virginia	1990, c. 276		Code 1950, §§ 8.01-456.6 to 8.01-465.13.
Washington	1975, c.240, 1st Ex.Sess.	6-26-1975	West's RCWA 6.40.010 to 6.40.915.

CHAPTER 2

THE JUDGMENT DEBTOR

§ 2.1 Introduction

In any judgment enforcement case, knowledge about the debtor is essential for successful collection efforts. Plaintiff's counsel must be willing to spend some time learning about the individual debtor and his routines and habits. If the debtor is a corporation, plaintiff's counsel should learn its business structure and routines of doing business. It is important to know how to locate and trace the debtor who has absconded. This Chapter will focus on the debtor, the debtor's routines and habits, and discuss some important preliminary strategy.

§ 2.2 Reviewing the Client's Files on the Debtor

When a plaintiff's attorney recovers a judgment for his client, he must take certain basic steps in the judgment enforcement process. First, if necessary, the judgment must be registered in any foreign districts. [See **Chapter 1.**] Second, wherever the judgment is registered, it must be recorded as a lien in any county where the defendant, now a judgment debtor, resides or owns property. [See **Chapter 1.**] In fact, he may file liens on the defendant's property in several locations. Third, after those initial steps, it is helpful to gather all necessary background information on the judgment debtor.

When he commences suit, all the plaintiff's counsel needs is information concerning the contract, account, or note on which the defendant is allegedly liable, including the original documents, and the address of the debtor for service of process. After recovering a judgment for his client, plaintiff's counsel needs information on the judgment debtor's financial ability and location of the judgment debtor's assets. To begin the process of gathering information for postjudgment collection, the judgment creditor's attorney must educate himself about the judgment debtor.

The attorney should interview the plaintiff's representative in charge of the defendant's account. A personal interview is best. The plaintiff's attorney should request the representatives of the plaintiff to bring all available defendant's files to his office. He should obtain background information on the defendant by reviewing files and any applications or credit histories given to the plaintiff at the time of the original loan or contract. These files on the defendant may contain valuable information on the defendant's financial background, business assets, present and former addresses, social security number, names and addresses of relatives, present and past employers, and the like.

The plaintiff's counsel faces a different kind of defendant with each judgment he attempts to collect. A judgment enables the plaintiff's attorney, for perhaps the first time in the litigation process, to attempt to locate a defendant's assets through postjudgment discovery. Each defendant and each case will present him with unique problems. In the easy case, plaintiff's attorney recovers the judgement, and in about 30 days he will have a check in the mail from the judgment debtor. This is not the type of case analyzed in this book.

This book focuses on the problematic judgment enforcement case, which requires good planning, strategy, and tactics to find and trace assets for successful resolution. During this process there are often difficult legal and investigative problems that arise. This book is intended to assist the busy practitioner by giving ideas for recovery of assets, for meeting discovery problems, execution and judicial sales problems, and for generating new and creative ideas for motions and trials to enforce and collect the judgement. Also this book contains materials to assist in receivership cases, to assist in strategy for post-judgment motions and in developing theories for recovery. The main focus of this book concerns problems in judgment enforcement in federal court, but the plaintiff's attorney will realize that the methodology and tactics discussed also apply to judgment enforcement cases in state court. Additionally, since Federal Rule of Civil Procedure 69(a) follows practice and procedure of the state in which the district court is located, there is specific discussion of the applicable state laws in a number of areas.

In this book the plaintiff's attorney is given ideas for tracing assets, techniques for discovery, methods for execution against various types of assets, sale of those assets by execution sale or judicial sale, applicable remedies to recover assets, and principals of trials on plaintiff's suits to enforce judgments. Furthermore, the book will present an overview of the requirements of the United States in enforcing a judgment under the Federal Debt Collection Procedures Act which became effective in May 1991, and is codified in 28 U.S.C. §§ 3001–3308.

Plaintiff's counsel, in enforcing judgments, should strive to understand the habits and routines of the defendant-debtor. This will assist counsel in developing ideas of when, where, and how the debtor may have hidden assets. The debtor may be very cunning, and has the advantage of time and the knowledge that someone may later be searching for these assets. Often judgment enforcement litigation requires the plaintiff's counsel to search for assets using documents obtained from the debtor or from some other source. It requires the plaintiff's attorney to develop an understanding of the methods and routines of the defendant-debtor's business. Usually the debtor has hidden assets in such a way to make the job of locating collectible assets very difficult. The officers and directors of the defendant company, or the individual debtor, know at the beginning of the litigation process, that eventually the plaintiff will recover a judgment. So, often, the defendant decides to transfer and hide assets, long before the plaintiff has a right to look for them.

> Even with the honest debtor," [Joseph] Braunstein adds, "collecting is an art, a science, a strategy. When debtors reach the point where they have to stall, they become very evasive. They have to stay alive, so they become extremely resourceful in trying to preserve what assets they have. They fraudulently conceal or transfer them." . . . . Stuart Brenner . . . agrees. "The dishonest debtor is a pro. . . . He's almost impossible to collect from, hiding behind corporations, skipping, creating fictitious disputes—the merchandise didn't arrive, or wasn't right. His tactics are delay and stall."[1]

When counsel starts to look for assets, he should strive to know as much as he can about the debtor. Very often enough he develops evidence through real estate records, corporate documents, and bank records to establish where the debtor has hidden assets. [See **Chapter 4.**] It is very important to gather information on where he can find this evidence. If he has an understanding of the debtor, a sense of the debtor's history from his client's files on the debtor, and a knowledge of the debtor's business, then he will be ready to begin a

---

[1] Anshaw, *Psychology: The Indispensable Collection Tool,* Commercial Law Bulletin, Sept. 12, 14 (Sept.–Oct. 1989).

proper investigation or be ready to begin informing his investigator of what information he needs to accumulate.

After the counsel interviews his client, the client's files on the debtor are an excellent place to start to look for evidence. The files contain information on the individual debtor or on the corporate debtor. The kind of data varies depending on his client's records keeping practices and the kind of business relationship involved with the debtor. After he reviews the documents the client maintains in its home office files, counsel should ask about any files in its branch offices, or files on the debtor which may be maintained by the client's subsidiaries or related businesses. Plaintiff's counsel must be sure to review and have copies of all pertinent files.

§ 2.3 Information from the Debtor's Files

Regardless of whether the debtor is an individual or a corporation, plaintiffs counsel will want to examine any documents which detail what the debtor's financial condition was like when the debtor first initiated business with his client. Information can be gleaned from financial statements, tax returns, and credit applications of the debtor. Counsel must focus on the financial history of the debtor and any previous list of assets the defendant provided his client at the beginning of their relationship.

If the debtor had these assets when the debtor began business with his client, then counsel will want to establish documentation and testimony to trace those assets through the business routines of the debtor over the last few years. Tracing assets begins with knowing what assets the debtor had at a particular point in time. Later, the debtor may plead insolvency and inability to pay his client's claim, and, in fact, be living comfortably on his hidden assets. Therefore, plaintiff's counsel should focus carefully on the debtor's financial transactions, and he may find that the assets are still in control of the debtor, but, for example, are now in the debtor's new business, or in a trust, which the debtor or his relatives control for the debtor's benefit.

Certainly information concerning the individual debtor's name, address, social security number, and relatives' addresses may serve to help counsel locate a debtor who absconds with the client's secured collateral. Cancelled checks or information on the debtor's bank name and account numbers help counsel trace funds drawn on that bank and deposited in another bank by the debtor in a attempt to place funds beyond the reach of creditors. Counsel must review correspondence, collection reports, employment history, and the client's telephone records which will often give him information on the debtor's personality, job experience, salary payments, and credit history. Tax returns, if available, give the attorney much information about the debtor, and his sources of income, savings accounts, stocks, interest payments, and deductions. If they are not available, they will be among the documents counsel seeks to have the debtor produce in post-judgment discovery. Of course, in some cases, plaintiff's counsel will find that the debtor was giving his client false or inflated financial statements and credit applications. Knowing this will save time in trying to trace assets that never existed.

If the judgment debtor is a business, plaintiff's counsel should adjust his approach accordingly. [See §§ **2.5** and **2.6.**] The information counsel wants on the business organization details the type of business, and its last known address and phone number. The information should contain the name and address of the principals. Counsel also needs financial information on the company as a starting point to reconstruct the financial history of the business. Importantly, counsel should obtain a list of the debtor's assets, including real estate, automobiles, trucks, furniture, fixtures, equipment, inventory, accounts receivable, and other assets. Any financial statements or tax returns will schedule the loans made from the corporation to its principals. Any such unpaid loans give plaintiff's counsel a possible avenue of collection. In post-judgment discovery, obtaining this information enables the plaintiff's attorney to trace assets and their disposition or current location. Plaintiff's counsel should obtain a list of the defendant-debtor's customers as part of the records obtained in post-judgment discovery. These customers may be a source of knowledge concerning the debtor's new business operations, may be a potential source of garnishment if they owe the debtor for past purchases and may be a source of information concerning an absconding defendant-debtor. [For a discussion of garnishment, see **Chapter 5.**]

Perhaps the plaintiff's files may contain a list of suppliers of services to the debtor. Counsel should also review those files. If the debtor has not paid the plaintiff, perhaps the debtor owes one of his suppliers. Often such a supplier of goods or services can assist counsel in his pursuit of the debtor or in his pursuit of his client's secured collateral. The supplier may have legal counsel who is also seeking to collect money from the debtor. Contact with the supplier's attorney may provide a useful avenue of information about the debtor.

In his investigation, plaintiff's counsel should review his client's files to see if they contain any information about other collection suits against the debtor. These other collections actions often provide some very useful information about the debtor's activities. If the court records are nearby, counsel should have a paralegal obtain these records.

Counsel may find that the debtor has access to money hidden in other businesses or trusts. In following the guidelines for judgment enforcement and tracing assets contained in this book, counsel will discover techniques for finding those assets. Perhaps the seemingly uncollectible judgment may be collectible when counsel knows where to look for the assets.

§ 2.4 Understanding the Individual Debtor's Habits

When plaintiff's counsel is pursuing the debtor he will find it worthwhile to make note of the debtor's habits and psychology. Counsel should try to think as the debtor would, knowing creditors are coming to find his assets. Counsel must look at the big picture, but must also examine even the small details he uncovers. Being a judgment creditor's lawyer is also being part detective or private investigator, or hiring someone to help you with the legwork of tracking down the debtor and tracing his assets.

Counsel will benefit by thinking like the debtor might think, assuming the debtor's moods and mindsets may give counsel information about the debtor. The creditor's lawyer should become familiar with the debtor's hobbies such as sailing, golfing, or skiing. This knowledge about the debtor's hobbies may lead counsel to assets the debtor owns or controls. The debtor will likely pursue his hobby despite problems with creditors. Information about the source of the debtor's funds for pursuit of these hobbies may lead counsel to hidden assets.

For example, in a past case of the author, the debtor enjoyed sailing. The debtor had filed bankruptcy, and after taking some discovery and receiving information from some of the debtor's family members, the author's client joined the bankruptcy trustee in a suit for relief against several of the debtor's alter ego companies. [See **Chapter 6.**] In discovery in the litigation, including depositions of the debtor, production of the debtor's documents and controlled company documents, and review of those documents, evidence of some of the debtor's habits became apparent. [See **Chapter 4.**]

The credit card accounts of the debtor's controlled companies were obtained by subpoena. [See **§ 2.10.**] Sure enough, the debtor continued sailing, despite his "bankruptcy." Behind the facade of his bankruptcy, the debtor used his controlled companies to continue his extravagant lifestyle, and hid his assets from creditors under the guise of his controlled companies. He came to the depositions with his arm in a sling and walking on crutches, while wearing an old yellow golf shirt and worn trousers. Despite the poor man image, the evidence of his spending habits indicated that outside the deposition room, the debtor lived the life of a wealthy business executive.

However, the debtor's controlled companies paid for dues at the New York Yacht Club, and for the rest of his elaborate lifestyle. The credit card receipts gathered in discovery indicated an expensive sailing trip down the intercoastal waterways from New York to the Bahamas. On the way, the debtor used company credit cards to pay for marine gas, groceries, and dinners at excellent restaurants. The credit cards showed other expenses paid by the corporate credit card, including personal items for the debtor's spouse and children and household items. This evidence became key indications that the debtor merely used the companies as shells to hide his personal income and assets. After several years of litigation, the case was settled and almost a million dollars recovered for creditors.

Checklist for the Individual Debtor Files

Plaintiff's counsel should check this list of items to examine and note as available from the individual defendant-debtor or places where the debtor has done business:

____ 1. name
____ 2. aliases
____ 3. date of birth
____ 4. social security number
____ 5. home address
____ 6. business address
____ 7. type of business
____ 8. form of the business organization
____ 9. evidence of the debt (such as a contract or loan)
____ 10. credit application records
____ 11. personal financial statements
____ 12. loan or credit history documents
____ 13. security agreement
____ 14. mortgage or deed of trust
____ 15. contract or loan settlement and closing documents
____ 16. security and mortgage filings
____ 17. copies of cancelled checks
____ 18. correspondence
____ 19. collection records
____ 20. loan reports
____ 21. telephone records
____ 22. employment records and resume
____ 23. federal and state income tax records
____ 24. spouses or relatives names and addresses
____ 25. bank account and safe deposit records
____ 26. life insurance records
____ 27. stock, brokerage and money-market records
____ 28. credit card records

[For methods on how to obtain this information see **Chapters 3** and **4** below.]

Practice Tip

Often the debtor will attempt to hide a lavish lifestyle from his creditors. In post-judgment discovery counsel should ask penetrating questions about his lifestyle, habits, and hobbies. [Discovery and the mechanics are more fully explained in **Chapters 3** and **4.**] Plaintiff's attorney can find out about the debtor's hobbies by asking the debtor, his spouse, relatives, or neighbors in the discovery process. [See **Chapter 4.**] Some of this investigation can be done informally, without cost to the client. [See **Chapter 4.**] Beware that in the case of the consumer debtor, counsel must comply with the requirements of the Fair Debt Collection Practices Act, 15 U.S.C. § 1692b. [See **Chapter 1.**] That law places certain restrictions and limitations on how a plaintiff's attorney acquires information on consumer debtors.

Checklist for Determining the Debtor's Lifestyles, Habits or Hobbies

____ 1. Determine the debtor's principal hobbies, for example, sports (such as skiing, tennis, sailing, golfing, hunting, football, baseball, rowing, rugby, boxing), and determine if he is a participant or a spectator; or the arts (such as theatre, opera, concerts, musicals), and determine whether the defendant-debtor may have a season ticket, box seat, and so forth; or woodworking or carpentry; or acquiring collectibles (like guns, jewelry, artwork, trains, coins, postage stamps, baseball cards, and so forth).

____ 2. Determine the debtor's marital status, and then determine the names and addresses of the spouse, ex-spouse, girlfriend, ex-girlfriend, and so forth.

____ 3. Determine the debtor's previous history of financial difficulties or family difficulties, if any, and review any available files on prior collection, bankruptcy, or divorce cases.

____ 4. Determine the debtor's participation in civic, political, or professional organizations or clubs.

____ 5. Determine whether the debtor has any prior criminal convictions, history of dependency on alcohol or drugs, employment difficulties, or other reoccurring problems.

Understanding the debtor's lifestyles, hobbies, and habits will give plaintiff's counsel information, insights, and data which may indicate the likelihood of difficulties in collection, sources of assets for collection, or places and patterns to observe for collection potential.

If the debtor does business under a business name, and claims to have no other business or corporate involvement, check the local business filings or state corporate records to see if the debtor may have involvement in other businesses or corporations under similar names. [See **Chapter 4.**] For example, in the past, the debtor may have used a business name such as "National Security Services." It is suggested that counsel search public records for other "National" business the debtor may be operating. Also check similar names like "Transnational Investment," "National Insurance Services," or "Transnational Security Services." Upon further investigation, counsel, his investigator, or his paralegal may uncover other likely names to search.

Of course, since the individual debtor knows creditors are pursuing him, the debtor will probably arrange for his controlled companies to pay his spouse or children, but not him directly. For services to the company, the debtor may only receive the use of the company-paid car, medical insurance and other fringe benefits, but no salary. The debtor may still render the principal management or sales services to the new company, but to the outside observer, it appears that the debtor's spouse or children are actually running the company. The problem for the plaintiff's counsel will be to convince the court of this likely fraud on creditors, and have the court, in supplementary proceedings, order the company to make regular payments to plaintiff based on the judgment against the debtor, and the evidence that the debtor actually controls the business. [For types of supplementary proceedings, injunctions, orders or theories of recovery, see **Chapters 4** and **6.**]

§ 2.5 Understanding the Business Structure of the Debtor

It is essential in pursuing judgment enforcement remedies that plaintiff's attorney understand the business structure of the debtor or the debtor company and any related entities. The situation may develop that after plaintiff contracts with the debtor, the debtor's business structure is changed. The plaintiff may have had no knowledge of the change. If the business is still operating, the plaintiff's representative should visit the business and verify if it is still operating under the same name. Perhaps the representative may learn that while the underlying litigation was ongoing, the company was abandoned or liquidated, and its assets dissipated or transferred to a new company controlled by the debtor. [See **Chapter 6.**]

If this has occurred, plaintiff's attorney can obtain evidence in discovery which may assist him in collecting the judgment from the successor company. Counsel will want to establish the time of the dissolution and liquidation of assets from the debtor corporation, and develop answers to some important questions which may establish a prima facie case under one or more theories of recovery as outlined in **Chapter 6.**

Checklist of Preliminary Questions

____ 1. Did the assets go to shareholders?

____ 2. Was the debtor's company insolvent at the time of the transfers of assets, or did the transfers render the corporation insolvent? (Insolvency means that the assets are less than the liabilities of the debtor corporation, including the debtor's debt to plaintiff.)

____ 3. Was the company merged, reorganized, or consolidated?

____ 4. Is there a successor corporation that may be liable for the judgment?

____ 5. Has the parent corporation controlled the operations of its subsidiary to such a degree as to make it liable for the debts of the subsidiary?

____ 6. Did the plaintiff have notice?

Checklist for Understanding the Business Structure

Plaintiff's counsel in trying to understand the business structure of the debtor company and information about its assets should obtain and examine the following information:

____ 1. business name

____ 2. business address

____ 3. type of business

____ 4. form of the business organization

____ 5. current names and addresses of officers and directors

____ 6. current names and addresses of shareholders

____ 7. current names and addresses of partners

____ 8. current names and addresses of joint venturers

____ 9. basis of the debt (such as contract or loan)

____ 10. credit application

____ 11. financial statement

____ 12. loan or credit history documents

____ 13. security agreements

____ 14. mortgages or deeds of trust

____ 15. minutes or votes authorizing borrowing

____ 16. memo to credit committee on loan approval

____ 17. contract or loan settlement and closing documents

____ 18. copies of cancelled checks

____ 19. correspondence

____ 20. collection records
____ 21. loan reports
____ 22. telephone records
____ 23. state and federal income tax returns
____ 25. profit and loss statements
____ 26. accountant reports or workpapers
____ 27. business licenses and permits
____ 28. Securities and Exchange Commission annual and quarterly reports
____ 29. annual reports to stockholders
____ 30. other reports required by government agencies

§ 2.6 Understanding the Corporation's Routines

In dealing with the corporate debtor, plaintiff's counsel should consult his client's representative to obtain information on the debtor's routine business practices. As the cash flow problems of the debtor begin, the business routines may be altered so the debtor can continue to do business and pay its necessary suppliers. Also, officers of the debtor corporation, recognizing that the company may not have much life remaining, may take selfish actions to satisfy their own needs to the detriment of the creditors of the business. Therefore, it is suggested that plaintiff's counsel must educate himself on the ordinary business routines of the debtor. If he does not understand the usual business practices, he will not understand the unusual.

Practice Tips

1. Unlawful transfers of cash, equipment, inventory and other assets often occur during the year before the downfall of the corporation. These transfers occur in a variety of ways.
2. Examine the period one year before the debtor corporation became insolvent, and take a financial snapshot, and then compare it to the previous year when the corporation had financial stability, and see if there is a change in business routines.
3. Call this period the "grab year."
4. Apply the applicable state or federal law to these kinds of transactions, and determine whether the "grab law" says these transfers are unlawful. [The applicable law and remedies to use are discussed in detail in **Chapter 6.**]
5. During the "grab year" corporate insiders take advantage of their position to engineer the movement of assets to themselves or their controlled entities.

6. The corporate insiders get greedy, and start to "grab" whatever is available to move from the financially troubled debtor. The creativity of the individual officers and their lawyers will determine the way the "grab" transaction is structured.

These schemes to denude the corporation of assets have been around since corporate business began. Actions to recover on fraudulent transfers have been around at least since the Statutes of Elizabeth, Chapter 5 (1570). A few years have passed since then, and the art of hiding assets from creditors has been developed and refined. In these years of computerized bookkeeping and electronic funds transfer, some corporate insiders have become more sophisticated in their methods of looting corporations.

Yet, no matter how things change, they remain the same. The bottom line for the plaintiff's counsel remains to uncover how the corporation was looted of its assets. If he can answer that question, plaintiff's counsel may find some assets to satisfy his client's judgment. He may be able to collect the judgment even though the corporation is insolvent. After all, as statutory and case law develops, these types of actions to loot corporations are still fraudulent.

As certainly as there are routines of the business that may have been altered to make the "grab," there are certain "grabs" that have become routine. It is suggested that plaintiff's counsel should look for certain common occurrences that will emerge in his discovery from corporate officers and corporate records. [See **Chapters 3** and **4.**]

Checklist of Schemes to Denude Corporate Assets

____ 1. The officers or directors take excessive salaries, bonuses, fringe benefits.

____ 2. Corporate insider's loans are repaid, notwithstanding the corporation's heavy indebtedness.

____ 3. Bogus sales are made to related entities, and the profits kept by corporate insiders or their related entities.

____ 4. Outright transfers of assets are made without consideration being paid to the corporation.

____ 5. Loans owed by related or affiliated entities are written off without justification.

____ 6. The corporation is dissolved before the creditor's debts mature and become judgments.

____ 7. During the dissolution period shareholders are paid liquidating dividends.

____ 8. These and other events at the time of the insolvency of the debtor corporation, or when the transfers render the debtor corporation insolvent, give rights to creditors to have these transactions set aside, or rights to a damage action, or both, against the corporate insiders.

§ 2.7 Locating the Judgment Debtor

Locating the debtor is a problem plaintiff's counsel often encounters in a judgment enforcement case. In many cases the debtor is not at his last known address. Counsel may discover the debtor's absence after a writ of execution is issued and the process server returns the writ unsatisfied. On the writ, the process server notes that the debtor has moved from the service address.

When counsel cannot locate the debtor, perhaps his client may have recent information concerning the debtor's location. Perhaps the client's employees may know the debtor's new address, or the client may use some of its internal investigators to follow leads to find the debtor's new address. If the client is a government agency, for example, the agency should have investigators to assist counsel in locating the debtor. If the client is a bank, it may have branches or affiliates in other cities which can assist in gathering information on the debtor's new location.

If the debtor cannot be located in the usual manner, then there are several things counsel can do to locate the debtor. First, check any available local phone book or perhaps a local or regional criss-cross street directory. In some states for a small fee, counsel can write the motor vehicle administration, or department of public safety, and obtain a copy of the debtor's address from the driver's license records. However, in some states this information from the motor vehicle administration is considered confidential. The requirements of some states on this matter are in **Appendix A.**

Plaintiff's counsel can hire a private investigator to assist him in the search for the debtor.[2] Counsel should arm the investigator with facts about the debtor from his client's files, including names of references, relatives, and neighbors. Inquiring with such persons may be a good starting point for the private investigator. Plaintiff's counsel should be sure to comply with the Fair Debt Collection Practices Act, 15 U.S.C. § 1692(b) on consumer debts. [See the discussion of this statute in **Chapter 1.**] Under § 1692(b) of the Fair Debt Collection Practices Act, if communicating with someone other than the consumer for purpose of locating the consumer, the investigator must identify

---

[2] Pankaw, *Check It Out! Everyone's Guide to Investigation,* Cloak & Data Press (1990). The author, Edmund I. Pankaw, is a private investigator located in Houston, Texas.

himself and that he is confirming or correcting the location information on the consumer. Only if expressly requested should he identify his employer. The investigator should not refer to the consumer's debt, and not talk to the same person more than once unless requested by such person. The other requirements for obtaining consumer information in § 1692(b) of the Fair Debt Collection Practices Act must also be considered.

Additionally, counsel can also consult national financial services companies, such as Equifax, Inc. or TRW Information Services, which specialize in obtaining information about debtors and their assets. The provide, on a fee for service basis, such services as obtaining credit reports, keeping track of consumers who have moved to new addresses, and information on the consumer's assets. Equifax, with offices around the country, will assist creditor's counsel in other ways, such as, title rundowns and insurance file searches. TRW Information Services offers software packages to assist counsel in obtaining on line information and credit reports.

In some cases, the process server can help plaintiff's counsel locate debtors. In one memorable case, the author was representing an out of state bank which had loaned the debtor a sizeable amount of money in Maryland to buy an expensive sailboat. The loan was in default, and the bank was unable to find the debtor or the collateral. The sailboat, under the terms of the security agreement, was to be kept at the port of Annapolis, Maryland. The author's firm was engaged to locate the debtor, the bank's collateral, and sue the debtor on the promissory note to obtain a judgment.

The initial suit was instituted in federal court in Maryland, but the debtor could not be located or served in Maryland. From the client's files the author learned that the debtor formerly owned some real property in the District of Columbia. A title company was contacted in Washington, D.C., and a preliminary search for property authorized in the District. The title company located a parcel of property there in the debtor's name, and also advised that the debtor had recently sold real property in the District of Columbia. A new action against the debtor was filed in the federal court for the District of Columbia, and, based on the fact of the debtor's recent sales of property in the District, an attachment before judgment was obtained to prevent further transfers of real property by the debtor.

Attempts to serve process on the debtor at the location of the real estate proved futile, at first. However, the process server informed the author that the debtor's son, a young adult, was living at the premises. The process server suspected that the debtor, and, perhaps, his wife were living there. The son denied this. However, the bank authorized the process server to stake out the debtor's home, and the next day, the debtor's wife returned to the home. The process server knocked on the door, and served the suit papers on the debtor's wife.

Further investigation into the debtor's background as a publisher, and contacts by the process server with neighbors of the debtor revealed that the debtor continued his corporate publishing enterprise in the District at another location. Attempts to serve the debtor at the publishing business also failed, but the names of several key employees were obtained by the process server. The process server also had the good sense to purchase the latest edition of the debtor's monthly publication, which contained useful information.

At this point, in consultation with the bank's vice president, it was decided to employ a strategy to bring the debtor out of hiding, so the sailboat could be located. A similar strategy is available in all postjudgment litigation. The debtor's son, and two key employees at the debtor's publication business were served with the deposition subpoenas. [See **Chapter 4.**] The deponents failed to attend the depositions, and so, subsequently, the author filed contempt motions under Federal Rule 37 against them [see **Chapter 4**]. Before the contempt motions could be heard by the court, the debtor called the author at his office. Very soon thereafter, the debtor obtained counsel who appeared in the lawsuit. The contempt motions were withdrawn when the debtor arranged with the author to surrender the bank's collateral. The sailboat had been moved by the debtor to Lewes, Delaware, to avoid the bank's repossession. Within a short time, the sailboat was auctioned to satisfy a portion of the bank's claim against the debtor. By flushing the debtor out of hiding, the collateral was returned, and later a judgment obtained against the debtor.

If the client is a government agency, the agency may have an internal method of obtaining the debtor's last known address from the debtor's state or federal tax returns. To follow this procedure it may be necessary to have the debtor's social security number. The methods for obtaining the debtor's current address would vary according to each government's internal policy.

If the debtor is a party to a court proceeding of some kind, such as a divorce, criminal action, or another collection action, counsel should check the court files for a recent address for the debtor. If there is a criminal conviction that includes probation, the debtor's probation officer may be a good source for the debtor's current location. Counsel may also ask the probation officer to advise him when the debtor will make his next visit to the probation office. Arrangements can be made to serve the debtor an judgment examination subpoena on his way in or out of the meeting with the probation officer. [The examination of the debtor is explained in the **Chapters 3** and **4.**]

Under another set of circumstances, the plaintiff's attorney may discover that the debtor has moved to a nearby city. In checking telephone information, the phone company advises counsel that the debtor's new number is unpublished. In that situation, it is suggested that counsel obtain a subpoena duces tecum for the appropriate telephone business or security office. In the subpoena, command the telephone company to bring any documents listing the current address and telephone number of the subscriber-debtor to the deposition or the place designated, if the attorney just wants the documents. [See the proposed form of deposition subpoena at **§ 2.9.**] Serve the subpoena in accordance with Federal Rules 5 and 45. If permissible, arrange by telephone conference or letter with the appropriate telephone manager for the phone company to accept the subpoena by mail.

Since the subpoena only requests "subscriber information" on the address and telephone number of the subscriber, the phone company should agree to mail counsel that information and save the expense of sending someone to a deposition. Of course, under the changes to Federal Rule of Procedure 45, nonparties are now required to produce documents upon issuance of the subpoena. The debtor does not have to be informed by the phone company about the subpoena, because the phone company only contacts the subscriber when it receives inquiries about long-distance records. If the phone company is located outside the jurisdiction of the judgment court, counsel may have to initiate a miscellaneous action in the other district to obtain jurisdiction to issue the subpoena. Once the subpoena is served, compliance with the subpoena is accomplished by the phone company's return letter containing the subject debtor's address and telephone number.

There is another source of information, if counsel knows the debtor has children. If the debtor has moved, counsel can subpoena the local school district, and see information on where the school records of the debtor's children have been forwarded. This information should enable counsel to locate the debtor in that new district.

Another common tracing tool is a letter to the local post office, requesting whether mail is still being received by the subject debtor at the last known address. If mail is not being received at that address, counsel should send a postal trace letter to check if a forwarding address is registered. [See the proposed form of postal trace letter at § **2.8.**]

Credit card records often contain valuable information on the individual debtor. Local state laws must be checked for any applicable restrictions on obtaining all or part of these consumer records. Assuming there are no restrictions, a subpoena can be issued, pursuant to Federal Rule of Civil Procedure 45, to the local office of that credit card company. Pursuant to Rule 45(c), if the records are all counsel needs, it may not be necessary to depose a person from the credit card company. In the duces tecum part of the subpoena, counsel should command information on the debtor's credit card account files and other data. [See the sample form at § **2.10.**] If counsel suspects the debtor uses a corporation as his alter ego, counsel should subpoena the corporate credit card records.

Surprisingly enough subpoenas for records of credit card companies usually prove very informative. Counsel often obtains the debtor's new address, and acquires much information about the debtor's recent spending habits, or use of corporate credit cards for personal expenses. If the credit card company keeps copies of checks paid on the account, counsel also receives information on the debtor's new bank, or about a new corporation the debtor has formed to hide personal assets and pay his debts. If it is necessary to register the judgment in the debtor's new district, then one of the first things counsel should do thereafter is obtain a writ of garnishment against the debtor's new bank. [See **Chapter 5** on procedures for garnishment.] Also, be certain to review the debtor's credit card application in the file. The debtor may list in the application some recent financial information which was previously unknown to plaintiff's counsel.

§ 2.8 —Sample Postal Trace Form

FORM 2–1
POSTAL TRACE FORM

Postmaster
[City, State]

Re: [name], Plaintiff v. [name], Defendant
[case number]
[name of court]

Dear Postmaster:

Our client, [plaintiff], has a judgment in the amount of [dollar amount] against [defendant] whose last known address was [last known address of the defendant]. Please advise if mail is received by [defendant] at that address. If mail is not received by [defendant] at that address, kindly advise us if a forwarding address is registered, and provide us with that address. We include a self-addressed stamped return envelope for your use.

We appreciate your assistance in this matter. Please direct your reply to the undersigned or call us at the number listed above.

Sincerely yours,

[attorney's name]
Attorney for Creditor

Enclosure: Envelope

§ 2.9 —Sample Form Subpoena to Telephone Company

FORM 2–2
SAMPLE DEPOSITION SUBPOENA

[Usual headnote information for civil deposition subpoena]

To: [Name of Telephone Company]
[Address of Telephone Company]

YOU ARE HEREBY COMMANDED to appear at the place, date, and time specified below to testify at the taking of a deposition in the above-entitled case.

PLACE	DATE AND TIME
ATTORNEY'S OFFICE FOR CREDITOR [attorney' office address]	[date and time]

YOU ARE ALSO COMMANDED to bring with you the following document(s) or object(s):

Any and all documents listing the current address and telephone number of [defendant], of [defendant's city] a subscriber of [Local Telephone Company] with an unpublished telephone number, as shown in your subscriber files.

[Fed. R. Civ. Pr. 30(b)(6) and Fed. R. Civ. Pr. 45 form language]

[Clerk's Seal]

This subpoena is issued upon the application of the:

Plaintiff's Attorney

[Under the changes to Federal Rules of Civil Procedure, only the subpoena may be necessary to require third parties to produce documents.]

§ 2.10 —Sample Form of Deposition Notice to Credit Card Company

FORM 2–3
SAMPLE DEPOSITION NOTICE

[Usual headnote information for deposition notice]

PLAINTIFF'S NOTICE OF DEPOSITION
OF CREDIT CARD COMPANY

Please take notice that at [time], on [date] at the offices of Creditor's Law Firm, [office address] pursuant to Fed. R. Civ. P. 30, 30(b)(6), 45, and 69, the plaintiff, [name], will take the deposition of [Credit Card Company of New City], upon oral examination before a notary public, or before some other officer authorized by law to take depositions. The oral examination will continue from day to day until completed. You are invited to attend and cross examine.

Please take notice notice that [Credit Card Company] will be served with a subpoena, pursuant to applicable procedures under Fed. R. Civ. P. 5 and 45, and a copy of this notice. This subpoena may command a representative of the [Credit Card Company] to appear and testify at the time and place specified above and to bring to the deposition or mail to plaintiff, for plaintiff's inspection and copying, the books, papers, documents, or tangible things in its possession, custody, or control which are described in Attachment "A" to the subpoena (served herewith).

[Followed by the signature line and certificate of service]

[If only the records are required and not testimony, the notice and subpoena should be amended accordingly pursuant to Fed. R. Civ. P. 45.]

ATTACHMENT A

[Introduction to matter, citation to rules and definitions of documents.]

Documents Subpoenaed for the Period —— to the Present.

1. Any and all documents describing, evidencing, or summarizing any travel related service agreements, credit card service agreements, line of credit agreements, accounts and/or other contracts between [Credit Card Company] and: [Insert here the name of the individual debtor, the business organization debtor and/or any related entities plaintiff's counsel wants information about from Credit Card Company.]

2. Any and all monthly statements, payment records, summary of payments, payment transmittal forms, computer records, microfiche records, microfilm records, graphic representations, charts, confirmation of payments, checks, wire transfers, check stubs, drafts, invoice slips, and any other records of payments to [Credit Card Company] from [name of the debtor].

3. Any and all records of charges, advances, loans, withdrawals, electronic or computer transfers and/or payments from [Credit Card Company] to the [name of the debtor].

4. Any and all documents, correspondence, letters, memoranda, and other records of communication between [Credit Card Company] and [name of the debtor], or between [Credit Card Company] and any and all persons acting for or on behalf of [name of the debtor].

[Be sure to attach to the Credit Card Company subpoena a copy of Attachment A].

§ 2.11 Size of the Judgment versus Strategy Employed

At different times in the history of the litigation, plaintiff's counsel can make long-range plans about the strategy to be employed in the case. This is to be distinguished from the tactics counsel employs during trial. When counsel considers postjudgment strategy, he has the advantage of time and planning. On the other hand, some trial tactics develop under the stress of courtroom circumstances, and require immediate decision-making.

Suggested strategy and tactics in the postjudgment litigation process are considered in this book. The larger and more complex the case, the more time counsel needs in planning strategy. In the smaller cases, say in the range under $25,000, the client usually cannot afford to pay for elaborate strategy and planning. However, if the size of the judgment and complexity of the case warrant, a client should envision that counsel will spend time in investigating the case and preparing strategy, as would be expected in any other large and complex litigation matter. The client should expect to pay for good planning and expect to take bigger risks to collect a large amount. Certainly a large case would be considered one where the amount to be collected exceeds $100,000.

However, all counsel enforcing judgments must consider the size of the judgment and collection prospects vis a vis reasonable budget for accomplishing postjudgment objectives, whether the lawyer's fees are paid on an hourly or percentage basis. Unless counsel is enforcing a government or private client program which has deterrence objectives, litigation expenses must always be reconciled with the total amount to be collected on the judgment, assuming a successful effort. In any planning on postjudgment strategy where the client is paying counsel on an hourly basis, the client should be given an estimate of the likely expenses to be incurred, so that the client can evaluate the risks involved versus the likelihood of success of the strategy. At any point in the process, the client may decide that the hourly fees have reached the limit to economically achieve judgment enforcement objectives. There is a point in postjudgment litigation that the client rightfully cuts losses, and sits on the judgment, and waits for other opportunities of enforcement.

Nevertheless, in many cases, a client relies on collection counsel for the experience and advice in helping the client evaluate overall expenses versus results in postjudgment strategy. The client depends on counsel to analyze the risks versus the costs. If counsel wants continued business from the client, counsel have to use good judgment in knowing when to take risks, and when not to take risks.

§ 2.12 Overall Strategy in the Small Judgment Case

In the small judgment case where the amount to be collected is under $25,000, counsel has to focus strategy on certain basic steps in the collection process. Counsel must find some method to get the debtor's attention. It is suggested that, first, counsel sends a demand letter to the debtor, requesting payment on the judgment. If the debtor responds, counsel may be able to work out payment in full, even if by installments. Many times the demand letter is ignored.

Next, counsel has to take some initial postjudgment discovery to find out what assets the debtor has to apply to your judgment. [see **Chapters 3** and **4.**] As openers in the discovery process, counsel may send out some interrogatories and requests for production of documents. Then he may take a postjudgment debtor examination, where counsel subpoenas basic records of the debtor's assets and income. Counsel's strategy is simple. He wants to reach the debtor at some vulnerable point, and hold on.

Counsel, therefore, must find some method to get leverage against the debtor, and apply pressure. Of course, counsel may have to consider overall strategy in view of the small judgment he is enforcing. It is important to take a quick look around and see what assets counsel finds to attach or lien. If the debtor is earning wages, counsel may attempt to garnish wages. If the debtor has a bank account, counsel may take a shot at garnishing the bank account. [See **Chapter 5** on garnishment and exemptions.] If counsel is successful, counsel should keep the garnishment current, and renew it as the appropriate law requires.

If the debtor has real property, counsel should file a judgment lien. It may not be worth much effort to execute and levy on the lien in the small judgment case. That process can be expensive. If there is equity in the property, the lien will give counsel security and leverage to use when most appropriate. [See **Chapter 5** on execution on the judgment.]

Remember the points addressed above in **§ 2.3** on the debtor's habits. Here's an example from the author's experience. In this case, plaintiff was a bank. The defendant-debtor defaulted on a loan for his business, and owed the bank about $25,000, on a promissory note. The debtor had numerous other creditors, none of whom had been satisfied. In fact, many had no success in collecting against this debtor. Suit was begun on behalf of the bank, and a summary judgment obtained. An investigation revealed that the debtor had a gun collection kept in his home.

The gun collection appeared to have some real value. So, the author met with the loan officer from the bank and advised him about the gun collection. The author recommended that, under the circumstances, the bank was justified in incurring further collection expenses. Based on the new information, a postjudgment attachment was ordered by the court. Importantly, the expense of moving and storing the property was also authorized by the bank.

The author planned the strategy with the local sheriff. The sheriff obtained a moving company representative to assist in taking the guns from the debtor's home. The sheriff, armed with the appropriate writs [See **Chapter 5,** on executing the judgment], and meeting no resistance, came into the house and took the gun collection from the family room wall.

After the guns have been moved to the moving company's warehouse, the guns were appraised. Much to author's delight, the appraiser estimated the guns were worth over $50,000. Of course, the debtor wanted to get his favorite gun collection back. In this case, the debtor found the cash and managed to pay the bank's judgment in full. In addition, the debtor paid the sheriff's fees and court costs, and also the moving and storage costs. In the process the author collected the bank's loan balance of $25,000, plus interest. Since author's actions had excellent results, he charged the bank the usual fee, plus a premium.

The lesson in this example is, that even in the small case, counsel may have success if leverage is found against some property the debtor really likes. If counsel has the debtor in a difficult position like this, the debtor either pays, or counsel has the sheriff or U.S. marshal sell the property to satisfy the judgment.

§ 2.13 Overall Strategy in the Large Judgment Case

Sometimes plaintiff's counsel starts with a large judgment to attempt to collect for his client. [A large judgment is assumed to be a judgment for $100,000 or more, but may vary according to the economic times.] First, in the large judgment case, counsel takes the same basic steps as with a small judgment, and goes through the process of having a demand and service of a writ of execution made on the debtor. Like the small case, the writ may be returned unsatisfied. Plaintiff's counsel should file judgment liens where applicable [see **Chapter 1**].

Unlike the small judgment case, however, if the client is paying him on an hourly basis, rather that on a percentage of the amount collected, counsel should ask the client for a larger budget in developing discovery. If there are large dollars involved, counsel should attempt to convince the client to let him do some preliminary discovery to see if debtor's assets were dissipated during the time the judgment was obtained. The specific strategy is to find records and information which will assist counsel in analyzing whether the debtor was manipulating assets before, during, or after the underlying litigation. Any postjudgment discovery is going to cost money. Counsel must choose his methods carefully. There is no easy way at the beginning to assure the client that the money spent in postjudgment discovery, and, if necessary, even new postjudgment litigation, will produce a recovery. But counsel can assure the client that if no attempts are made to trace assets, then any recovery from the debtor is unlikely.

Usually the preliminary postjudgment discovery attempts will tell counsel whether the pursuit is worthwhile. Counsel begins to acquire a sense about the debtor's activities, and whether there are any assets around to collect. Counsel reviews the documents produced by the debtor and examines the individual debtor, or one or two of the officers of the corporate debtor. Then counsel realizes, as he sifts through the evidence that the debtor's assets have been fraudulently transferred to avoid having to pay the client's judgment. Counsel now has an idea of how to locate them, and attach them before they are transferred again.

Counsel has to be adaptible and flexible, and consider the underlying facts and circumstances, before applying just any strategy. Counsel has examined the client's files and has discussed the matter with the client. Counsel, or an assistant, has examined all the pubic records available to get preliminary information about the case. Counsel has reviewed the pleadings in the underlying litigation files and notices did not move along to judgment very quickly. Or counsel notices that the debtor stalled at every opportunity. The evidence obtained so far indicates that the delay was necessary so the corporate treasury could be raided, and the pockets of corporate insiders lined with the proceeds of unlawful transfers of corporate assets. Or, perhaps it was so the individual debtor could make fraudulent transfers of assets, and hide them from pursuing creditors.

Counsel should remember that one sizable unlawful transfer is all counsel needs to start an action to recoup the assets, and satisfy part, or all, of his client's judgment. [See **Chapter 6** on new litigation to enforce judgments and **Chapter 4** on methods of discovery.] The strategy should be to attempt to freeze or attach the assets he finds so that the debtor cannot transfer them again. [See **Chapter 1** on maintaining the status quo, injunctions, and lis pendens.] Perhaps an injunction order or attachment will give the needed leverage to force payment on the judgment.

CHAPTER 3

DISCOVERY TO FIND THE DEBTOR'S ASSETS

§ 3.1 Introduction

The principles of discovery discussed in this chapter concern the enforcement of a judgment in federal court using the Federal Rules of Civil Procedure. Some discussion concerns the use of state procedural methods available, because under Federal Rule of Civil Procedure 69 plaintiff's counsel may use state procedural methods if she finds they are more advantageous than the federal rules.[1] Several different aspects of discovery are examined including first, the range of inquiry permissible; second, the application of

[1] El Salto, S.A. v. PSG Co., 444 F.2d 477, 484, n.3 (9th Cir.), *cert. denied,* 404 U.S. 940 (1971); United States v. Kulukundis, 329 F.2d 197, 199 (2d Cir. 1964); Strick Corp. v. Thai Teak Products Co., 493 F. Supp. 1210, 1211 (E.D. Pa. 1980); Ranney-Brown Distributors v. E.T. Barwick Indus., Inc., 75 F.R.D. 3, 5 (S.D. Ohio 1977). *See also* Burak v. Scott, 29 F. Supp. 775, 776 (D.D.C. 1939).

privileges raised by the debtor; and third, the evidence necessary to assist in the enforcement of the judgment.

It should be clear from the outset that postjudgment discovery differs in many respects from prejudgment discovery. Because counsel has a judgment, she has expanded rights to inquire about the debtor, the debtor's financial transactions, and the debtor's assets. In prejudgment collection cases, plaintiff's counsel is suing on the note or contract, but may not have the right to inquire about the debtor's ability to pay on the note or contract at this stage of the litigation. As a result of the judgment, the debtor will have limited availability of evidentiary privileges to shield inquiry about the assets of the judgment debtor and their location.

The objective of the postjudgment discovery is to see whether the debtor has assets, or whether there may be methods available for collecting assets from third parties as a result of their activities with the debtor. The evidence assembled in discovery may become the basis for new litigation against third parties, the basis for instituting supplementary proceedings against the third parties, or the basis for exercising execution remedies against assets of the debtor, even if the assets have been fraudulently transferred to other third parties.

§ 3.2 Broad Range of Inquiry

Federal Rule 26 will not permit the discovery of information concerning the financial condition of the defendant during the prejudgment stages of litigation.[2] When the creditor has a judgment against the debtor, federal cases interpreting the scope of discovery under Rule 69 of the Federal Rules of Civil Procedure recognize a broad range of inquiry to develop information about the debtor.[3] Creditor's counsel may inquire about what assets exist or what assets may have been concealed or fraudulently transferred.[4]

Under Rule 69, the judgment creditor may initiate discovery concerning the location or disposition of the debtor's property. Discovery may proceed against the judgment debtor or from third persons without the need of filing a new suit against the third person. The judgment debtor or third person may seek a protective order if it appears that the discovery is being used as a

---

[2] Ranney-Brown Distribs. v. E.T. Barwick Indus., Inc., 75 F.R.D. 3, 5 (S.D. Ohio 1977); Sanderson v. Winner, 507 F.2d 477 (10th Cir. 1974), *cert. denied,* 421 U.S. 914 (1975).

[3] Ranney-Brown Distribs. v. E.T. Barwick Indus., Inc., 75 F.R.D. at 5; Magnaleasing, Inc. v. Staten Island Mall, 76 F.R.D. 559, 561 (S.D.N.Y. 1977); Caisson Corp. v. County W. Bldg. Corp., 62 F.R.D. 331, 334 (E.D. Pa. 1974); Monticello Tobacco Co. v., American Tobacco Co., 12 F.R.D. 344 (S.D.N.Y. 1952), *aff'd on other grounds,* 197 F.2d 629 (2d Cir.), *cert. denied,* 344 U.S. 875 (1952); Davis v. Acoustical Corp. v. Skulnik, 131 N.J. Super. 87, 92, 328 A.2d 633, 635–36 (App. Div. 1974).

[4] Caisson Corp. v. County W. Bldg. Corp., 62 F.R.D. 331, 334 (E.D. Pa. 1974).

means for harassment.[5] One court has held that before discovery can be conducted against third parties, the judgment creditor should first seek execution against the judgment debtor's assets.[6] The court's reasoning for this is that such a requirement prevents any hardship against the third party, and requires the judgment debtor to first seek satisfaction of the judgment against the debtor.[7]

Therefore, even though there is a broad range of inquiry permitted, counsel should first check on the necessity of having to obtain a writ of execution and attempting to satisfy it, in whole or in part, from the judgment debtor.[8] The right to discovery against third parties does not include the right to inquire about the assets of the third parties, but the examination should be limited to an inquiry about the assets of the judgment debtor.[9] In *Caisson Corp. v. County West*,[10] the court set forth the standards for allowing such inquiry:

> There is no doubt that third parties can be examined in relation to the financial affairs of the judgment debtor. The appropriate manner to afford third parties protection is not to require that questions be phrased in a legalistically conclusory manner but rather to allow questions as to their personal activities, within limits, yet requiring some showing of the relationship that exists between the judgment debtor and the third party from which the court on a motion for protective order can determine whether the examination has a basis. We think that this is the appropriate manner for balancing the potentially conflicting legitimate interests both of parties in satisfying judgments, in light of the difficulty of such tasks at times, and of third parties in protection from baseless harassment.[11]

In *Caisson Corp.*, a vigorous discovery examination was permitted against an officer of the judgment debtor corporation when there was sufficient question about the bona fides of the transfer of assets between the judgment debtor and corporation and other entities with which it had financial relationship.[12] Similarly, in *Magleasing, Inc. v. Staten Island Mall*,[13] the court allowed discovery against the controlling shareholder of two judgment debtor corporations, the joint venturers of the Staten Island Mall development, when it was alleged that the controlling shareholder received payments from the corporations to

---

5 Hartmann v. United States, 79 F.R.D. 705, 707 (E.D. Wis. 1978).

6 *Id.* at 707.

7 *Id.*

8 Caisson Corp. v. County W. Bldg. Corp., 62 F.R.D. 331, 334 (E.D. Pa. 1974); Burak v. Scott, 29 F. Supp. 775, 776 (D.D.C. 1939); Davis Acoustical Corp. v. Skulnik, 131 N.J. Super. 87, 92, 328 A.2d 633, 636 (App. Div. 1974).

9 Caisson Corp. v. County W. Bldg. Corp., 62 F.R.D. 331, 335 (E.D. Pa. 1974).

10 *Id.*

11 *Id.*

12 *Id.* (For a discussion of "alter ego," *See* **Chapter 6** "Piercing the Corporate Veil Claim.")

13 76 F.R.D. 559, 562 (S.D.N.Y. 1977).

strip them of any assets that might satisfy the judgment. It was proper under those circumstances to allow discovery concerning the consideration received by the shareholder from the corporate lender in connection with the transfer of certain properties of the corporate debtors to the lender in the settlement of a foreclosure action against the Mall properties.

When there is a claim concerning a close relationship between the judgment debtor and the third parties to form the basis for allowing discovery, that claim must be shown before the court will allow discovery to proceed. Counsel for Strick Corporation served a writ of execution and interrogatories against Thai Teak Products Company and Forest Products Company, judgment debtors, in *Strick Corp. v. Thai Teak Products Co.*[14] Counsel for Strick Corporation served a writ of execution and interrogatories on Bangkok Industries, Inc., and also attempted to garnish the assets of Dumrong Trading Co. and Dumrong Phanich Sawmill Company. The Complaint filed for Strick Corporation alleged that these two companies were the "alter egos" of the judgment debtors. Bangkok did not challenge the process Strick Corporation served upon it under Pennsylvania practice, but it challenged "Strick's authority to attach debts owned to the alleged 'alter egos' and to compel answers to interrogatories directed to relationships with those companies."[15] The Court denied the discovery directed to the Dumrong companies, as there was no factual basis before the court to show the alleged alter ego relationship.[16]

Practice Tips. The careful plaintiff's attorney will refuse the temptation to stretch the broad range of inquiry allowed to Rule 69. The *Strick Corp. v. Thai Teak Products Co.* case,[17] provides a good example of overreaching. Before plaintiff's counsel issues a subpoena to a third party, she must examine the basis for the subpoena and the relationship of the third party of the defendant judgment debtor. Counsel should have sufficient facts to present to the court about the relationship which will overcome any protective order raised by the third party. If she does not, she will most probably lose the motion for protective order and have wasted time in the discovery process. Other avenues of developing the information on the judgment debtor and location of her assets may also be tried.

Remember, when the judgment debtor is a corporation it is appropriate to examine officers of the corporation concerning its activities. However, the officer must be subpoenaed to compel her to testify.[18]

---

[14] 493 F. Supp. 1210 (E.D. Pa. 1980).

[15] *Id.* at 1218.

[16] El Salto, S.A. v. PSG Co., 444 F.2d 477, 484 (9th Cir.), *cert. denied,* 404 U.S. 940 (1971).

[17] 493 F. Supp. 1210 (E.D. Pa. 1980).

[18] Ryan v. Commissioner, 568 F.2d 531, 543 (7th Cir. 1977), *cert. denied,* 439 U.S. 820 (1978); G-Fours, Inc. v. Miele, 496 F.2d 809, 812–13 (2d Cir. 1974); Barsky v. United States, 339 F.2d 180, 182–83 (9th Cir. 1964).

§ 3.3 Judgment Debtor's Privileges Are Limited

In prejudgment litigation, the defendant, in many circumstances, will be able to raise various privileges to thwart the discovery process. Once a judgment is entered, Federal Rule of Civil Procedure 69, as explained below, permits a broad range of inquiry to discover the locations of assets, the location of concealed and fraudulently transferred assets, and the debtor's financial relationships with third parties. In view of this principle established by case law that Rule 69 permits a broad range of inquiry into the judgment debtor's activities, there has been a corresponding development that a judgment debtor's privileges are limited when used to shield or protect discovery about those assets. This development in federal cases governed by Federal Rule of Evidence 501, and the federal common law, is discussed in §§ **3.4** through **3.8.**

§ 3.4 Spousal Privilege in Postjudgment Discovery

The federal rule of husband-wife privilege in criminal cases was considered by the United States Supreme Court in *Trammel v. United States.*[19] *Trammel* applied a limited husband-wife privilege in a criminal case for information privately disclosed between husband and wife in the confidence of the marital relationship and swept away the restrictive privilege that had previously been applied in *Hawkins v. United States:*[20]

> Our consideration of the foundation for the privilege and its history satisfy us that "reason and experience" no longer justify so sweeping a rule as that found acceptable by the Court in *Hawkins.* Accordingly, we conclude that the existing rule should be modified so that the witness-spouse alone has a privilege to refuse to testify adversely; the witness may neither be compelled to testify nor foreclosed from testifying.[21]

Even before *Trammel* the marital privilege was not considered applicable to information about the income and assets of the marital partners because these were not considered as "intimate marital communication," and, therefore, fell outside the privilege.[22] However, when the testimony between spouses involves business matters, the presumption of confidentiality ordinarily

---

[19] 445 U.S. 40 (1980).

[20] 358 U.S. 74 (1958).

[21] 445 U.S. 40, 53 (1980).

[22] Computerland Corp. v. Batac, Inc., No. 88 Civ. 8624 (S.D.N.Y. April 26, 1990) (LEXIS, Genfed Library, Dist File); Atlantic Richfield Co. v. Triad Petroleum, Inc., 120 F.R.D. 471, 473 (S.D.N.Y. 1988).

applicable to spousal communications applies and must be rebutted.[23] In *Computerland Corp. v. Batac, Inc.*,[24] the court stated that the presumption is rebutted by "a showing of probable cause to believe a crime or fraud has been committed and that the communications in issue were in furtherance if it."

Moreover, federal courts have consistently held that the husband-wife privilege cannot be used as a shield behind which assets are fraudulently hidden or transferred away from judgment creditors.[25] The Second Circuit in *G-Fours, Inc. v. Miele* recognized this principle:

> After the marshal's execution obtained only $783.40 from a bank account, G-Fours began supplementary proceeding to discover hidden or fraudulently transferred assets. Plaintiff served information subpoenas and interrogatories upon judgment debtor Charles Miele, his wife, Ethel, and his wholly-owned corporation, Infinco, Inc., and all three failed either to respond or to move to obtain a protective order. . . . Mrs. Miele also refused to answer some questions which sought information regarding her husband's bank accounts and property and recent transfers to her by her husband of property or money, "on the grounds of the privilege between husband and wife.". . . To the extent that the Mieles have attempted to conceal their assets from plaintiff, therefore, we think, New York would follow the lead of other jurisdictions which have held that the marital privilege is not available to refuse disclosure of communication designed to perpetrate frauds on third parties.[26]

This principle is illustrated in another case. A debtor in his postjudgment deposition testimony stated that he was totally supported by his wife who lived in the Dominican Republic. At his examination, he refused to answer questions about the source of her income and assets. The court found that the debtor did not purge himself of contempt in refusing to answer these questions, as the questions were plainly proper to uncover information about fraudulent transfers of assets to the debtor's wife.[27]

In *Computerland Corp. v. Batac, Inc.*,[28] the court analyzed a series of questions posed by the plaintiff, which illustrate the application of the spousal privilege in civil litigation. Plaintiff Computerland commenced an action

---

[23] G-Fours, Inc. v. Miele, 496 F.2d 809, 812 (2d Cir. 1974); Fraser v. United States, 145 F.2d 139 (6th Cir. 1944), *cert. denied,* 324 U.S. 849 (1945); Federal Deposit Ins. Corp. v. Alter, 106 F. Supp. 316, 318 (W.D. Pa. 1952).

[24] No. 88 Civ. 8624 (S.D.N.Y. April 26, 1990).

[25] Cerami v. Robinson, 85 F.R.D. 371 (S.D.N.Y. 1980.)

[26] G-Fours, Inc. v. Miele, 496 F.2d 809, 810, 812-13. *See* Kine v. Forman, 205 Pa. Super. 305, 209 A.2d 1 (1965); Fraser v. United States, 145 F.2d 139, 143–144 (6th Cir. 1944), *cert. denied,* 324 U.S. 849 (1945); Tobias v. Adams, 201 Cal. 689, 258 P. 588, 592 (1927); Eddy v. Bosley, 324 Tex. Civ. App. 116, 78 S.W. 565 (1903). *But see* Stalcup v. Jepsen, 118 Neb. 240, 224 N.W. 16 (1929).

[27] Ranney-Brown Distribs. v. E.T. Barwick Indus, Inc., 75 F.R.D. 3, 5 (S.D. Ohio 1977).

[28] No. 88 Civ. 8624 (S.D.N.Y. April 26, 1990).

against Mr. L. and several corporations he controlled for breach of a franchise agreement and fraud, in that Mr. L. and his corporations allegedly failed to pay for a large quantity of inventory, and then secreted the equipment, or disposed of it, hiding the proceeds. During the discovery proceedings, the plaintiff deposed Mr. L.'s wife. Mr. L.'s attorney raised the spousal privilege to a series of 15 questions during the depositions. Computerland brought a motion to compel her testimony.

The court reviewed the application of the spousal privilege to the 15 questions one by one. If the question was directed to uncovering a fraudulent transfer of assets to frustrate creditors, the court required Mrs. L. to answer the question. If the question concerned the basis for a claim of privilege, it did not invade the privilege, and must be answered. If the plaintiff offered no basis to invade the presumptively confidential spousal communication, the court did not require the witness to answer the question.

Based on this review of cases concerning application of the spousal privilege, it is evident that this privilege will not effectively thwart postjudgment discovery designed to uncover hidden or fraudulently transferred assets or designed to uncover information about the debtor's business activities and income. The debtor will often raise other privileges in attempt to stall inquiry by the judgment creditor.

§ 3.5 Attorney-Client Privilege in Postjudgment Discovery

Another privilege frequently raised by defendant's counsel in postjudgment discovery is the attorney-client privilege. If the attorney-client privilege is presented by defendant's counsel at a deposition of the debtor or other third parties, or is presented in objections to answering interrogatories or producing documents, plaintiff's counsel should be prepared to respond to restrict the improper use of this privilege to thwart postjudgment inquiry. When defense counsel raises the attorney-client privilege it should be a signal to plaintiff's counsel that she is inquiring into areas where the debtor and her counsel do not wish her to proceed. But, assuming the privilege is raised as a shield to prevent plaintiff's counsel from finding out about unlawful transfers of assets, she should press on and obtain a motion to compel discovery under Federal Rule of Civil Procedure 37. Counsel should know that a claim of privilege cannot be used to hide assets and prevent execution on her judgment.[29]

For example, a motion to compel discovery pursuant to Rule 37 was used to compel production of a settlement agreement between the defendant-judgment debtors and Chase Manhattan Mortgage and Realty Trust (Chase)

---

[29] Magnaleasing, Inc. v. Staten Island Mall, 76 F.R.D. 559, 560–61 (S.D.N.Y. 1977).

in *Magnaleasing, Inc. v. Staten Island Mall.*[30] The judgment creditor realized that certain information in this settlement agreement might give leads about the location of property that might satisfy the $156,769.99 judgment. Before Magnaleasing could obtain its judgment, the defendants had settled a mortgage foreclosure action with Chase. Chase argued that portions of the settlement agreement were protected from disclosure under the attorney-client privilege or work-product doctrine. However, Magnaleasing, urging the court to review the document *in camera,* submitted that the settlement agreement contained information about "improper transfers of assets to and from defendants and that production of the agreement would aid plaintiff in locating defendants' assets."[31]

The district court inspected the settlement agreement *in camera* and found the agreement did contain considerable information about property of the defendants that could satisfy plaintiff's judgment. Despite the claims of privilege, the court decided that relevant portions of the settlement agreement could be disclosed without offending either the work-product doctrine or the attorney-client privilege. Coming to the essence of the matter, the court stated:

> In the instant case, the settlement agreement, insofar as we have ordered disclosure, relates merely to the transfer to assets between defendants and Chase. The relevant portions embody no communications concerning the manner or substance of the parties' joint or common defense of the actions brought by the other tenants. Therefore, even assuming that New York law would recognize a privilege for communications among the attorneys of co-defendants, the relevant portions of the settlement agreement would not fall within the privilege.[32]

Under some circumstances, when the document may have been turned over to plaintiff's counsel in discovery, any applicable attorney-client privilege may have been waived (see § **3.4**).

§ 3.6 Crime-Fraud Exception to the Attorney-Client Privilege

The attorney-client privilege and the work-product privilege are not absolute privileges. For example, in the cases discussed below, the attorney-client or work-product privileges, when raised to shield inquiry about documents

---

[30] *Id; Cf.* Natural Gas Pipeline v. Energy Gathering, Inc., 2 F.3d 1397 (5th Cir. 1993) (attorney required to turn over document he held of his client, a judgment creditor.)

[31] Ranney-Brown Distribs., Inc. v. E.T. Barwick Indus., Inc., 75 F.R.D. 3, 6 (S.D. Ohio 1977); Underwater Storage Inc. v. United States Rubber Co., 314 F. Supp. 546, 549 (D.D.C. 1970); Duplan Corp. v. Deering Milliken, Inc., 397 F. Supp. 1146, 1191 (D.S.C. 1975).

[32] Magnaleasing, Inc. v. Staten Island Mall, 76 F.R.D. 559, 564 (S.D.N.Y. 1977).

produced from the debtor's or debtor's attorney's files, did not prevent plaintiff's counsel from inquiring into the very planning of the fraudulent transfers by the debtor or her counsel to hide assets. This evidence of the planning of the fraudulent transfers becomes a very powerful tool in litigation to set aside the fraudulent transfers. See the discussion of fraudulent transfer litigation in **Chapter 6.** The evidence may become the linchpin whereby plaintiff's counsel can successfully attach plaintiff's judgment lien to the newly discovered assets of the debtor for the purpose of successful collection of the judgment.

The crime-fraud exception is an exception to both the attorney-client privilege and work-product privilege, if those privileges are used in an attempt to hide or conceal criminal or fraudulent conduct. The Second Circuit Court of Appeals discussed the policies of these privileges and the issue of the necessity of protection of confidential communications when the advice is sought to further a crime or fraud.

The rationale for the exclusion is closely tied to the policies underlying these privileges. Whereas confidentiality of communications and work product facilitate the rendering of sound legal advice, advice in furtherance of a fraudulent or unlawful goal cannot be considered "sound." Rather advice in furtherance of such goals is socially perverse, and the client's communications seeking advice are not worthy of protection.[33]

Trying to hide or conceal fraudulent transfer of assets is sufficient fraud to invoke the application of the crime-fraud exception. There were fraudulent transactions involved in *In re Grand Jury Subpoena Duces Tecum dated September 15, 1983*. In that case, Intervenor, Marc Rich & Co. A.G. (A.G.) appealed the district court's order denying a motion to quash a subpoena served on Proskauer, Rose, Goetz & Mendelsohn (Proskauer), A.G.'s former counsel. Proskauer and A.G. claimed that many of the documents requested in the subpoena were attorney-client or work-product privileged. However, the district court held that the documents were not privileged because they related to business, rather than legal advice, and were communications in furtherance of an ongoing crime or fraud. The Second Circuit affirmed, as to certain documents, under the theory of furtherance of a fraud.

In this case, A.G. had previously been assessed contempt fines for failure to comply with a subpoena. On July 15, 1983, the district court ordered A.G. to pay $1 million in accrued contempt fines. On July 20, 1983, the United States learned of an agreement between A.G. and its chief executive officer, R. Alec Hackel, some 13 days before, in which A.G. sold all of its stock in its wholly owned American subsidiary, Marc Rich & Co. International to Hackel, for a price to be fixed at a subsequent date. The court concluded that the sale of stock may have been a fraudulent conveyance under Section 276 of the New York Debtor and Creditor Law.

---

[33] *In re* Grand Jury Subpoena Duces Tecum dated September 15, 1983, 731 F.2d 1032, 1038 (2d Cir. 1984) (citations omitted).

In another fraudulent transfer case, *In re Blier Cedar Co., Inc.,*[34] the Blier Cedar Company declared bankruptcy. The trustee sought to invalidate certain real estate transactions made by the Bliers, owners and operators of the company, alleging that the transactions were fraudulent conveyances meant to hinder, delay, and defraud existing and future creditors. The trustee subpoenaed documents of Philip Parent, Esquire to assist in establishing fraudulent conveyances.

The court, after a hearing, concluded that Parent's testimony and the joint affidavit of the Bliers, were insufficient to determine whether the attorney-client privilege could be invoked. The court then proceeded to conduct an *in camera* inspection of the subpoenaed documents. The court found that "[t]he clear statements and implications of the documents coupled with pertinent testimonial evidence" lead the court to conclude "that the Blier's enlisted Parent's assistance in furtherance of a wrongful act."[35] The court also noted that the burden of proof that a communication is not in aid of an unlawful act is upon the party asserting the privilege.[36]

The intent of the client is the controlling factor.[37] Even if the attorney is completely innocent the privilege may be lost. It is not necessary that the crime or fraud actually be committed, but there must be more than mere allegations.[38] It is obvious that it would be absurd to say that the privilege could be got rid of merely by making a charge of fraud.[39]

The Supreme Court of the United States, in the case of *United States v. Zolin,*[40] has recently considered the crime-fraud exception. This decision by the Supreme Court has resolved the differences of approach to this issue taken by several circuit courts. In *Zolin,* the basic general question at issue concerned whether the crime-fraud exception had to be established by "independent evidence," or whether the court could resolve the issue by reference to the privileged material.

---

[34] 10 B.R. 993 (Bankr. D. Me. 1981).

[35] *Id.*

[36] *Id.* at 999–1000, n.14. *Cf. In re* International Sys. & Controls Corp. Sec. Litigation, 693 F.2d 1235 (5th Cir. 1982) (dealing with the work-product privilege); *In re* Sealed Case, 754 F.2d 395 (D.C. Cir. 1985) (court stated that "[c]ommunications otherwise protected by the attorney-client privilege are not protected if the communications are made in furtherance of a crime, fraud, or other misconduct." 754 F.2d at 399. The court further noted at 399, n.4. (quoting Judge Wright in the case of *In re Sealed Case*, 676 F.2d 793, at 812) "[a]n exception or waiver of the work product privilege will also serve as an exception or waiver of the attorney-client privilege, since the coverage and purposes of the attorney-client privilege are completely subsumed into the work product privilege").

[37] *In re* Grand Jury Proceedings, 604 F.2d 798, 802 (3d Cir. 1979).

[38] Coleman v. American Broadcasting Co., Inc., 106 F.R.D. 201, 207 (D.D.C. 1985); *In re* Blier Cedar Co., 10 B.R. 993, 999 (Bankr. D. Me. 1981).

[39] Clark v. United States, 289 U.S. 1, 14, 53 S. Ct. 465, 468 (1933).

[40] 491 U.S. 554, 109 S. Ct. 2619 (1989).

> The . . . issue concerns the testimonial privilege for attorney-client communications and, more particularly, the generally recognized exception to that privilege for communications in furtherance of future illegal conduct—the so-called "crime-fraud" exception. The specific question presented is whether the applicability of the crime-fraud exception must be established by "independent evidence" (i.e., without reference to the content of the contested communications themselves), or, alternatively, whether the applicablity of that exception can be resolved by an in camera inspection of the allegedly privileged material. We reject the "independent evidence" approach and hold that the district court, under circumstances we explore below, and at the behest of the party opposing the claim of the privilege, may conduct an in camera review of the materials in question.[41]

The Supreme Court noted that the attorney-client privilege is not without its limitations and explained the purpose of the attorney-client privilege compared to the crime-fraud exception. Justice Blackmun, writing an opinion in which all other members joined, except Justice Brennan who took no part in the consideration or decision of the case, stated that the attorney-client privilege "protects the confidences of wrongdoers," but the reason for that protection—the centrality of open client and attorney communication to the proper function of our adversary system of justice—"ceas[es] to operate at a certain point, namely, where the desired advice refers not to prior wrongdoing, but to future wrongdoing." It is the purpose of the crime-fraud exception to the attorney-client privilege to assure the "seal of secrecy," . . . between lawyer and client does not extend to communications "made for the purpose of getting advice for the commission of a fraud" or crime.[42]

Based on this review, therefore, the attorney-client privilege will not be a stumbling block to your inquiry about fraudulent transfers when the crime-fraud exception can be used as a wedge to pry into fraudulent planning.

§ 3.7 Accountant-Client Privilege in Postjudgment Discovery

Assume the plaintiff's counsel has obtained a judgment in federal district court in a diversity action or under some federal statute, or have obtained a judgment in a federal bankruptcy court. Counsel begins discovery to enforce the judgment, and subpoenas the judgment debtor's accountant and his accounting papers. The judgment debtor's attorney moves for a protective order that the discovery not be held on the basis of the state accountant-client privilege. Consider the application of this privilege in federal court.

---

41 United States v. Zolin, 491 U.S. 554, at 556–57, 109 S. Ct. 2619, 2623 (1989).

42 *Id.*, 109 S. Ct. at 2626 (citations omitted.).

Yes, you should win. In about half the states there is no accountant-client privilege statute. However, some form of accountant-client privilege is recognized in twenty-four states, namely: Arizona, Colorado, Florida, Georgia, Idaho, Illinois, Indiana, Kansas, Kentucky, Louisiana, Maine, Maryland, Michigan, Mississippi, Missouri, Montana, Nevada, New Mexico, Pennsylvania, Puerto Rico, Rhode Island, Tennessee, Vermont and Washington.[43] In some of those states, namely, Arizona, Kentucky, Louisiana, Maine, Mississippi, Montana, Rhode Island, Vermont and Washington, the privilege does not apply if the accountant is subpoenaed to testify.[44]

However, if plaintiff's counsel seeks to enforce a federal judgment based on some federal statute, there is no federally recognized accountant-client privilege. State created privileges are not recognized in federal cases. "[W]e note that no confidential accountant-client privilege exists under federal law, and no state-created privilege has been recognized in federal cases."[45] This will be true where there are federal claims in a case which also presents state claims, because the federal rule favoring admissibility governs any state privilege.[46]

---

[43] *See* D. Causey, & F. McNair, *An Analysis of State Accountant-Client Privilege Statutes and Public Policy Implications for the Accountant-Client Relationship,* 27 Am. Bus. L.J. 535 (1990) (article lists full statutes and citations.)

[44] *Id.* at 538.

[45] Couch v. United States, 409 U.S. 322, 335, 93 S. Ct. 611, 619 (1973) (criminal case); United States v. Arthur Young & Co., 465 U.S. 805, 819, 104 S. Ct. 1495, 1503 (1984) (IRS enforcement action); *In re* International Horizons, Inc. (International Horizons, Inc. v. The Committee of Unsecured Creditors), 689 F.2d 996, 1004 (11th Cir. 1982) (bankruptcy case); United States v. Arthur Andersen & Co., 623 F.2d 725, 729 (1st Cir.), *cert. denied,* 449 U.S. 1021, 101 S. Ct. 588 (1980) (action enforcing IRS summons); Brink v. DaLesio, 82 F.R.D. 664, 673–674 (D. Md. 1979) (labor case); Osterneck v. E.T. Barwick Indus., 82 F.R.D. 81, 87–88 (N.D. Ga. 1979) (federal securities law and common law of Georgia); Federal Deposit Ins. Corp. v. Mercantile Nat'l Bank of Chicago, 84 F.R.D. 345, 349 (N.D. Ill. 1979) (federal securities law and claims under Illinois law); Belke v. Merrill Lynch, Pierce, Fenner and Smith, 78 F.R.D. 736, 737 (S.D. Fla. 1978) (federal securities law); Mitsui & Co. (U.S.A.) Inc. v. Puerto Rico Water Resources Auth., 79 F.R.D. 72, 78–79 (D.P.R. 1978) (diversity case); Lewis v. Capital Mortgage Inv., 78 F.R.D. 295, 313 (D. Md. 1977) (securities fraud case); United States v. Schmidt, 360 F. Supp. 339, 345–346 (M.D. Pa. 1973) (action enforcing IRS summons); *In re* Grand Jury (Jaskiewicz), 362 F.2d 942 (3d Cir. 1966) (criminal tax case); United States v. Bowman, 236 F. Supp. 548, 550–551 (M.D. Pa. 1964), *aff'd,* 358 F.2d 421 (3d Cir. 1966) (action to enforce an IRS summons).

[46] William T. Thompson Co. v. General Nutrition Corp., Inc., 671 F.2d 100, 103–04 (3rd Cir. 1982); Federal Deposit Ins. Corp. v. Mercantile Nat'l Bank of Chicago, 84 F.R.D. 345, 349 (N.D. Ill. 1979); Osterneck v. E.T. Barwick, 82 F.R.D. 81, 87–88 (N.D. Ga. 1979).

§ 3.8 Fifth Amendment Privilege in Postjudgment Discovery

When pursuing postjudgment discovery, counsel occasionally finds that the judgment debtor makes a blanket invocation of the Fifth Amendment Privilege. Such a blanket invocation of the Fifth Amendment Privilege is improper in the circumstances of a Federal Rule of Civil Procedure 69 civil discovery matter designed to discover assets of a judgment debtor.[47]

In a Federal Rule of Civil Procedure 69 discovery deposition a judgment debtor is required to offer additional explanation as to why responses to certain seemingly innocuous questions might prove incriminating.[48] "[T]he pendency of criminal proceedings does not by itself excuse a witness of his obligation to give testimony in civil proceeding. Some nexus between the risk of criminal conviction and the information must exist."[49] If the questions would form a link in a chain of evidence leading to a conviction for some crime, the defendant can properly invoke his Fifth Amendment privilege.[50] "Once the court determines that the answers requested would tend to incriminate the witness, it should not attempt to speculate whether the witness will in fact be prosecuted."[51]

However, the cases have held that the trial court must make a determination from the facts of the case whether or not the assertion of the Fifth Amendment privilege is justified.[52] In *Hoffman v. United States*, the Supreme Court established the criterion for evaluating a Fifth Amendment privilege claim which must be considered as to each question asked: "[I]t need only be evident from the implications of the question, in the setting in which it is asked, that a responsive answer to the question or an explanation of why it

---

47 United States v. Hatchett, 862 F.2d 1249, 1251 (6th Cir. 1988); Mertsching v. United States, 704 F.2d 505 (10th Cir. 1983), *cert. denied,* 464 U.S. 829 (1983); Baker v. Limber, 647 F.2d 912 (9th Cir. 1981); Martin-Trigona v. Gouletas, 634 F.2d 354 (7th Cir.), *cert. denied,* 449 U.S. 1025 (1980); Capital Prods. Corp. v. Hernon, 457 F.2d 541, 542 (8th Cir. 1972). *See* Heidt, *The Conjurer's Circle—The Fifth Amendment Privilege In Civil Cases,* 91 Yale L.J. 1062 (1982) (comprehensive analysis of the Fifth Amendment privilege in civil litigation).

48 Brunswick Corp. v. Doff, 638 F.2d 108, 110 (9th Cir.), *cert. denied,* 454 U.S. 862, 102 S. Ct. 319 (1981); Baker v. Limber, 647 F.2d 912, 919 (9th Cir. 1981); Capital Prods. Corp. v. Hernon, 457 F.2d 541, 544 (8th Cir. 1972).

49 Martin-Trigona v. Gouletas, 634 F.2d 354, 360 (7th Cir.), *cert. denied,* 449 U.S. 1025 (1980).

50 United States v. Jones, 703 F.2d 473, 476 (10th Cir. 1983); Federal Deposit Ins. Corp. v. Sovereign State Capital, Inc., 557 F.2d 683, 686 (9th Cir. 1977).

51 United States v. Jones, 703 F.2d 473, 478 (10th Cir. 1983).

52 Baker v. Limber, 647 F.2d 912, 917 (9th Cir. 1981); Martin-Trigona v. Gouletas, 634 F.2d 354 (7th Cir.), *cert. denied,* 449 U.S. 1025 (1980); Capital Prods. Corp. v. Hernon, 457 F.2d 541, 547 (8th Cir. 1972).

cannot be answered might be dangerous because injurious disclosure could result."[53]

If the Court determines that defendant's refusal to answer some or all of the questions has no connection or nexus to a valid Fifth Amendment privilege claim, then the Court should order defendant to answer those questions, and in lieu of answer, the Court can exercise its contempt power, and hold the defendant in contempt for such refusal.[54] In *United States v. Hatchett,*[55] the debtor was held in contempt for failing to fully respond to interrogatories served by the government in postjudgment collection proceedings. The court reasoned:

> In the present case, it is not self-evident that every disclosure of a disposition of appellant's assets would form a link in the chain of evidence of some crime. Hatchett concededly did not pay his taxes, but he had filed returns, and the Government already has obtained a judgment against him. The interrogatory is apparently aimed at enforcing the judgment, and it is unclear from the record why appellant believes answering the interrogatory might further incriminate him. On remand, Hatchett must explain how the interrogatory raises a reasonable fear of incrimination. A mere blanket assertion of the privilege will not suffice. He has already answered that he made no transfers in 1987. It is not readily apparent what earlier transfers would be incriminating. Some—for example gifts—would seem to pose no threat at all. Therefore, appellant must "seek judicial determination on each claim of privilege" with respect to each specific category or type of transaction he deems incriminatory.[56]

In *Baker v. Limber,*[57] trustees were appointed for a group of related companies "pursuant to a final judgment of permanent injunction entered in a securities fraud suit brought against the companies and their managers by the Securities Exchange Commission. Under the terms of the judgment, the trustees were authorized to bring suit for recovery of assets loaned, wasted, or misappropriated by the former officers and directors of the trusteeship companies."[58] The discovery by the trustee under Rule 69 of the Federal Rules of Civil Procedure was for the purpose of discovering assets from which the judgment could be satisfied. The trustee noticed appellant Fendler to inquire whether he had authorized a sham loan from one of the companies to appellant Limber. On two different occasions, Fendler, in his depositions, was asked about the amount or location of his assets, but Fendler refused to

---

[53] 341 U.S. 479, at 486, 487 (1951).

[54] Baker v. Limber, 647 F.2d 912, 919 (9th Cir. 1981); Martin-Trigona v. Gouletas, 634 F.2d 354, 355 (7th Cir.), *cert. denied,* 449 U.S. 1025, 101 S. Ct. 593 (1980); *cf.* Heinold Hog Market, Inc. v. McCoy, 700 F.2d 611, 613 (10th Cir. 1983).

[55] 862 F.2d 1249 (6th Cir. 1988).

[56] *Id.* at 1251.

[57] 647 F.2d 912 (9th Cir. 1981).

[58] *Id.* at 914.

answer, claiming his Fifth Amendment privilege each time. After the second refusal, the district court entered sanctions against him, including striking his counterclaim and entering a default judgment against him. The Ninth Circuit Court of Appeals found that Fendler did not attempt to explain the connection between an ongoing federal grand jury investigation and his refusal to answer questions. "A danger of incrimination is not evident from the implications of the questions, nor did appellant provide any basis for believing that a responsive answer or an explanation for his refusal would raise such a danger."[59]

In *Capitol Products Products Corp. v. Hernon,*[60] Capitol Products obtained a judgment against Hernon for $75,000. After noticing his deposition, Hernon was asked a series of questions on several subjects, including the following:

1. Whether any criminal proceedings were filed against him or might be filed
2. What were the names and addresses of his wife and children
3. What was his present and past employment
4. Was he acquainted with certain persons whose names were identified
5. What were his assets, including bank accounts, automobiles, sheep, jewelry, and furniture
6. Whether he had brought with him certain financial records, such as income tax returns, and bank and checking account records
7. Whether he had an interest in certain named business.

Hernon appeared at the deposition, but, relying on his privilege against self-incrimination, he would not answer the questions that were put to him.[61] The district court ordered Hernon to answer two of 105 questions put to him. However, on appeal, the Eighth Circuit did not find any substantial threat of incrimination and found the questions innocuous. The court of appeals remanded the matter to the district court with instructions to order the defendant to answer all questions unless he established a real danger of incrimination with respect to each question.[62]

Based on this analysis, it is evident that the Fifth Amendment privilege should not be a stumbling block to a judgment debtor inquiry, unless there is an actual threat that an answer may incriminate the debtor. If the threat is real, then the district court will have to consider the matter on a question-by-question basis. If questions concerning the debtor's assets do not present a basis for invoking the Fifth Amendment privilege, then they should be ordered answered.

---

[59] *Id.*

[60] 457 F.2d 541 (8th Cir. 1972).

[61] *Id.*

[62] *Id.*

§ 3.9 Evidence in Examination of Individual Debtor

There are no real secrets when plaintiff's counsel examines the individual judgment debtor. Counsel should look for evidence that establishes the debtor's ability to pay her client's judgment. First, inquiry should include whether the debtor has the present ability to pay the judgment. Second, inquiry should include whether the judgment debtor has the present ability to pay the judgment, or the ability to pay the judgment in the future, out of future earnings, or by installments. Third, inquiry should include whether the judgment debtor has the present or future ability to pay the judgment, or whether the debtor has the ability to pay the judgment in the past, and then transferred assets away to avoid payment of the debt. A checklist of evidence to consider obtaining and reviewing is given in the following section.

§ 3.10 —A Checklist for Postjudgment Discovery from Individual

For the individual plaintiff's counsel should seek evidence and information as follows:

_____ 1. Ownership of real property.
_____ 2. Encumbrances or liens against the real property.
_____ 3. Business ownerships or beneficial interests.
_____ 4. Ownership of stocks, bonds, or other securities.
_____ 5. Ownership or beneficial interests in bank accounts.
_____ 6. Location and contents of safe-deposit boxes.
_____ 7. Type and amount of insurance and cash values.
_____ 8. Nature of any claims the debtor has against others.
_____ 9. Title, case number, and amount of any judgments the debtor owns against a third party.
_____ 10. Property held by others for the debtor.
_____ 11. Any property held in trusts.
_____ 12. Accounts or loans receivable held by the debtor.
_____ 13. Property disposed by the debtor in the last few years.
_____ 14. Legacies or bequest owed to the debtor or expected to be paid to the debtor.
_____ 15. Transactions with the debtor's family members or others.
_____ 16. Creditors of the debtor.
_____ 17. Exemptions claimed by the debtor.
_____ 18. Books and records maintained by or on behalf of the debtor.

____ 19. Financial statements maintained or filed by the debtor.
____ 20. Appraisals of the debtor's property.
____ 21. Title reports on the debtor's real property.
____ 22. Ownership of jewelry, furs, artworks, artifacts, stamps, guns, dolls, or other valuable collections or properties.

§ 3.11 Evidence in Examination of Corporate Debtor

It is the same approach with the corporate debtor, as with the individual. Plaintiff's counsel should search for evidence that indicates the corporate debtor's ability to pay the judgment. Plaintiff's counsel should seek answers to three basic questions. First, does the corporate debtor have the present ability to pay the judgment? Second, does the corporate debtor have future earnings capacity which indicates the corporation will have the ability to satisfy the judgment in full at some time in the future, or will it have the ability to pay the judgment by installments? Third, did the corporation have the ability to pay the judgment in the recent past, and then the corporate officers, directors and/or shareholders transferred corporate assets to themselves or other entities to avoid payment of the judgment? A checklist of evidence to consider obtaining and reviewing is given in the next section.

§ 3.12 —A Checklist for Postjudgment Discovery from Corporate Debtor

For the corporation plaintiff's counsel should seek evidence from the following:

____ 1. Corporate ownership of real property.
____ 2. Encumbrances or liens against the real property.
____ 3. Ownership of stocks, bonds, or other securities.
____ 4. Ownership or beneficial interests in bank accounts.
____ 5. Ownership of inventory, materials, or work-in-process.
____ 6. Ownership of equipment, tools, trucks, automobiles, trailers, boats, tractors, planes, or other personal property.
____ 7. Types and amounts of corporate insurance.
____ 8. Profit and loss statements over the last five years.
____ 9. Balance and income statements over the last five years, including income and expenses by year for each year during the relevant period, including total volume of production, gross sales, net sales, other income, costs and expenses, taxes, net income, per common share, dividends paid, and depreciation.

____ 10. Corporate financial statements over the last five years, whether prepared internally or prepared externally.
____ 11. Location and contents of corporate safe-deposit boxes.
____ 12. Nature of any claims the corporation has against others.
____ 13. Title, case number, and amount of any judgments the corporation owns against a third party.
____ 14. Property held by others for the corporation.
____ 15. General and subsidiary ledgers of the corporation.
____ 16. Accounts receivable owned by the corporation.
____ 17. Loans or mortgages receivable owned by the corporation.
____ 18. Rents receivable owned by the corporation.
____ 19. Contracts, patents, trademarks, or other intangible property owned by the corporation.
____ 20. Corporate federal and state tax returns for the last five years.
____ 21. Creditors of the corporation.
____ 22. Appraisals of corporate property.
____ 23. Title reports on any corporate real property.
____ 24. All reports filed with the Securities and Exchange Commission, including, but not limited to SEC 10K and SEC 10Q reports.
____ 25. Certificates of title on all automobiles, trucks, planes, ships, boats, etc.
____ 26. All business operating licenses and permits, including, but not limited to liquor licenses, environmental permits, and other specialized business permits and licenses.
____ 27. Ownership of the corporation by shareholders, or parent corporations.
____ 28. Projections, estimates, or plans for future production, sales, expenditures of business operations, physical expansion, or modernization.
____ 29. Average number of persons employed during the year their names and addresses, and the number of employees laid off at any time during the year and their names and addresses.
____ 30. Identification of the officers, directors, and shareholders of the corporation over the last five years.
____ 31. Corporate official records, like the articles of organization, corporate minutes, and votes.
____ 32. Current and past list of corporate customers.

With respect to corporate transactions the examination by plaintiff's counsel should include the following items to uncover whether payments, repayments, loans, or transfers were made to officers, directors, shareholders, parents, subsidiary corporations, or other affiliated parties or entities.

____ 1. Payments of dividends.
____ 2. Repayments of loans.
____ 3. Repayment of other debts.
____ 4. Transfers of assets.
____ 5. Loans to closely related parties.
____ 6. Write-offs or forgiveness of debts of closely related parties.
____ 7. Advances to affiliate parties.
____ 8. Sales to closely related parties for less than fair value.

If one or more of the above events has occurred, they may be unlawful, when coupled with other events.

____ 9. Insolvency when the events occur.

The establishment of insolvency is important, because very often this is an element of a prima facie case in the enforcement of postjudgment remedies and statutes. (See **Chapter 6.**)

____ 10. Date officers, directors, or shareholders had actual or imputed knowledge of creditor's debt.
____ 11. Listing of creditor's debts on corporate financial statements, whether actual or contingent.

Either the actual or imputed knowledge of the debt will establish another element of the usual case, the existence of the debt and knowledge of the debt by a corporate officer or other corporate insiders.

____ 12. Comparison of the tax returns, financial statements, income statements, general and subsidiary ledgers, and other applicable corporate records.
____ 13. Whether financial statements, etc., list any assets, and at what value.
____ 14. From the end of one corporate year to the beginning of the next corporate year, whether there has been a change in assets from year end to beginning of the new year, and why.
____ 15. Any missing inventory, equipment, land, buildings or other property, and what is the explanation.
____ 16. Any of the events listed above occur during the relevant period of your examination for fraudulent transfers, etc.

____ 17. Any accounts or loans receivable from related parties or entities that were cancelled or written off on the books of the company.

Checking these items will assist plaintiff's counsel in determining what particular assets, if any, were transferred or dissipated, and at what period of time. The time is important if a federal or state statute of limitations is applicable to the particular creditor remedies plaintiff's counsel plans to use to attack the transactions and recover the assets. (See **Chapter 6.**)

____ 18. Whether there has been a transfer, dissipation, or merger of all, or substantially all, of the corporate debtor's assets or sale of assets to another corporation in basically the same business.

Some remedies may only apply if a substantial part or all of the debtor's assets are transferred, dissipated, or merged. In some situations, the event may occur in one transaction, and, in other cases, the events you seek to set aside may occur in a series of transactions.

____ 19. Whether there has been just a change of name in the corporation, and the new corporation does business at or has:

- _____ The same location.
- _____ The same assets.
- _____ The same officers and directors.
- _____ The same customer lists.
- _____ The same employees.

If one or more of these events are applicable from the list above, the court may apply the plaintiff's judgment debt directly to the other corporation as the successor or mere continuation of the debtor corporation.

Often establishment of these events may require an on-site visit, and other related discovery. But sometimes if the business is in proximity to the creditor, or creditor service company, an agent of the creditor may be able to establish some of these facts.

____ 20. If any of the corporate debtor's assets have been transferred, merged or sold, has the transfer or sale been to a related party.

Examination of these facts will establish whether the sale has been a genuine third-party transaction, or whether the close relationship of the entities or parties will be considered part of the prima facie case in transferring plaintiff's judgment debt to the new entity.

____ 21. Whether there is evidence of dealing with the corporation as a single identity of ownership and interest by related parties or entities.

____ 22. Whether any officer or director has breached a fiduciary duty to the corporation.

____ 23. Whether any officer or director has taken a business opportunity belonging to the corporation.

____ 24. Whether any related parties or entities directed their debts, or debts of related entities, paid as a preference.

____ 25. Whether there have been any large or unusual payments to lawyers, accountants, or other corporate service providers.

____ 26. Whether there have been any loans to officers, subsidiaries, or related companies without evidence of debt or without proper security.

____ 27. Whether there are suspected "kickbacks" on any sales or other contracts.

____ 28. Whether there have been any corporate sales to the business "straws" or "dummy" corporations of a related party or entity, rather than to legitimate third parties.

§ 3.13 Discovery Strategy

After plaintiff's counsel has completed the basic steps, such as recording and registering the judgment, locating the debtor and evaluating the debtor's routines or business organization, as discussed in **Chapters 1** and **2,** counsel is ready to think about a discovery strategy for her particular case. In the sections above plaintiff's counsel has been given some useful checklists to consider for sources of information about the individual or corporate debtor. In the sections that follow—methods of discovery, targets of discovery, handling unfair litigation tactics and analyzing the information obtained—will be topics for consideration as plaintiff's counsel develops and molds her strategy to her case.

The strategy will depend on a number of variables that apply to her judgment enforcement problem. Among the variables will be:

1. The size of the judgment
2. The assets the debtor has
3. Or the assets concealed
4. The kind of business of the debtor

5. The amount of time and expense your client authorizes for pursuit of discovery
6. The deterrent affect or policies behind the enforcing of the judgment
7. The complexity of the legal, business, and practical problems encountered in discovery.

If plaintiff's counsel has a limited budget for discovery, then she will want to chose the inexpensive methods of discovery as discussed in the sections that follow, such as production of documents, interrogatories, garnishment of third parties, or informal discovery. If cost is not a factor in her discovery strategy, and her initial inquiries of the judgment debtor indicate conduct to hide or conceal assets, then plaintiff's counsel will want to pursue the more costly and time-consuming methods of discovery, such as supplementary proceedings to examine the debtor and review documents produced, deposition of the judgment debtor, depositions of third parties, or a combination of one or more of these options to uncover information about those hidden or concealed assets.

As with any other litigation matter, planning a strategy is an important tool for success. In the simple case, counsel may only need to have the debtor produce his business and financial records during a judgment debtor examination following state statutory supplementary proceedings. In the more complex case involving a judgment debtor corporation that has suddenly been denuded of assets, for example, counsel's inquiry naturally has to include the third-party recipient of the assets, and may also include the officers who authorized the transfers and the accountants or lawyers who assisted in planning the fraudulent transfers. Also, as with any litigation, counsel's discovery strategy will develop more clearly with each additional document and witness she uncovers. The chief task of plaintiff's counsel will be to analyze the information she develops and to focus the direction her discovery takes. The following chapter should prove useful to plaintiff's counsel in undertaking those tasks.

CHAPTER 4

METHODS OF IMPLEMENTATION OF DISCOVERY TO TRACE ASSETS

§ 4.1 Supplementary Proceedings

Supplementary proceedings are created by state law to aid a judgment creditor to discover assets of the judgment debtor which may be applied to satisfy the judgment. Depending on the particular state law applicable, supplementary proceedings may or may not require the return of an unsatisfied execution before the process may be used. Supplementary proceedings should not be confused with the postjudgment discovery process. Discovery is just that, discovery of information. Plaintiff's counsel may want to initiate some sort of postjudgment discovery, such as interrogatories or requests for production of documents from the judgment debtor, before resorting to the state procedures for supplementary proceedings. In many jurisdictions, the procedures on postjudgment discovery are provided in the same statutory sequence for other postjudgment remedies, such as supplementary proceedings. However, supplementary proceedings are much more than discovery, because the court can require the debtor or a third parties to appear before the court at a hearing and comply with one or more orders which will facilitate the collection of a judgment.

In general, plaintiff's counsel initiates supplementary proceedings in the same action in which he has obtained the judgment. In most states a motion or application for supplementary proceedings is filed with the court, with a memorandum of law giving statutory and caselaw support for the proceedings. Additionally, counsel's pleadings for supplementary proceedings should include an affidavit that a writ of execution has been returned unsatisfied (if that is necessary under state law before instituting supplementary proceedings), and the pleadings should also contain proposed orders for the relief sought. In some states the process is begun by service of a citation to discover assets issued by the clerk of court.

Usually proposed orders or citations will include one or more of the following:

1. An order or citation for the examination of the judgment debtor to prove his assets and income
2. Show cause orders, citations and/or subpoenas for third parties who hold property belonging to the judgment debtor that ought to be turned over for application to the creditor's judgment or for third parties who have information concerning such property
3. Orders, citations and/or subpoenas for the examination of other witnesses and documents to prove the debtor's actual financial condition, unlawful transfers of assets by the debtor or the hiding of concealed assets by the debtor. Third parties who are called before the court are generally entitled to due process, including notice and summons to appear for the supplementary proceedings, an opportunity for a full hearing before the court, representation by counsel, an opportunity to confront and cross examine witnesses and an opportunity to appeal the court's ruling.

The provisions of state law concerning supplementary proceedings will vary from state to state, and using Federal Rule of Civil Procedure 69 in a federal district court, the practice and procedures will follow the state law. "Rule 69(a) stipulates the law of the place where the district court is held will govern supplementary proceedings." *Water Technologies Corporation v. Calco, Ltd.*[1] Therefore, to understand some of the similarities and differences in various state practices and how they apply to an action to collect a judgment in a federal district court, some analysis of particular state practice is useful.

Colorado

Colorado Rule of Civil Procedure 69, as amended, provides for procedures on both execution and supplementary proceedings in Colorado.[2] In summary, these rules provide some of the common procedures available to the judgment creditor in proceedings subsequent to judgment.

1. Process to enforce the judgment is by writ of execution. Colorado Rule of Civil Procedure 69(a). (Exception for garnishment as provided in Colorado Rule of Civil Procedure 103.)
2. A person indebted to the judgment debtor can be directed to pay the sheriff the amount necessary to satisfy the execution. Colorado Rule of Civil Procedure 69(c)
3. Interrogatories may be served on the judgment debtor. Colorado Rule of Civil Procedure 69(d)
4. A subpoena may be served on a judgment debtor for his examination to produce documents and testify before the court, master, or referee, including possible issuance of a bench warrant for his failure to appear. Colorado Rule of Civil Procedure 69(e)(1) and (2)
5. Also, a subpoena for appearance of a judgment debtor and production of documents where the amount of debt exceeds $500. Colorado Rule of Civil Procedure 69(f)
6. The court may order under its contempt power any nonexempt personal property of such person or other person, or owed the judgment debtor to be applied to satisfy the judgment. Or the judgment creditor may file a creditor's bill. Colorado Rule of Civil Procedure 69(g)
7. In the supplementary proceedings, witnesses may be subpoenaed to appear and testify. Colorado Rule of Civil Procedure 69(h)
8. Also, depositions may be taken of any person in accordance with the Rules. Colorado Rule of Civil Procedure 69(i).

---

[1] 132 F.R.D. 670, 674 (N.D. Ill. 1990); United States *ex rel.* Goldman v. Meredith, 596 F.2d 1353, 1357 (8th Cir.), *cert. denied sub nom.* Goldman v. Merrill, Lynch, Pierce, Fenner & Smith, Inc., 444 U.S. 838 (1979); H.H. Robertson Co. v. V.S. DiCarlo Gen. Contractor, Inc., 789 F. Supp. 998 (E.D. Mo. 1992), *aff'd,* 994 F.2d 476 (8th Cir. 1993) (supplementary proceedings under Missouri law).

[2] Hudson v. American Founders Life Insurance Co., 160 Colo. 420, 417 P.2d 772, 775 (1966).

It is clear that §§ (d), (e), and (i) grant the judgment creditor rights to discovery, and §§ (c), (g), and (h) give teeth to the supplementary proceedings hearing process.[3] In reviewing the supplementary proceedings process under Colorado Rule of Civil Procedure 69, the Colorado Supreme Court explained:

> Rule 69 contemplates that three types of individuals may be required to appear in the proceedings: (1) the judgment debtor, (2) the debtor of the judgment debtor, and (3) such other witnesses as are needed to testify on matters relating to the proceedings.[4]

In *First National Bank of Denver v. District Court*[5] the Supreme Court of Colorado noted that issuance of a writ of execution is not the only procedure available under Colorado Rule of Civil Procedure 69(a). In the matter below, the trial court, using the procedures provided in Colorado Rule of Civil Procedure 69(f) (now section (g) as amended), entered a subsequent ex parte charging order, modifying a prior charging order, pursuant to the Uniform Partnership Act[6] against defendants' interest in a partnership directing payment of the partners' shares of profits to the judgment creditor to apply on the judgment. The Colorado Supreme Court affirmed the trial court's power to enter such an order under section (f) (amended section (g)), but vacated the order to require notice and hearing before issuance of the modified order as required by the "due application" language in § 7-60-128 of the Uniform Partnership Act.

However, a supplementary proceeding under Colorado Rule of Civil Procedure 69 to have money allegedly owed to the judgment debtor applied to satisfy the judgment creditor's debt, may not be considered as due process and equal protection when the third party denies the debt. In that case, the judgment creditor must bring a creditor's bill to enable the third party "to plead responsively, setting forth his denials and/or defenses."[7]

Florida

In *Conrad v. McMechen*[8] the Court discusses the difference between Florida Rule of Civil Procedure 1.560, providing for discovery in aid of execution and § 56.29, Florida Statutes (1975) on supplementary proceedings. The court quoting from Kline, *Supplementary Collection,* 25 University of Miami Law Review, p. 596, 608–609, states:

---

[3] *Cf.* Hudson v. American Founders, 160 Colo. 470, 417 P.2d 772, 775 (1966).

[4] Stubblefield v. District Court, 198 Colo. 569, 603 P.2d 559, 560 (1979).

[5] 652 P.2d 613 (Colo. 1982).

[6] Colo. Rev. Stat. § 7-60-128(1) (1973).

[7] Equisearch, Inc. v. Lopez, 722 P.2d 426, 429 (Colo. Ct. App. 1986) (presenting an excellent history and philosophy of Colorado supplementary proceedings at 428–29).

[8] 338 So. 2d 1306 (Fla. Dist. Ct. App. 1976).

> [T]he discovery process does not have the teeth of supplementary proceedings for it operates only as a discovery device and no orders are made by the court requiring persons to produce property or show cause why the property should not be produced. On the other hand, in supplementary proceedings, the judge may order third parties to pay the judgment creditor's judgment and this order may be enforced through the court's power of contempt. The discovery procedure provided by the Florida Rules is a flexible and inexpensive supplement to supplementary proceedings but it does not operate to supplant these proceedings.[9]

In Florida supplementary proceedings contain the following procedures:[10]

1. Supplementary proceedings can only begin after the sheriff holds an unsatisfied writ of execution for the judgment creditor. § 56.29(1)
2. Motion by judgment creditor for court to order judgment debtor to appear before it or master in debtor's county of residence to be examined concerning his property. § 56.29(2)
3. Examination of an individual or corporation by an officer specified in the order. Also, examination of witnesses shall be as at trial and any party may call other witnesses § 56.29(4)
4. Court may order any property of the judgment debtor in hands of another person, and not exempt, or due to the judgment debtor, to be applied to the judgment. § 56.29(5)
5. Personal property titled to or paid for by debtor, within one year before service of process on him, to which his wife or any relative or person on confidential terms with debtor claims title and right of possession at time of examination, debtor has burden to establish that it was not made to hinder, delay or defraud creditors, and if so, can be ordered void and execution levied against it. §§ 56.29(6)(a), (b)
6. Answers may not be used to incriminate any person; the court may enter orders to subject property of any defendant to execution; the court may order contempt for failure to obey its orders; and, may tax costs, fees, and attorney's fees § 56.29(8), (9) and (10)

"Under decisional law interpreting § 56.29, the two jurisdictional prerequisites for supplementary proceedings are (1) an unsatisfied writ of execution and (2) an affidavit averring that the writ is valid and unsatisfied along with a list of person to be impleaded."[11] Impleading third parties is necessary to

---

[9] Conrad v. McMechen, 338 So. 2d at 1307.

[10] References are to Fla. Stat. § 56.29 (1987).

[11] Allied Indus. Int'l, Inc. v. AGFA-Gevaert, Inc., 688 F. Supp. 1516, 1518 (S.D. Fla.), *aff'd,* 900 F.2d 264 (11th Cir. 1988); Wieczoreck v. H&H Builders, Inc., 450 So. 2d 867, 871 (Fla. Dist. Ct. App. 1984).

acquire jurisdiction over them and to afford due process to the parties impleaded, including the usual due process concepts of: (1) a hearing, (2) before an impartial magistrate or judge, (3) fair notice of the charges and allegations, and (4) an opportunity to present your own defense.[12]

In *Allied Industries International, Inc. v. AGFA-Gevaert, Inc.,*[13] the court using § 56.29(5), allowed impleading of a successor corporation and its officers and fashioned equitable relief to allow judgment against a new corporation, United, as the alter ego of the judgment debtor corporation, Allied; to hold new corporation's (United's) shareholder liable to the extent of his interest in its stock; and to hold judgment debtor's former shareholder and employee liable for her excessive "sales commissions" from United. Additionally, supplementary proceedings pursuant to § 56.29(4), Fla. Stat. (1985) and Florida Rule of Civil Procedure 1.280 allow a judgment creditor broad discovery into a judgment debtor's businesses and financial matters.[14]

In Florida supplementary proceedings the more diligent creditor is rewarded following the general principle that, where two or more judgment creditors levy against property of the judgment debtor, the creditor who pursued the debtor, and set aside the fraudulent transfer of a boat, transferred from the debtor to his wife, should reap the rewards of its pursuit, and have its lien first satisfied.[15]

Illinois

The provisions for supplementary proceedings in Illinois are contained in Illinois Revised Statutes 1981, ch. 110, § 2-1402. The Illinois supplementary proceedings provisions include the following:

1. Judgment creditor can prosecute supplementary proceedings to examine the judgment debtor or any other person to discover assets or income of the judgment debtor, and the procedure can be commenced

---

[12] Ryan's Furniture Exch., Inc. v. McNair, 120 Fla. 109, 162 So. 483, 486–88 (1935) (rights include right to jury trial where appropriate); Wieczoreck v. H&H Builders, Inc., 450 So. 2d 867, 871 (impleading a third party as the recipient of a fraudulent transfer); Tomayko v. Thomas, 143 So. 2d 227, 229 (Fla. Dist. Ct. App. 1962) (wife of judgment debtor denied due process when orders entered against her in supplementary proceedings to return money she held in trust, although she was not made a party to the proceedings).

[13] 688 F. Supp. 1516, 1518 (S.D. Fla.), *aff'd,* 900 F.2d 264 (11th Cir. 1988). *But cf.* Advertects, Inc. v. Sawyer Indus., Inc., 84 So. 2d 21, 23–24 (Fla. 1955) (no alter ego or fraudulent conduct shown against officers).

[14] Jim Appley's Tru-Arc, Inc. v. Liquid Extraction Sys. Ltd. Partnership, 526 So. 2d 177, 179 (Fla. Dist. Ct. App. 1988).

[15] Salina Mfg. Co. v. Diner's Club, Inc., 382 So. 2d 1309, 1310–11 (Fla. Dist. Ct. App. 1980).

before the judgment is returned unsatisfied. The procedure is commenced by service of a citation issued by the clerk. § 2-1402(a)

2. The court may order the judgment debtor to deliver up, and apply to the satisfaction of the judgment, money, choses in action, property, or effects in his possession. § 2-1402(b)(1)
3. The court may order the judgment debtor to pay the judgment in installments with a portion of his or her income. § 2-1402(b)(2)
4. The court may compel a third person to deliver up assets in satisfaction of the judgment when those assets could be recovered by the judgment debtor in an action against the third party. § 2-1402(b)(3)
5. The court may enter any order upon or judgment against the person cited that could be entered in a garnishment action. § 2-1402(b)(4)
6. The court may order any person cited to execute assignments of choses in action or conveyances of real or personal property. § 2-1402(b)(5)
7. The court may authorize the judgment creditor to file an action to collect debts owed the judgment debtor and forbid the transfer or other disposition of the debt until the action can be commenced and prosecuted to judgment. § 2-1402(b)(6)
8. The court may make such further turnover, injunctive or contempt orders to effectuate the supplementary proceedings process. § 2-1402(c), (d) and (e).

Under Illinois supplementary proceedings, personal service of the citation to discover assets is necessary.[16] However, service of the citation to discover assets on the attorneys who represented the judgment debtor in defense of a contempt proceedings which resulted in the judgment was sufficient for due process purposes.[17] the process set forth by the Illinois statute for a citation to discover assets provides more than mere discovery, in that the "statute also provides that the judgment creditor is 'entitled to . . . compel the application of non-exempt assets or income discovered toward payment of the amount due under the judgment or decree'."[18]

In the case of *Second New Haven Bank v. Kobrite, Inc.*[19] a judgment creditor issued a citation to the insurers of the judgment debtor seeking to recover the proceeds of debtor's fire insurance policy. In the proceedings the insurers were free to present any defenses they had to the claim, such as arson, and in absence of a proper defense, the judgment creditor could collect on the judgment debtor's policy and was not precluded from making the claim simply because the judgment debtor had not made the claim. However, in *Stevenson*

[16] Manley Motor Sales Co. v. Kennedy, 95 Ill. App. 3d 199, 419 N.E.2d 947 (1981).

[17] Martin v. C.D. Gray, Inc., 110 F.R.D. 398, 401 (N.D. Ill. 1986).

[18] Textile Banking Co. v. Rentschler, 657 F.2d 844, 851 (7th Cir. 1981).

[19] 86 Ill. App. 3d 832, 408 N.E.2d 369, 370 (1980).

v. Samkov[20] the judgment debtor's homeowner's policy was held not to be an asset which the judgment creditor could garnish based on the debtor-insured's cause of action for bad faith against the insurance company.

Some questions asked of third parties in the citation process are proper, but some may not be proper. In *Shatkin Investment Corporation v. Connelly*[21] respondents appealed from orders of the circuit court holding them in contempt for failing to answer certain questions by the judgment creditor during a citation proceedings. In *Shatkin Investment,* the Illinois Appellate Court examined the process:

> The five questions in the first group are not sufficiently related to the location of judgment debtor's assets to warrant a contempt citation. For example, knowledge of Morton's home address, whether he resides in DuPage County or about the names of Churchfield's employees is not relevant to the location of judgment debtor's assets absent additional information. The second group, however, contains questions which are material to the inquiry. For example, judgment creditor asked whether Churchfield had ever done business with the judgment debtor, had ever been owed money by or owed money to judgment debtor, had ever employed or received things of value from judgment debtor, and asked other questions relating to Churchfield's past relationship with judgment debtor.[22]

In supplementary proceedings in Illinois, employers may be summoned to appear in court to answer questions concerning the judgment debtor's income, and the court has the power to order the employer to apply the nonexempt portion of the income toward the payment of the underlying judgment.[23]

There is some confusion in the case law in Illinois about whether the service of a citation to discover assets creates a lien on intangible personal property.[24] Some courts hold that the service of a citation to discover assets does create a lien on intangible personal property.[25] While other courts hold that the service of a citation does not create a lien on intangible personal property.[26]

---

20 142 Ill. App. 3d 293, 491 N.E.2d 1318, 1321–22 (1986).

21 128 Ill. App. 3d 518, 470 N.E.2d 1230 (1984).

22 470 N.E.2d 1230, 1234.

23 Kauk v. Matthews, 100 Ill. App. 3d 107, 426 N.E.2d 552, 555 (1981).

24 Water Technologies Corp. v. Calco, Ltd., 132 F.R.D. 670, 674–77 (N.D. Ill. 1990).

25 Asher v. United States, 570 F.2d 682 (7th Cir. 1978); Rochford v. Laser, 91 Ill. App. 3d 769, 414 N.E.2d 1096, 1102 (1980); *In re* Waner Corp., 89 B.R. 751, 755 (Bankr. N.D. Ill. 1988); *In re* Fowler, 90 B.R. 375, 377 (Bankr. N.D. Ill. 1988); *In re* Foluke, 38 B.R. 298, 301 (Bankr. N.D. Ill. 1984); *In re* Hormovitis, 57 B.R. 471, 475 (Bankr. N.D. Ill. 1985).

26 Water Technologies Corp. v. Calco, Ltd., 132 F.R.D. 670, 674–77 (N.D. Ill. 1990); Barnett v. Stern, 93 B.R. 962, 975 n.3 (N.D. Ill. 1988), *rev'd on other grounds,* 909 F.2d 973 (7th Cir. 1990); *In re* Weatherspoon, 101 B.R. 533 (Bankr. N.D. Ill. 1989); *In re* Jaffe, 111 B.R. 701 (Bankr. N.D. Ill. 1990).

Michigan

In Michigan, supplementary proceedings are permitted even if execution has not been returned unsatisfied, and, in fact, supplementary proceedings may be commenced even if execution has not been issued.[27] Under that law, after judgment for money is entered, the judge may, on motion in that action or in a subsequent proceeding:

1. Compel a discovery of any property or things in action belonging to a judgment debtor, and of any property, money, or things in action due to him, or held in trust for him
2. Prevent the transfer of any property, money or things in action, or the payment or delivery thereof to the judgment debtor
3. Order the satisfaction of the judgment out of property, money, or other things in action, liquidated or unliquidated, not exempt from execution
4. Appoint a receiver of any property the judgment debtor has or may thereafter acquire
5. Make any order as within his discretion seems appropriate in regard to carrying out the full intent and purpose of these provisions to subject any nonexempt assets of any judgment debtor to the satisfaction of any judgment against the judgment debtor.

Minnesota

Supplementary proceedings in Minnesota are contained in §§ 575.01–575.07 of the Minnesota Statutes. In summary, the following procedures may be utilized by a judgment creditor:

1. After issuance of an execution against property, any person indebted to the judgment debtor may pay the amount of the debt to the sheriff, and thus discharge his debt to the judgment debtor. Minn. Stat. § 575.01 (1986)
2. When an execution against the judgment debtor is returned unsatisfied, in whole or in part, the judgment debtor may obtain an order from the court to examine the judgment debtor. § 575.02 (1986)
3. Upon affidavit, if it appears that the debtor will leave the state or hide, the judge may issue a warrant to have the sheriff arrest the debtor, and bring him in for an examination of his property before the court. The court may require the debtor to post a bond for further attendance before the court, and be enjoined from disposing of his nonexempt

[27] Mich. Stat. Ann. § 27A.6104.

property, and, in default of the bond, may be committed to jail for contempt. § 575.03 (1986)

4. The examination of the judgment debtor shall be before the judge or referee, and witnesses may testify on behalf of either party. The statute also grants use immunity for testimony which would tend to convict the person of the commission of fraud. § 575.04 (1986)
5. The court may order the judgment debtor's property in the hands of the judgment debtor, except his wages necessary for support of his family for the preceding 30 days, or property in the hands of other persons, not exempt from execution, applied to the satisfaction of the judgment. The court may appoint a receiver of the debtor's unexempt property, or forbid transfer or other disposition of the property. § 575.05 (1986).

In *Anchor Gas, Inc. v. Border Black Top, Inc.*[28] the court decided that Minnesota Rule of Civil Procedure 69, expanded the discovery rules to allow a judgment creditor to examine an officer of the judgment debtor corporation in postjudgment discovery, even though the writ of execution had not yet been returned unsatisfied, as required by Minnesota Statute § 575.02. Defendant who refused to testify at supplementary proceedings under Minnesota Statute § 575.04, where he had use immunity on any of his answers relating to mail fraud and other crimes against the federal government, was properly held in civil contempt of the court order.[29] Under Minnesota supplementary proceedings, creditors had the option of proceeding with a direct suit against the transferee of the judgment debtor's property, or requesting the court for the appointment of a receiver to bring suit.[30]

§ 4.2 —Form Motion and Memorandum for Supplementary Proceedings and Proposed Order

[Usual headnote information for caption of the case.]

MOTION FOR SUPPLEMENTARY PROCEEDINGS

Plaintiff, ________________, through its undersigned attorneys, moves this Court for Supplementary Proceedings and An Order to Show Cause under Federal Rule of Civil Procedure 69(a) and under ________________ (applicable state law and procedures). For its reasons, Plaintiff attaches hereto and

---

28 381 N.W.2d 96, 98 (Minn. Ct. App. 1986).

29 Production Credit Ass'n v. Good, 303 Minn. 524, 228 N.W.2d 574, 579–80 (1975).

30 Longueville v. Olson, 369 N.W.2d 537, 539 (Minn. Ct. App. 1985).

incorporates by reference its Memorandum in Support of this Motion, Affidavit of __________, its Attorney, and ____________ (other documents required under state law and procedures.)

Respectfully submitted,

SIGNATURES

[Usual headnote information for caption of the case.]

MEMORANDUM IN SUPPORT OF MOTION FOR SUPPLEMENTARY PROCEEDINGS

I. Factual Background

On __________ (date), the Plaintiff, _________________, filed suit in this Court against _________________, Defendant, for ______________ (cause of action).

On ______________ (date of alleged unlawful activity or transfers, or other grounds for supplementary proceedings), while this suit was pending, ______________, Defendant, ____________, made a number of transfers of property which transferred title to these properties from her individual name to herself and her husband, ______________. On this same date, the Defendant assigned mortgages receivable, due to her alone, for the purpose of creating estates by the entireties.

Subsequently, on ___________ (date of judgment), this Court rendered final judgment against the Defendant in the amount of $ __________, plus interest at the rate of ______ per annum until paid, together with costs and disbursements of $ __________.

Plaintiff has collected $ ________ on this judgment leaving unpaid the total sum of $ _________, plus interest.

On __________ (date), the United States Marshal served a writ of execution issued by this Court on the Defendant, _____________, demanding payment of the judgment, and payment was refused. The writ of execution was returned unsatisfied on ___________ (date). [In some states, this paragraph is unnecessary, since return of an unsatisfied writ of execution is not a prerequisite prior to commencement of supplementary proceedings.]

II. Legal Justification for Allowance of Supplementary Proceedings

Under Fed. R. Civ. P. 69(a), the procedure to enforce a judgment of a Federal Court shall be in accordance with the practice and procedure of the state in which the District Court is held. The applicable procedures under Florida law for supplementary proceedings are contained in Florida Statutes, §§ 56.29(1), et seq.

In respect to the Florida Statute, the Florida Supreme Court has stated that supplementary proceedings are designed to be an aid in determining through judicial process what property the Defendant may have or others have for her that could be subjected to execution. *Young v. McKenzie,* 46 So.2d 184, 185 (Fla. 1950).

The Federal courts have afforded relief to judgment creditors by setting aside assets that have been fraudulently transferred to a third party. *Mission Bay Campland, Inc. v. Sumner Financial Corp.,* 72 F.R.D. 464 (M.D. Fla. 1976). In the instant case, Plaintiff submits that the Defendant, ________________, has fraudulently transferred property to third parties, including her husband, __________________. Therefore, supplementary proceedings are necessary to give Plaintiff appropriate opportunity to reach the assets transferred to satisfy its judgment.

CONCLUSION

Based upon the foregoing, Plaintiff requests the Court to issue the proposed Order for Supplementary Proceedings and issue an Order to Show Cause against __________________, Defendant, and to her husband, _____________.

[Add to the form any necessary third parties, and consider whether any restraining orders or freeze orders are necessary to prevent the property from being transferred again.]

Respectfully submitted,

SIGNATURES

[Usual headnote for the caption of the case.]

ORDER

The Court, after considering the Plaintiff's Motion for Supplementary Proceedings,

HEREBY ORDERS AS FOLLOWS:

1. Defendant, __________ and _____________, her husband are ordered to appear and answer concerning their property before this Court on the _____ day of _______________, 19__, in Courtroom # _______.

2. _____________ (husband's name) is ordered impled as an involuntary counterclaim Defendant in this case, and Defendant, _________ and ________

(her husband) are ordered to show cause why the transfer of certain real property and assignments of certain mortgages receivable on __________, and on other dates if it so appears, should not be set aside as fraudulent.

3. Defendant, ____________, and _______________, involuntary counterclaim Defendant, are ordered to produce all of their deeds, mortgages, mortgage accounts receivable, papers, books, notes, checks, accounting and financial documents, or other records reflecting the transfer of real or personal property from ______________ (date) to the present.

4. Defendant, ____________, is ordered to produce any other documents or records reflecting, supporting, and documenting the existence of any of her assets, whether real or personal, tangible or intangible, and any documents reflecting any transfers of her assets from ____________ (date) to the present.

5. Defendant, _____________, is ordered to produce any other documents or records and financial data pertaining to the ________ (year) sale by her of the _________ shares of stock in the _________________ (name of corporation.)

6. After examination of the Defendant, ______________, and involuntary counterclaim Defendant, __________________, such other witnesses called by the parties and examination of the documentary evidence, the Court may make such other and further orders necessary to satisfy the Plaintiff's judgment against Defendant, ____________.

[If appropriate, list any temporary restraining orders or freeze orders granted by the Court on application of Plaintiff, at the time the supplementary proceedings are commenced.]

SO ORDERED this __________ day of ___________, 19__.

____
United States District Judge

§ 4.3 Interrogatories

Pursuant to Rule 69(a), Federal Rule of Civil Procedure, a judgment creditor who has obtained a money judgment may serve interrogatories on the judgment debtor, and the procedures for the interrogatories may follow Rule 33, Federal Rules of Civil Procedure, or the rule on interrogatories applicable to the case by state procedures.[31] Rule 69 of the Federal Rules states:

[31] G-Fours, Inc. v. Miele, 496 F.2d 809, 810 (2d Cir. 1974); United States v. McWhirter, 376 F.2d 102 (5th Cir. 1967); Magnaleasing, Inc. v. Staten Island Mall, 76 F.R.D. 559, 560–61 n.1 (S.D.N.Y. 1977); Ranney-Brown Distribs., Inc. v. E.T. Barwick Indus., Inc., 75 F.R.D. 3, 5 (S.D. Ohio 1977).

> In aid of the judgment or execution, the judgment creditor or a successor in interest when that interest appears of record, may obtain discovery from any person, including the judgment debtor, in the manner provided by these rules or in the manner provided by the practice of the state in which the district court is held.

As decided in *United States v. McWhirter*[32] based on a motion to compel by the United States, the Fifth Circuit overruled the district court, which had denied the United States the right to take postjudgment interrogatories under Rule 69(a), and held "that Rule 69(a) was intended to afford a postjudgment method of securing information concerning the assets of judgment debtors and that to effectuate that intent the rule should be construed to allow the use of the inexpensive device of written interrogatories to secure that information." The Circuit Court reversed and remanded the case to the district court requiring the interrogatories to be answered. It should be noted that the Fifth Circuit's decision in *McWhirter* was made before the 1970 amendment to Rule 69(a) which changed the words "may examine any person" to "may obtain discovery from any person." (emphasis added.) The decision in *McWhirter,* the 1970 amendment to Rule 69(a), and the subsequent cases cited, should leave no doubt that under the Rule 69(a), a judgment creditor may use the full choice of discovery under Rules 26–37, or the discovery procedures provided under state law.

Interrogatories may be limited by the local rule in prejudgment proceedings, but usually are not limited in a postjudgment proceedings. However, even if there is a limit under local rules to a certain number of postjudgment interrogatories, plaintiff's counsel may find this method of discovery inexpensive and informative. Review the information on the judgment debtor in the creditor's file, or in the prejudgment litigation file. Reviewing that information from the creditor's file and the litigation file will sharpen the focus of the interrogatories plaintiff's counsel prepares. The primary focus of postjudgment interrogatories is on the debtor's assets. Counsel will want to focus on what assets the debtor had during a specified period prior to the commencement of the litigation, what assets the judgment debtor has now, and what happened to those assets during the course of the litigation. Several suggested forms of interrogatories are contained in the following Sections of this Chapter.

Some general suggestions may be helpful in focusing these interrogatories. If the judgment debtor has real estate, counsel will want a description and location of each parcel. Counsel needs to know if it is encumbered, and if so, the amount of the liens against each parcel. Counsel should review the last few years, and inquire about what real property the debtor has transferred away after the debt to the client was incurred. This may be the foundation evidence for a fraudulent transfer claim.

---

[32] 376 F.2d 102, 105–06, (5th Cir. 1967).

Plaintiff's counsel should inquire about the judgment debtor's business interests. [See **Chapter 2** above, concerning understanding the habits and routines of the judgment debtor.] If the debtor owns a business, counsel needs to know the form of the business entity, the kind of business and its profitability. The business may be in the form of a corporation, partnership, joint venture, trust or sole proprietorship. Counsel should also determine the form in which the debtor holds his or her interest. Counsel also needs to know how much the debtor earns from the business in the way of salary, bonuses, stock options, and other fringe benefits. A short history of this information is necessary to see if there has been a change in what salary and benefits the debtor now derives compared to what salary and benefits were paid a few years ago, before incurrence of the recent judgment debt. If the business is still as profitable, and the debtor gives the same services to the business, perhaps the change in the way the money is being paid out is to protect the debtor from his creditors.

For example, if counsel obtains these answers, and notices such a change, he may be able to make out a case that more money is available from the business, and should rightfully be paid to creditors. This may be the type of relief that a supplementary proceedings action could obtain for the client, once the preliminary evidence is developed from the interrogatories, and other less expensive discovery methods, such as requests for the production of documents. [Supplementary proceedings are explained in the preceding sections.]

Plaintiff's counsel should also inquire in the initial interrogatories about the debtor's ownership of stocks, bonds, money market certificates, other securities, or brokerage accounts. Counsel needs particularized information concerning all these assets. Naturally, the interrogatories will include questions concerning where the debtor has done banking business over the last few years, and counsel should develop information concerning the name and location of the bank, the account numbers, and account balances. The answers to these interrogatories will give counsel the information necessary to file postjudgment execution against the debtor and postjudgment garnishment against third parties. [Procedures for execution and garnishment are explained in **Chapter 5.**]

Additional interrogatories should inquire about the judgment debtor's interest in safe deposit boxes, insurance policies, claims of any kind, property held by others, accounts receivable, and legacies or bequests. Then the interrogatories should focus on disposition of property by the debtor in the last few years before the judgment, and should examine transactions with family members or business associates during that time for possible unlawful transfers to avoid claims of creditors.

If the judgment debtor refuses to answer appropriate interrogatories, then a motion to compel should be filed, and other sanctions sought.[33] [Motions

[33] United States v. McWhirter, 376 F.2d 102 (5th Cir. 1967).

to compel and contempt sanctions are discussed, and forms given in §§ **4.26** to **4.34.**]

§ 4.4 —Form of Interrogatories for Financial Information from an Individual

There may be limits under the Federal Rules of Civil Procedure or the local rules for the number of interrogatories that may be served. These limits are usually construed to apply to prejudgment litigation, not postjudgment litigation.

SAMPLE INTERROGATORIES FOR FINANCIAL INFORMATION FROM AN INDIVIDUAL

Interrogatory 1.

What is your full name, age, Social Security number, address, and telephone number:

Interrogatory 2.

By what other name or names are you known?

Interrogatory 3.

What are the names, ages, relationships, and addresses of your spouse and dependents?

Interrogatory 4.

Describe the premises which you occupy, give the address, and tell how long you have lived there.

Interrogatory 5.

If you rent the premises you occupy, state how much rent you pay and when it is payable.

Interrogatory 6.

What is your landlord's name and address?

Interrogatory 7.

State the nature or amount of any security deposited with your landlord and the terms of the deposit.

Interrogatory 8.

If you own the premises where you live, state the legal description, who paid for it (i.e., whose money or trade-in was used), in whose name or names title is held, and whether it is held by joint tenancy, tenancy by the entireties, or otherwise.

Interrogatory 9.

State the date upon which your home was purchased, the purchase price, the present assessed valuation, and its present fair market value.

Interrogatory 10.

State the address, area, legal description, and fair market value of any property presently claimed by you as a homestead in accordance with state law, and describe the improvements included thereon.

Interrogatory 11.

State the name and address of your employer, the position held by you, the dates upon which you are compensated for your services, and the amount you are paid therefor.

Interrogatory 12.

If you have other employment, state the name and address of your employer, the position held by you, the dates upon which you are compensated for your services, and the amount you are paid therefor.

Interrogatory 13.

Are you self-employed or do you own all or any part of a business as sole owner, partner, or stockholder?

Interrogatory 14.

If your answer to the previous question is in the affirmative, state the name and address of the business, the nature of your ownership interest, and how and when you draw money from it.

Interrogatory 15.

Give an accurate account of the financial condition of this business for the last three years, including a statement of assets, inventories, liabilities, gross and net income, and the amount of any undistributed profits in the business.

Interrogatory 16.

If your spouse or any dependent claimed by you is employed, state his or her name, employer, the position held, and the amount paid for his or her services.

Interrogatory 17.

If your spouse or any dependent claimed by you is self-employed or owns all or any part of a business, state the name and address of the business, the nature of his or her ownership interest therein, and the amount of income derived therefrom.

Interrogatory 18.

State the source and amount of any income received by (1) you, (2) your spouse, and (3) your dependents, other than that stated heretofore.

Interrogatory 19.

When and where did you last file a federal income tax return, and what was the amount of gross income reported therein?

Interrogatory 20.

Describe, give the present license number, value, and ownership of any motor vehicles owned by (1) you, (2) your spouse and (3) your dependents.

Interrogatory 21.

Describe the jewelry owned by (1) you, (2) your spouse, and (3) your dependents, and state where it may be found and its value.

Interrogatory 22.

Identify and give the amount and location of any uncashed checks or cashier's checks issued to your order or for your benefit or that of your spouse or dependents.

Interrogatory 23.

What accounts receivable, notes receivable, mortgages, liens, leases, royalties, or pledges of personalty do (1) you, (2) your spouse, or (3) your dependents own or hold, whether in your name or in the name of another; what is their value, and where are the evidences of ownership located?

Interrogatory 24.

What other personal property, including stocks, bonds or other securities, do (1) you, (2) your spouse, or (3) your dependents own or hold as pledgee or otherwise, whether held in your name or in the name of another; where is such property located, and what is its value?

Interrogatory 25.

Do (1) you, (2) your spouse, or (3) your dependents rent or use a safe-deposit box, either alone or together with one or more other persons? If so, state where the safe-deposit box is located in whose name it is listed, how it is numbered or otherwise identified and give its contents, their ownership, and value.

Interrogatory 26.

Describe and state the ownership and value of any account or shares held by (1) you, (2) your spouse, (3) your dependents, or (4) anyone on your or their behalf in any bank, building and loan association, savings institution, cooperative, or credit union.

Interrogatory 27.

Other than as stated heretofore, do (1) you,(2) your spouse, or (3) your dependents own cash or other personal property either hidden or in the possession of any person, form, or corporation?

If so, state the location, value, and ownership thereof.

Interrogatory 28.

What money or personal property have (1) you, (2) your spouse, or (3) your dependents received from anyone since the date of the judgment herein (or the last disclosure hearing) and what have you or they done with it?

Interrogatory 29.

State the names and addresses of all insurers with whom you have policies of life or accident insurance; give the date, face value, and cash surrender value of each policy, and specify which policies are payable to your estate.

Interrogatory 30.

Have you made or do you hold or own, or have you a lien upon, any claim by suit or otherwise against the United States or any other party? If so, state against whom the claim is or will be filed, the amount claimed, and the basis for the claim.

Interrogatory 31.

Are you in receipt of any pension, disability compensation, retirement pay, or other benefits from the United States or any other source?

Interrogatory 32.

If your answer to the preceding question is in the affirmative, describe and give the amount thereof and state whether you are willing to voluntarily assign all or any part thereof for application upon the indebtedness herein.

Interrogatory 33.

Give the address, nature of interest, date of acquisition cost, assessed value, fair market value legal description, and the income derived from any real estate or interest therein owned in whole or in part by (1) you, (2) your spouse, or (3) your dependents, whether in your name or that of another, wherever located, and state who paid for it (i.e., whose money or trade-in was used).

Interrogatory 34.

Do you expect to receive anything by inheritance or from any existing decedent's estate or otherwise? If so, state what, when, and from whom, and give its probable value.

Interrogatory 35.

Do you have any vested or contingent future interest in any property, or to the payment of any money, for any reason whatsoever? If so, state the nature and source of such interest, the location of the property, the identity and address of any person or institution that may be involved, the circumstances that will cause the property or money to inure to your benefit, and the probable value or amount thereof.

Interrogatory 36.

Is any money or property held in trust for (1) you, (2) your spouse, or (3) your dependents? If so, state the name and address of the trustee or other fiduciary, identify the trust, state what monies or property are held in trust, the value thereof, and the date upon which the trust is to terminate.

Interrogatory 37.

If monies or property are held in trust for (1) you, (2) your spouse, or (3) your dependents, state the amount of income which is or may be received therefrom, the timing of such payments; give the value of the corpus of the trust which may be distributed to (1) you, (2) your spouse, or (3) your dependents, and the expected date of distribution.

Interrogatory 38.

What other sources of income or property, a actual or potential do (1) you, (2) your spouse, or (3) your dependents have, which you have not disclosed in answer to previous questions, and what is the value or potential value thereof?

Interrogatory 39.

What cash have (1) you, (2) your spouse, or (3) your dependents paid out, what checks have you or they written, what property in your name or that of another have you or they sold, transferred, or given away since you incurred the obligation upon which the judgment herein is based, and what was the consideration received therefor, if any? Since the first date of demand for payment? Since the date of the judgment? Since service of notice of the taking of this deposition? Give full details as to dates, names, addresses, consideration, who uses, who has possession, who receives the income therefrom, and who pays the taxes and insurance thereon in each instance.

Interrogatory 40.

Have (1) you, (2) your spouse, or (3) your dependents closed any bank or other account or withdrawn any cash, bonds, or other assets from a safe-deposit box since the suit giving rise to the Government's judgment was filed against you? If so, give the name and address of the bank or other institution and state the monies, bonds and other assets withdrawn therefrom and their value.

Interrogatory 41.

Have you in any fashion transferred, assigned, sold, or conveyed any asset that you would have held longer, or for which you would have demanded more money or value, if you had not been, or did not expect to become, indebted to the United States or any agency thereof? If so, describe the asset, identify the transferee(s), and state the date, circumstances, and facts of the transaction in detail.

Interrogatory 42.

Are any suits or judgments pending against you? If so, state full details including the dates and amounts of recent payments thereon made by you and whether your salary has been garnisheed and by whom.

Interrogatory 43.

State the dates and amounts of any mortgages, deeds of trust, or other liens outstanding against any properties owned by (1) you, (2) your spouse, or (3) your dependents, giving the name and address of the mortgagee, trustee, or lienor, the remaining term thereof, the unpaid balance thereof, and the specific property affected in each instance.

Interrogatory 44.

Give the date, amount, and purpose of each fixed installment obligation now being paid by you.

Interrogatory 45.

What other legally enforceable obligations do you owe, to whom, and in what amounts?

Interrogatory 46.

What other fixed monthly or periodic living expenses are you paying and for what?

§ 4.5 —Form of Interrogatories to Corporate Officer Regarding Transfer of Assets, Repayment of Loans from Corporations

SAMPLE INTERROGATORIES FOR FINANCIAL INFORMATION FROM A CORPORATE OFFICER

Interrogatory 1.

State your name, current address, and current place of employment.

Interrogatory 2.(a).

Were you at any time an officer, director or shareholder of ________________ [insert name of corporation.]

2.(b).

If the answer to part (a) above is yes, for each position held list the following:

(1) Dates during which you held such position in the corporation.

(2) The title, office or directorship held in the corporation, and/or the number of shares of stock held in the corporation.

(3) Salary, bonuses, dividends or other compensation paid for each position held in each of the years.

Interrogatory 3.(a).

List the names and current addresses of all other former officers, directors and shareholders of the corporation during the last three years.

3.(b).

List the duties and compensation of each officer and director and state the dates between which each officer and director of the corporation was in such office or directorship.

Interrogatory 4.(a).

State the date on which the articles of organization were filed with the Secretary of State or other state corporate records office.

4.(b). State the date on which the corporation adopted by-laws, held its first corporate minutes or meetings, and recorded its first corporate records and books.

4.(c). Which of these corporate records are now available, and where are the records located, and identify the custodian of the records?

Interrogatory 5.(a).

Did the corporation file federal and/or state corporate tax returns for the last three years?

5.(b).

If the answer to (a) above is yes, list the types of returns filed, the dates when the returns were file, and state which officer or director of the corporation signed any of the returns, and identify such officer or director.

5.(c).

Give the names and address of the individual or company who prepared the tax returns for the corporation.

5.(d). Was any accountant the preparer of the returns, and if so, identify the location of his license and the location of his business address.

Interrogatory 6.(a).

Explain and describe in detail regarding the sale of assets of the corporation to ______________ (list the name of the party who purchased assets from the corporation) the following:

6.(b).

What real, personal, tangible or intangible assets of the corporation were sold to __________________ (purchaser).

6.(c).

What consideration was received by the corporation as a result of the sale?

Interrogatory 7.(a).

Explain and describe in detail whether you ever sold any individual or jointly held real, personal, tangible or intangible assets to ____________ (purchaser) during the period.

7.(b).

List for the assets sold, the purchaser, the sales price, the date of the sale, and the method of payment for the purchase.

Interrogatory 8.

Did the ________________ (purchaser) make or transfer any payment of money to you by check or otherwise, during the period ____________ (list the dates applicable.)

Interrogatory 9.

For each transfer or payment, list the type of transfer or payment, the date of the payment or transfer, the amount of consideration paid, the method of payment and the location of the account where the money or checks were deposited.

Interrogatory 10.

Has anyone from the corporation paid money to you for deposit in your personal checking, savings or other account?

Interrogatory 11.

If the answer to interrogatory 10 is yes, state the time and place of the transaction and explain and describe in detail the amount of money, the arrangements, if any, for payment to the corporation, and whether any repayment has been made.

Interrogatory 12.

Did you maintain any personal, joint or other checking, savings or trust accounts during the period ________________ (list the applicable dates.)?

Interrogatory 13.

If the answer to Interrogatory 12 is yes, state for each account, the type of account, the name of the bank or other financial institution where the account was maintained, and the account number.

Interrogatory 14.

On any of the tax returns you filed and signed on behalf of the corporation, did the balance sheet entries on such returns ever list an asset "loan to stockholders?"

Interrogatory 15.

If the answer to Interrogatory 14 was yes, explain and describe in detail for each such entry:

(a) The nature of this loan to stockholders.

(b) Whether this entry was made from supporting data in the corporate books of the company.

(c) The identity of the person who prepared the returns.

(d) Did the preparer use the the corporate books and records to prepare the return.

(e) The names and addresses of the corporate shareholders, and the number and/or percentage of shares held by each.

(f) The amount of the entry indicated on each tax return.

Interrogatory 16.

What payments, services, property or money has been paid or given by the corporation to you or your family members during the period from ____________ to ____________, and if any, explain, identify and describe in detail?

Interrogatory 17.

What amount of money has been loaned to you by the corporation during the time you were an officer, director or shareholder of the corporation?

Interrogatory 18.

If the answer to Interrogatory 17 is yes, state the date of any such loan, the amount of the loan, the rate of interest on the loan, the terms and evidence of repayment of the loan, and state whether the loan was reflected in a note or other instrument of indebtedness.

§ 4.6 —Form of Interrogatories on Fraudulent Sale of Assets Between Related Corporations

SAMPLE INTERROGATORIES ON FRAUDULENT SALE OF ASSET

Interrogatory 1.

Please indicate the name, address and current employment of each person who was a member of the Board of Directors of the selling corporation from __________ (date) to _________ (date), and indicate the period during which each person was a director.

Interrogatory 2.

Please indicate the name, address and title of each person who was an officer of the selling corporation from _______ (date) to __________ (date), and state the period or periods during which each person held such position.

Interrogatory 3.

Please indicate the name and address of each person who was employed as a certified public accountant for the selling corporation during the period from ______ (date) to ___________ (date), and indicate the relevant period during which each person was employed in that capacity.

Interrogatory 4.

Please indicate the name of each person who was employed as legal counsel of the selling corporation from _______ (date) to _________ (date), and indicate the relevant period during which each person named was employed in that capacity.

Interrogatory 5.

Were any of the persons named in the answer to Interrogatory No. 2 a member of the Board of Directors of the purchasing corporation during the period from _________ to date? If so, please indicate the name of each such person and indicate the the relevant period during which each person named was a director of the purchasing corporation.

Interrogatory 6.

Were any of the persons named in the answer to Interrogatory No. 1 a member of the Board of Directors of the purchasing corporation during the period from _______ to date? If so, please indicate the name of each such person and indicate the relevant period during which each person named was a director of the purchasing corporation.

Interrogatory 7.

Were any of the persons named in the answer to Interrogatory No. 1 an officer of the purchasing corporation during the period from ________ to date? If so, please indicate the name of each such person who was an officer of the purchasing corporation and the relevant period during which each person named held such title.

Interrogatory 8.

With respect to the sale in ________ (date) of substantially all the assets [or of a particular valuable asset, or series of assets] of the selling corporation, please describe the asset or assets sold, and indicate the consideration paid for each asset by the purchaser.

Interrogatory 9.

With respect to the sale or sales identified in Interrogatory 8, identify the purchasing corporation, each sale document used to transfer title of the asset, and the person who executed the documents for the selling corporation.

Interrogatory 10.

With respect to the sale or sales identified in Interrogatory 8, identify any federal, state or local government agency where any of such sale documents were filed, and identify any and all persons receiving a copy of such documents so filed.

Interrogatory 11.

With respect to the sale or sales identified in Interrogatory 8, please explain and describe in detail whether the selling corporation complied with the State Bulk

Sales Laws, Article 6 of the Uniform Commercial Code, or similar law, where a list of creditors is prepared and notice of the sale of assets given to creditors of the selling corporation.

Interrogatory 12.

During the period from _________ (date) to ________ (date), did the selling corporation file Federal income tax returns?

Interrogatory 13.

With regard to any such federal income tax returns, please indicate whether the selling corporation recognized any gains or loss from the sale or sales identified in Interrogatory 8.

Interrogatory 14.

With respect to the purchasing corporation, please identify each document prepared during the period from _________ to the present, which sets forth the financial condition, assets, liabilities, net worth, surplus, income, loss or the result of its operations.

Interrogatory 15.

With respect to the selling corporation, please state the name and address of each of its creditors to whom a debt (of an amount or value over $3,000) was outstanding during the period from one year prior to the year after the sale, state the amount of each such debt and the date incurred, and identify each document which evidences or reflects such debt.

Interrogatory 16.

With respect to each debt identified in Interrogatory 15, please state the date on which the debt was paid or liquidated, and identify each document which evidences or reflects such payment or liquidation.

Interrogatory 17.

As a result of any sales or transfers identified in Interrogatory 8 between the selling corporation and purchasing corporation, was any outstanding debt, lien, mortgage, encumbrance, or guaranty of the seller to the purchaser satisfied or paid as part of the transaction? If so, identify, describe and explain in detail.

Interrogatory 18.

As a result of any sales or transfers listed in Interrogatory 8 between the selling corporation and purchasing corporation, was any outstanding debt, lien, mortgage, encumbrance, or guaranty of the purchaser to the seller satisfied or paid as part of the transaction? If so, identify, describe and explain in detail.

Interrogatory 19.

Identify each person who has knowledge and identify each document which contains information concerning any of the factual issues concerning the sales or transfers listed in these interrogatories, or in any pleadings in this case.

§ 4.7 Requests for Production of Documents

Federal Rule of Civil Procedure 69(a) permits requests for production of documents under Federal Rule of Civil Procedure 34, or under the state discovery procedures concerning document requests.[34] As the Court indicates in *Magnaleasing*[35] there once was some doubt about whether Rule 69 allowed production of documents under Rule 34 as part of the postjudgment discovery devices available to judgment creditors.[36] However, the 1970 amendment to Rule 69(a) clarified that all federal discovery measures are available under Federal Rules 26-37, including the production of documents under Rule 34.[37]

In *Magnaleasing,* the plaintiff Magnaleasing, sought discovery in aid of its federal judgment under Rule 69(a), for the production of a settlement agreement between the defendants and Chase Manhattan. It was alleged by Magnaleasing that "the settlement involved improper transfers of assets to and from defendants and that production of the agreement would aid plaintiff in locating defendants assets."[38] The court ordered production of documents, under Federal Rule of Civil Procedure 34, of those portions of the settlement agreement that would be useful to plaintiff in obtaining information concerning the location of property from which the judgment could be satisfied.

---

[34] Magnaleasing, Inc. v. Staten Island Mall, 76 F.R.D. 559, 560–61 (S.D.N.Y. 1977); Fed. R. Civ. P. 34(c) has been amended to allow production from persons not parties to the action. *Cf.* Natural Gas Pipeline Co. v. Energy Gathering, Inc., 2 F.3d 1397 (5th Cir. 1993) (attorney ordered to produce documents he held belonging to his client, a judgment debtor).

[35] 76 F.R.D. at 560 n.1.

[36] *See* M. Lowenstein & Sons, Inc. v. American Underwear Mfg. Co., 11 F.R.D. 172, 173 (E.D. Pa. 1951).

[37] 76 F.R.D. at 560 n.1. *See* Note of the Advisory Committee, Rule 69. *Cf.* G-Fours, Inc. v. Miele, 496 F.2d 809, 810 (2d Cir. 1974); Ranney-Brown Distribs., Inc. v. E.T. Barwick Indus., Inc., 75 F.R.D. 3, 5 (S.D. Ohio 1977); Strick Corp. v. Thai Teak Prods. Co., Ltd., 493 F. Supp. 1210, 1211 (E.D. Pa. 1980). *Cf.* United States v. McWhirter, 376 F.2d 102, 105–06 (5th Cir. 1967).

[38] 76 F.R.D. at 560–61.

Where discovery, including production of documents, is related to obtaining information concerning the debtor's financial condition and ability to pay or satisfy the judgment, state privileges concerning incriminating testimony will not prevent the debtor from answering questions and producing documents.[39] Also, where a judgment creditor furnished enough information to raise doubts as to whether a judgment debtor's father owned property rather than his son, an order compelling the son to produce documents was affirmed.[40]

The first set of postjudgment requests for production of documents, under Federal Rule of Civil Procedure 34, should cover all areas of financial information of the individual or corporate debtor. The requests should also require production of documents concerning transfers of assets to related parties. As with any litigation, the requests should be prepared and tailored to the needs of the particular case. Several suggested forms are contained in the following sections.

§ 4.8 —Form of Requests for Documents from a Corporation

SAMPLE REQUESTS FOR DOCUMENTS FROM A CORPORATION

[Caption of the case]

Plaintiff, XYZ Banking Corporation (XYZ), pursuant to Federal Rule of Civil Procedure 69 and 34, requests defendant, ABC Trucking Co., Inc. (ABC), to produce and permit XYZ to inspect and copy any and all documents on the list attached hereto. Said production is called for to be made, and the inspection shall be made at 9:30 a.m. On Tuesday, the _______ day of __________, 19__, at the office of XYZ's attorneys, _________________________. At the appointed time and date, representatives of Plaintiff will physically inspect and make photostatic copies of the material produced.

INSTRUCTIONS AND DEFINITIONS

a. Unless otherwise indicated, this Request for Discovery of Documents and Property refers to the time, place, and circumstances of the occurrences mentioned or complained of in the pleadings, in any agreements between the parties, or in the judgment rendered herein.

---

39 First Fed. Sav. & Loan Ass'n of Rochester v. Fisher, 422 F. Supp. 1, 3–4 (N.D. Ga. 1976).

40 Davis Acoustical Corp. v. Skulnick, 131 N.J. Super. 87, 328 A.2d 633, 636–37 (Super. Ct. App. Div. 1974).

b. Where a document or documents in the possession of a party is requested, such request includes documents in the possession of the party's agents, representatives, and, unless privileged, the party's attorneys.

c. The pronouns "you" and "your" refer to the party to whom the Request for Discovery of Documents and Property is addressed and the persons mentioned in clause "b" hereinabove.

d. The term "person" means any natural person, corporate entity, partnership, association, or sole proprietorship.

e. The term "document" means any written, recorded or graphic matter, however produced or reproduced, including all nonidentical copies containing notations not contained on the original therefor, and including all punchcards, tapes, or recordings used in data and/or word processing together with the programming together with the programming instructions and other materials necessary to understand such media. The term "__________" means [define any terms necessary for this case.]

f. All documents which are not produced under a claim of privilege, under a claim that such documents form a part of the attorney's work product, or under a claim that such documents were prepared in anticipation of litigation shall be identified in sufficient detail to permit a request for *in camera* inspection of each document in the event any such claim is disputed.

g. Whenever appropriate in this Request for Discovery of Documents and Property, the singular form of a word shall also be interpreted as its plural.

h. The terms "and" as well as "or" shall be construed either disjunctively or conjunctively as necessary to bring with the scope of this Request for Discovery of Documents and Property any information which might otherwise be construed to be outside its scope.

i. The term "relevant period: means the period from January 1, 19__ to the present.

[Add other definitions as appropriate to this litigation.]

DOCUMENTS REQUESTED

For the relevant period:

1. Any and all real estate deeds, leases, mortgages, mortgage notes, deeds of trust, deeds of trust notes, payment schedules, lease payments, lease accruals, mortgage payments, and checks to individuals, partnerships, corporations, banks, or other financial institutions for payments of any and all leases, mortgages or deeds of

trust on property leased or owned by ABC, or held for the corporation beneficially by any person or trustee.

2. Any and all corporate federal and state tax returns.

3. Any and all financial statements, profit and loss statements, balance and income statements, balance sheets, trial balance sheets, ledgers, journals, accounting statements, accounting reports or other documents designed to present the financial condition of the corporation in summary form, prepared by its officers or directors, or on its behalf by any person or entity, or submitted to any financial institutions.

4. Copies of any and all checks, money orders, cashiers checks, wire transfers, electronic transfers, instruments of payments, negotiable instruments, or other documents representing payments or transfers of assets from the corporation to any of its officers, directors, shareholders, or companies or entities owned or controlled by these officers, directors or shareholders.

5. Any and all bank statements, money market account statements, stock broker account ledgers, passbooks, entry ledgers, computer printouts, or other graphic representations of whatever kind, which reflect money or property held by the corporation at any financial institution, brokerage house, bank, savings institution, safe deposit and trust company or other financial or credit company.

§ 4.9 —Form of Request from Individual

SAMPLE REQUEST FOR DOCUMENTS FROM AN INDIVIDUAL

[Caption of the case]

Now comes Plaintiff, by its undersigned attorneys and requests that the Defendant produce and permit a representative of Plaintiff to inspect and copy, pursuant to Federal Rules of Civil Procedure 34 and 69, each of the following documents in his custody, possession or control, including all documents in the custody or under control of any of his agents or representatives. Unless otherwise agreed to by the parties, the time and place of inspection and copying will be [date] at [time] at the offices of [Plaintiff's Representative].

REQUEST FOR PRODUCTION

1. The United States passport and immigration card for Defendant for the period [dates].

2. Any and all individual, partnership and/or joint federal income tax returns and wage statements for the period [date] to the present.

3. Any and all individual and/or joint state income tax returns for the period [date] to the present.

4. Any and all records concerning ownership, rental, mortgage, security or use by Defendant, or anyone on his behalf, of [property] during the period [date] to the present.

5. Any and all financial statements, loan applications or other documents prepared by or presented by Defendant to any bank, financial institution, lender, mortgage company, or other creditor during the period [date] to the present.

6. Any and all records concerning any real or personal property owned by Defendant from [date] to the present.

7. Any and all records concerning any stocks, bonds, debentures, bank accounts, money market accounts, certificates of deposit or other financial accounts owned by Defendant, individually or jointly, from [date] to the present.

8. Any and all records concerning ownership of any stock by Defendant in [corporation] from [date] to the present.

§ 4.10 —Form of Request for Documents from Trustee of Fraudulently Transferred Property

SAMPLE REQUEST FOR DOCUMENTS FROM A TRUSTEE OF FRAUDULENTLY TRANSFERRED PROPERTY

[Caption of the case]

Plaintiff, pursuant to Federal Rules of Civil Procedure 34, requests that you produce the following documents for inspection and copying at the office of [counsel], at [time], on [date]:

Any and all tangible material, for the period 1972 to present, in any way relevant to the trust which is involved in this law suit, including but not limited to:

1. Any and all consideration paid by the trustee, the beneficiaries of the trust or any other person or entity for the formation of the trust;

2. Any and all trust receipts or disbursements, including but not limited to state and federal tax returns prepared for the trust and bank records regarding the trust;

3. The original promissory notes or documents executed by the trust;

4. Any and all correspondence between or among any beneficiary, trustee and/or grantor regarding the trust;

5. Any and all documents relevant to the financial condition of trust for [period of time];

6. Any and all ledgers, journals, books, and accounts maintained by you for the trust;

7. Any and all bills, invoices, statements reflecting accounts paid by you from trust funds regarding the trust;

8. Any and all probate papers, records, pleadings, correspondence, tax papers, receipts, disbursements, real property records, personal property records, bank accounts or other documents reflecting the probate and assets of the trust;

9. Any and all automobiles owned by you as trustee for the trust;

10. Any or all records of any life insurance purchased for, by or on behalf of beneficiary;

11. Any or all records of any and all correspondence with [companies];

12. Any or all records of yachts, boats or other vessels owned for, by or on behalf of beneficiary or said trust;

13. Any and all records reflecting receipt by beneficiary or her trust of real or personal property from the grantor.

14. Any and all stocks, bonds or other securities of any class owned by beneficiary or by you as trustee of the trust.

§ 4.11 Kinds of Documents Available from Public Depositories

Documents filed with government agencies can be very useful in helping uncover a judgment debtor's assets. These records are usually quite accessible.

The expense to get public documents is usually very reasonable. Government records are available at local, state and federal departments.

County Records

Registry or Recorder of Deeds. There are a variety of records available at the county level of local government. The real estate records maintained at the Registry or Recorder of Deeds in the county provide a good starting point to determine if the judgment debtor owns any real property in the county. The registry or recorder's files will also contain information on mortgages or deeds of trust filed as liens against the property. The information concerning the mortgage will identify a lending institution where the debtor may also maintain a bank account. The mortgage or the deed may also contain information concerning the title company involved in the sale. The title company and the records it maintains on the sales transaction, such as the closing or settlement sheet, may be the source of identification of further financial information about the judgment debtor. Often, title companies may retain copies of the checks or other financial instruments the judgment debtor used at the real estate closing.

Clerk of Courts or Lien Offices. The county, parish, or municipal courthouse will be an excellent source of information about the debtor, since it contains records of all civil or criminal cases in the county, parish or city. The names of these courts will depend on the particular state, and may be called the District Court, County Court, Circuit Court, Superior Court, City Court or Court of Common Pleas, for example. If the judgment debtor has other liens or judgments recorded against it, you will want to know this information. This information will not only contain information regarding county, parish or municipal actions, but generally any federal tax liens or judgments will have to be filed in the office of the clerk of court or the lien office, as well. Very often, the clerk of court will be the source of records filed under the state Uniform Commercial Code indicating security agreements or financial statements on personal property maintained by the debtor or his business. In some states these records may be kept in the Town or Borough Clerks office, as well.

Probate, Family or Surrogate Court Records. Part of any local court system will contain a court clerk's office for filing administration or probate of estates for deceased persons, divorce proceedings and custody disputes. Often usual information about the debtor or his family will be located in any cases in which the debtor is a party or an heir.

County Tax Assessor's Office. The county tax assessor's office, or other such office, will contain information on who pays the taxes on the property.

The records should also contain information on where the tax bill is sent. These taxing authority records may contain information on a bank account maintained by the debtor which has not previously been identified.

Licensing and Inspection Offices. Many business or professional offices will have to obtain licenses or inspections from a local or state agency, such as the county health department or the county weights and measures department. Often to obtain such license or inspection, the debtor may have filed a financial statement or other information which will be useful in tracing assets.

State Records

Corporate Records. The Secretary of State's Corporation Division or Bureau, or such other state office of corporate registry, will also be an important source of information. The requirements of the kind of records which the state gathers on corporations doing business within the state will vary from jurisdiction to jurisdiction. Most offices will require registration of the corporate name, the date of incorporation, and identification of the purpose of the corporation in articles of organization or a corporate charter. Often the state assigns the corporation an identification number for easy access to its computerized records on the corporation. The state may require filing of an annual report which will often contain names of the corporate officers and directors, and perhaps information on the corporate shareholders and their percentage of ownership. Some states have cross-referenced indexes where individuals' names are given in alphabetical order, and then cross-referenced to corporations in which they are officers, directors or shareholders. The basic corporation information should also contain information on the registered agent, or agent for service of process, for the corporation. This is a normal requirement whether the corporation is either a domestic or foreign corporation.

State Regulatory Boards or Licensing Agencies. Depending on the type of judgment debtor plaintiff's counsel is pursuing, information from one of the state regulatory or licensing agencies, such as the state department of labor and industry, may be useful. Often the various state agencies that license, inspect or regulate will contain sources of information on businesses or professional associations. Licenses are often required for accountants, architects, attorneys, auctioneers, beauticians, cosmetologists, chiropractors, physicians, podiatrists, and psychologists. Furthermore, states often require inspection or audits of various kinds of business activity, and this information may be useful in discovering hidden assets of the judgment debtor.

State Department of Taxation. Many state tax records may not be available to the public, but some information provided in public records may contain vital information. The department may require businesses to have sales tax licenses. In obtaining these licenses, the business may have to file an application. The application may be available as a public record. If this is so, the information may be of assistance to you. Of course, if you are involved with a local, state or federal law enforcement agency, you may be able to have access to individual, partnership and corporate returns under statutory access or by ex parte court process. Access to corporate tax returns will provide information on loans to and from stockholders, loans to and from corporate officers, directors, or shareholders, and information on liabilities such as mortgages, notes and bonds. Interest payments may also indicate a source of payment, such as a bank or other financial institution. The tax return may also indicate an accountant who prepared the return.

Federal Records

U.S. Securities and Exchange Commission (SEC). Federal records are maintained by a variety of agencies. If information is sought for a public corporation, the records of the United States Securities and Exchange Commission (SEC) will provide an excellent source. Public corporations in the United States are required to file, among other things, SEC annual reports (called 10K's) and SEC quarterly reports (called 10Q's). These reports contain a variety of detailed financial and operational information on the corporation.

Federal Court Records. Like state courts, the various levels of federal courts, such as the United States District Courts, United States Courts of Appeal, the United States Supreme Court, the United States Claims Court, the United States Tax Court, the United States Bankruptcy Court, and other federal courts and federal administrative bodies, provide useful sources of information.

Department of Transportation. Federal Aviation Administration (Aircraft) Records on the title and encumbrances on aircraft in the United States are maintained at the Department of Transportation, Federal Aviation Administration, F.A.A. Aircraft Registry, in Oklahoma City, Oklahoma. All attachments, executions and judgment liens against aircraft should also be filed there in accordance with 49 U.S.C. § 1403.

Department of Transportation. U.S. Coast Guard (Ships) Records on Ships are maintained by the Secretary of the Department of Transportation and are available for public inspection. 46 U.S.C. § 31302. Ships are considered to be vessels over 21 tons. All bills of sale, conveyances, mortgages, assignments or related instruments maintained for ships must be filed in accordance with 46 U.S.C. § 31321, et seq. One of the ways of finding these instruments is to check the filing at the home port of a vessel with the U.S. Coast Guard. A certified copy of the preferred ship's mortgage should be kept on the vessel and be available for inspection. 46 U.S.C. § 31324. A preferred ship's mortgage includes the whole of a vessel, and is defined as such in 46 U.S.C. § 31322. The Secretary of Transportation can certify that certain state titling systems comply with the Secretary's guidelines for a titling system under § 13106(b)(8) of 46 U.S.C. *See,* 46 U.S.C. § 31322(d)(1)(A). Vessels under 21 tons should be titled according to state law.

Federal Banking Agencies. The Federal Reserve Board, Comptroller of the Currency, Federal Deposit Insurance Corporation, and Resolution Trust Corporation. Federal Banking Agencies maintain a variety of reports on national and state financial institutions. If counsel believes that any such information may be helpful in enforcing a judgment, he should contact the particular agency to find out what publicly filed reports may assist in developing the information sought.

Other Federal Agencies. There are many other federal agencies which regulate business and industry. Many of the agencies maintain public files and records which will be valuable sources of information regarding particularized searches.

§ 4.12 Informal Discovery

Not enough can be said of the benefits, including cost savings, of informal discovery in approaching a judgment enforcement problem. The client's file on the debtor and its contents always provide information and clues about the debtor and his habits. [See **Chapter 2.**] Plaintiff's counsel should become familiar with the history of the litigation and the history of the judgment debtor. Very often the relationship between the debtor and the plaintiff began with some kind of business transaction. At the beginning of the transaction, the debtor may have given the plaintiff a financial statement or paid by check from a certain bank for a product. There may be helpful information in some of the correspondence in the client's files which will provide financial information about the debtor.

Perhaps counsel should look in the phone book for the debtor's place of business. Does the debtor have an ad in the yellow pages that may provide some clues about other related businesses the debtor may own? Call the number. Is the debtor's place of business still operating?

Other informal discovery might include calling local attorneys who in the past may have had claims against the debtor, or are presently enforcing claims against the debtor. Naturally such inquiries have to be discreet, and not disclose privileged information, but very often in the collection field, there is much information to be exchanged among attorneys pursuing the same debtor which may help both parties collect on their respective claims.

For example, plaintiff's counsel may review the debtor's records that the client, a bank, has provided, to assist in a collection action against the debtor. The records indicate that the debtor lost money on some purchase transactions over the last year. In reviewing the invoices concerning the purchase of raw materials that the debtor presented to the bank in accordance with its financing agreement, counsel notices that several months ago, a new supplier started to appear on the invoices. This raises suspicions about these transactions, because the bank's loan specialist noticed discrepancies in the company's remaining inventory, versus the amount of finished goods sold. Counsel learns that the debtor was short on raw materials and corresponding product sales, compared to the ratio of raw materials allegedly purchased. According to the invoices reviewed, the company allegedly shipped certain raw materials to the debtor, and claimed to be a sub-specialist of a certain trading industry. Counsel should to verify these suspicions.

It is advisable to check the name of the company with the national trading association for that industry. Is the company a recognized company on the rolls of the trading association? If not, counsel may have uncovered a fraud, namely, the debtor's bogus purchases of raw materials. The company doing the selling of raw materials to the debtor may not be giving the debtor any raw materials at all, and, in fact, later formal discovery may indicate that the money from the debtor was split among certain dishonest officers or directors of the debtor company, as a way of siphoning off assets of the debtor and the client bank unpaid. Certainly if such information is uncovered, it may indicate that formal discovery from the third parties is necessary to trace what happened to the sales proceeds. This formal discovery may lead counsel to avenues of recovery against third parties for fraudulent transfers or other theories of recovery. [See **Chapter 6** on Remedies and **Chapter 7** on Receivership.]

TARGETS OF DISCOVERY

§ 4.13 Examination Process for the Debtor

State law usually gives a judgment creditor an opportunity to conduct supplementary proceedings or to take a judgment debtor examination. [See §§ **4.1** and **4.2** on Supplementary Proceedings.] Under Federal Rule of Civil Procedure 69, the judgment creditor, after the recovery of the judgment, always has the right to take the examination of the debtor, whether under the state discovery rules, or the Federal Rules.[41] Under the Federal Debt Collection Procedures Act of 1990 (FDCPA), codified in Title 28, the Federal Rules of Civil Procedure apply regarding the enforcement of a judgment by the United States. 28 U.S.C. §3003(f). Therefore, the principles of examination of the debtor and discovery of the debtor's financial condition under Federal Rule 69, including supplementary proceedings and discovery under state practice and procedure, are still available to the United States, as long as the state law is not inconsistent with a provision of the FDCPA.[42] Under FDCA, § 3015(b), the United States even has the right to take financial discovery of the debtor in prejudgment cases where there is a reasonable chance of recovering a debt exceeding $50,000. Before taking any action to enforce a remedy under the FDCPA, however, the United States has to comply with the notice provision of § 3202(b).

In the examination process of the individual debtor, be sure to check **Chapter 3** above for information on what to look for in the examination. Also, the form interrogatories [Form in § **4.4**], and the form request for production of documents [Form in § **4.9**] will give you information to form a basis for the examination of the individual debtor. If you have not previously requested this information, your subpoena duces tecum directed to the judgment debtor for examination should contain a list of these documents for the debtor to bring to the examination.

The main purpose of the examination is to obtain information concerning the financial condition and assets of the judgment debtor, and information about any assets that may have been fraudulently transferred by the judgment debtor to avoid payment to creditors.[43] Inquiry should include all sources of past, present and future income, including the name and address of the debtor's past and current employers. If the debtor says he is totally supported by his wife, he has to answer questions concerning the source of her income and assets, since the questions may uncover fraudulent transfers of assets to his spouse.[44] The income information should be explored to ascertain if the debtor has any rent, interest or royalty income, in addition to any income

---

41 United States v. Kulukundis, 329 F.2d 197, 199 (2d Cir. 1964); Evans v. Chicago Football Franchise Ltd. Partnership, 127 F.R.D. 492, 493–94 (N.D. Ill. 1989); Caisson Corp. v. County W. Bldg. Corp., 62 F.R.D. 331, 334 (E.D. Pa. 1974).

42 28 U.S.C. §§ 3001(d), 3015(a); United States v. Kulukundis, 329 F.2d 197, 199 (2d Cir. 1964). *Cf.* Evans v. Chicago Football Franchise Ltd. Partnership, 127 F.R.D. 492, 493–94 (N.D. Ill. 1989).

43 G-Fours, Inc. v. Miele, 496 F.2d 809 (2d Cir. 1974); United States v. McWhirter, 376 F.2d 102, 105–06 (5th Cir. 1967); Caisson Corp. v. County W. Bldg. Corp., 62 F.R.D. 331, 334–36 (E.D. Pa. 1974).

44 Cerami v. Robinson, 85 F.R.D. 371, 373 (S.D.N.Y. 1980). *See* Magnaleasing, Inc. v. Staten Island Mall, 76 F.R.D. 559, 561 (S.D.N.Y. 1977).

from salary, wages, and bonuses. Documents from the client's files and information given by the debtor on his initial financial statement at the start of the relationship with the client, if available, should be compared to the debtor's present financial circumstances.

All documents produced by the debtor should be identified and explained by the debtor. Tax returns, bank records and business records should be produced and examined. The debtor's records concerning real and personal property should be examined, and special attention given to any recent transfers of interest in property to another person. The examination should include information concerning any cause of action pending for or against the debtor, and information concerning any loans, notes, or accounts payable owing to the debtor.

Inquiry should be made about the debtor's spouse and dependents, and their sources of support other than the debtor.[45] If the debtor has dependents in college or a private elementary or high school, questions should be formulated to ascertain the method of payment of these tuitions. In some instances, counsel may discover that a corporation in which the debtor is a principal pays these tuitions directly on behalf of the debtor. Such payments may give counsel a basis for piercing the corporate veil of the corporation, and alleging that the debtor is the alter ego behind the corporation, or may provide further evidence for the court to support a writ of garnishment against the corporation for the nonexempt portion of the debtor's wages, which includes the amount the debtor reports, plus any other amounts he receives as part of his compensation package from the corporation. [See **Chapter 6** on Piercing the Corporate Veil and **Chapter 5** on Garnishment.]

Credit card records are another source of information concerning the debtor and the business activities in which the debtor engages. In some cases, where the debtor reports little personal income, counsel may find the debtor is using a credit card, paid for by a corporation he controls, to maintain his rather lavish lifestyle. Some debtors use such credit cards, arguably for business purposes only, to pay for such potentially nonbusiness expenses as suits, socks, microwave ovens, tennis rackets, pantyhose, and stereo sets. Credit card account statements, whether corporate or personal, are evidence of the debtor's spending habits, and they can help counsel trace the debtor's travels during a particular period of time. The records may demonstrate that the debtor stopped at a marina for food and gas, using a boat he does not claim to own. The records on the boat may show it is another asset of his closely controlled corporation that he uses at will, providing further information to show that the corporation is the debtor's alter ego. This and other information you develop may prove that the debtor uses this corporation as a personal "piggy bank."[46]

---

[45] G-Fours, Inc. v. Miele, 496 F.2d 809 (2d Cir. 1974). *Cf.* Cerami v. Robinson, 85 F.R.D. 371, 373 (S.D.N.Y. 1980).

[46] *But cf.* El Salto, S.A. v. PSG Co., 444 F.2d 477, 483 (9th Cir.), *cert. denied,* 404 U.S. 940, 92 S. Ct. 273, 30 L. Ed. 2d 253 (1971).

Judges usually will not be sympathetic to this kind of corporate abuse and will allow counsel to pierce the corporate veil when the corporation is merely a shell to protect the debtor's personal assets from creditors, as long as counsel presents sufficient facts justifying such a remedy.[47] Alternatively, the court may enter a monthly payment order on plaintiff's judgment, based on the debtor's noncash "income" derived from his services to the corporation.

Inquiry of the judgment debtor corporation will have to be made through officers, directors or shareholders of the corporation in their capacity as an officer or managing agent of the corporation. Sanctions cannot be imposed on a corporation for failure of its officer to appear when he was served with notice only in his individual capacity.[48] "It would be anomalous to impose sanctions on Greenberg when it was the corporation's deposition that was sought and sanctions could not be imposed on the corporate party itself."[49]

Here is an example of a deposition of a corporate officer, in a federal judgment case, where the line of inquiry centers on whether there may have been sales of product from the judgment debtor to a partnership that the corporate officer controlled. The partnership then turned around and sold the product to former customers of the judgment debtor at a significant mark-up and pocketed the profits which should have belonged to the judgment debtor. The process was just part of a scheme to keep the judgment debtor from making a profit and paying on the judgment.

Question: (hereinafter "Q" [Question is addressed to an officer of the judgment debtor. The transcript has been edited for use in this book, but is based on an actual transcript of a deposition taken by the author.])

Q: When was the contract dated?
Answer: (hereinafter "A")
A: August 22, 1989. Sold to AEC Company, 176 bales of smoke sheets of crude rubber. This rubber was purchased from the RPM Company [the judgment debtor] on August 6, 1989.
Q: At what price was it purchased from RPM Company?
A: At 32 and 1/2 cents a pound.
Q: And you signed the contract marked as Plaintiff's Exhibit No. 5, did you not?
A: Yes.
Q: And who signed the contract for the JAE partnership if you know?
A: JAE signed it himself.

---

47 *Cf.* Strick Corp. v. Thai Teak Prods. Co., Ltd., 493 F. Supp. 1210, 1218 (E.D. Pa. 1980). See **Ch. 6** on Piercing the Corporate Veil.

48 *See* Gillam v. A. Shyman, Inc., 22 F.R.D. 475 (D. Alaska 1958). *See also* Pioche Mines Consol., Inc. v. Dolman, Janney & Dolman, 333 F.2d 257 (9th Cir. 1964), *cert. denied,* 380 U.S. 956, 85 S. Ct. 1081, 13 L. Ed. 2d 972 (1965).

49 El Salto, S.A. v. PSG Co., 444 F.2d 477, 484 (9th Cir. 1971).

Q: He was one of the partners of JAE?
A: Yes.
Q: And what was the quantity of the rubber to be delivered?
A: 44,000 pounds.
Q: And I show you what has been marked as Plaintiff's Exhibit No. 6, and ask you to identify that document?
A: It is an invoice showing a sale by JAE.
Q: To what company was the sale made?
A: It was made to AEC Company.
Q: What is the date of that sale?
A: It was made on August 22, 1989.
Q: And it is that same number of bales of rubber, correct?
A: That is correct.
Q: The same classification of rubber?
A: Yes, sir.
Q: It is the same pounds of rubber?
A: Yes, it is.
Q: And the period of time from August 6th to August 22, 1989, is how many days, sir?
A: About 16 days.
Q: And the rubber was originally purchased by RPM at 32 and 1/2 cents per pound?
A: Yes, sir.
.....
Q: And the total contract price between RPM and JAE was $14,200, was it not?
A: Yes, sir.
Q: And it is true, is it not, that on August 22, 1989, the same rubber was sold by JAE to AEC Company for $19,300?
A: Yes, sir.
Q: So the difference between those two prices is over $5,000, is it not?
A: Yes, sir.
Q: And the difference between the sale dates is only 16 days, as you have testified, is it not?
A: Yes, sir.

[The questioning went on for contract after contract, and invoice after invoice. It turned out that the officer of RPM was a partner of JAE, and he and JAE were just pocketing the profits, and siphoning off the profits of RPM. The litigation against the officer, JAE and several others was later settled for $450,000. The original judgment against RPM was for $750,000. See **§ 4.39.**]

§ 4.14 Examination of the Debtor's Spouse or Relatives

Many times the examination of the judgment debtor will not provide all the answers counsel needs. It will be obvious that counsel must depose a person not a party to the lawsuit. Under Federal Rule of Civil Procedure 69, such discovery is permitted.[50] [See the discussion of the Broad Range of Inquiry under Rule 69 in **Chapter 3.**] However, this right is not unfettered, and some courts may require that counsel seek execution first against the judgment debtor's assets before permitting discovery against third parties. Also, to compel a third party and his documents, counsel must use a subpoena.[51] Generally, it is said that the inquiry must be kept pertinent to the goal of discovering concealed assets of the judgment debtor and not be allowed to become a means of harassment of the debtor or third persons.[52]

So, even though plaintiff's counsel may inquire about the third party's transactions with and the financial affairs of the judgment debtor, the third party cannot be required to disclose his own assets.[53] Of course, if the debtor indicates he is totally supported by his wife, he must answer questions about the sources of her income or assets, since the creditor may use this information to uncover fraudulent transfers of assets to her.[54] Also, if there is a question about the debtor's business affairs, and receipt by the spouse of bank accounts or property from the judgment debtor, then the spouse has to answer concerning these matters, despite the claim of husband-wife privilege.[55] [See the discussion of Spousal Privilege in Postjudgment Discovery in **Chapter 3.**]

---

[50] Hartmann v. United States, 79 F.R.D. 705, 707 (E.D. Wis. 1978).

[51] El Salto, S.A. v. PSG Co., 444 F.2d 477, 484 (9th Cir.) *cert. denied*, 404 U.S. 940, 92 S. Ct. 273, 30 L. Ed. 2d 253 (1971); Fed. R. Civ. P. 30 and 45. However, when only documents are needed, Fed. R. Civ. P. 34(c) now permits production of documents from persons not parties to the action.

[52] Caisson Corp. v. County W. Bldg. Corp., 62 F.R.D. 331, 334 (E.D. Pa. 1974); Monticello Tobacco Co. v. American Tobacco Co., 12 F.R.D. 344 (S.D.N.Y.), *aff'd on merits,* 197 F.2d 629 (2d Cir.), *cert. denied,* 344 U.S. 875 (1952); Davis Acoustical Corp. v. Skulnick, 131 N.J. Super. 87, 328 A.2d 633, 635–36 (Super. Ct. App. Div. 1974).

[53] Caisson Corp. v. County W. Bldg. Corp., 62 F.R.D. 331, 334–35 (E.D. Pa. 1974); Strick Corp. v. Thai Teak Products Co., Ltd., 493 F. Supp. 1210, 1218 (E.D. Pa. 1980); Burak v. Scott, 29 F. Supp. 775, 776 (D.D.C. 1939).

[54] Cerami v. Robinson, 85 F.R.D. 371, 373 (S.D.N.Y. 1980).

[55] G-Fours, Inc. v. Miele, 496 F.2d 809, 812–13 (2d Cir. 1974); *cf.* Computerland Corp. v. Batac, No. 88 Civ. 8624, 1990 U.S. Dist. LEXIS 4920 (S.D.N.Y. Apr. 26, 1990).

In *Davis Acoustical Corp. v. Skulnick*[56] Davis Acoustical Corp. (Davis) had acquired a judgment against Louis Skulnick (Louis) for $55,880.10 on May 4, 1967. In supplementary proceeding, Louis claimed that his son Martin saved $10,000 to $15,000 while working in college, and used these funds to start a steel products business on Long Island, New York. [See the discussion of Supplementary Proceedings above at § **4.1**] Louis also testified that the East Paterson, New Jersey house in which he lived was a gift given to him by Martin. Suggesting a strong pattern of fraudulent transfers, the attorneys for Davis moved for an ex parte order compelling Martin to attend a discovery proceeding and produce documents. Among documents requested were "'any and all correspondence, cancelled checks, checkbooks, pass books for savings accounts or bank accounts, and any and all other documentation which he possesses to establish the purchase of the United Steel Products Co. with his own funds' and 'documents reflecting his ownership of the premises, 2 Donner Avenue, East Paterson, New Jersey as well as statement of closing title, cancelled checks and any and all other evidence indicating the consideration paid by him therefore.'"[57] Martin moved to modify the order by only allowing his examination concerning Louis's assets, not his own. On July 30, 1973, the court denied the motion.

Martin appealed from the order. During arguments in the appellate court, attorneys for Davis indicated Martin formed the company within a year of the judgment by Davis against Louis. Further, the company moved to New Jersey in 1971, had machinery worth $150,000, and did business with a steel company in which Louis was an officer and director. Also, counsel for Davis indicated that the Louis testified falsely that he was not involved with any corporations in New Jersey or elsewhere. However, the Secretary of State of New Jersey corporate records revealed Louis was president and director of a New Jersey steel company, called Shelf-It Steel Products, Inc., at the time he made the statement. There was, in addition, a discrepancy between Louis's deposition testimony, and Martin's affidavit, on how Martin acquired the house in East Paterson.

The appellate court upheld denial of Martin's motion, noting the following:

> Here, sufficient information was furnished by the judgment creditor to raise a reasonable doubt of the ownership of the properties in question and to raise a sufficient possibility that the judgment debtor had interests in the properties. These factors would render the issue of ownership and interest amenable to clarification or substantiation through reasonable discovery. The trial judge's ruling in this respect is consistent with the liberal purpose and spirit of discovery under the court rules and does not constitute an abuse of discretion. . . . There is no doubt that third parties can be examined in relation to the financial

[56] 131 N.J. Super. 87, 328 A.2d 633 (Super. Ct. App. Div. 1974).

[57] 328 A.2d 633, 635.

affairs of the debtor. The appropriate manner to afford third parties protection is not to require that questions be phrased in a legalistically conclusory manner but rather to allow questions as to their personal activities, within limits, yet requiring some showing of the relationship that exists between the judgment debtor and the third party from which the court on a motion for a protective order can determine whether the examination has a basis.[58]

§ 4.15 Examination of the Debtor's Accountant

Often counsel will find that a deposition of the debtor's accountant will be a valuable and worthwhile undertaking, especially if the judgment debtor has been engaged in a business or if the judgment debtor is a corporation. There is no accountant-client privilege in federal cases.[59] [See the discussion of the Accountant-Client Privilege in Postjudgment Discovery in **Chapter 3** and a suggested form of subpoena in § **4.19.**]

Counsel will often have problems with the judgment debtor who "loses" some of the crucial business records sought in postjudgment discovery. Some of the excuses for losing records are preposterous in themselves, and the plaintiff's attorney will hear them all. For example, judgment debtor's record disappear by being stolen, being burned in the trunk of a car, falling off a truck during a move and being damaged by a flood, lightning, or a tornado. Counsel will wonder at the tremendous opportunity for tragedy to strike the debtor's records, and will be amazed that such events often occur shortly before judgment is acquired, or within a week of issuing a subpoena to the judgment debtor for these records. Therefore, finding other sources for the same records or different records accumulating the same kinds of information becomes an essential task of plaintiff's counsel.

The debtor's accountant is an excellent target for a subpoena in a federal case, although you will find this avenue may be blocked in a state case where the debtor has the availability of the state accountant-client privilege. When dealing with state accountant-client privilege laws, be sure to check the statute, because in some states the privilege does not apply when a subpoena is issued in litigation, or under some other appropriate circumstance.

When counsel issues the subpoena to the accountant, it will become apparent that the accountant maintains a wide variety of records on the individual

---

[58] Davis Acoustical Corp. v. Skulnick, 131 N.J. Super. 87, 328 A.2d 633, 636–37 (Super. Ct. App. Div. 1974). *Cf.* Caisson Corp. v. County W. Bldg. Corp., 62 F.R.D. 331, 335 (E.D. Pa. 1974).

[59] United States v. Couch, 409 U.S. 322, 93 S. Ct. 611, 34 L. Ed. 2d 548 (1973); United States v. Arthur Young & Co., 465 U.S. 805, 104 S. Ct. 1495, 79 L. Ed. 2d 826 (1984); United States v. Arthur Andersen & Co., 623 F.2d 725 (1st Cir.), *cert. denied,* 449 U.S. 1021, 101 S. Ct. 588, 66 L. Ed. 2d 483 (1980).

judgment debtor, or the corporate judgment debtor. The accountant should have copies of the debtor's tax returns. The accountant should have financial statements on the corporate debtor, and perhaps even on the individual debtor. The accountant should have profit and loss statements on the corporate debtor. When he produces the financial statements and tax returns, the accountant often will have a drawer filled with supporting documents and papers called "accountant work papers" or "tax accrual workpapers." These files should contain valuable sources of information used in preparing tax returns, financial statements, and other financial documents for the debtor.

Often to support the preparation of tax returns or financial statements the accountant will preserve copies of the underlying corporate minutes, corporate transactional documents, or other records of the judgment debtor. Sometimes among the accountant's work papers may be a "smoking gun" or other useful document which will assist in proving the postjudgment litigation to set aside fraudulent transfers or piercing a corporate veil. [See **Chapter 6.**]

In recent federal court litigation to recover over a million dollars of fraudulent transfers from a corporation, the author, representing the Plaintiff, deposed the accountant of the judgment debtor corporation. After much resistance from the accountant, and a flurry of pleadings by the attorneys for the accountant and the judgment debtor trying to quash the subpoena to the accountant, the court ordered the accountant to produce his records. Subsequently, the accountant produced about five file drawers of records. The records were essential to establish evidence of the underlying financial transactions which indicated the corporation had been liquidated, and the assets transferred to the shareholders and other related parties. The effort in deposing the debtor's accountant is usually worth the results.

§ 4.16 Use of an Expert Accountant in Financial Discovery

In most cases involving proof of fraudulent transfers of a financial nature, plaintiff's counsel may need your own accounting expert to assist in unraveling those transactions. In § **4.15,** the author discusses a recent case where the accountant produced five file drawers of records. Many attorneys who collect judgments are not accountants, and need experts to assist in evaluating the financial records that may assist in judgment collection. The accountant can assist in preparing financial interrogatories and requests for production of documents. The accountant can assist in developing questions for the judgment debtor's accountant, evaluating the accountant's testimony after the deposition, or assisting in the actual deposition.

In most postjudgment litigation cases counsel may find that the bottom line in the litigation may come down to a battle of plaintiff's experts against the experts for the judgment debtor to prove that the judgment debtor was insolvent at the time of the transfers, to prove the amount and kind of transfers made, and to simplify the presentation of these issues to the judge or jury. In some cases plaintiff's counsel may need more than one expert, and may need an economist or financial analyst to assist in the expert proof. Whatever the case, the assistance will be very valuable. Counsel may be surprised at what experts find in their examination of the financial documents. Also, the expert and the assistance provided will help free counsel from some of the tasks of looking through reams and reams of documents that counsel may not have the time or expertise to evaluate and analyze.

The recent federal court litigation the author discussed in § **4.15** provides an excellent illustration on how valuable expert assistance can be and, sometimes, how surprising that assistance can be. In that case, some time had elapsed between the production of the five file drawers of documents by the defendant's accountant, and the time for a thorough examination of the records by an accountant hired by the Plaintiff. Late one afternoon, the accountant walked into the author's office waving a document from the files of the defendant's accountant. The document turned out to be a very informative letter from counsel of one of the judgment debtor's officers, planning the very fraudulent transfers the plaintiff sought to set aside. The letter discussed the plans at some length and detail. In the opinion of the author, the letter was positive proof of actual fraudulent intent. The letter was the kind of "smoking gun" that a plaintiff's lawyer dreams about.

§ 4.17 Examination of the Debtor's Attorney

In some situations, plaintiff's counsel will uncover facts or information which will indicate that taking the deposition of the debtor's attorney will be worthwhile. An evaluation should be made as to whether the attorney-client privilege will prevent counsel from obtaining useful information. [See the discussion in **Chapter 3** on the Attorney-Client Privilege in Postjudgment Discovery.] If counsel suspects that the prior defendant's attorney has assisted in the planning of the fraudulent transfers counsel seeks to set aside, the court may allow the subpoena to the judgment debtor's attorney, and require a Motion for in Camera Inspection by the court of the attorney's records. Perhaps the attorney-client privilege may be waived, or is not applicable because of the crime-fraud exception. [See the discussions in **Chapter 3** on the Attorney-Client Privilege and on the Crime-Fraud Exception to the Attorney Client Privilege.]

If plaintiff's counsel obtains such discovery, and finds the attorney was involved in planning the fraudulent transfers, here are some practice tips on what to look for in the attorney's files.

Practice Tips

1. Look in the attorney's files for planning memoranda where meetings were held with corporate officers of the judgment debtor, or with the individual debtor, to discuss the fraudulent transfers and distribution of the assets.
2. Look for research on the law regarding fraudulent transfers, the constructive trust fund doctrine, and so on, where the attorney was attempting to find a way around application of the law.
3. Look for memoranda from partners in the firm to associates regarding planning to protect individual officer's real estate from creditors, since the individual officers also might have potential liability on other aspects of the litigation.
4. Look for calculations of the value of the assets to be transferred, and correspondence or memoranda that indicate that the accountant was an essential participant to complete the financial recordation of the transfers on the books of the corporation, or assisting the individual in planning the tax aspects of the transfers.
5. Consider whether, if the transfers were supposed to be "gifts", do the attorney's or accountant's files contain copies of the gift tax returns.
6. Consider whether, if the transfers were supposed to be for "estate planning" purposes, the estate plan makes good practical sense and actually saves estate taxes.
7. Look for the "smoking gun" which will help counsel establish the fraudulent transfer case. It may be a piece of correspondence, a memorandum, or work notes that the attorney can identify.
8. Try to get the court to allow access to more documents after the court completes its in camera inspection of the attorney's files in accordance with the case of *United States v. Zolin.*[60] [See the discussion at **Chapter 3** above.]
9. Look for settlement agreements between the judgment debtor and other parties which may disclose fraudulent transfers.[61]

§ 4.18 Examination of the Debtor's Bank Records

Another third-party source of information concerning the judgment debtor is the judgment debtor's bank records. Often counsel may find that all or a portion of

---

[60] 491 U.S. 554, 109 S. Ct. 2619, 2623, 105 L. Ed. 2d 469, 481 (1989); cf. Natural Gas Pipeline Co. v. Energy Gathering, Inc., 2 F.3d 1397 (5th Cir. 1993) (district court has inherent power to require attorney to turn over records related to his client, a judgment debtor).

[61] Magnaleasing, Inc. v. Staten Island Mall, 76 F.R.D. 559 (S.D.N.Y. 1977).

the debtor's bank account records have been "lost" or "misplaced." So using discovery available under Federal Rule of Civil Procedure 69, a postjudgment document production request or subpoena to the debtor's bank under Federal Rule of Civil Procedure 34(c) or 45 and a deposition notice of the bank under Federal Rule of Civil Procedure 30(b)(6) may need to be issued. [A form of deposition notice to a bank is given in § **4.20,** which includes a suggested list of documents to subpoena. The same list may be an adequate request for production of documents under Rule 34(c). Of course, the list of documents used will depend on the particular facts of the case, and what records are sought.]

If plaintiff is a federal government agency, the defense counsel may file a protective order claiming that the subpoena is filed in violation of the Right to Financial Privacy Act of 1978 (12 U.S.C. §§ 3401 *et seq.,* Financial Privacy Act). In fact, § 3413(e) of the Financial Privacy Act excepts such a subpoena from the statutory provisions. "Nothing in this chapter shall apply when financial records are sought by a Government authority under the Federal Rules of Civil Procedure . . . In connection with litigation to which the Government authority and the customer are parties." 12 U.S.C. § 3413(e). If the bank has other grounds to challenge the subpoena, counsel may face a motion to quash the subpoena under Federal Rule of Civil Procedure 45(b), which is a proper method for the bank to challenge the subpoena, if the bank has any grounds to do so.[62]

The judgment debtor has no standing to challenge the subpoena to the bank, since the bank records are not the debtor's records, but are business records of the bank.[63]

> Accordingly, the bank customer has no inherent right to assert ownership, possession, or inferentially, control over the release of a bank's records of his transactions. . . . Nothing in the Act [Financial Privacy Act], however, shields the records from discovery in a civil suit.[64]

"[A] bank customer, has no "legitimate 'expectation of privacy'" in the contents of checks, deposit slips and other banking documents.[65] These records are not confidential communications but instruments of commercial transactions.[66]

Therefore, the bank subpoena should be an effective method for looking at the judgment debtor's financial transactions over the last few years. Review

---

62 Clayton Brokerage Co. v. Clement, 87 F.R.D. 569, 570 n.1 (D. Md. 1980).

63 United States v. Miller, 425 U.S. 435 (1976); Clayton Brokerage Co. v. Clement, 87 F.R.D. 569, 571.

64 Clayton Brokerage Co. v. Clement, 87 F.R.D. 569, 571.

65 United States v. Miller, 425 U.S. 435, 442.

66 87 F.R.D. 569, 571.

the checklist in **Chapter 3,** and consider for the individual and the corporate judgment debtor what facts the bank records may help prove plaintiff's remedy in postjudgment litigation. [See **Chapter 6** for various remedies.]

§ 4.19 —Form of Subpoena to an Accountant

[Caption of the case]

NOTICE OF DEPOSITION

TO DEPONENT AND ALL COUNSEL OF RECORD:

You are hereby notified that Plaintiff, ________________, will take the oral deposition under oath of _______________, C.P.A., of _______________ Street, _______________, _______________, pursuant to Rules 30 and 45 of the Federal Rules of Civil Procedure, on, _______________, 19__, commencing at ______ A.M.(P.M.) before a shorthand reporter or other person duly authorized to administer oaths, at the office of ________________, __________________. This deposition shall continue from day-to-day thereafter until completed.

Pursuant to Rule 30 and 45 of the Federal Rules of Civil Procedure, _______________, C.P.A., will bring to the deposition any and all documents listed in Exhibit A, which are in his (her) possession, custody and control, and be prepared to testify about the matters specified in the attached Exhibit A.

YOU ARE INVITED TO ATTEND AND CROSS-EXAMINE.

Dated the _______ day of _______________, 19__.

Respectfully submitted,

EXHIBIT A

Any and all cancelled checks, deposit orders and deposit tickets, withdrawal tickets, invoices, money orders, wire transfers, monthly bank account statements, loan records, correspondence, notes, guarantees, lines of credit, security agreements, mortgages, repayment schedules, savings account records, account ledgers, checking account records, repayment schedules, time certificates of deposit, cashier's checks, money market accounts, debentures, contracts, correspondence, memos, telephone conversation notes and memos, calendar notes and memos, corporate minutes and votes, corporate agreements, inter or intracompany transfers or orders, statements of debts and collateral, profit and loss statements, income statements, balance sheets, statements of change of financial position, accountants, opinions or comments, accounting workpapers, internal audit reports, and bluebacks to management regarding inventories, accounts receivable, contracts receivable, intercompany accounts, fixed assets and reclassification of expenses and balance sheet items, security and inventory listings, subordinations, assignments, releases, purchase orders, master agreements, beneficiary lists for any trusts, all trust agreements, all deeds, deeds of trust, trust documents, all trust accounts, receipts and disbursements for all trust accounts and other financial records relating to or pertaining to same.

§ 4.20 —Form of Deposition Notice to a Bank

SAMPLE NOTICE OF DEPOSITION

NOTICE OF DEPOSITION

TO DEPONENT AND ALL COUNSEL OF RECORD:

You are hereby notified that Plaintiff, [name], hereby sets the oral deposition under oath of a person or persons designated by ____________ Bank of ____________, pursuant to Rule 30(b)(6), 45 and 69 of the Federal Rules of Civil Procedure, commencing at [time] before a shorthand reporter or other person duly authorized to administer oaths, at the office of ____________, ______________________________. This deposition shall continue from day-to-day thereafter until completed.

RULE 30(b)(6) DESIGNATION

Pursuant to Rule 30(b)(6), 45 and 69 of the Federal Rules of Civil Procedure, ________________ Bank shall designate one or more of its officers, directors, managing agents or other persons who has knowledge of and will testify upon oral examination on behalf of ________________ Bank with respect to the matters specified in the attached Exhibit A. Pursuant to the Federal Rules of Civil Procedure, ________________ Bank shall bring with it to this deposition any records, documents or notes listed in Exhibit A.

YOU ARE INVITED TO ATTEND AND CROSS-EXAMINE.

Dated the ______ day of ______________, 19__.

EXHIBIT A

1. Any and all cancelled checks, deposit orders and deposit tickets,

2. withdrawal tickets, invoices, money orders, wire transfers,

3. monthly bank account statements, loan records,

4. correspondence, notes, guarantees, lines of credit, security agreements,

5. mortgages, repayment schedules, savings account records, account ledgers, checking account records,

6. time certificates of deposit, cashier's checks, money market accounts,

7. debentures, contracts, memos, telephone conversation notes and memos, calendar notes and memos,

8. corporate minutes and votes, corporate agreements, inter- or intra-company transfers or orders,

9. statements of debts and collateral, profit and loss statements, income statements, balance sheets,

10. statements of change of financial position, accountants, opinions or comments, accounting workpapers,

11. internal audit reports, and bluebacks to management regarding inventories, accounts receivable, contracts receivable,

12. intercompany accounts, fixed assets, and reclassification of expenses and balance sheet items,

13. security and inventory listings, subordinations, assignments,

14. releases, purchase orders, master agreements and also specifically checking or savings accounts as listed.

and other financial records relating to or pertaining to same.

§ 4.21 —Form of Deposition on Written Questions to Debtor's Accountant

NOTICE OF DEPOSITION UPON WRITTEN QUESTIONS

This is notice that the [plaintiff], the plaintiff and judgment creditor in this action, in aid of its judgment and execution, will obtain discovery of and from you pursuant to Fed. R. Civ. P. 69(a) and 31.

This discovery will be by a deposition upon written questions, and a copy of the questions which will be asked is enclosed with this notice.

The deposition will be taken before:

____

(Officer before whom deposition to be taken.)

at

____

(Time and location of deposition)

A Subpoena Duces Tecum will be served upon you as provided by Rule 45, Fed. R. Civ. P., to compel your attendance at the time and place designated.

The subpoena will require you to bring with you the documents listed on Exhibit "A" attached to this notice.

Date of Notice: ______________

EXHIBIT A

Documents to be subpoenaed

1. Any and all copies of certified or uncertified balance and income statements, appraisals, inventories, audits, asset valuations, or analyses of income prepared for or on behalf of [company] from [date] through the present.

2. Any and all preparer copies for Federal or State tax returns for [company] from [date] through the present.

3. Any and all copies of loan applications, notes receivable, notes payable, accounts payable, accounts receivable, journals, ledgers, books, or other records of Monroe Garment Company for the period [date] to the present.

4. Any and all copies of records of [company] in connection with loans to shareholders for the period [date] to the present, including but not limited to corporate votes on such loans, journal or ledger entries of such loans, notes or other documents reflecting the notes receivable by the corporation from shareholders.

5. Any and all copies of correspondence, notes, diaries, calendar memos, telephone memos, telegrams, reports, statements or any other documents of any kind, which you prepared for and/or sent to any person or entity, or received from any person or entity in the period from [date] to [date], in connection with any payment or distribution of assets of any kind made by [company] to [name], or any other officer, director or shareholder of [company].

6. Any and all copies of correspondence, notes, diaries, calendar memos, telephone memos, telegrams, reports, statements or other documents of any kind, which you prepared for and/or sent to any person or entity, or received from any person or entity in the period from [date] to [date], in

connection with the sale and/or transfer of assets from [company] to [new company] on or about [date], whether such documents would be prepared before or after that date.

7. Any and all copies of records of any sums of money received by [name] as a result of the sale of their assets, and the assets of [company], to [new company], Inc., on or about [date], and all records of the distribution and accounting of those funds.

8. Any copies of documents, correspondence, notes or other records regarding notes or notes payable to [name] and copies of any records of payment.

WRITTEN QUESTIONS TO [CPA] FOR A DEPOSITION
UPON WRITTEN QUESTIONS

1. What is your full name and current address?

2. What is your current occupation, business address, and how long have you been so employed?

3. If applicable, what was your former place of employment, former business address, and length of such former employment?

4. Have you ever been employed as an accountant for [company]? If so, please state period of such employment.

5. Have you ever been employed as an accountant for ______________? If so, please state the periods of such employment.

6. Have you ever prepared Federal Corporate Income Tax Returns for [name of company]? If so, please state the calendar or fiscal year for each such tax return you have prepared, and state whether or not you signed the return, and state what officer of the corporation signed the return.

7. Have you ever prepared any [name of state] Corporate Income Tax Returns for [company]? If so, please state the calendar or fiscal years for which you prepared such returns, and state whether or not you signed the return, and state what officer of the corporation signed the return.

8. Were you employed as an accountant for [company] at the time [company] transferred certain of its assets to [name], on or about [date]? If you were so employed, please attach copies of all correspondence, notes, diaries, calendar memos, telephone memos, telegrams, reports, statements or other documents of any kind, which you prepared for, or

sent to any person or entity, or received from any person or entity, from the period [date] to [date] in connection with said sale or transfer of assets from [company] to [name]. For each document listed, please explain your involvement in the preparation of that document, the purpose of the document and the person who ultimately received the original of such document.

9. Do you have any documents or records of whether or not [name] received any payment as a result of the sale of their assets, and the assets of [company], to [name] on or about [date]? If so, please list each document or record, and explain who prepared the document, the purpose of the document, and who ultimately received the original of such document.

10. Have you prepared, or received copies of documents, correspondence, notes or other records regarding accounts or notes payable to [name] from [company] and/or [name], Inc. during the period [specify]? If so, please explain and attach a copy of such document to your answer.

11. Have you ever prepared, certified or uncertified, balance and income statements, appraisals, inventories, audits, asset valuations, or analyses of income, for or on behalf of [company] for the period [date] through the present? For each such document prepared, please state the date on which you prepared the document, the purpose of such document, and the person or entity who ultimately received the original of such document. Attach a copy of said document to your answer.

12. Do you have any copies of loan applications, notes receivable, notes payable, accounts payable, accounts receivable, journals, ledger books or other records of [company] for the period of [date] to the present? If your answer is yes, please attach copies of these documents with your answer. If your answer is no, please explain and describe in detail, what happened to these records, if you know.

13. Do you have any copies of records of [company] in connection with loans to shareholders for the period [date] to the present, including but not limited to corporate votes on such loans, journals, or ledger entries of such loans, notes, or other documents reflecting the notes receivable by the corporation from shareholders? If you do have such copies, please attach them to your answer. If not, please explain what happened to these documents, if you know.

14. The Federal Corporate Income Tax Returns for [company], for the period [date] through the present, list a loan to shareholders as an asset on the balance sheet of the corporation filed as part of the returns. Please explain and describe in detail this entry on the balance sheet,

and attach any and all work papers, trial balances and other documents used in preparing and entering this item on the corporate balance sheets in each and every one of those tax returns as applicable.

15. If you deny that there was a loan to shareholders listed as an asset on the balance sheet of the corporate tax returns, for the period [date] through the present for each year that you deny such entry, please explain and describe in detail the reasons for your denial.

16. The Federal Corporate Income Tax Returns of [company] for the years [date], list as an asset of the corporation on the balance sheet a loan to shareholders. Please state whether or not you prepared and signed any or all of those returns. Also explain and describe in detail whether or not you had access to all of the books and records of the corporation in preparing any or all of these tax returns for each of those years. If not, explain and describe in detail, and explain your answer as it relates to your signature and certification statement on each of the said tax returns, as applicable.

17. If you prepared Federal Corporate Income Tax Returns or State Income Tax Returns for [company], for any of the years between [date] and the present, please explain who asked you to prepare such returns, what documents you had access to or were provided with in connection with the preparation of those returns, and please explain who or what entity paid for your services in connection with the preparation and filing of those tax returns for [company].

§ 4.22 —Form of Deposition Notice to a Lawyer

NOTICE OF DEPOSITION

TO DEPONENT AND ALL COUNSEL OF RECORD:

You are hereby notified that Plaintiff, ______________________________, will take the oath deposition under oath of ______________, Esquire of ________________, ________________, and ____________________, pursuant to Rules 30, 45 and 69 of the Federal Rules of Civil Procedure, on the ____ day of ______________, 19 __, at the office of __________________________ (address) __________________________. This deposition continue from day to day until completed. The deponent shall bring with him the documents listed on Exhibits A and the Subpoena served upon him pursuant to Fed. R. Civ. P.45.

Dated the _____ day of ______________, 19__.

HANDLING UNFAIR LITIGATION TACTICS IN POSTJUDGMENT DISCOVERY

§ 4.23 The Nonexistent Privilege

Plaintiff's counsel must learn to handle unfair litigation tactics in postjudgment litigation. A few practical examples from actual litigationmay be helpful. In the following example, one of the judgment debtor's accountants is being examined.

PROBLEM OF THE NONEXISTENT PRIVILEGE
BY MR. BROWN:
Q. Could you state for the record your name?
A. [States name, Mr. X]
Q. And, your current address?
A. Home or business?
Q. Home address?
A. [Gives the address.]
Q. And, could you state for the record your current place of employment?
A. [States his employment with a C.P.A. firm in (state).]
Q. And, what position do you hold with that company, sir?
A. I'm a partner.
Q. Are you a licensed CPA in the State of ______________?
A. Yes.

[At this point the accountant was asked several relevant questions about the financial statement of the corporate judgment debtor. After each question, the lawyer representing the accountant had the same objection.]

MR. DEFENSE COUNSEL:
Objection, and I instruct the witness not to answer on the basis of the applicable provisions of the (state) Certified Public Accountant's Law, which is codified at (state) Statutes, entitled Privileged Communication, which in my judgment precludes Mr. X from any further testimony on this subject.

As the attorney representing the judgment creditor in this federal district court litigation, plaintiff's counsel may consider recessing and going to the magistrate.

MR. BROWN:
Note for the record that at this time, I would like to take a recess of the deposition and consult with a magistrate and get a ruling with regard to the evidence questions that have been posed by counsel for the accountant.
(In front of Magistrate)

THE COURT:

Let's have an introduction of this matter. First of all, this is the case of— [Case and counsel introduced by Mr. Brown, and the matter at issue explained.]

THE COURT:

You have the financial statement?

MR. BROWN:

I have the financial statement, yes, Your Honor. It was previously disclosed to me. . . . So, with regard to their claim of the accountant's privilege under (state) Statute, I would claim that at least with regard to this document that has been previously disclosed by the defendants, that they have waived the privilege with regard to that document. Secondly, I claim that the privilege under the (state) Statutes does not apply because this is an action [state the nature of the federal court action and the basis for the postjudgment claim or collection action.] Now, I refer the court to the case of *United States v. Schmidt,*[67] which is mentioned in our notations following the (state) Statute. [Under this case] [and other relevant cases] . . . I would argue that the (state) Statutory accountant-client privilege law does not apply in this action. [ETC.]

MR. DEFENSE COUNSEL:

[States his argument why the statute should apply.]

THE COURT:

[Denies the claim of the (state) Statutory Accountant-Client Privilege Law, and orders the accountant to answer the questions.]

Once plaintiff's counsel calls defense counsel's bluff on the improper instruction not to answer based on a nonexistent privilege, counsel will probably not have to go to the magistrate again during this series of depositions. After earning defense counsel's respect, they will recognize that plaintiff's counsel will call their bluff if there is insufficient basis for the claim of privilege.

§ 4.24 Disruptive Tactics

Plaintiff's counsel may have to face the situation in which defense counsel becomes obstructive. Following are some examples of ways to handle this situation. [The proposed changes to Federal Rules of Civil Procedure 26 and 30 may alleviate some of this conduct.]

Problem # 1.

Here is an example from a postjudgment case from a federal district court, in which the witness is the principal officer for the judgment debtor.

---

67 360 F. Supp. 339 (M.D. Pa. 1973).

BY MR. BROWN:
Q: You never fought the case?
A: No.

[At this point counsel notices the attorney for the witness has his hand in front of the witness as if to stop him from answering further, or signalling the witness. To handle this situation, let the signal be clearly reflected on the record.]

MR. BROWN:
Note for the record that counsel's hand is in front of the witness kind of like holding him back from testifying openly. Is that the gesture?
MR. DEFENSE COUNSEL:
My hand is in front of the witness, not holding him back from testifying openly.
MR. BROWN:
Is that a signal?
MR. DEFENSE COUNSEL:
I am telling him I am getting ready to object and not to answer until I have a chance to do so. If you are going to ask him about the lawsuit—

[This shows that the witness may have not been properly instructed before he attended the deposition. However, after this statement was placed on the record, the hand was dropped from in front of the witnesses face, and was not used again.]

Problem # 2.

How does counsel handle the instruction to the witness with a qualification? How does counsel handle this disruptive tactic? Here is an example of how to handle this problem.

COUNSEL FOR THE JUDGMENT CREDITOR:
Q. [A question is asked an accountant which gives support to a financial topic about the judgment debtor, but is peripheral.]
COUNSEL FOR THE JUDGMENT DEBTOR:
Objection, and I am instructing you not to answer unless I know the relevance of this whole line of questioning. Do not answer the question.
COUNSEL FOR THE JUDGMENT CREDITOR:
The relevance of this line of questioning is [the relevance is explained briefly.] Now, I would like the question read back for the witness.
(The question was read by the reporter.)
COUNSEL FOR THE JUDGMENT DEBTOR:
How long are you going to remain on this topic?
COUNSEL FOR THE JUDGMENT CREDITOR:
I don't know.

COUNSEL FOR THE JUDGMENT DEBTOR:

Objection. Don't answer. I will take one question at a time then. This one don't answer. [Counsel may sense in counsel's voice the bluff and hesitation.]

COUNSEL FOR THE JUDGMENT CREDITOR:

I believe that if you want to prevent him from answering these questions, the burden is on you to get a protective order. I feel that they are very necessary to be answered. I am nearing the end of our deposition. I think I will be forced to suspend here and get an order compelling the answers so I can continue in an orderly progress.

COUNSEL FOR THE JUDGMENT DEBTOR:

I think this line is utterly absurd. I will permit a few more questions, but you better get to the point or I am going to cut it off. [The ususal threat! The question, now pressed, after the threats, etc., is read back again. Counsel has won this point, and the examination now continues without interruption.]

Problem # 3.

How does plaintiff's counsel handle the disruptive tactic where defense counsel instructs the witness not to answer, asking that the question be rephrased. In some cases, have the question read back. Perhaps counsel has made a mistake in phrasing the question, and it can be rephrased to be more precise, or not leading, for example. However, the question may be okay as it stands, but the defense counsel uses this tactic to interrupt counsel's line of thought and flow of questioning.

COUNSEL FOR THE JUDGMENT DEBTOR:

[To an officer of the judgment debtor corporation.]

Have you exercised any ownership rights as a result of possessing share certificates in the corporation?

COUNSEL FOR THE JUDGMENT CREDITOR:

The question calls for a legal conclusion. I instruct the witness not to answer the question unless you rephrase the question. You can ask her what she has done.

COUNSEL FOR THE JUDGMENT CREDITOR:

What have you done to exercise your ownership rights as a result of the possession of the corporate certificates of the judgment debtor corporation?

COUNSEL FOR THE JUDGMENT DEBTOR:

You are asking again a legal conclusion. You can ask her what acts she did. I don't think she is required in this deposition to characterize what those legal acts were in the terms of exercising ownership. That is a legal conclusion.

COUNSEL FOR THE JUDGMENT CREDITOR:

Are you instructing her not to answer?

COUNSEL FOR THE JUDGMENT DEBTOR:

Yes, I am asking you to rephrase the question. You can ask her what she did, but I don't think she is required in a deposition without analysis to determine whether or not those facts amounted to an exercise of ownership, whatever that might be, in your question. I am not instructing her not to answer. I am only saying that I think the question is improper so far as it calls for legal chaacterization of those actions.

COUNSEL FOR THE JUDGMENT CREDITOR:
You did instruct her not to answer?

COUNSEL FOR THE JUDGMENT DEBTOR:
She can state what she did.

COUNSEL FOR THE JUDGMENT CREDITOR:
What actions did you take on behalf of the corporation prior to obtaining the stock certificates?

OFFICER OF THE JUDGMENT DEBTOR:
I don't think I took any action on behalf of the corporation.

In this example, a slight change in emphasis in the question resolves the conflict, and gets the desired answer. Opposing counsel may have had a point well taken, and the corrected question just asked for facts rather than legal conclusions.

Problem # 4.

Then there is the objection from the lawyer who has not been involved in much postjudgment discovery, and does not understand the broad scope of discovery.

MR. BROWN:
Can you tell me the bank that holds the mortgage or other company that might hold the mortgage on Mr. X's property [the judgment debtor's property]—

THIRD PARTY WITNESS:
I believe —

COUNSEL FOR THE THIRD PARTY WITNESS:
Just a second. I am going to object to that question. I am not sure the extent to which questioning along these lines may be more in the nature of a supplementary proceeding, as opposed to a discovery deposition. Perhaps you could illuminate a little bit as to that question.

MR. BROWN:
This is a postjudgment discovery deposition under Federal Rule 26, 30 and 69. I am inquiring about the debtor's assets. I note your objection and instruct the witness to answer the question.

COUNSEL FOR THE THIRD PARTY WITNESS:
She can answer.

THIRD PARTY WITNESS:
(Name) Bank holds the mortgage.

MR. BROWN:
Do you have any other mortgages on the [judgment debtor's] property, besides the mortgage to (name) Bank?

THIRD PARTY WITNESS:
Not to my knowledge.

Sometimes plaintiff's counsel must remind opposing counsel that in post-judgment discovery there is a broad scope of discovery under Rule 69, to inquire into the debtor's assets. Opposing counsel will usually back off. If not, counsel may have to seek a duty magistrate to make a ruling, or get as much answered as possible, and move to compel the unanswered questions.

Problem # 5.

Then there is the old standby objection, "Asked and answered," which is used as a method of interrupting counsel's concentration. Here is a way to respond:

MR. BROWN:
And you didn't have any misunderstanding about that contract term that when they were talking about, quote, "with proceeds payable to bank and borrower," end quote, that they were talking about the proceeds payable from the contractor on the equipment sold, did you?
DEBTOR'S COUNSEL:
I'm going to object to that. He has asked and answered that question four times now, I kept track. It's repetitious and it's argumentative, and I'm going to tell him that he has answered it numerous times. [Getting angry by the end of the question.]
MR. BROWN:
I'll let you answer it one more time.
DEBTOR'S COUNSEL:
I'm going to tell him not to answer it one more time, he has answered it four times.
MR. BROWN:
I don't believe he has answered it one time, nevertheless, four times, Mr. Counsel. This is an important question, it's crucial to the case. And the fact that I just read him his deposition testimony and answer, my question is a very simple one that can be repeated again. And, if you would repeat the question I would like the witness to answer it.
(QUESTION READ)
WITNESS:
Mr. Brown, I'm aware we took a contract of XYZ Manufacturing . . . and we should have received the proceeds from the contract in the normal flow.

Sometimes counsel must pursue the answer even if the opposing counsel says it has been asked and answered. In some situations counsel may want to rephrase the question if the point being sought is different than what opposing counsel thinks it is. In any case, do not be afraid to ask the question again.

§ 4.25 The Witness Review Notes

Imagine deposing a witness when suddenly the witness pulls some notes from a folder in front of him, and starts to use the notes seemingly to refresh his recollection. Counsel should ask to see the document. Counsel may not have a right to see the whole document, but can certainly see that portion of the document the witness is using to refresh his recollection.

But before counsel can obtain documents used by a witness prior to his testifying in a deposition or trial, there are three conditions:

1. the witness must use the writing to refresh his memory
2. the witness must use the writing for the purpose of testifying
3. the court must determine that production is necessary in the interests of justice[68]

If access to the document is denied by counsel for the witness, which in most cases it may be, plaintiff's counsel can adjourn the deposition pending a ruling from the magistrate, or from the court. Federal Rule of Evidence 612 provides that "an adverse party is entitled to have the writing produced at the hearing, to inspect it, to cross-examine the witness thereon, and to introduce in evidence those portions which relate to the testimony of the witness." If a portion of the document does not relate to the testimony the court should examine the document in camera, and delete those portions, and order delivery to the adverse party.[69]

The *Costner* case, although not a judgment enforcement case, is illustrative of the principal. In that case, in order to refresh his memory during his testimony, defendant's witness consulted a portion of a written report he had made concerning defendant's activities. After his testimony, the defense requested to have a portion of the report admitted into evidence. The prosecutor requested admission of the whole report. The court allowed the entire document to be shown to the jury. The basis for admitting the whole report was that the defense had introduced part of the report, and the prosecution had the right to compel admission of all of the report. The defendant appealed.

The court of appeals held that pursuant to Federal Rule of Evidence 612, the trial court had the duty to inspect the report in camera, and excise any part of the document not related to the subject matter of the testimony. The appeals court ruled that the prosecutor did not have the right to see, much less, introduce into evidence, any parts of the document not dealing with the subject matter of the testimony. The case was reversed and remanded for a new trial.

---

68 Fed. R. Evid. 612, Sporck v. Peil, 759 F.2d 312, 317–18 (3d Cir. 1985).

69 United States v. Costner, 684 F.2d 370 (6th Cir. 1982).

Counsel should consider what to do if the document is claimed to be privileged. Here are some practice tips:

1. General rule is that there is a waiver.
   The general rule is that when a document is used to refresh recollection, there is a waiver of privileges regarding the document.[70] For example, under certain situations, the deponent may use work product in preparation for his testimony in a case, and thus, waive the privilege.[71]
2. Some courts apply a balancing test.
   However, some courts have applied a balancing test between Rule 612, favoring disclosure of documents used to refresh recollection, and Federal Rule of Civil Procedure 26(b)(3) requiring a party to show substantial need for the privileged materials.[72]
3. Some courts hold the privilege is not waived.
   Other courts have held, meanwhile, that privileges are not waived.[73]
4. Some courts read Rule 612 and Rule 26(b)(3) in harmony.
   Other courts believe Federal Rule of Evidence 612 and Federal Rule of Civil Procedure 26(b)(3) may be read in harmony with each other.[74] That is, if materials qualify as work product, they are discoverable "only upon a showing that the party seeking discovery has substantial need of the materials in the preparation of his case and that he is unable without undue hardship to obtain the substantial equivalent of the materials by other means." Federal Rule of Civil Procedure 26(b)(3). When, however, a witness has used such materials to refresh his recollection prior to testifying Fed. R. Evid. 612 weights the balance in favor of finding that the "substantial need" exists, because of the policy in favor of effective cross-examination.[75]

---

[70] Laxalt v. McClatchy, 116 F.R.D. 438, 454 (D. Nev. 1987); United States v. 22.80 Acres of Land, 107 F.R.D. 20, 25 (N.D. Cal. 1985); S.& A. Painting Co. v. O.W.B. Corp., 103 F.R.D. 407, 409 (W.D. Pa. 1984); Wheeling Pittsburgh Steel v. Underwriters Lab., Inc., 81 F.R.D. 8, 10 (N.D. Ill. 1978).

[71] *In re* Joint E. & S. Dist. Asbestos Litig., 119 F.R.D. 4, 5–6 (E.D.N.Y. and S.D.N.Y. 1988); Berkey Photo, Inc. v. Eastman Kodak Co., 74 F.R.D. 613, 616 (S.D.N.Y. 1977).

[72] *In re* Joint E. & S. Dist. Asbestos Litig., 119 F.R.D. 4, 5 (E.D.N.Y. and S.D.N.Y. 1988).

[73] Bogosian v. Gulf Oil Corp., 738 F.2d 587, 595 n.3 (3d Cir. 1984) ("Rule 612 . . . does not displace the protections of Federal Rule of Civil Procedure 26(b)(3)."); Leucadia, Inc. v. Reliance Ins. Co., 101 F.R.D. 674, 679 (S.D.N.Y. 1983) (mere fact that a witness looked at an attorney-client privileged document in preparation for deposition does not destroy attorney-client privilege).

[74] *In re* Comair Air Disaster Litig., 100 F.R.D. 350, 353 (E.D. Ky. 1983).

[75] *Id.*

Obviously, if plaintiff's counsel believes the document is discoverable, it is worth trying to go after disclosure under Rule 612, because in some jurisdictions counsel may even get access to otherwise privileged documents on which the privilege has been waived.

§ 4.26 Moving to Compel for Failure to Provide Postjudgment Discovery

Postjudgment discovery is no different from prejudgment discovery in terms of the application of a motion to compel under Federal Rule of Civil Procedure 37, for failure to provide postjudgment discovery. In *Evans v. Chicago Football Franchise Limited Partnership*[76] the district court granted Evans' (a football player) motion to compel against the Chicago Football Franchise, and others, based on the player's default judgment. After the default judgment, Evans filed a request for production of documents directed to all three defendants in the case, and served a subpoena and notice on O'Malley, the accountant for the football franchise. Interpreting Federal Rule of Civil Procedure 69(a), the court stated that Evans could use the federal rules to gather information regarding the defendant's assets. Additionally, the court granted the motion to compel despite the defendant's argument that the discovery was untimely under Illinois procedures.

A motion to compel under Rule 69 was granted in *A.F.L. Falck v. E.A. Karay*[77] to compel production of a debtor's books and records, including corporate minutes and corporate tax returns in supplementary proceedings. A motion to compel production of a settlement agreement between the judgment debtors and a third party was granted in a proceedings in aid of execution by a judgment creditor. *Magnaleasing, Inc. v. Staten Island Mall.*[78] A judgment creditor moved for an order requiring the sole stockholder of the judgment debtor to answer certain questions on his ownership of, interest in, or employment by corporations other than the judgment debtor, where there is evidence that the judgment debtor has financial relationships with the other entities.[79]

The United States filed a motion to compel against judgment debtors to answer certain written interrogatories served under Rule 69(a) which related to the debtor's financial condition. The district court denied the motion to compel, and the government appealed. In *United States v. McWhirter*[80] the

---

[76] 127 F.R.D. 492 (N.D. Ill. 1989).

[77] 131 F.R.D. 46, 48–50 (S.D.N.Y. 1990).

[78] 76 F.R.D. 559, 564 (S.D.N.Y. 1977).

[79] Caisson Corp. v. County W. Bldg. Corp., 62 F.R.D. 331, 334–35 (E.D. Pa. 1974).

[80] 376 F.2d 102, 106 (5th Cir. 1967).

Fifth Circuit overruled the district court, and concluded "that Rule 69(a) authorized the government to propound written interrogatories to the appellees [judgment debtors] under Rule 33." (material in brackets added.)[81]

§ 4.27 —Form of Motion to Compel Discovery

MOTION TO COMPEL ANSWERS TO INTERROGATORIES

Plaintiff moves this Court pursuant to Fed. R. Civ. P. 37(a) to compel answers to interrogatories from defendant ______________ and for reasonable costs and attorneys fees incurred and necessitated by the filing of this motion.

For its reasons, plaintiff attaches its Memorandum in Support of this Motion.

§ 4.28 —Form of Memorandum in Support of Motion to Compel Discovery

MEMORANDUM IN SUPPORT OF PLAINTIFF'S MOTION TO COMPEL ANSWERS TO INTERROGATORIES

Plaintiff is a judgment creditor of defendant, [name], by virtue of a judgment of $[amount] obtained against him in this Court on [date]. In aid of execution of the judgment, plaintiff mailed interrogatories to defendant which were received by defendant on [date]. At defendant's request, in addition to the thirty-day (30) required time period for his response under Rule 33 of the Federal Rules of Civil Procedure, he was given an additional forty-five days (45) in which to answer. As of now, the defendant has had six months in which to respond to the plaintiff's interrogatories and has not responded.

Rule 69(a) of the Federal Rules of Civil Procedure provides in relevant part:

> In aid of the judgment or execution, the judgment creditor or his successor in interest when that interest appears of record, may obtain discovery from any person, including the judgment debtor, in the manner provided in these rules or in the manner provided by the practice of the state in which the district court is held.

Among the discovery devices available "in the manner provided in these rules" are interrogatories to a party under Rule 33 of the Federal Rules of Civil Procedure. The 14 interrogatories in the plaintiff's First Set of Interrogatories to defendant related to the judgment debtor's financial resources and are reasonably calculated to lead to discovery of such financial

---

81 *Cf.* McElveen v. Carib Inn Int'l, Inc., 71 F.R.D. 193, 194–95 (S.D. Tex. 1976); United States v. Earl Phillips Coal Co., 66 F.R.D. 101 (E.D. Tenn. 1975).

resources to aid in execution of the judgment. *See* Rule 26(b) of the Federal Rules of Civil Procedure.

Fed. R. Civ. P. 37(a) provides that a party may apply for an order compelling an answer to interrogatories where a party fails to answer. This Rule further provides that the Court may require the party whose conduct necessitated the motion to pay reasonable attorney fees and expenses.

Based upon the foregoing, plaintiff requests the Court to issue the proposed Order requiring defendant to answer plaintiff's interrogatories, and for reasonable costs and attorney fees incurred and necessitated by the filing of this motion as set forth in plaintiff's accompanying Affidavit.

§ 4.29 —Form of Order Compelling Discovery

ORDER

This cause having come before the Court on motion to compel answers to interrogatories filed by plaintiff pursuant to Fed. R. Civ. P. 37(a), and the defendant having failed to answer interrogatories propounded by the plaintiff within the time required by Fed. R. Civ. P. 33(a) and the Court having the motion, it is therefore

ORDERED AND ADJUDGED that said motion is hereby granted and the defendant shall file sworn answers to interrogatories propounded by the plaintiff within _________ days of this Order, and pay the plaintiff _________ as reasonable costs and attorneys fees incurred and necessitated by this motion.

If the defendant fails to answer the interrogatories within the time provided, the Court will consider him in contempt of this Order and thereafter will consider sanctions against him as appropriate.

Done and ordered at [city, state] this _________ day of _________ 19__.

§ 4.30 Dealing with the Recalcitrant Witness

In federal cases, the district court can take advantage of a specific statute for dealing with the recalcitrant witness. In 28 U.S.C. § 1826(a), the statute provides:

> Whenever a witness in any proceeding before or ancillary to any court or grand jury of the United States refuses without just cause shown to comply with an order of the court to testify or provide other information, including any book, paper, document, record, recording or other material, the court, upon such refusal, or when such refusal is duly brought to its attention, may summarily

order his confinement at a suitable place until such time as the witness is willing to give such testimony or provide such information. No period of such confinement shall exceed the life of—

1 the court proceeding, or

2 the term of the grand jury, including extensions, before which such refusal to comply with the court order occurred, but in no event shall such confinement exceed eighteen months. . . .

When the witness can show no good cause for failure to comply with a subpoena duces tecum, the witness will be held in contempt for failure to comply. An example of this statute's application is found in cases where the judgment debtor relied on his Fifth Amendment privilege claim in refusing to answer the plaintiff's questions, and if the Court finds that defendant's refusal has no connection to a valid Fifth Amendment claim, then the Court can exercise it power to hold the defendant in contempt for such refusal, as a recalcitrant witness, until such time as the witness is willing to give such testimony.[82]

In *Martin-Trigona v. Gouletas,* the Seventh Circuit stated:

It may also be fairly assumed that he has a motive not to answer questions in order to shield his assets from execution. His claim must be viewed in the light of his conduct during the course of these proceedings. Trigona has proved to be an extremely uncooperative litigant. He failed to answer the appellees' counterclaim leading eventually to the entry of a default judgment against him. He at first failed to respond to appellees' requests to appear to answer questions in these supplementary proceedings, and he responded only after he had been found in contempt. The appellees' initial attempts to question him were met with what the trial court found was a blanket invocation of the Fifth Amendment. Against this background of intransigence, the trial court had good reason to question Trigona's credibility.[83]

The record in this case indicated that Martin-Trigona was purposely evading answers to questions.[84] The Circuit Court upheld the District Court's ruling that Martin-Trigona was a recalcitrant witness.[85]

Additionally, if the witness fails to be sworn or answer a question after being directed to do so by the court, the Court may hold the witness in contempt, upon the opposing party's proof that the witness has failed to comply

---

[82] 28 U.S.C. § 1826; Baker v. Limber, 647 F.2d 912, 919 (9th Cir. 1981); Martin-Trigona v. Gouletas, 634 F.2d 354, 355 (7th Cir. 1980) (supplemental proceedings to discover assets of the judgment debtor at the time of the claim of Fifth Amendment privilege for pending state criminal charges for alleged theft and forgery, and a federal grand jury on charges of mail fraud).

[83] *Id.* at 357 (7th Cir. 1980).

[84] *Id.* at 357–58.

[85] *Id.* at 362.

with a valid court order.[86] A pretrial deposition hearing is considered ancillary to the court, and thus, the Recalcitrant Witness Act applies.[87]

Of course the district court is always able, under its traditional contempt powers and Rules 69(a) and 37, to hold a judgment debtor in contempt for repeated failure to provide discovery to the judgment.[88] Also, third parties may find themselves the unwilling objects of the court's contempt power. For example, in *G-Fours, Inc. v. Miele,* the Second Circuit affirmed a contempt order and $1,500 in attorneys' fees for refusal of a judgment debtor's wife to answer written interrogatories concerning her husband's assets.[89]

§ 4.31 —Form of Motion for Contempt

PLAINTIFF'S MOTION FOR ORDER TO SHOW CAUSE WHY DEFENDANT [NAME] SHOULD NOT BE HELD IN CONTEMPT FOR REFUSING TO TESTIFY AND FOR AN ORDER ASSESSING REASONABLE EXPENSES AGAINST DEFENDANT AND HIS COUNSEL

Plaintiff, United States of America, by its undersigned attorneys, moves this Court for an Order to Show Cause why defendant [name] should not be held in contempt for refusal to testify and for an order assessing reasonable expenses against the defendant and his counsel.

§ 4.32 —Form of Memorandum in Support of Motion for Contempt

MEMORANDUM IN SUPPORT OF PLAINTIFF'S MOTION FOR ORDER TO SHOW CAUSE WHY DEFENDANT [NAME] SHOULD NOT BE HELD IN CONTEMPT FOR REFUSING TO TESTIFY AND FOR AN ORDER ASSESSING REASONABLE EXPENSES AGAINST DEFENDANT AND HIS COUNSEL

On [date], this Court Ordered that defendant [name] make himself available for deposition by the plaintiff on [date], pursuant to Fed. R. Civ. P. 69 and 30.

---

86 Heinold Hog Mkt., Inc. v. McCoy, 700 F.2d 611, 615 (10th Cir. 1983).

87 United States v. Johnson, 752 F.2d 206, 210 (6th Cir. 1985).

88 Cerami v. Robinson, 85 F.R.D. 371, 373 (S.D.N.Y. 1980).

89 496 F.2d 809 (2d Cir. 1974).

This Order was entered after consideration of plaintiff's motion to compel and of defendant failure to appear at two previously noticed postjudgment discovery depositions. At the appointed day and time defendant and his counsel [name] appeared at the deposition. Except for the defendant giving his name and address, he refused to testify and, on advice of counsel, plead the Fifth Amendment privilege against self incrimination to each and every other question at the deposition. (Deposition transcript of defendant, dated [date], with exhibits, attached hereto as Exhibit "A," hereinafter "Deposition").

The Federal Rules of Civil Procedure provide for sanctions by the Court, including contempt, for failure to comply with a court order. Fed. R. Civ. P. 37(b). [List applicable case citations.] On [date], this court Ordered the defendant to appear and testify and stated that sanctions would be imposed if [name] failed to adhere to that Court Order. ". . . 'To make a prima facie showing of contempt, however, the government need prove only that the defendant has failed to comply with a valid court order. It need not prove that defendant is able to comply.'" *Heinold Hog Market, Inc. v. McCoy,* 700 F.2d 611, 615 (10th Cir. 1983).

Additionally, Federal Rule 37(b)(2)(E) states that ". . . The court shall require the *party failing to obey the order or the attorney advising him or both to pay the reasonable expenses,* including attorney's fees, caused by the failure, unless the court finds that the failure was substantially justified or that other circumstances make an award of expenses unjust." (emphasis supplied.)

Plaintiff submits that a blanket invocation of the Fifth Amendment privilege is improper in the circumstances of a Fed. R. Civ. P. 69 deposition to discover assets of a judgment debtor, and the facts of this case. *Baker v. Limber,* 647 F.2d 912 (9th Cir. 1981); *Martin-Trigona v. Gouletas,* 634 F.2d 351 (7th Cir. 1980); *Capital Products Corporation v. Hernon,* 457 F.2d 541, 542 (8th Cir. 1972). At the defendant's deposition on [date], defendant introduced a grand jury subpoena duces tecum served upon him as his only reason for not answering further questions beyond giving his name and address. (Deposition, Defendant's Exhibit ___ attached thereto.) The defendant did not offer additional explanations as to why responses to questions asked by plaintiff's counsel might prove incriminating. Many of the questions asked had previously been answered by defendant by Written Interrogatories filed under oath in the instant case on [date]. (Deposition, Plaintiff's Exhibit __). Therefore, any Fifth Amendment privilege claim regarding this inquiry and line of questioning had been waived.

However, in a Rule 69 discovery deposition a judgment debtor is required to offer additional explanation as to why responses to certain seemingly innocuous questions might prove incriminating. *Capital Products Corporation v. Hernon, supra,* 457 F.2d, 544. "[T]he pendency of criminal proceedings does not by itself excuse a witness of his obligation to give testimony in civil proceeding. Some nexus between the risk of criminal conviction and the information requested must exist." *Martin-Trigona v. Gouletas,* 634 F.2d 354, 360, (7th Cir. 1980).

The cases have held that the trial court must make a determination from the facts of the case whether or not assertion of the Fifth Amendment Privilege is justified. *Baker v. Limber,* 647 F.2d 912, 917 (9th Cir. 1981); *Martin-Trigona v. Gouletas, supra,* at 357–362; *Capital Products Corporation v. Hernon,* 457 F.2d 541, 543 (8th Cir. 1982).

Therefore, plaintiff requests that the Court examine the defendant at a hearing before the Court, following the line of questions posed by the Plaintiff during the deposition testimony of defendant on [date], and that the Court determine after such hearing whether the defendant has properly invoked a blanket Fifth Amendment privilege against self incrimination under the present facts. If the Court determines that defendant's refusal to answer some or all of the questions has no connection or nexus to a valid Fifth Amendment privilege claim, then plaintiff requests that the Court Order defendant to answer those questions, and in lieu of answer, that the Court exercise its power to hold defendant in contempt for such refusal, as a recalcitrant witness, until such time as he is willing to give such testimony. 28 U.S.C. § 1826[1] *Baker v. Limber,* 647 F.2d 912, 919 (9th Cir. 1981). *Martin-Trigona v. Gouletas,* 634 F.2d 354, 355 (7th Cir. 1980); Cf. *Heinold Hog Market, Inc. v. McCoy,* 700 F.2d 611, 613 (10th Cir. 1983).

The *Martin-Trigona* case, *supra,* is clearly very similar to the instant case, since at the time of the supplemental proceedings to discover assets of the judgment debtor in that case, state criminal charges had already been larged against Martin-Trigona for alleged theft and forgery, and a federal grand jury in the Central District of Illinois had indicted Martin-Trigona on charges of mail fraud. *Martin-Trigona v. Gouletas,* 634 F.2d 354, 359, (7th Cir. 1980). (In the instant case, defendant Rubin's grand jury subpoena indicates a pending grand jury investigation regarding mail fraud. Deposition, Defendant's Exhibit One.) Despite the pending state criminal charges and the federal grand jury indictment, the court in *Martin-Trigona* found that the pendency of these criminal proceedings did not by itself excuse a witness of his obligation to give testimony, where the witness failed to establish some nexus between the risk of criminal conviction and the information requested. "The ultimate question of whether the privilege is properly invoked is one for the judge." *Id.,* p. 360.

Furthermore if the Court determines that defendant [name] improperly invoked the blanket Fifth Amendment privilege against self-incrimination at his deposition on [date], and failed to establish a basis between the Fifth Amendment claim, and the questions asked by plaintiff's counsel, plaintiff requests the Court to assess reasonable expenses, including attorney's fees, against the defendant, and against his counsel who improperly advised him, for his failure to testify as previously Ordered by the court on [date]. Fed. R. Civ. P. 37(b)(2)(E). An Affidavit of Plaintiff's counsel for reasonable time and travel expenses is attached hereto. Also, in support of its Motion, the plaintiff submits a Certificate of Compliance with Local Rule ____, attached hereto. [Submit any required certificate indicating the appropriate conference with defense counsel.]

CERTIFICATE OF COMPLIANCE WITH LOCAL RULE ___

Plaintiff, United States of America, by its undersigned counsel, respectfully submits this Certificate of Compliance, pursuant to Rule ___ of the Local Rules of practice of this Court, in support of its Motion for Order to Show Cause Why Defendant [name] Should Not Be Held in Contempt for Refusal to Testify and for an Order Assessing Reasonable Expenses Against the Defendant and His Counsel.

Plaintiff's counsel has conferred with defendant's counsel and agreed to a preliminary briefing schedule for these motions and briefs, subject to the approval of the court. It has been agreed that plaintiff's counsel would file its Motion for Order to Show Cause and Brief on [date], and defense counsel would file their Responsive Briefs by [date].

Thereafter, if it was agreeable by the court, a hearing is requested on the motion with respective counsel, and defendant present for examination, on [dates], if the Court's calendar would provide time for such a hearing on either of those days. A proposed briefing schedule and order to show cause is attached to this motion.

§ 4.33 —Form of Order to Show Cause for Contempt

BRIEFING SCHEDULE AND ORDER TO SHOW CAUSE

This matter having been brought by Motion of ________________, plaintiff herein, for an Order to Show Cause Why Defendant [name] Should Not Be Held in Contempt for Refusal to Testify and for an Order Assessing Reasonable Expenses Against the Defendant and His Counsel, for good cause shown, it is on this _________ day of [date]:

1. Ordered that the defendant shall file his Brief in response to this motion on or before [date], and it is hereby Ordered that the defendant [name], and his counsel, [name] of the law firm of [name of firm], herein will show cause before this court at a hearing on the _________ day of [date], at _________, in Court room number _________, why he should not be held in contempt for refusal to testify and why an order should not issue for plaintiff against the said defendant and his said counsel for reasonable expenses and attorneys' fees in accordance with the affidavit of plaintiff's counsel attached to plaintiff's motion, and Fed. R. Civ. P. 37(b)(2)(E).

2. It is further Ordered that the Clerk of Court shall mail a copy of this Order to Show Cause to defendant [name], at [address], and upon [counsel name and address], within _________ day hereof.

§ 4.34 —Form Application and Proposed Order Regarding Contempt for Failure to Obey Injunction

PLAINTIFF'S APPLICATION FOR ORDER TO SHOW CAUSE WHY DEFENDANTS SHOULD NOT BE HELD IN CONTEMPT FOR REFUSAL TO COMPLY WITH COURT ORDER AND INJUNCTION

Plaintiff, ______________, by its undersigned counsel, applies for the entry of an Order to Show Cause Why [defendants] should not be held in contempt for refusal to comply with this Court's Order and Permanent Injunction of [date]. In support of its Application, Plaintiff represents as follows:

1. This Court issued its Memorandum Decision in this case on [date], entering judgment that [recite contents of judgment].

2. Additionally, on the same date this Court entered a Permanent Injunction requiring [party], within fifteen days of the injunction, to do certain specified acts to assist the plaintiff in enforcing and perfecting its judgment rights.

3. In its Memorandum Decision, this Court found that [recite decision].

4. The last day for [party] to comply with the injunction of this Court was [date], and no action was taken by [party], its controlling parties, liquidator, and/or officers to comply with this injunction.

WHEREFORE, Plaintiff, [plaintiff], applies for entry of an Order to Show Cause Why [defendants] should not be held in contempt for refusal to comply with the Court Order and Permanent Injunction of [date], and further ordering them to reimburse Plaintiff for its attorneys fees, costs, and expenses incurred by reason of bringing this application.

§ 4.35 —Form of Court Order Denying Postjudgment Protective Order

-ORDER-

THIS MATTER is before the Court on several Motions related to proceedings under Rule 69 of the Federal Rules of Civil Procedure initiated by the plaintiff to collect on a judgment against the defendants. Defendant filed a Motion to Quash a Deposition Subpoena on [Date]. Alternatively, she sought Protective Orders to Limit the Scope of Her Deposition. The financial corporation, and the plaintiff filed a Joint Motion for Protective Order on [Date]. This Motion requested that the subpoenas issued either be quashed or, in the alternative, that a protective order be issued limiting the scope of any depositions taken. After a careful review of the record in this matter, including the briefs submitted by the parties, we are of the view that the various Motions should be *DENIED* in part and *GRANTED* in part.

This action originated in the United States District Court for the _________ District of _________. The plaintiff sued the defendants to recover certain funds as a result of the defendants' personal guaranty of a loan made in participation with the _________ Bank to [Company].

The defendants were principals of this business entity. A default judgment was obtained against the plaintiffs on [Date] in the amount of $[amount] plus interest and costs. In [Date] this judgment was registered in this Court, for purposes of collection, as _______, pursuant to 28 U.S.C. § 1963. In [Date] defendant filed a bankruptcy petition in the United States Bankruptcy Court for the District of _________. At that time the plaintiff ceased collection efforts as to the defendant-wife, but continued its efforts as to the defendant-husband.

In _________ of 19___ the plaintiff served a series of subpoenas duces tecum upon various persons and institutions seeking information about the assets and finances of defendant-husband. Among those individuals and entities receiving subpoenas were defendant-wife, financial corporation executive, and an officer of certain of the corporate third parties. Finally, on or about [Date], the plaintiff issued a subpoena and notice of deposition to [banking institution] to seek information about the defendant-husband's finances and assets. In addition information relating to the assets of certain of the third party corporate entities was sought from [banking institution]. At the deposition which took place on [date] the plaintiff requested that the representative of [banking institution] contact [lending institution] and have [lending institution] search its records concerning the defendant-husband and the third party corporate entities.

The defendant-wife challenged the subpoena issued to her on the grounds that the information sought from her is protected under the "marital privilege." The subpoena issued to plaintiff is challenged on the grounds that the information sought falls within the accountant-client privilege recognized by statute in the state of ________________. The various third party corporate entities challenge the subpoenas issued to them on the grounds that the inquiry is outside the scope permitted under Rule 69. The third party corporate entities also seek to have the request made to [banking institution] quashed for the same reason; it is outside the scope permitted under Rule 69.

At the outset we must determine whether state law or the common law, as interpreted by the Courts of the United States, applies in the case at hand. It is the view of the Court that the common law interpreted by the federal courts governs the issues presented by the instant case. We are of the view that Rule 69 of the Federal Rules of Civil Procedure read in conjunction with Rule 501 of the Federal Rules of Evidence dictates this result. Rule 69 states that

> . . . and in proceedings supplementary to and in aid of a judgment, and in proceedings on and in aid of execution shall be in accordance with the practice and procedure of the state . . . *except* that any statute of the United States governs to the extent that it is applicable. In aid of the judgment or execution, the judgment creditor . . . may obtain discovery from any person . . . In the manner provided by *these rules or* in the manner provided by the practice of the state in which the district court is held. (emphasis added).

The Tenth Circuit Court of Appeals has held that "any statute" includes the Federal Rules of Civil Procedure, *Rumsey v. George E. Failing Co.,* 333 F.2d 960 (10th Cir., 1964). Rule 26 of the Fed. R. Civ. P. has been read to state that the question of "privilege" during discovery is controlled by Rule 501 of the Federal Rules of Evidence, Wright and Miller, *Federal Practice and Procedure* § 2016 pp. 23, (1970). Indeed, Rule 1101(c) of the Fed. R. Evid. states that Rule 501 applies at all stages of all actions, cases, and proceedings. Under Rule 501, state law privileges apply only where state law would provide the rule of decision as to a claim or defense. In the instant case, there is no claim or defense at issue. The terms claim or defense necessarily refer to the issue of liability or "fault" in a civil action. In the case before us liability has already been determined. Further, the defendants were sued pursuant to federal law and federal law would control the substantive issues at trial had there been one. It is clear that at trial the federal common law of privileges would have applied. We read Rule 501 as continuing that application in post-trial or post-judgment proceedings. It is the view of this Court that the common law as interpreted by the federal courts controls the issue of privilege presented by the Motions to Quash.

Under the common law as interpreted by the federal courts no Accountant-Client privilege has been recognized, *Couch v. United States,* 409 U.S. 332, 335 (1973). We are of the view that this is true whether the privilege is asserted at trial or in postjudgment proceedings. Accordingly, the Motion to Quash as it relates to the subpoena issued to the plaintiff is *DENIED.*

While the common law does not recognize the Accountant-Client privilege a marital privilege has long been acknowledged. As the defendant, defendant-wife, correctly points out, the testimonial privilege that permits one spouse to refuse to testify against the other has not been abolished, *Trammel v. United States,* 445 U.S. 40 (1980). It is also true that, in civil proceedings, the testimonial privilege has come under increasing attack and limitation. We are of the view that the analysis described in *Ryan v. Commissioner,* 568 F.2d. 531 (7th Cir., 1977), *cert. denied* 439 U.S. 820 (1978), provides the best approach in dealing with the testimonial privilege. The competing interests must be weighed against each other and a decision made based on the unique facts of each case.

In the instant case, it is the view of the Court that the facts support the position taken by the plaintiff. The defendant-wife does not assert that the exercise of the privilege is necessary to protect her marriage nor is it alleged that the information sought from her relates to intimate marital discussions. There is nothing to suggest that the information will be used in future criminal proceedings against the plaintiff. The information is sought simply to aid the plaintiff in satisfying a valid, enforcible judgment entered against both defendants. Finally, while by no means conclusive, the record before us suggests that the assets of the defendants have been and continue to be hidden from the plaintiff. Given the circumstances of this case as described, we are of the view that the defendant-wife's interests in claiming the privilege are outweighed by the competing interests of the plaintiff and society as a whole. Accordingly, the defendant-wife's Motion to Quash is *DENIED.*

The last issue presented to the Court by the various Motions relates to the scope of discovery permitted under Rule 69. Specifically, the issue has to do with the information that may be sought from non-parties who may have some connection with the judgment debtor. In the case before us the non-party corporate entities seek to prevent any further depositions of the corporate executive, and the plaintiff, a certified public accountant employed by the corporations. The non-party corporate entities point out that proceedings under Rule 69 may not be used to acquire information about the finances or assets of non-parties. While this is a correct statement of a general rule, Wright and Miller, *Federal Practice and Procedure*; § 3014 pp 72 (1970), it is also true that non-party status cannot be used to conceal assets of the judgment debtor. We are of the view that the various cases cited to the Court by the parties stand for the proposition that where the judgment debtor has close financial connections with certain non-party individuals or entities, those non-parties can be examined as to these financial connections. This is the case despite the fact that during the course of such an examination the finances of the non-party are revealed. To preclude such an examination would invite the judgment debtor to conceal assets by placing them with or routing them through non-parties. This is the central thrust of the various cases dealing with the scope of Rule 69 proceedings, *Strick Corp. v. Thai Teak Products Company, Ltd.*, 493 F. Supp. 1210, (E.D. Pa. 1980); *Magnaleasing, Inc. v. Staten Island Mall,* 76 F.R.D. 559 (S.D.N.Y., 1977); *Caisson Corp. v. County West Building Corp.,* 62 F.R.D. 331 (E.D. Pa., 1974).

As we read the various Notices of Deposition issued by the plaintiff it appears that what is sought is information relating to financial transactions or transfers between the judgment debtor and the nonparties. It is clear that the plaintiff is concerned that certain transfers and/or transactions involve assets that may be available to satisfy the judgment against the defendant's husband. Unlike the facts in *Strick Corp., supra,* the plaintiff has presented more than "mere allegations" of close ties between the non-party corporate entities and the defendant-husband. In *Strick Corp.* the Court stated that discovery of the assets of a non-party would be permissible where the relationship between the non-party and the judgment debtor was sufficient to raise reasonable doubts about the validity of certain fund transfers. We are of the view that the plaintiff has made a such a showing. That being the case, we cannot preclude the plaintiff from taking the desired depositions, particularly where the Notices issued state that the information sought involves the accounting and financial records of the defendant's husband individually and/or in connection with the corporate non-parties. Accordingly, the Motion to Quash the subpoenas issued to an officer of the various corporate non-parties and the Motion to Quash the subpoena issued to the plaintiff are *DENIED*.

In sum, all Motions to Quash or for Protective Orders filed on [Date] by the defendant-wife and the various corporate non-parties are *DENIED*. This Order does not preclude the filing of any Motions for Protective Orders in the future as they may relate to specific questions propounded at depositions or as to specific requests for production of documents.

ANALYZING INFORMATION OBTAINED IN POSTJUDGMENT DISCOVERY

§ 4.36 Relating the Evidence to the Financial Condition of the Debtor

As plaintiff's counsel takes postjudgment discovery from the debtor and other parties, he must begin to relate the evidence to the financial condition of the debtor, and what happened to the judgment debtor's assets. Counsel should be able to accumulate sufficient information about this information after a short round of postjudgment discovery. If counsel discovers assets have been transferred, he must analyze how difficult it is going to be to get those assets back. Keep in mind that one valuable piece of fraudulently transferred real estate, or a valuable piece of personal property, if easily reached in a subsequent suit or in a supplementary proceedings, may make counsel's judgment enforcement action worth pursuing. Shortly after the preliminary discovery proceedings, counsel must sit down and examine the evidence to see if further discovery or subsequent proceedings will be fruitful in satisfying the judgment.

§ 4.37 Expert Assistance in Analyzing Financial Evidence Obtained in Postjudgment Discovery

As with any litigation matter, an analysis of the potential use of expert witnesses is necessary. In postjudgment discovery and postjudgment litigation plaintiff's counsel will most often need an accountant, economist, or financial analyst to assist in the case. Of course, the type of litigation may necessitate other experts. Counsel must also decide if the cost of the expert is warranted in view of the size of the potential recovery. To keep costs down, counsel may want to use an expert from his client's staff when available. However, as with any litigation, despite the costs, it is always beneficial to use a disinterested expert.

When counsel chooses experts, he should consider whether the expert has experience in tracing assets, analyzing fraudulent transfers, and determining whether individuals or corporations are insolvent, plus experience in testifying in such matters. In postjudgment litigation these matters are most frequently encountered, and become the battleground where the case is won or lost.

Naturally, before employing the professional expert to assist in postjudgment litigation, counsel should obtain an estimation of the fees and costs to be incurred, and have those fees and costs approved by the client. Before contacting the client, have the name, resume of the expert, and the anticipated cost analysis ready for discussion. Be prepared to evaluate the cost of the expert versus the size of the potential recovery and risks of collection.

§ 4.38 Technique of Diagraming the Transfers of Assets and Parties Receiving Transfers

In postjudgment litigation plaintiff's counsel may find himself trying to figure out where the assets have gone from the individual or corporate debtor. If there are only one or two transfers, and only one or two parties, counsel probably will not need a diagram to depict the transfers. However, as the number of transfers and number of parties increase, he may want to diagram the transfers, or use charts, graphs, or other demonstrative evidence to help understand what happened. Remember, this diagram, or other demonstrative evidence, will also be a potential tool at trial, either in the opening statement, or as part of the case, to describe to the judge or jury what happened to the judgment debtor's assets. Counsel's expert may be able to prepare these diagrams, charts, models, or graphs and testify from them. It will be useful to consider the kinds of demonstrative evidence counsel can use effectively as a trial tool.[90]

It may also be useful to diagram or chart the different entities used by the judgment debtor to conceal transfers when dealing with a series of transfers through a number of different entities. To show the corporate judgment debtor's control of these transfers and the relationships of these other entities to the judgment debtor, it will be effective to combine the visual power of diagrams, charts or graphs, with the oral testimony received at trial. To assist the judge or jury in understanding the controlling parties handling these

---

[90] *See* M. Dombroff, Dombroff on Demonstrative Evidence (John Wiley & Sons, Inc. 1983).

transfers, it may be necessary to depict what offices, directorships or shares they held in the related entities. Certainly in the alter ego case, such a diagram or chart will be essential, to communicate these often complex relationships in simple picture form.

§ 4.39 Sample Diagram to Understand Financial Transactions

Depicted below are three diagrams which illustrate, in progression, a series of financial transactions. [See § **4.13.**] **Figure 4-1** is the normal sales pattern of XYZ and ABC companies. **Figure 4-2** illustrates how profits were diverted to two companies, Seller Trading Co. and Tricky Joe Co., controlled by one of the principal officers of XYZ and ABC. **Figure 4-3** illustrates how additional profits were diverted to a third company, Lazy Construction Co. [Gerry Pell, Ph.D., is acknowledged for his assistance in developing the diagrams in **Chapter 4.**]

§ 4.40 Relating the Evidence to Theories of Recovery of the Unlawfully Transferred Assets

After accumulating, documenting, and analyzing the evidence, and diagramming the transactions and the parties, counsel is ready to relate the evidence to the theories of recovery of the unlawfully transferred assets.

Return to the checklists in **Chapter 3** for the individual debtor and the corporate debtor. Relate the evidence that has been accumulated. Compare the basic guidelines for the major theories of recovery in **Chapter 6** and see how the evidence stacks up to the prima facie case for fraudulent transfers, the constructive trust fund theory, piercing the corporate veil, or the Federal Priority Statute claims. If one or more of the theories are applicable, counsel is ready to file a new suit to enforce the judgment.

Alternatively, counsel may be able to bring the judgment to a successful conclusion by moving for supplementary proceedings under state law. [See §§ **4.1** and **4.2.**]

DIAGRAM ONE

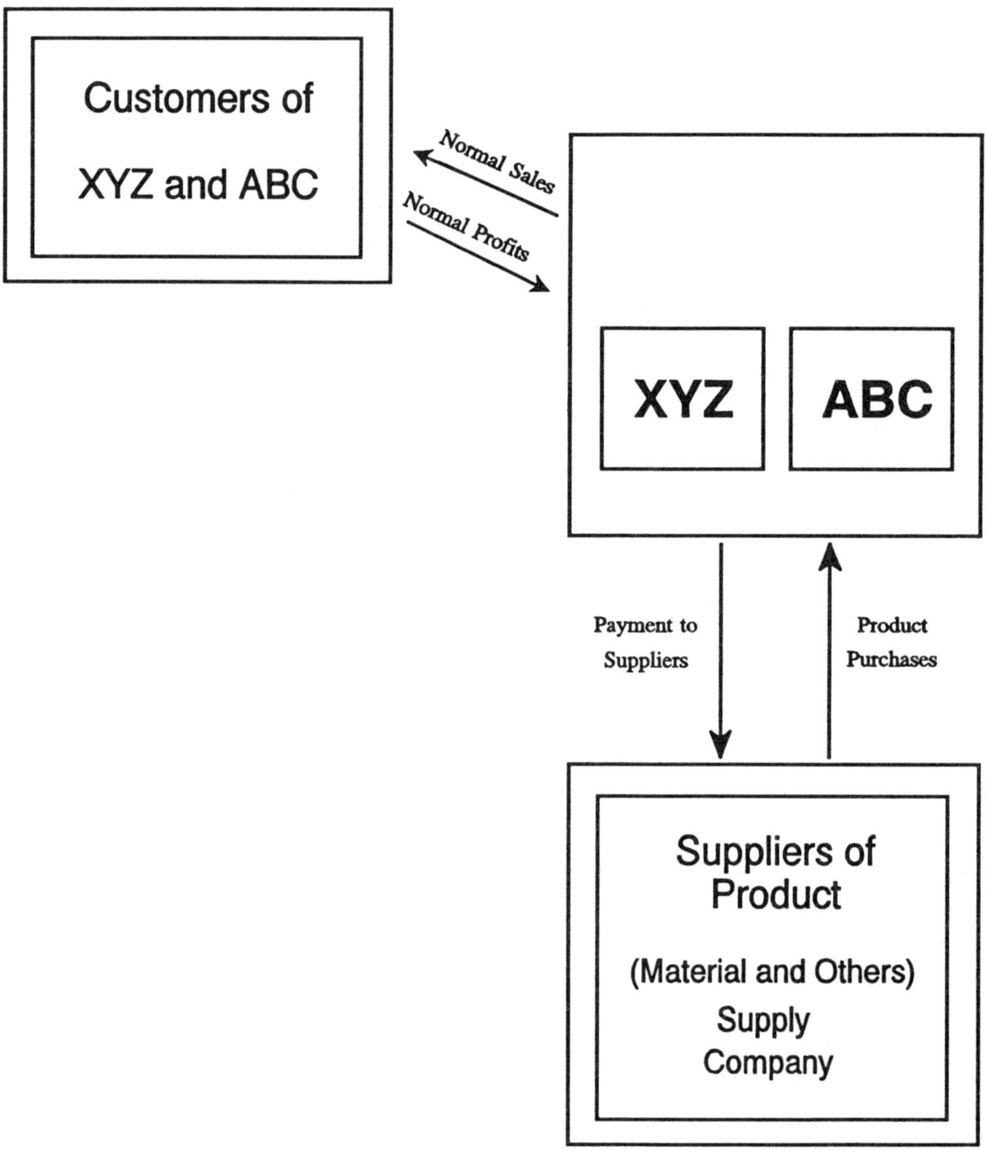

Figure 4-1. Normal sale pattern.

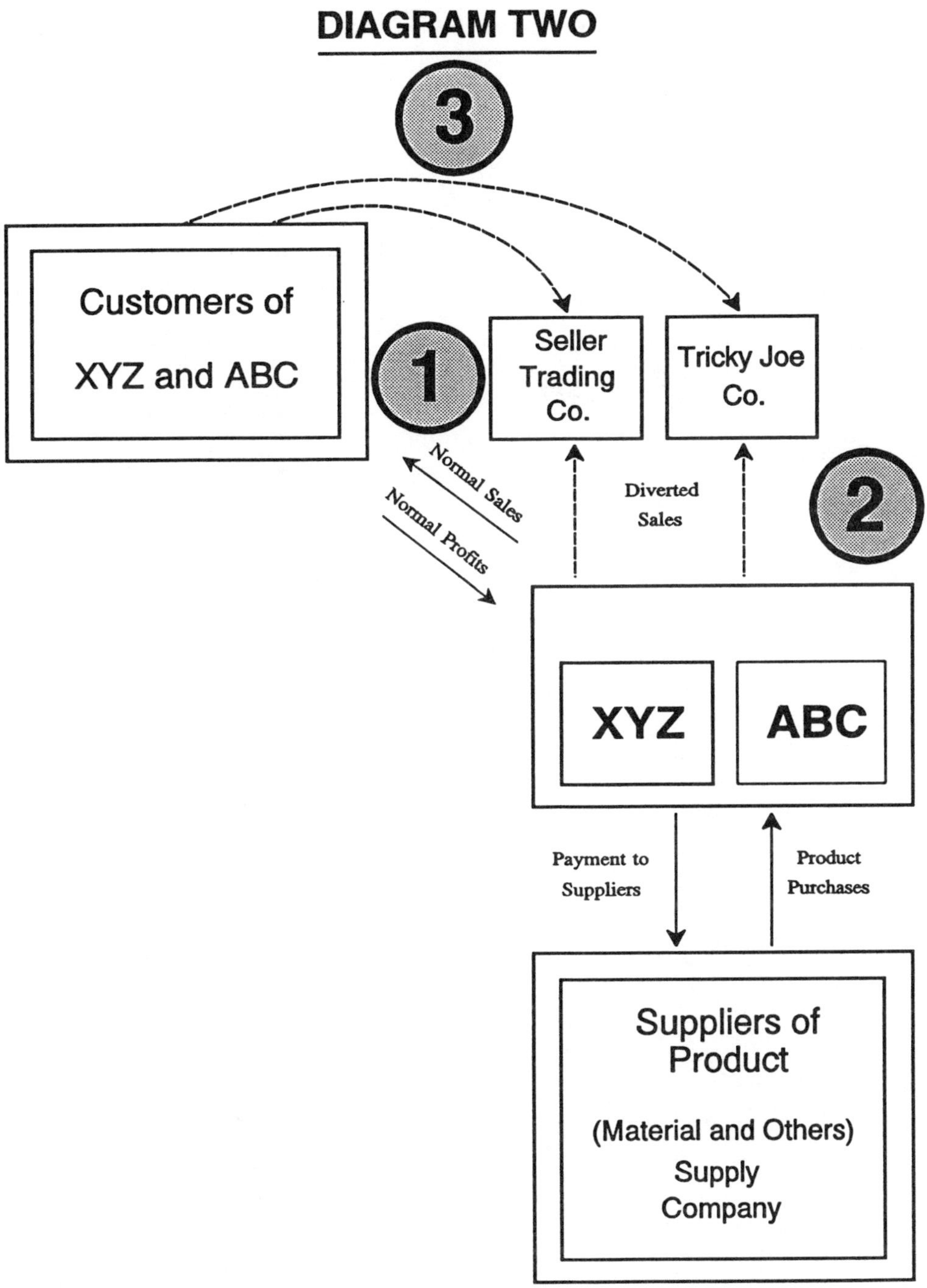

Figure 4-2. Diversion of profits.

DIAGRAM THREE

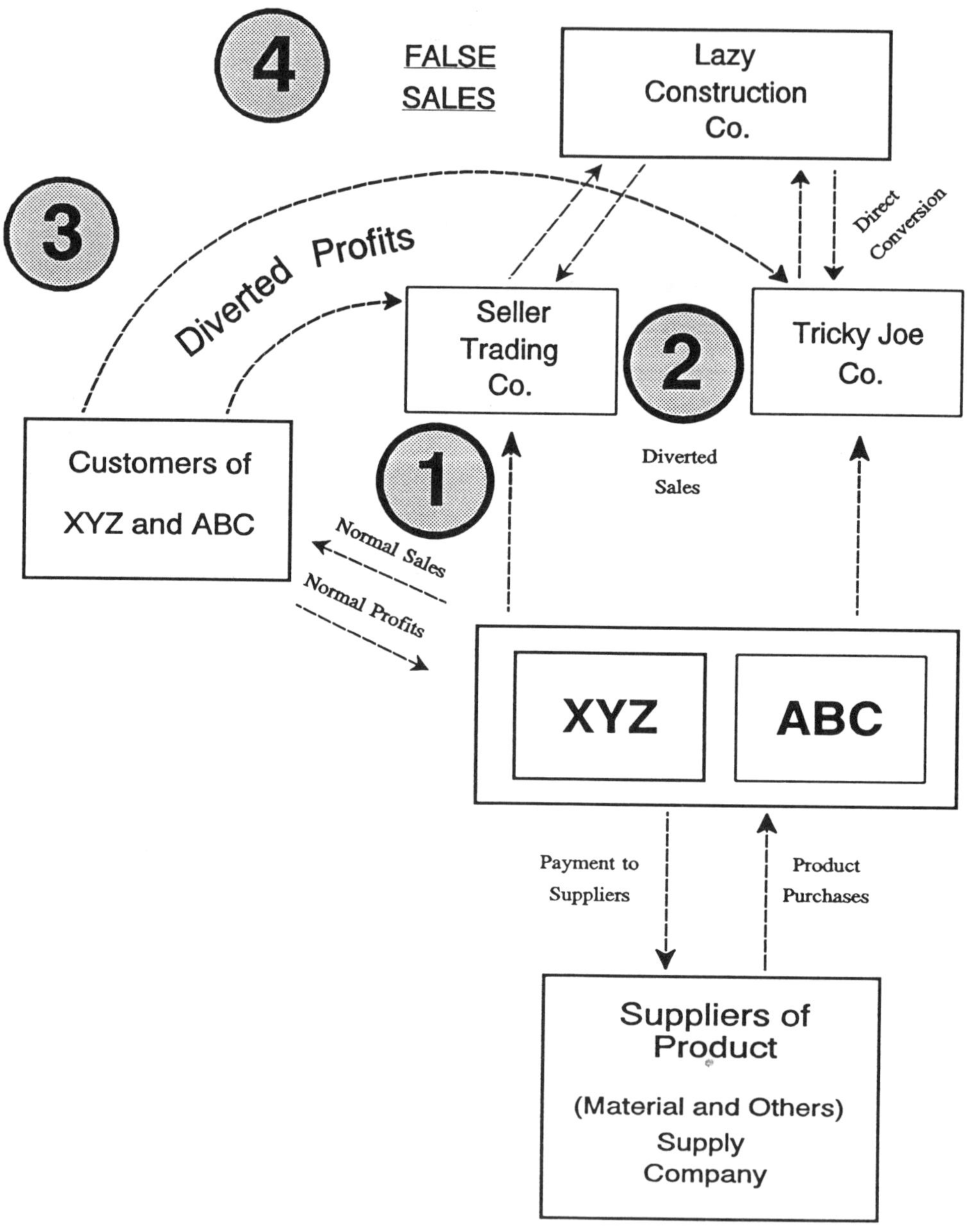

Figure 4-3. Diversion of additional profits.

CHAPTER 5

EXECUTING ON THE JUDGMENT*

* The author is indebted to Claude D. Brown for allowing the use of his outline as a basis for some of the materials in this chapter.

§ 5.1 Introduction

This Chapter considers the process for executing on the judgment. This Chapter is intended to give a basic primer on federal execution practice on a federal judgment. Part of this process is governed by federal law, and part of the process may be governed by the law of the particular state in which the judgment is enforced.

It is not the purpose of this Chapter to give a definitive explanation of all the different state execution, attachment, and garnishment statutes available for use in protecting or securing collection on a federal judgment. That task would be impossible in a book of this size. Instead, the Chapter is designed to give an overview of several aspects which are basic in the execution, attachment, and garnishment process, and their application under federal law. This material reviews some of the practices in several different states, and addresses the legal and practical considerations to analyze with any federal judgment before writs of execution, attachment or garnishment are issued.

This Chapter contains discussion and analysis of postjudgment writs available under federal law and state law. Essential to this discussion is the effect of the Federal Debt Collection Procedures Act of 1990, codified at Title 28, United States Code, §§ 3001–3308, on the execution, attachment, and garnishment process of the United States.

§ 5.2 Prejudgment Attachment

Under Federal Rule of Civil Procedure 64, if a state law permits prejudgment attachment of property, then attachment is available for any nonfederal creditor in a federal district court action. Of course, state law may provide for other prejudgment remedies such as garnishment or sequestration. Usually, the remedy employed will have to meet the same prejudgment process requirements. Of course, the nonfederal creditor must follow the attachment procedures provided by the current state law in which the federal district court is held. The prejudgment attachment requirements for the United States as a federal creditor are set forth in § **5.2.**

Under the usual prejudgment attachment process, a writ of attachment is obtained from the court for the purpose of securing satisfaction of the judgment ultimately obtained. As discussed below, under some circumstances, it may be necessary to have a hearing before the attachment is issued. Once the writ of attachment is served upon the debtor by a sheriff, U.S. Marshal, or other attaching officer, the attaching officer may take possession of the property or attach a copy of the writ to the property if it is too bulky to move. If the property is real estate, a copy of the writ should be recorded in the city or county land records to perfect the attachment.

Of the 50 states in the United States, 49 states have prejudgment attachment statutes, the lone exception being Pennsylvania.[1] In any prejudgment litigation, it is recommended practice to review the particular state prejudgment attachment statute for its applicability and use in the action. Naturally, if a creditor can obtain a prejudgment attachment (or other prejudgment remedy), this remedy will provide security for any judgment later obtained in the action.

"Prejudgment attachment was a remedy unknown at common law."[2] "[I]t traces its origin to the Custom of London, under which a creditor might attach money or goods of the defendant either in the plaintiff's own hands or in the custody of a third person, by proceedings in the mayor's court or in the sheriff's court."[3] In *Connecticut v. Doehr,*[4] the Supreme Court, in reviewing the state law attachment process, surveyed different state attachment provisions and compared them to Connecticut's provisions to determine what safeguards were needed to prevent unconstitutional deprivation of property.

> A survey of state attachment provisions reveals that nearly every State requires either a preattachment hearing, a showing of some exigent circumstance, or both, before permitting an attachment to take place. (See appendix.) Twenty-seven States, as well as the District of Columbia, permit attachments only when some extraordinary circumstance is present. In such cases, prejudgment hearings are not required but postattachment hearings are provided. Ten States permit attachment without the presence of such factors but require prewrit hearings unless one of those factors is shown. Six States limit attachments to extraordinary circumstance cases but the writ will not issue prior to a hearing unless there is a showing of some even more compelling condition. Three States always require a preattachment hearing. Only Washington, Connecticut, and Rhode Island authorize attachments without a prior hearing in situations that do not involve any purportedly heightened threat to the plaintiff's interests. Even those States permit ex parte deprivations only in certain types of cases: Rhode Island does so only when the claim is equitable; Connecticut and Washington do so only when real estate is to be attached, and even Washington requires a bond.[5]

In *Connecticut v. Doehr,* the majority opinion of the Supreme Court held that the Connecticut prejudgment attachment statute failed to comply with due process, because Connecticut's statute failed to provide for a preattachment hearing without at least requiring a showing of some exigent circumstance.[6] In the *Doehr* case, Justices Marshall, Stevens, O'Connor, and White,

---

1 Connecticut v. Doehr, 501 U.S. 1, 115 L. Ed. 2d 1, 17–18 and n.6 (1991) (See the chart of state prejudgment attachment statutes in the Appendix to that decision, 115 L. Ed. 2d, at 22–23.)

2 Connecticut v. Doehr, 501 U.S. 1, 115 L. Ed. 2d 1, 17 (1991).

3 Ownbey v. Morgan, 256 U.S. 94, 104 (1921).

4 Connecticut v. Doehr, 501 U.S. 1, 115 L. Ed. 2d 1 (1991).

5 Connecticut v. Doehr, 501 U.S. 1, 115 L. Ed. 2d 1, 17–18 (1991).

6 *Id.,* 115 L. Ed. 2d 1, 18–21.

deemed it appropriate to consider whether due process also requires the plaintiff to post a bond or other security in addition to requiring either a preattachment hearing or a showing of some exigency.[7] These Justices believed that due process requires 1) a preattachment hearing; 2) a showing of some exigency, or both; 3) a postattachment hearing when the hearing has been made ex parte; and 4) the filing of an attachment bond by the plaintiff.[8]

§ 5.3 Prejudgment Attachment by the United States

The prejudgment remedies available to the United States are governed by the Federal Debt Collection Procedures Act of 1990. Subsection 3101(a) authorizes the United States to apply for a prejudgment remedy at any time after filing of the action. The United States has a right to prejudgment attachment in accordance with the procedures and requirements of 28 U.S.C. § 3102. Before prejudgment attachment by the United States is available, the United States must comply with the procedures contained in 28 U.S.C. § 3101, and show reasonable cause to believe that the prejudgment remedy is needed to preserve property pending judgment. Also, before allowance of the prejudgment attachment, counsel for the United States must file an application which states the grounds for the attachment. The application must include an affidavit which establishes the probable validity of the debt and the right of the United States to recover the amount demanded in the application.

Provided that the United States shows reasonable cause under one or more of the grounds stated in § 3101(b), the provisions of the Federal Debt Collection Act indicate that an expedited prejudgment remedy may be granted without prior notice to the debtor before the writ issues. However, under § 3004(c) of the Act, counsel for the United States is required to serve, with reasonable diligence after the time when the prejudgment remedy is put into effect, a notice on the debtor, or other person in possession, custody, or control of the property. The Act does not define "reasonable diligence," and thus, presumably the courts will interpret what is reasonable diligence under particular circumstances.

Once the prejudgment attachment is issued, the debtor must have an opportunity for notice and hearing on the matter.[9] The statute contains a suggested form of notice, but the form and content of a particular jurisdiction's notice must be approved by a majority of the chief judges of the federal districts in the state in which the court is located. The notice provided in the statute establishes procedures for requesting and conducting a hearing on the

---

[7] *Id.*

[8] *Id.*, 115 L. Ed. 2d, at 21.

[9] 28 U.S.C. § 3101(d).

prejudgment remedy. Sections 3101(d)(2)(A)–(D) also prescribes limits on the issues to be raised at the hearing, including:

1. the probable validity of the claim for the debt for which such remedy was granted and of any defense or claim of exemption asserted by such person
2. compliance with any statutory requirements for the issuance of the prejudgment remedy granted
3. the existence of any grounds set forth in section 3101(b) for prejudgment remedies
4. the inadequacy of alternative remedies (if any) to protect the interests of the United States.

Counsel for the United States prepares the particular form of notice required in that district, and the clerk issues the notice for service on the debtor whose property will be attached, and for service on any other person in possession, custody, or control of that property. The debtor or custodian must receive triplicate copies of the notice. The notice must provide the name of the debtor, the amount of the debt, the reason for the debt and indicate that a lawsuit has been filed to collect the debt. Also, the notice must contain the major exemptions which apply in the state where the property is located and notify the debtor that a hearing may be requested by notifying the clerk of court in writing and sending a copy of the request to an attorney for the United States.

Practice Tips on Debtor's Notice

1. Use the appropriate form of notice required for the district.
2. Serve the notice on the debtor in triplicate.
3. Enter the proper data required for the notice.
4. List in the notice the exemptions which apply in that state.

Receivership, garnishment, and sequestration are other prejudgment remedies provided for the United States in the Federal Debt Collection Procedures Act in §§ 3103–3105. The process to apply for any of these prejudgment remedies is the same as the process required in applying for a prejudgment attachment.

Any application for issuance of a prejudgment remedy must be approved by the court, and cannot be issued by the clerk of court acting alone. Under § 3101(a)(3), the application for such remedies by the United States must "(A) state that the debtor against whom the prejudgment remedy is sought shall be afforded an opportunity for a hearing; and (B) set forth with particularity that all statutory requirements under this chapter for the issuance of the prejudgment remedy have been satisfied. Section 3101(b)(1) sets for the grounds for issuance of the prejudgment attachment by the United States under court approval.

Over the years, common grounds that have developed both in case law and in model state statutes, which have become a basis in the Federal Debt Collection Act for granting provisional remedies before judgment. The grounds include:

1. the debtor is about to leave the jurisdiction of the United States
2. the debtor is about to assign, dispose, remove, conceal, ill treat, waste, or destroy property
3. the debtor is about to convert property into money, securities, or evidence of debt in a manner prejudicial to the United States
4. the debtor has evaded service of process by concealing himself or has temporarily withdrawn from the jurisdiction of the United States.[10]

This statute, although passed prior to the Supreme Court's decision in *Connecticut v. Doehr,*[11] meets the constitutional safeguards required before the issuance of prejudgment attachment because the statute requires the United States to show exigent circumstances before the issuance of the prejudgment remedy, and requires an opportunity for the debtor for notice and a hearing regarding the attachment within five days after the clerk receives the debtor's request for a hearing under 28 U.S.C. § 3101(d). In addition, the United States must specify in the notice the debtor's right to claim exemptions as provided in § 3014. Therefore, the requirements provided in the Federal Debt Collection Act before issuance of a prejudgment remedy comply with the constitutional safeguards demanded by the Supreme Court in *Doehr.*

Practice Tip

1. Once the writ of attachment is issued, the U.S. Marshal should proceed without delay to levy upon the property specified pursuant to § 3102(d). A levy is merely the seizure of property by the U.S. Marshal or other levying officer for the purpose of satisfying the judgment by selling the property.
2. Levy upon real estate is made by entering the property and posting the writ and notice in a conspicuous place upon the property, in accordance with § 3102(d)(3).
3. Levy upon personal property, according to § 3102(d)(4) is made by taking possession of it.

---

[10] 28 U.S.C. § 3101 (b)(1)(A)–(D).

[11] 501 U.S. 1 (1991).

4. If the personal property is too large to move without great expense or inconvenience, § 3102(d)(4) permits the levy to be made by placing a copy of the writ and levy on the property or in a conspicuous place in vicinity of the property describing the property by quantity and sufficient detail to identify the property on which the levy is made.

Under the Act, the notice of levy of the United States is filed in the same manner as required under state law. Here's how it works. First, when the levy is made, the Marshal pursuant to § 3102(d)(5), "shall file a copy of the notice of levy in the same manner as provided for judgments in § 3201(a)(1)." Second, the Marshal then serves the writ and notice of levy on the debtor or person in possession of the property in the same manner as a summons is served in a civil action. Third, once served, the Marshal records the time, date and place of levy and returns a copy to the issuing court.

Section 3201(a)(1) requires the filing of the notice of levy by the U.S. Marshal in the same manner as the filing of a notice of tax lien under paragraphs (1) and (2) of § 6323(f) of the Internal Revenue Code of 1986.[12] Section 6323(f) of the Internal Revenue Code of 1986 requires the notice of the United States to be filed in accordance with state law in the city or county land records to protect the lien position of the United States. Such filing of the levy of attachment creates the lien position of the United States on the property in accordance with § 3102(f)(1) of the Federal Debt Collection Procedures Act. Basically § 3102(f)(2) codifies the principal, established in the *United States v. City of New Britain,*[13] that the first lien to be filed is the first in right. The lien of the United States "shall be ranked ahead of any other security interest perfected after the later of the time of levy and the time a copy of a notice is filed under subsection (d)(5)."[14]

EXECUTION PROCESS

§ 5.4 Basic Execution Process

Under the Federal Debt Collection Procedures Act, the judgment debtor's nonexempt interest in property is subject to levy pursuant to a writ of execution, when that debtor is indebted to the United States.[15] This new debt collection statute carries forth the historical procedure of using a writ of execution

12 28 U.S.C. § 3201(a)(1).

13 *See* United States v. City of New Britain, 347 U.S. 81 (1954).

14 28 U.S.C. § 3102(f)(2).

15 28 U.S.C. § 3203(a).

long recognized in both state and federal courts of the United States for the process by which a judgment is collected.[16]

> An execution is a judicial writ issuing from the court where the judgment is rendered, directed to an officer thereof, and running against the body or goods of a party, by which the judgment of the court is enforced. It has also been defined as . . . a writ which authorizes the officer to carry a judgment into effect; the process by which the debt, or damages, or other things recovered, and the costs adjudged, is obtained. . . ."[17]

The basic execution process for both the United States and other nonfederal creditors who recover money judgments in the federal courts follows the procedures contained in Federal Rule of Civil Procedure 69(a). Under Federal Rule of Civil Procedure 69(a), a writ of execution is the usual process for the enforcement of a final money judgment.[18] However, the procedure on execution for a nonfederal creditor follows state law.[19]

> The procedure on execution, in proceedings supplementary to and in aid of a judgment, and in proceedings on and in aid of execution shall be in accordance with the practice and procedure of the state in which the district court is held, existing at the time the remedy is sought, except that any statute of the United States governs to the extent that it is applicable.[20]

As with attachment, discussed above in § **5.3** and garnishment as discussed in § **5.8,** execution procedures must comply with constitutional due process.[21]

---

16 *Cf.* Custer v. McCutcheon, 283 U.S. 514, 515–16 (1930).

17 33 C.J.S. *Executions* § 1 (1955).

18 Weir v. United States, 339 F.2d 82, 85–6 (8th Cir. 1964); *see* Whiteleather v. United States, 264 F.2d 861 (6th Cir. 1959). "Process to enforce a judgment for the payment of money shall be a writ of execution, unless the court directs otherwise." Fed. R. Civ. P. 69(a).

19 Marshal v. Green, 746 F.2d 927, 930 (2d Cir. 1984); *see* Duchek v. Jacobi, 646 F.2d 415 (9th Cir. 1981); United States *ex rel.* Goldman v. Merdith, 596 F.2d 1353 (8th Cir. 1979).

20 Fed. R. Civ. P. 69(a).

21 *See* Note, *Constitutional Law—Writ of Execution Statutes Held Unconstitutional—Has Due Process Notice Requirement Left Creditors Out In The Cold?* 13 U. Ark. Little Rock L.J. 293 (1991); *Cf.* Duhan v. Gravett, 302 Ark. 358, 790 S.W. 2d 155 (Ark. 1990); Dunham, *Postjudgment Seizures: Does Due Process Require Notice And Hearings?* 21 S.D.L. Rev. 78 (1976).

§ 5.5 Notice of Enforcement by the United States

Pursuant to the Federal Debt Collection Procedures Act, the United States, on the commencement of an action or proceedings to obtain a remedy to enforce a judgment, must follow the notice procedures contained in 28 U.S.C. § 3202(b). Counsel for the United States must prepare the notice which the Federal District Court Clerk issues. The form of the notice is provided in § 3202(b), and unlike the prejudgment notice required in § 3101(d), this subsection contains no requirement that the form of this notice must be approved by a majority of the chief judges of the federal districts in the State in which the court is located. This procedure is new, and prior to the Federal Debt Collection Procedures Act of 1990, it was not necessary for the United States to give a judgment debtor notice before commencing collection action.

The notice must identify the property seized by the United States, and identify the debt owed to the United States for which it was seized. The notice must include the potential exemptions available to the debtor, and must notify the debtor of the right to a hearing and formal claim of any exemptions chosen in accordance with § 3014. If the judgment is a default judgment, the debtor should be notified of the right to deny the debt, if the debtor believes the money is not owed to the United States. If the notice is for issuance of a writ of execution, the debtor should be informed that if a hearing is not requested within 20 days of receiving the notice, the property may be sold at public auction.

§ 5.6 Judgment Debtor's Right to Hearing on Notice by the United States

Within 20 days after the debtor receives notice of commencement of a remedy to enforce a judgment from the United States, the debtor may move to quash the order granting such remedy. The court that issued such order shall hold a hearing within five days or as soon thereafter as possible. The statute provides limitations on the issues at such hearing.

The first issue concerns the validity of the debtor's claim to exemptions. The debtor's right to claim exemptions is contained in § 3014. Basically rather than limit the debtor's right to exemptions, this section provides the debtor a choice of the following exemptions to claim:

1. The exemptions under the Bankruptcy Code in section 522(d) of title 11
2. Any property that is exempt under federal law other than the Bankruptcy Code exemptions

3. State or local law of the debtor's domicile that is applicable on the date the remedy application was filed by the United States

The second issue at the hearing may concern compliance by the United States with any statutory requirements or the issuance of the postjudgment remedy granted. The third issue at the hearing may concern the probable validity of the claim for the debt which is merged into the judgment and the existence of good cause for setting aside the judgment. These issues may only be heard if the judgment is a default judgment, and the Constitution or some other law of the United States provides a right to a hearing. Section 3202(d) by its terms clarifies that if the judgment debtor already had one hearing on these issues, § 3202(d)(3) does not afford opportunity for a second hearing, unless the Constitution or another law of the United States so provides.

By its terms, the statute is clear that if the judgment was obtained after trial, or on summary judgment, and thus, not a default judgment, the debtor has no right to a hearing on the probable validity of the claim for the debt which is merged into the judgment and the existence of good cause for setting it aside. This section by its terms, however, appears to extend the one year period for a debtor's opportunity to move for relief from judgment under Federal Rule of Civil Procedure 60(b). The Federal Debt Collection Procedures Act provides for the application of the Federal Rules of Civil Procedure, except as otherwise provided in the Act.[22] Federal Rule of Civil Procedure 60(b) provides for relief from judgment by a motion filed by the debtor "within a reasonable time, and for reasons (1), (2) and (3) not more than one year after the judgment, order, or proceedings was entered or taken." A default judgment can be set aside for any of the reasons contained in Rule 60(b).[23] Under the prior civil rules, therefore, the debtor must have filed a motion for relief from judgment within one year to obtain relief for the reasons states in Rule 60(b)(1), (2), and (3). After that date the motion by the debtor would be untimely by the limitations set in the rule.

However, the United States may attempt to enforce a default judgment obtained over a year before and notice is sent by counsel for the United States to the judgment debtor seeking enforcement of a remedy by the United States. Assuming the debtor never had a hearing on the prior default judgment, and even though more than a year has elapsed, the debtor has a right to a hearing under 28 U.S.C. § 3202(d), and can show good cause by providing the grounds listed at Federal Rules of Civil Procedure 60(b)(1), (2), and (3). This provision under § 3202(d), therefore, extends the definition of what is meant by a final default judgment by the United States. Of course, if the United States previously served the debtor for the prior Rule 60(b) hearing,

---

22 28 U.S.C. § 3003(F).

23 *Cf.* Fed. R. Civ. P. 55(c).

and the debtor failed to appear, counsel for the United States should argue at the § 3202(d) hearing that the debtor had the right to appear at the prior Rule 60(b) hearing, and chose not to exercise that right. Section 3202(b) is specific about guaranteeing the debtor the "right" to a hearing, but not a right to more than one such hearings.

§ 5.7 Right of the United States for Installment Payment Order

The requirements and procedures for the United States to obtain an installment payment order from a judgment debtor is provided by § 3204 of the Federal Debt Collection Procedures Act. Section 3204(c) clarifies that an order for installment payments may not be issued if a writ of garnishment is already in effect against the debtor's earnings, and also provides that any installment payment order may issue only against nonexempt disposable earnings of the debtor. However, an installment payment order may issue under certain conditions.

To have an installment payment order issue, the United States must demonstrate that the debtor will receive substantial nonexempt disposable earnings from self-employment that are not subject to garnishment or that the debtor is diverting or concealing substantial earnings from any source or property in lieu of earnings. Disposable earnings are defined in § 3002(5) as that part of earnings remaining after all deductions required by law have been withheld. Section 3002(6) defines earnings as compensation paid or payable for personal services, denominated as wages, salary, commission, bonus, or otherwise, and includes periodic payments pursuant to a pension or retirement program. Section 3002(9) defines nonexempt disposable earnings as 25 percent of disposable earnings, subject to § 303 of the Consumer Credit Protection Act.[24]

This section limits the types of debtors on which installment payment orders may be obtained. The debtors must be self-employed like doctors, accountants, and lawyers. The type of debtor would also include the debtor who controls a family business through a corporation, to which the debtor provides important services thereto, but may be paid no salary, to prevent creditor's from garnishing the same. In turn, the corporation pays for the debtor's expenses, such as medical expense, insurance expense, car expense, and other types of support expenses. In the past, this type of debtor has been difficult to collect against under traditional methods. Now § 3204 provides a method of reaching these concealed earnings.

Under the statute, the United States serves notice on the debtor and moves the court for an installment payment order. Notice of the motion must be

[24] 15 U.S.C. § 1673.

served on the debtor in the same manner as a summons, or served by registered or certified mail, return receipt requested. Subsequently, the court holds a hearing on the installment payment motion.

At the hearing the court considers several factors in fixing the amount of payment. Among the factors are:

1. The income, resources, and reasonable requirements of the judgment debtor and the judgment's dependents
2. Any other payments the judgment debtor is making on other judgments
3. The amount due on the judgment in favor of the United States

Any order issued is subject to later modification under § 3204(b), either on motion of the United States or of the judgment debtor, if the judgment debtor's financial circumstances have changed or previously undisclosed assets are discovered.

§ 5.8 Procedures for Garnishment

Garnishment is a statutory remedy which did not exist at common law.[25] Garnishment is a remedy with many uses, and is readily defined by caselaw. "Garnishment is a legal proceeding brought by a creditor (garnishor) of a person (the debtor) against a third party (garnishee) to obtain property of the debtor in the hands of the third party to satisfy the garnishor."[26] (See §§ **5.9** through **5.12** and **5.17** for futher discussion of this topic and related topics.) Garnishment has also been defined as "a statutory remedy which may be used by a creditor to obtain satisfaction of an indebtedness out of credits of the defendant debtor in the possession of a third party, the garnishee."[27] Simply explained, garnishment is the process where an obligation of a third party to the judgment debtor is reached by a writ of garnishment.[28] In some states the actual garnishment may be accomplished with a writ of attachment served on the garnishee.[29]

Federal Rule of Civil Procedure 64 recognizes that garnishment is one of the procedures available to seize property in a federal district court proceeding.

---

[25] United States v. Morris, 754 F. Supp. 185, 186 (D.N.M. 1991).

[26] Millard v. United States, 916 F.2d 1, 3 (Fed. Cir. 1990); *see* Harris v. Balk, 198 U.S. 215, 226 (1905). (See also §§ **5.9–5.12** and **5.17** for further discussion of this topic and related topics.)

[27] Stena Rederi AB v. Comision De Contratos Del Comite, 923 F.2d 380, 391 (5th Cir. 1991)

[28] Skevofilax v. Quigley, 810 F.2d 378, 390 (3d Cir.) (en banc), *cert. denied,* 481 U.S. 1029 (1987).

[29] Monarch Life Insurance Company v. Elam, 918 F.2d 201, 203 (D.C. Cir. 1990) (Applying D.C. Code § 16-546).

This procedure may be available in appropriate circumstances in both prejudgment and postjudgment proceedings in accordance with the practice of state law.[30]

Although Rule 64 of the Rules of Civil Procedure, 28 U.S.C., following § 723c, provides only for garnishment "for the purpose of securing satisfaction of the judgment *ultimately to be entered,* it is sanctioned practice of this District to issue garnishment after judgment as "proceedings supplementary to and in aid of judgment" under Rule 69(a), "in accordance with the practice and procedure" of the State of Michigan."[31]

The facts in the case of *Monarch Life Insurance Company v. Elam,*[32] illustrates how effective the use of a writ of garnishment can be in enforcing a judgment. Monarch obtained a judgment against Martha Elam in August 1988. Elam settled a tort suit with Sonya Steele on October 26, 1988, in the Federal District Court in the District of Columbia. The day before the settlement Monarch had filed a certified copy of its judgment against Elam in that Court. Monarch requested an attachment on judgment pursuant to D.C. Code § 16-546 (method of garnishment under state law), made applicable by Rule 69(a) of the Federal Rules of Civil Procedure. Monarch had the attachment served on Steele's insurance company, Government Employees Insurance Company on October 27, 1988. Monarch filed a motion for judgment in condemnation of the attached property with the court. Elam opposed the motion, asserting the claims of her attorney and certain assignees. On March 21, 1989, the court granted Monarch's motion. On appeal, the United States Court of Appeals certified the question of whether the settlement agreement created an attorney's charging lien on the settlement fund. However, the case illustrates the utility of garnishment in reaching the debtor's funds held by third parties.

In some instances, however, state law may make it easier to seize the judgment debtor's third party claim by way of supplementary proceedings. In supplementary proceedings, once the judgment debtor's right to the third party's claim is known, the third party should be impled as a defendant in the supplementary proceedings, and, after hearing, the claim is seized and ordered sold to satisfy the judgment.[33]

The authorities are unanimous that a federal court maintains ancillary jurisdiction to enforce its judgments, and it is not necessary that the federal court possess an independent basis of subject matter jurisdiction over a garnishee

---

30 Skevofilax v. Quigley, 810 F.2d 378, at 384–87 (3d Cir.) (en banc), *cert. denied,* 481 U.S. 1029, (1987); Schram v. Carlucci, 41 F. Supp. 36 (E.D. Mich. 1941).

31 Schram v. Carlucci, 41 F. Supp. 36, at 37 (E.D. Mich. 1941); *cf.* United States v. Pauly, 725 F. Supp. 923, 925–26 (W.D. Mich. 1989).

32 918 F.2d 201 (D.C. Cir. 1990).

33 *See* Wetherington, *Proceedings Supplementary To Seize The Judgment Debtor's Third Party Claim,* 65 Fla. B. J. 26 (1991); *see also* Supplementary Proceedings discussed in **Ch. 3.**

before allowance of the garnishment process.[34] However, the federal court must have "jurisdiction over either property that the court can apply to the satisfaction of the defendant's debt or persons who themselves owe an obligation to the defendant that the court can apply to the satisfaction of the debt."[35] "In garnishment cases, the court may exercise quasi in rem jurisdiction to the extent that it has jurisdiction 'over a person who is indebted to, or owes a duty to the defendant.'"[36]

Constitutional issues have long been present in garnishment cases, and still are a concern in the issuance of garnishment case, and still are a concern in the issuance of garnishment today. A brief history of some of the constitutional issues in garnishment cases will illustrate the importance of these issues. In 1924 the Supreme Court in *Endicott-Johnson Corp. v. Encyclopedia Press, Inc.,*[37] addressed the issue of whether due process required notice and an opportunity to be heard prior to the issuance of a writ of garnishment of a judgment debtor's wages. In that case, the court stated that the judgment debtor "has had his day in court" in the action, and must "take notice of what will follow."[38]

Over fifty years later in *Finberg v. Sullivan,*[39] in analyzing the Pennsylvania postjudgment garnishment procedures before garnishment of a bank account, the court reviewed the development of four recent prejudgment seizure opinions by the Supreme Court on due process, and held that garnishment might deprive a debtor of exempt property.

> We conclude that the four prejudgment seizure cases control the due process issue before us now. . . . The principles established in the controlling Supreme Court decisions [*Sniadach v. Family Finance Corp.,* 395 U.S. 337 (1969); *Fuentes v. Shevin,* 407 U.S. 67 (1972); *Mitchell v. W.T. Grant Co.,* 416 U.S. 600 (1974); *North Georgia Finishing, Inc. v. Di-Chem, Inc.,* 419 U.S. 601 (1975)], to summarize, are that notice and an opportunity to be heard before an attachment are absolutely necessary. However, the available procedures must afford the debtor adequate protection against erroneous or arbitrary seizures.

---

34 Skevofilax v. Quigley, 810 F.2d 378, 384 (3d Cir.) (en banc), *cert. denied,* 481 U.S. 1029, (1987); Blackburn Truck Lines, Inc. v. Francis, 723 F.2d 730, 732 (9th cir. 1984); Chambers v. Blickle Ford Sales, Inc., 313 F.2d 252, 256 (2d Cir. 1963); RCA Corp. v. Tucker, 696 F. Supp. 845, 850 (E.D.N.Y. 1988); American Safety Table Co. v. Schreiber & Goldberg, Inc., 320 F. Supp. 603, 604 (S.D.N.Y. 1970).

35 Stena Rederi AB v. Comision De Contratos Del Comite, 923 F.2d 380, 391 (5th Cir. 1991).

36 *Id.;* Belcher Co. of Alabama, Inc. v. M/V Maranatha Mariner, 724 F.2d 1161, 1164 (5th Cir. 1984).

37 226 U.S. 285 (1924).

38 *Id.,* at 288. (For further discussion of garnishment of a debtor's wages, see also §§ **5.12** and **5.17.**)

39 634 F.2d 50 (3d Cir. 1980).

> The procedural protection is adequate if it represents a fair accommodation of the respective interests of creditor and debtor.[40]

The Third Circuit in *Finberg v. Sullivan* reviewed the due process procedures of the Pennsylvania postjudgment garnishment statute, including the requirements for 1) a prompt postseizure hearing, 2) notice, and 3) preliminary affidavit, bond, and judicial issuance. First, the court found that the Pennsylvania statute did not provide the debtor a prompt hearing and adjudication on the debtor's claim of exemptions.[41] Second, in this case, the notice of garnishment was constitutionally defective, in that it did not inform Mrs. Finberg of her rights to exemptions for Social Security benefits or the $300 exemption under Pennsylvania law.[42] Third, the court did not find due process violations for the absence of the requirement to post a bond to compensate the judgment debtor or that a judge or magistrate issue the writ of execution.[43] Also, the Third Circuit held that the Pennsylvania postjudgment garnishment rules conflicted with the Social Security Act exemption, and thus were invalid under the supremacy clause of Article Six of the Constitution.[44]

Subsequent to the *Finberg* decision a number of courts held state garnishment statutes unconstitutional for not requiring notice and a prompt hearing after the garnishment of a judgment debtor.[45] It appears evident that the

---

40 634 F.2d 50, 58.

41 *Id.* at 59–61.

42 *Id.* at 61–62.

43 *Id.* at 62.

44 *Id.* at 62–63.

45 McCahey v. L.P. Investors, 774 F.2d 543 (2d Cir. 1985); Dionne v. Bouley, 583 F. Supp. 307 (D.R.I. 1984), *aff'd as modified,* 757 F.2d 1344 (1st Cir. 1985) (debtor's bank account garnished and contained Social Security exempt funds, but debtor not notified of the exemption for Social Security funds); Deary v. Guardian Loan Co., 534 F. Supp. 1178 (S.D.N.Y. 1982); Harris v. Bailey, 574 F. Supp. 966 (W.D. Va. 1983); Betts v. Tom, 431 F. Supp. 1369 (D. Haw. 1977); Clay v. Fisher, Inc., 584 F. Supp. 730 (S.D. Ohio 1984); Green v. Harbin, 615 F. Supp. 719 (D.C. Ala. 1985); Neeley v. Century Finance Co. of Arizona, 606 F. Supp. 1453 (D. Ariz. 1985); Davis v. Paschall, 640 F. Supp. 198 (E.D. Ark. 1986); Follette v. Vitanza, 658 F. Supp. 492, 512 (N.D.N.Y. 1987) (debtor needs notice of special exemptions to garnishment); Kirby v. Sprouls, 722 F. Supp. 516 (C.D. Ill. 1989) (due process requires notice of the garnishment proceedings, notice of exemptions and notice and opportunity for prompt judicial review); *cf.* Hutchinson v. Cox, 784 F. Supp. 1339, 1342–44 (S.D. Ohio 1992) (Ohio's postjudgment statutory procedure for execution on personal property declared unconstitutional where statute permitted execution without giving debtor notice of potentially available exemptions and procedures for claiming them); Duhon v. Gravett, 302 Ark. 358, 790 S.W.2d 155 (Ark. 1990); *See* Note *Constitutional Law—Writ of Execution Statutes Held Unconstitutional—Has Due Process Notice Requirement Left Creditors Out In The Cold,* 13 U. Ark. Little Rock L.J. 293 (1991); Note, *Constitutional Law—Due Process—Garnishment Procedures Must Provide For Notice To Postjudgment Debtor,* 9 U. Ark. Little Rock L.J. 517 (1987); *but see* Brown v. Liberty Loan Corp.,

Supreme Court, faced with a case similar to the *Finberg* facts would hold that due process requires notice of exemptions and the opportunity for a prompt judicial review for the debtor on the exemptions issue. The Supreme Court decision on prejudgment attachment is evidence of its intent to prevent unconstitutional deprivation of property, especially where the burden on the creditor is not very great to serve the writ on the debtor, notify the debtor of the right to exemptions, and then require the district courts to give a prompt hearing.[46]

Practice Tips

Wages and salaries, bank account deposits, and contract rights, such as insurance proceeds or cash surrender value are some of the debts most frequently garnished by creditors.

1. For a specific discussion of garnishment of bank accounts, see Bailey, *What Lawyers Should Know About the Garnishment of Bank Accounts,* 32 Prac. Law 27 (1986) (Part I); 32 Prac. Law 45 (1986) (Part II).
2. For a specific discussion of garnishment of contract rights, see Henderson, *Garnishment and Execution of Contract Rights,* 24 Idaho L. Rev. 1 (1987–88) (Part I) and 24 Idaho L. Rev. 183 (1987–88) (Part II); Israeloff, *Postjudgment Enforcement and Collection Actions Within 30 Days After Entry of Judgment,* 51 Texas B. J. 126, 127 (1988).
3. For a specific discussion of garnishment of wages and salaries, see Martaus, *Garnishment of Employee Wages in Ohio: Whose Money Is It Anyway?,* 18 Ohio N.U.L. Rev. 197 (1991); Toben and Toben, *Using Turnover Relief to Reach the Nonexempt Paycheck,* 40 Baylor L. Rev. 195 (1988).

§ 5.9 Postjudgment Garnishment by the United States

The postjudgment garnishment remedies available to the United States have recently been renovated by passage of the Federal Debt Collection Procedures Act of 1990. According to the requirements of 28 U.S.C. § 3205, the United States has a right to postjudgment garnishment against nonexempt property in which the debtor has an interest and which is in the possession,

---

539 F.2d 1355 (5th Cir. 1976) (Florida garnishment statutes constitutional even though they require neither notice to the debtor nor an opportunity for a hearing prior to garnishment); Haines v. General Motors Corp., 603 F. Supp. 471 (S.D. Ohio 1983).

[46] Connecticut v. Doehr, 501 U.S. 1 (1991). (See the discussion of the due process issues in the *Doehr* case in § **5.2** above.)

custody, and control of a person other than the debtor. This section authorizes garnishment of the judgment debtor's wages, but consideration must be given to the Consumer Credit Protection Act, 15 U.S.C. § 1673, which limits garnishment to 25 percent of the debtor's disposable earning and to 28 U.S.C. § 3014 which authorizes the debtor to elect exemptions. The restrictions on garnishment in 15 U.S.C. § 1673 specify that, except as provided in subsection (b) of that section,

> the maximum part of the aggregate disposable earnings of an individual for any work week which is subjected to garnishment may not exceed: (1) 25 percentum of his disposable earnings for that week, or (2) the amount by which his disposable earnings for that week exceed thirty times the federal minimum hourly wage prescribed by section 206(a)(1) of Title 29 in effect at the time the earnings are payable, whichever is less.

Under § 3205, a court may issue simultaneous separate writs of garnishment to several garnishees. The statute provides general and specific requirements for the form of the writ in §§ 3205(b)(1) and (c)(2), and provides specific requirements for a particular property to be garnished in § 3205(b)(2). The Federal Debt Collection Procedures Act, in § 3205(c)(3), requires service of the writ on both the garnishee and the judgment debtor. Under § 3205(c)(3), counsel for the United States shall certify to the court that this service was made.

Naturally, when the writ of garnishment is served on the debtor, it must be accompanied by a notice of enforcement as required by § 3202(b) and contain a notice concerning the debtor's right to claim the exemptions provided either by federal law or state law as contained in § 3014. The notice shall also notify the debtor of a right to a hearing within five days after the request is made with the clerk of court. these procedures required in §§ 3205 and 3202 for notice to the debtor, notice of the debtor's right to claim exemptions, and the right to a prompt postseizure hearing appear to comply with constitutional due process in accordance with the line of cases such as *Finberg v. Sullivan,*[47] and the other cases mentioned in this section.

A writ of garnishment issued on behalf of the United States may be served in any state an enforced by the court which issued the writ, in accordance with § 3004(b). This has long been a right of the United States to have longarm execution and garnishment under 28 U.S.C. § 2413.[48] Under the Federal Debt Collection Procedures Act, the debtor may request, in accordance with

---

[47] 634 F.2d 50 (3d Cir. 1980).

[48] United States v. Thornton, 672 F.2d 101, 217 U.S. App. D.C. 248 (D.C. Cir. 1982); United States *ex. rel.* Marcus v. Lord Electric Company, 43 F. Supp. 12 (W.D.Pa. 1942); *cf.* United States v. Palmer, 609 F. Supp. 544 (E.D. Tenn. 1985); *see* Brown, *An Analysis: Federal Registration Of Judgments vs. Federal Longarm Execution,* 91 Comm. L.J. 283 (1986).

§ 3004(b)(2), that the proceeding on the writ of garnishment be transferred to the district court for the district in which the debtor resides.

§ 5.10 Answering and Discharge on Garnishment

In the garnishment process, once the garnishee has been served, the particular garnishment law provides the procedure required for answering.[49] Under § 3205(c)(4), the garnishee having been served a writ of garnishment by the United States shall answer by filing with the court and serving a copy of the answer on the debtor and counsel for the United States. As provided in § 3205(c)(4), the answer shall state under oath

> (A) the garnishee has custody, control or possession of such property; (B) a description of such property and value of such interest; (C) a description of any previous garnishments to which such property is subject and the extent to which any remaining property is not exempt; and (D) the amount of the debt the garnishee anticipates owing to the judgment debtor in the future and whether the period for payment will be weekly or another specified period.

The judgment debtor or the United States, within 20 days of receipt of the answer, may file a written objection to the answer and request a hearing. The objecting party must include the grounds for the objection and bears the burden of proof for such grounds at the hearing.[50] If the garnishee fails to answer the writ of garnishment or to withhold property in accordance with the writ, the United States may, by petition, seek to require the garnishee to answer the writ and to withhold property before the appearance date. If the garnishee fails to appear or fails to show good cause for failure to comply with the writ, the court shall enter a judgment against the garnishee.[51] The judgment is limited to the value of the judgment debtor's nonexempt interest in such property (including nonexempt disposable earnings).

If the garnishee files an answer and no timely hearing is requested, the court shall enter an order directing the garnishee to dispose of the judgment debtor's nonexempt interest in the property. If there is a hearing requested, the court shall enter an order within five days of the hearing, or as soon thereafter as is practical.[52] Garnishments issued under § 3205 shall have priority over writs which are issued later in time, but judicial orders and garnishments for

---

[49] *Cf.* 28 U.S.C. § 3205(c)(4).

[50] 28 U.S.C. § 3205(c)(5).

[51] 28 U.S.C. § 3205(c)(6).

[52] 28 U.S.C. § 3205(c)(7).

the support of a person have priority over § 3205 writs.[53] The United States is required to give an annual accounting on the garnishment to the judgment debtor and the garnishee.[54]

The garnishment terminates:

1. by an order of the court terminating the writ
2. by exhaustion of the property subject to the writ
3. satisfaction of the debt for which the writ was issued.[55]

The United States must give a cumulative written accounting to the judgment debtor and the garnishee of all property it received under the writ of garnishment within 10 days after the garnishment terminates. The judgment debtor or garnishee may file a written objection within 10 days after such accounting and request a hearing.[56] Any person who pays or delivers to the United States money or other personal property of the judgment debtor is discharged from an obligation to the judgment debtor to the extent of the payment or delivery.[57]

§ 5.11 Exemptions Available under the Federal Debt Collection Procedures Act

Section 3014 of Title 28 specifies the types of property and interests in property which are protected from seizure by any other procedure used by the United States under the Federal Debt Collection Procedures. Under this section the individual debtor may elect one of two alternatives. Section 3014(a) permits a judgment debtor to elect either the exemptions listed in § 522(d) of the Bankruptcy Code or the exemptions applicable under other federal law, as well as exemptions available under the law of the state where the debtor has been domiciled for 180 days, and any interest the debtor had, prior to filing the exemption application, in joint, entirety, or community property.[58] The Bankruptcy Code permits the debtor to exempt $7,500 in equity in a residence, $1,200 in equity in a motor vehicle, $500 in jewelry and $4,000 in personal property.[59] If the debtor does not own a residence, or has less than $7,500 in equity in the residence, the debtor may exempt an additional

[53] 28 U.S.C. § 3205(c)(8).

[54] 28 U.S.C. § 3205(c)(9)(A).

[55] 28 U.S.C. § 3205(c)(10)(A), (B), and (C).

[56] 28 U.S.C. § 3205(c)(9)(B).

[57] 28 U.S.C. § 3206.

[58] 28 U.S.C. § 3014(a)(1) and (2)(A) and (B).

[59] 11 U.S.C. § 522(d).

$3,750 in personal property.[60] The Bankruptcy Code permits additional exemptions for such items as insurance contracts, pensions, and various benefits such as Social Security.[61] The state law concerning exemptions will vary according to the particular state law.

The statute sets forth a procedure for a debtor to claim and a creditor to contest the exemption claim in § 3014(b). This section will help to prevent fraud and abuse in the exemption process when the debtor attempts to prevent collection by claiming exemptions which do not apply. Under that section, the United States or the debtor may request a hearing by the court to determine the applicability of any exemption claimed by the debtor. The debtor bears the burden of proof at the hearing, unless it is reasonably evident that the exemption applies. The court will decide the issue on which, if any, exemptions apply. The court may order the debtor to file under oath a statement with regard to any claimed exemption, describing each item of exempt property, the basis for its value, and the nature of the debtor's interest. Similar procedures for challenging exemption claims are contained in 11 U.S.C. § 522 of the Bankruptcy Code and Bankruptcy Rule 4003.

§ 5.12 Restrictions on Execution and Garnishment

Of course, each state has statutes which restrict execution, levy, attachment, garnishment, or other legal process because of specific state restrictions or exemption laws. These state provisions are extensive and varied. It is beyond the scope of this book to discuss each specific state exemption law.

As has been discussed in **§ 5.11,** the Bankruptcy Code provides certain exemptions in 11 U.S.C. § 522 of the Bankruptcy Code. However, there are certain federal laws which restrict execution and garnishment by creditors.

First, with an exception as noted below, no money paid as Social Security benefits is subject to garnishment, among other things.[62] For example, Virginia postjudgment garnishment procedures which permitted a judgment creditor to freeze a debtor's social security benefits deposited to her bank account were held to violate the supremacy clause because they conflict with the Social Security exemption in 42 U.S.C. § 407(a).[63] This section of the Social Security Act provides:

---

[60] 11 U.S.C. § 522(d)(5).

[61] 11 U.S.C. § 522(d)(7)–(11).

[62] 42 U.S.C. § 407(a).

[63] Harris v. Bailey, 574 F. Supp. 966, 972 (W.D. Va. 1983); *cf.* Demp v. Emerson Enterprises, 504 F. Supp. 281, 284 (E.D. Pa. 1980).

> The right of any person to any future payment under this subchapter shall not be transferable or assignable, at law or in equity, and none of the moneys paid or payable or rights existing under this subchapter shall be subject to execution, levy, attachment, garnishment, or other legal process, or to the operation of any bankruptcy or insolvency law.

However, there is an exception to this restriction. The exception is provided in 42 U.S.C. § 659 wherein:

> The United States waived its sovereign immunity from state garnishment actions directed at federal employees. The statute simply removed the bar of sovereign immunity to one narrow class of actions: enforcement of garnishment writs issued by state courts. . . . The language of § 659 waives Government immunity only from legal process 'brought for the enforcement . . . of [the] legal obligations to provide child support of make alimony payments.[64]

Another restriction on garnishment concerns annuities authorized to federal judges and their survivors which are also exempt from garnishment or other legal process.[65] Section 376(n) of Title 28 of the United States Code provides: "No annuity authorized under this section shall be assignable, either in law or in equity, except as provided in subsections (s) and (t), or subject to execution, levy, attachment, garnishment, or other legal process."

Another federal statute, the Consumer Credit Protection Act, also provides for certain restrictions on garnishment.[66] Under the Consumer Credit Protection Act, *garnishment* is defined as "any legal or equitable procedure through which the earnings of any individual are required to be withheld for payment of any debt."[67] The restrictions provided in § 1673 restrict garnishment of disposable earnings to an amount not to exceed 25 per cent of the disposable earnings for the week, or the amount by which a debtor's disposable earning for the week exceed 30 times the federal minimum hourly wage prescribed by the Secretary of Labor under § 206(a)(1) of Title 29 in effect at the time the earnings are payable, whichever is less.[68] Section 1673(b) provides for certain exceptions. The exceptions include state support orders, wage earner plans under Chapter 13 of the Bankruptcy Code, and any debts

---

64 Overman v. United States, 563 F.2d 1287, 1291 (8th Cir. 1977); *cf.* Diaz v. Diaz, 568 F.2d 1061, 1063 (4th Cir. 1977); Lamerand v. Lamerand, 499 F. Supp. 1109, 1111 (C.D. Calif. 1980); Bank of Denver v. Romstrom, 496 F. Supp. 242, 244 (D. Colo. 1980).

65 28 U.S.C. § 376(n).

66 15 U.S.C. § 1673.

67 15 U.S.C. § 1672(c).

68 15 U.S.C. § 1673(a)(1), (2).

due for taxes to a state or the federal government.[69] Furthermore, under the supremacy clause, the garnishment restrictions provided in the Consumer Credit Protection Act preempt state laws when state laws would permit recovery in excess of the 25 percent without other exceptions applying.[70]

§ 5.13 *Writ Ne Exeat Republica*

Federal courts are authorized to issue a *writ ne exeat republica* pursuant to 28 U.S.C. § 1651 when the circumstances warrant. Where the debtor owes a debt that is positively due, certain in amount, and is threatening or about to leave the jurisdiction, federal courts may issue this writ to prevent such departure and require the U.S. Marshall, or other appropriate law enforcement agent, to seize and bring the debtor before the court. Section 1651 is often described as the "All Writs Act." 28 U.S.C. § 1651 states:

> (a) The Supreme Court and all courts established by Act of Congress may issue all writs necessary or appropriate in aid of their respective jurisdictions and agreeable to the usages and principles of law.
>
> (b) An alternative writ or rule nisi may be issued by a justice or judge of a court which has jurisdiction.

In the historical and revision note to this section of Title 28, it is indicated that § 1651 is a consolidation of three prior Code sections, §§ 342, 376, and 377 of Title 28, U.S.C. (1940). Prior § 376 provided:

> *Writs of ne exeat* may be granted by any justice of the Supreme Court, in case where they might be granted by the Supreme Court; and *by any district judge,* in cases where they might be granted by the district court of which he is a judge. But no writ of ne exeat shall be granted unless a suit in equity is commenced, and satisfactory proof is made to the court or judge granting the same that defendant designs quickly to depart from the United States. (emphasis supplied.)[71]

The function of the writ was described by the Supreme Court of the United States in the following language in the case of *D. Ginsberg & Sons, Inc. v. Popkin:*[72]

---

69 Snapp v. U.S. Postal Service-Texarkana Management Sectional Center, 664 F.2d 1329, 1331 (5th Cir. 1982); Midlantic National Bank/North v. Reif, 732 F. Supp. 354, 358 n.2 (E.D.N.Y. 1980).

70 *Cf.* Donovan v. Hamilton County Municipal Court, 580 F. Supp. 554, 556 (S.D. Ohio 1984); Hodgson v. Hamilton Municipal Court, 349 F. Supp. 1125, 1140 (S.D. Ohio 1972).

71 *Cf. In Re* Foster Construction Corporation, 50 F.2d 693 (2d Cir. 1931).

72 285 U.S. 204 (1931).

> Speaking for the Supreme Court of Wisconsin in *Davidor v. Rosenberg,* 130 Wis. 22, 109 N.W. 925, Mr. Justice Winslow described the writ of *ne exeat* as follows (p. 29): 'At common law it was simply a writ to obtain equitable bail. It was issued by a court of equity on application of the complainant against the defendant when it appeared that there was a debt positively due, certain in amount, or capable of being made certain, on an equitable demand not suable at law (except in cases of account and possibly some other cases of concurrent jurisdiction), and that the defendant was about to leave the jurisdiction, having conveyed away his property, or under other circumstances which would render any decree ineffectual.[73]

Justice Winslow's description of the writ sets forth the two basic requirements for issuance of the *Writ Ne Exeat Republica,* as has been established by cases applying federal common caw principles. Federal courts have upheld the use of such writs when the circumstances present meet the requirements for issuance of such a writ.[74] First, there is a debt positively due and certain in amount. Second, there is a threatened or impending departure of the defendant from the jurisdiction.[75] "The power of a district court to issue a *writ ne exeat republica,* though seldom exercised, is not questioned."[76] The writ is constitutional if issued for proper reasons.[77] Since the writ naturally interferes with the debtor's right of travel, the burden is always on the moving party to show that exceptional circumstances exist which warrant the relief requested.[78] The burden is not like that for issuance of an injunction under Federal Rule of Civil Procedure 65.[79]

---

[73] *Id.* at 208–09.

[74] United States v. Shaheen, 445 F.2d 6 (7th Cir. 1971); United States v. Lipper, 86,880 U.S. Tax Cas. (CCH) par. 9330 (N.D. Cal. 1981); United States v. McNulty, 446 F. Supp. 90 (N.D. Cal. 1978); United States v. Clough, 33 AFTR 2d 74-650 (N.D. Cal. 1974); United States v. Robbins, 235 F. Supp. 353 (E.D. Ark. 1964); National Automobile and Casualty Insurance Co. v. Queck, 405 P.2d 905 (Ct. App. Ariz. 1965); Summers v. District Court, Second District, Washoe County, 227 P.2d 201 (Sup. Ct. Nev. 1951).

[75] United States v. Lipper, 86,880 U.S. Tax Cas. (CCH) ¶ 9330 (N.D. Cal. 1981) (besides § 1651 of Title 28, the Lipper court also relied on § 7402(a) of Title 26, the Internal Revenue Code provision which specifically permits issuance of such writs in aid of tax collection).

[76] United States v. Shaheen, 445 F.2d 6, 9 (7th Cir. 1971); United States v. Robbins, 235 F. Supp. 353, at 355 (E.D. Ark. 1964).

[77] United States v. Lipper, 86,880 U.S. Tax Cas. (CCH) ¶ 9330, at 86,884; United States v. Shaheen, 445 F.2d 6, at 9–10.

[78] *Id.*

[79] United States v. Shaheen, 445 F.2d 6, at 10.

§ 5.14 —Form of *Writ Ne Exeat Republica*

FORM 5-1
WRIT NE EXEAT REPUBLICA

[Usual headnote of the Court and Caption of the Case]

WRIT NE EXEAT REPUBLICA

THE PRESIDENT OF THE UNITED STATES OF AMERICA to the UNITED STATES MARSHALL, any DEPUTY UNITED STATES MARSHALL, or any SPECIAL AGENT of the FEDERAL BUREAU OF INVESTIGATION in any District in which [Name], defendant, may be found.

It is represented to this Court on behalf of the United States, that the above captioned action has resulted in the entry of a final judgment in favor of the United States and against [Name], defendant, personally in the sum of [Amount], including interest, which sum has remained unpaid since the entry of the judgment.

It appears to the Court, upon affidavits and evidence presented by the United States, that the said defendant, [Name], plans to leave the limits and jurisdiction of the United States, and as a result would leave the judgment owing to the United States unpaid.

To prevent this injustice, WE HEREBY COMMAND YOU to without delay cause the said defendant, [Name], to be taken into your custody in order that he shall come before the United States Magistrate Judge and give sufficient bail or security, in the sum of [Amount], that the defendant [Name], so that defendant shall not go, or attempt to go, into parts beyond the limits of the United States, beyond the jurisdiction of this Court, without the leave of this Court. Furthermore, you are authorized to seize and retain any passport which you may find in the possession of said defendant, [Name], until further order of this Court.

If the said defendant, [Name], shall refuse to give such bail or security, then you are to commit him, the said defendant, [Name], to jail, there to keep him in safe custody until he shall do so on his own accord. Then, when you have taken such security, you are forthwith to make and return a signed certificate of the same to this Court, together with this Writ.

[Seal]

____
CLERK OF THE UNITED STATES
DISTRICT COURT FOR THE
DISTRICT OF ____________

RETURN

I CERTIFY that I have caused the within-named [Name], defendant, to be arrested at [Time] o'clock on [Date] in the ____________ District of ____________. In addition, I have / have not seized any passport found in the possession of [Name], the defendant.

1. That he has given security in the sum required by the command of this Writ.

2. That he has failed to give security as required by the command of this Writ, and has been confined to jail in this District.

____
Title: ____________________
__________ District of _____

DATE: _____________ 19__.

§ 5.15 Execution on Real Estate

Sections 5.15 through **5.20** in this book address execution against different kinds of property. Certain general rules concerning execution can be made. Generally, the types of property subject to execution and the method of levy as to each are as diverse as there are states and territories. Generally, the law of the state where the property is situate controls the type of property subject to execution and the procedure and not the law of the state where the owner resides or where the judgment was rendered. Another general rule is that all property or interest in property, not exempt by statute that the debtor can voluntarily transfer, sell, convey, mortgage, pledge, or assign is subject to execution.

Real estate, if not otherwise exempt, is subject to execution in nearly all jurisdictions. In some states, the creditor may proceed against realty or personalty as the creditor chooses. In other states, the creditor must first proceed against personal property to attempt to satisfy the judgment, and only after the personal property is exhausted, may the real estate be executed upon and sold. The purpose of this book is to give an overview and comparison of some of the federal and state laws concerning the execution process. Because of the variety and complexity of the federal and state laws and procedures concerning the execution process, it would be impossible to discuss all of them in detail. Specific federal and state laws and rules of procedure should be consulted for specific execution problems.

Practice Tips

1. Before attempting to execute against real estate, be certain to obtain an accurate description of the property from the appropriate county recorder's office or registry of deeds.
2. Review the state or federal procedures applicable, and be certain to follow them step by step.
3. Determine what exemptions are applicable to this particular parcel of real estate, particularly state homestead exemptions, if any.
4. Determine what previous liens and encumbrances attach to the property and what probable equity remains in the property to make the sale of real property worthwhile.
5. Have a writ of execution issued by the applicable court clerk or other administrator of the court as required by law.
6. Give the sheriff or U.S. Marshal specific instructions for the execution process by completing the instructions for a service form, such as a USM-285 form or other instructional document required for use in the issuing court.
7. Ascertain if the sheriff or U.S. Marshal should file the levy of execution, and suspend the process, or whether under the applicable law the executing officer must follow through with levy, execution, and sale of the real property within a specific time frame, or release the property from the execution process.
8. If the executing officer requires any advance fees, be certain that the executing officer is given checks or other money instruments to pay for any required fees to process the levy and execution at the appropriate recording office.

Selected Statutes and Procedures for Real Estate Execution

United States. Under the Federal Debt Collection Procedures Act of 1990 all property in which the judgment debtor has a substantial nonexempt interest shall be subject to levy pursuant to a writ of execution.[80] What is exempt property is determined by the judgment debtor's election under § 3014 of the statute. However, *substantial* is not defined in the definitional part of the Act in § 3002. Substantial will likely be defined by the courts to be some minimum monetary value, below which execution on real estate shall not be allowed by the United States. The exact meaning of *substantial* may likely become an issue for litigation, and there will likely be disagreement on its meaning among different courts. Prior to the Federal Debt Collection Procedures Act there had not been such a requirement for the United States before issuance of a writ of execution.

---

[80] 28 U.S.C. § 3203.

Since the United States must prepare a notice for the clerk to issue under § 3202(b) before execution can issue and the debtor has an opportunity for a hearing, it is likely that the judgment debtor can raise at the hearing the issue of whether the debtor has a "substantial" interest in any real estate that is nonexempt. Although not specifically addressed under § 3202(b) as an item on the agenda for a hearing, these hearing are the obvious forum where judicial determinations will define what is the meaning of "substantial."

Unlike some state laws, the Federal Debt Collection Procedures Act does not require execution on personal property before execution is allowed against real property. Under § 3203(c)(1), multiple writs may issue simultaneously, and successive writs of execution may issue before the return date of a writ previously issued. An execution lien, effective from the time of the levy, is created in favor of the United States once the real property is levied on under a writ of execution.[81]

Federal law requires a specific form of a writ of execution by the United States. The execution writ must contain the following:

1. The specific date the judgment is entered
2. The court in which it is entered
3. The amount of any money judgment
4. The amount of any costs
5. The amount of any interest due
6. The sum due as of the date the writ is issued
7. The rate of post judgment interest
8. The name of the judgment debtor
9. The judgment debtor's last known address.

California. The California Civil Code permits execution against real estate. California has detailed statutes providing for the enforcement of money judgments, and the specific statutes should be consulted regarding execution against specific property. Except as otherwise provided by law, all property that is subject to enforcement of a money judgment pursuant to Article 1 (commencing with § 695.010) of Chapter 1 is subject to levy under a writ of execution to satisfy a money judgment.[82]

Judgment creditors, however, may execute only to the extent of the judgment debtor's actual interest in the real property.[83] The steps in the real estate execution and sale process have been explained by the court as follows:

[81] 28 U.S.C. § 3203(b).

[82] Cal. Civ. Code § 699.710 (West 1983).

[83] Jose v. Pacific Title and Procelain Company, 251 Cal. App. 2d 141, 58 Cal. Rptr. 880, 883 (Cal. Dist. Ct. App. 1967).

> The first step for execution on a dwelling house if for the judgment creditor to have the superior court issue a writ of execution. (§§ 699.510, 699.520.) The judgment creditor then delivers the writ to the levying officer with instructions for service to enforce the money judgement. (§§ 699.520 and 699.530.) Next, the officer levies on the real property. After the levy, the officer is required to promptly serve notice on the judgment creditor that the levy has been made. (§ 704.750, subd.(a).) Within 20 days after the notice is served, the judgment creditor must apply for an order of sale or the property will be released. (Ibid.) The application must state whether the dwelling is a homestead and must also state the amount of any liens or encumbrances on the dwelling. (§ 704.760.) If the court thereafter determines that the dwelling is exempt, it must also determine the fair market value and make an order for its sale subject to the homestead exemption. (§ 704.780, subd. (b).) If no bid is received at the sale which exceeds the amount of the homestead exemption plus the amount needed to satisfy all liens an encumbrances, the homestead cannot be sold. (§ 704.800, subd. (a).) Finally if no bid in excess of 90 percent of the fair market value of the dwelling (as determined pursuant to section 704.780) is received, the creditor must return to court and seek an order permitting the sale for the highest bid that exceeds the total amount of the homestead exemption and all liens and encumbrances. (§ 704.800 subd. (b).)[84]

In California, leasehold interest are subject to levy and seizure pursuant to a writ of execution, and the lessee's interest in real property may be applied to satisfy a money judgment.[85] The interest of one cotenant may be levied against to satisfy a judgment rendered against that cotenant.[86]

Florida. In Florida, real property that is not otherwise exempt, is subject to execution. "Lands and tenements, goods and chattels, equities of redemption in real and personal property, and stock in corporations, shall be subject to levy and sale under execution."[87] Under this section, lands and tenements, not otherwise exempt, such as homesteads, are subject to levy and sale under a writ of execution.[88] The lien of an execution operates upon and binds real property which is subject to levy and sale as the order requires.[89] A real estate mortgage is not subject to execution as it is considered only a contract right.[90] A seller's interest under an executory real estate sales contract is subject to being executed and sold, since until full payment on the sales price legal title remains in the seller.[91]

---

84 Kahn v. Berman, 198 Cal. App. 3d 1499, 244 Cal. Rptr. 575 (Cal. Dist. Ct. App. 1988).

85 Archibald v. Iacopi, 120 Cal. 2d 666, 262 P.2d 40 (Cal. 1953).

86 Moore v. Hall, 250 Cal. App. 2d 25, 58 Cal. Rptr. 70 (Cal. Dist. Ct. App. 1967).

87 Fla. Stat. § 56.061 (1967).

88 Evins v. Gainesville National Bank, 80 Fla. 84, 85 So. 659 (1920).

89 *Id.*

90 *Id.;* Ratliff v. Nowery, 80 Fla. 84, 85 So. 659 (1920).

91 Latin-American Bank v. Rogers, 87 Fla. 147, 99 So. 546 (1924).

Maine. In Maine, if the judgment debtor owns nonexempt real property, the judgment creditor can obtain turnover and sale orders from the court, and the property may be ordered sold in full or partial satisfaction of the judgment.[92] Any order entered pursuant to this section, and properly recorded with the registry of deeds, constitutes a lien against the property and the proceeds of any disposition of the property by the judgment debtor which occurs at any time after entry of the order.[93] Once taken on execution, the real estate must be appraised by three disinterested persons. These persons are chosen, one each, by the creditor, the debtor, and the officer charged with the execution for service. Each appraiser, besides signing the back of the execution, gives a value of the real estate and describes it thereon, or on a document annexed to the writ of execution.[94]

Maryland. In Maryland, a sheriff receiving a writ of execution may seize and sell real property held by the judgment debtor.[95] The recordation of the money judgment in the appropriate Maryland county gives the creditor a lien on real estate in that county.[96] Under the Maryland Code, the sheriff is permitted to execute the writ, conduct the sale and distribute the proceeds.[97]

Nevada. Nevada is an example of a state which requires a writ of execution to be satisfied first out of personal property of the debtor, and, if sufficient personal property cannot be found, then out of the real property of the judgment debtor.[98]

New York. In New York, a sheriff who receives a writ of execution may seize and sell real estate of the judgment debtor to satisfy a judgment.

> Section 5230 sets forth the requirements for obtaining an execution. It provides that a judgment creditor's attorney or the clerk of the appropriate court may issue an execution. The execution is mailed or delivered to an enforcement officer, such as a sheriff or a city marshall, and directs the officer to satisfy the judgment out of the real and personal property of the judgment debtor. *McCahey v. L.P. Investors,* 593 F. Supp. 319 (E.D.N.Y. 1984), *aff'd,* 774 F.2d 543 (2d Cir. 1985).[99]

---

92 Me. Rev. Stat. Ann. tit. 14 § 3131(1), (2).

93 Me. Rev. Stat. Ann. tit. 14 § 3131(9).

94 Me. Rev. Stat. Ann. tit. 14 §§ 2001–2003.

95 Md. Cts. & Jud. Proc. Code Ann. § 11-501 (1983); *cf.* Buckeye Development Corporation v. Brown & Shilling, Inc., 243 Md. 224, 220 A.2d 922 (1966).

96 Md. Cts. & Jud. Proc. §§ 2-625, 3-625.

97 *Id.*

98 Nev. Rev. Stat. § 21.020 (1985).

99 N.Y. Civ. Prac. Law § 5230 (McKinney Supp. 1983); N.Y. Civ. Prac. Law § 5236 (McKinney 1978); United States v. Paccione, 948 F.2d 851, 856 (2d Cir. 1991) (New York law authorizes the sale of real property to satisfy a money judgment).

A levy of real estate docketed with the county clerk's office subjects the real property to a lien which is valid for 10 years.[100]

Ohio. In Ohio, real estate, not otherwise exempt, is subject to levy and sale upon a writ of execution.[101]

Texas. Real property of the judgment debtor is subject to execution and levy on a money judgment in Texas.[102] Homesteads are exempt under the Texas Constitution.[103] In Texas, however, the sheriff is first required to ask the defendant to designate property upon which the execution can be levied. If defendant fails to designate property, then the sheriff may levy on any property of the judgment debtor subject to execution.[104]

> [I]n Texas the statutory term 'execution' includes writs of possession which . . . may include an order to the sheriff, in addition to the direction to place a successful party to a land action in possession, to make on execution any damages or costs of suit that may be awarded the successful party.[105]

Execution on a judgment must be issued within ten years or else the judgment is dormant if not revived.[106]

Virginia. In Virginia, personal property must be levied on before real estate.[107] However, if the state is the plaintiff, execution can issue against real estate, as well as personal property.[108]

---

100 N.Y. Civ. Prac. Law § 5203(a).

101 Ohio Rev. Code Ann. § 2329.01 (1953); *cf.* National Bank v. Tennessee Coal, Iron & C. Co., 62 Ohio St. 564, 57 N.E. 450 (1900).

102 Tex. R. Civ. P. 630, 637; *cf.* Pace v. McEwen, 617 S.W.2d 816 (Tex. Civ. App. 1981) (the Texas Turnover Statute, Tex. Rev. Civ. Stat. Ann. § 3827a (Vernon Supp. 1983–84), now codified in Tex. Civ. Prac. Code Ann. § 31.002 (Vernon 1986), was used to establish the procedure by which the court determined whether or not money wrongfully obtained was used to purchase a homestead; and whether or not the property was actually a homestead and thereby exempt from execution).

103 Tex. Const. Art. VII, § 22 (1845); *See* McKnight, *Protection Of The Family From Seizure By Creditors: The Sources And Evolution Of A Legal Principle,* 86 S.W. Hist.Q. 364, 375 (1983).

104 Tex. R. Civ. P. 637.

105 Williams v. Masterson, 306 S.W.2d 152, 155–56 (Tex. Civ. App. 1957); Tex. R. Civ. P. 622, 629, 632.

106 Tex. Civ. Prac. Code Ann. § 34.001 (Vernon 1986).

107 Va. Code § 8.01–203.

108 Va. Code § 8.01–201.

§ 5.16 Execution on Tangible Personal Property

The general rule on tangible personal property is that all personal property that the debtor can voluntarily transfer is subject to execution unless exempt by statute. The usual method of execution and levy on personal property is to take possession or such control that would be a trespass except for the writ of execution. However, "California, Connecticut, and Maine have recently developed statutes that enable a judgment creditor to get a non-possessory lien on a debtor's personal property by filing a simple document in an appropriate state office."[109] In analyzing these new statutory methods, Professor Woodward states:

> California, Connecticut, and Maine have each made it inexpensive and easy for a judgment creditor to get a judgment lien on personalty. In each state, a judgment creditor can, by filing an appropriate document in the correct office, state a claim to much of the debtor's personal property. The lien created by this procedure will secure the judgment creditor's priority in the personalty against many later claimants. Obtaining a judgment lien in these states is possible without using the sheriff, without removing the property from the debtor's control, and without much of the risk and cost one must sustain in other states to get a similar priority advantage.[110]

§ 5.17 Execution on Wages and Salaries

In many jurisdictions, wages and salaries may be reached by garnishment proceedings or special execution procedures peculiar to wages and salaries.[111] In some states, wages and salaries are exempt from execution or other judicial process. Of course, the exemption may be lost when the wages and salary have been received by the employee (debtor) and are commingled with the debtor's other property. Moreover, federal law preempts conflicting provisions of state law concerning the maximum amount of wages which can be garnished.[112]

---

109 Woodard, *New Judgment Liens On Personal Property: Does "Efficient" Mean "Better,"* 27 Harv. J. on Legis 1 (1990). (Professor Woodward presents an excellent, comprehensive discussion of the statutes and their implications, including a cost and risk analysis and a discussion of their impact on the debtor-creditor system and a comparison with the sometimes cumbersome and costly methods in other states.)

110 *Id.*, at 7.

111 See **§ 5.8** on procedures for garnishment and **§ 5.9** on postjudgment garnishment by the United States for a more detailed explanations.

112 15 U.S.C. § 1673; 29 C.F.R. § 870.1-57.

California. If wages are not subject to a prior earnings withholding order or wage assignment for support, then a creditor may levy against 25 percent of the wages, with the balance being exempt. If a prior wage assignment or withholding order has been entered against the debtor for support, then all of the paid earnings are exempt. [113]

Florida. In Florida, the wages for personal labor and services of a head of a family of a state resident are exempt from garnishment, including wages traceable to a debtor's bank account.[114]

Maine. Wages and salary are subject to garnishment subject to the limitations on amounts provided in 14 Maine Revised Statutes Annotated § 3127. The limitation when an individual debtor is supporting a spouse or dependent child is that the garnishment shall not exceed 50 percent of the debtor's disposable earnings for that week. If the debtor is not supporting a spouse or dependent child, then the garnishment shall not exceed 60 percent of the debtor's disposable earnings for that week. *Disposable earnings* are that part of the earnings of a judgment debtor remaining after the deduction of any amounts required by law to be withheld.[115]

New York. In New York, income execution for installments, not to exceed 10 percent of the amount and other limitations set forth in the statute, is permissible when the judgment debtor is receiving or will receive disposable earnings for the week from any person which exceed 30 times the federal minimum hourly wages prescribed in the federal Fair Labor Standards Act of 1938.[116] The income execution must be delivered to the sheriff, and the sheriff must serve the writ on the debtor within 20 days. The execution must contain the statement required by New York Civil Practice Law and Rules § 52319(g).

Pennsylvania. In Pennsylvania, a creditor may not garnish the wages, salaries and commissions of the debtor as they are exempt from execution or other process, except in an action for support.[117]

Texas. In Texas, a debtor's current wages for personal services rendered to an employer are not subject to garnishment, except for the enforcement of court ordered child support payments.[118] It is not important whether the compensation

---

[113] Cal. Code Civ. Proc. § 704.070 (West 1984).

[114] Fla. Stat. 222.11; § 77.0305.

[115] 14 Me. Rev. Stat. Ann § 3121(2).

[116] N.Y. Civ. Prac. L. & R. § 5231(b).

[117] 42 Pa. Stat. Ann. § 8127.

[118] Tex. Const. Art. XVI § 28 (1876, amended 1983); Tex. Civ. Prac. & Rem Code Ann. § 63.004 (Vernon).

is called wages or salary, the controlling issue is whether it is considered compensation for personal services.[119] Wages lose their current status and may be subject to a turnover order for part of the proceeds, once paid to the judgment debtor by an employer.[120]

§ 5.18 Execution on an Airplane

The Federal Aviation Act requires the Secretary of Transportation to establish and maintain a recording system for any conveyances which affect title to any interest in any civil aircraft in the United States.[121] "Airplanes are uniquely mobile, and the Federal Aviation Act provides a uniform national means of registering aircraft ownership and security interests."[122]

> The purpose of section 1403 of the Federal Aviation Act is "to create a 'central clearing house for recordation of titles so that a person, wherever he may be, will know where he can find ready access to the claims against, or liens, or other legal interests in an aircraft.'"[123]

The Federal Aviation Act provides that a conveyance or instrument which is required to be recorded under § 1403(a)(1) of Title 49, shall not be valid against third parties who lack actual notice of the interest until recorded with the Federal Aviation Administration (FAA).[124]

---

119 King v. Floyd, 538 S.W.2d 165 (Tex. Civ. App. 1976); Davidson Texas, Inc. v. Garcia, 664 S.W.2d 791 (Tex. Civ. App. 1984).

120 Raborn v. Davis, 33 Tex. Sup. Ct. J. 249 (1990); Tex. Civ. Prac. & Rem. Code Ann. § 31.002 (Vernon 1986 & Supp. 1990); *see* Commentary, *Raborn v. Davis—Paycheck In Employee's Possession: A Limitation Of The Current Wage Exemption In Texas,* 21 St. Mary's L.J. 939 (1990); *but cf.* Barlow v. Lane, 745 S.W.2d 451, 454 (Tex.App.—Waco 1988, writ denied); Toben and Toben, *Using Turnover Relief To Reach The Nonexempt Paycheck,* 40 Baylor L. Rev. 195, 221 (1988).

121 49 U.S.C. App. § 1401(a)(1) and (h) (1988); South Shore Bank v. Tony Mat, Inc., 712 F.2d 896, 897 (3d Cir. 1983).

122 Sun Bank, N.A. v. Snell (*In re* Cone), 11 Bankr. 925 , 929 (Bankr. M.D. Fla. 1981); *see* Reiley, *Preemption Of Article 9 By The Federal Aviation Act: New Meaning To "Buyer Beware,"* 18 UCC L.J. 242 (1986).

123 Aircraft Trading and Services, Inc. v. Braniff, Inc., 819 F.2d 1227, 1231 (2d Cir. 1987) citing Philko Aviation, Inc. v. Shacket, 462 U.S. 406, 411 (1983) (quoting Hearing on H.R. 9738 before the House Committee on Interstate and Foreign Commerce, 75th Cong., 2d Sess. 407 (1938) (testimony of F. Fagg, Director of Air Commerce, Dep't. of Commerce)).

124 49 U.S.C. § 1403(c); *Cf.* Philko Aviation, Inc. v. Shacket, 462 U.S. 406, 413 (1983); Aircraft Trading and Services, Inc. v. Braniff, Inc., 819 F. 1227, 1231 (2d Cir. 1987); Compass Insurance Company v. H.P. Moore, 806 F.2d 796, 798 (8th Cir. 1986); Sun Bank v. Snell (*In re* Cone), 11 Bankr. 925, 929–30 (Bankr. M.D. Fla. 1981).

Therefore, once a United States Marshall has levied or seized an aircraft as required in accordance with the state execution law, the Marshall must also record the execution with the Federal Aviation Administration at its recordation office in Oklahoma City, Oklahoma, pursuant to 49 U.S.C. § 1403, for the creditor to have "perfected" a judgment lien against the aircraft.[125]

The facts in *Sun Bank v. Snell*[126] illustrate this principal. Cooper Industries obtained a default judgment for $86,606.72 against Cone in the United States District Court for the Northern District of Texas on June 19, 1980. The judgment was registered pursuant to 28 U.S.C. § 1963 in the Middle District of Florida on August 1, 1980. A writ of execution was issued from that court on August 12, 1980, and directed the U.S. Marshall to levy upon all real and personal property of Cone sufficient to satisfy the judgment. Cone purchased an aircraft on September 17, 1980, and Sun Bank finance the aircraft and perfected its security interest thereon on September 24, 1980, by filing with the appropriate office of the Federal Aviation Administration. On November 26, 1980, the U.S. Marshall levied upon and seized the aircraft pursuant to the writ of execution. Then, on December 18, 1980, Cone filed a voluntary petition in bankruptcy. Cone defaulted on his agreement with the bank. Sun Bank claimed a perfected security against the aircraft as of September 24, 1980, and Cooper Industries claimed a superior lien based on the docketing of its writ of execution with the U.S. Marshall on August 12, 1980.

Under Florida law, when a write of execution is delivered for docketing to the sheriff of the county in which the personal property is located, the creditor is considered to have a lien.[127]

> Florida law does not require a levy in order to perfect the lien created. As a result, the lien is created and perfected upon delivery of the writ of execution to the sheriff. The lien attaches to all personal property of the judgment debtor in the county in which the writ is docketed whether such personal property is then in existence or is later acquired by the judgment debtor.[128]

However, if the judgment lien of Cooper Industries attached upon the delivery of the writ to the sheriff it would defeat the purpose of the notice

---

[125] *Cf.* Philko Aviation, Inc. v. Shacket, 462 U.S. 406, 413 (1983); Sun Bank v. Snell (*In re* Cone), 11 Bankr. 925, 929–30 (Bankr. M.D. Fla. 1981); Marsden v. Southern Flight Service, Inc., 227 F. Supp. 411 (1964) (chattel mortgage recorded with FAA was entitled protection against purchaser of aircraft who failed to record his bill of sale with FAA until after mortgage); Crescent City Aviation, Inc. v. Beverly Bank, 219 N.E.2d 446 (Ind App. 1966) (any lien affecting aircraft would not be effective against property of third persons without knowledge unless the liens were recorded with the FAA); Wilson v. Barnes, 359 Mo. 352, 221 S.W.2d 731 (Sup. Ct. Mo. 1949) (attachment was valid, since made before sale of aircraft was recorded with the Civil Aeronautics Board).

[126] Sun Bank v. Snell (*In re* Cone), 11 Bankr. 925 (Bankr. M.D. Fla. 1981).

[127] Sun Bank v. Snell (*In re* Cone), 11 Bankr. 925, 927–28 (Bankr. M.D. Fla. 1981).

[128] *Id.* at 928.

scheme required by § 1403 of the Federal Aviation Act. As such, the court found that the Florida law was invalid as to the aircraft.[129] This decision is correct, because Congress in the Federal Aviation Act has preempted the field of registration and recording of title instruments affecting aircraft.[130] Under the facts in the *Sun Bank* case and the Federal Aviation Act provisions, the bank's security interest was perfected when the bank recorded its security interest with the Federal Aviation Administration.

The principle learned from the *Sun Bank* case is that to be effective against aircraft, writs of execution should be filed with the Federal Aviation Administration. Under the *Sun Bank* case, priority was determined by federal law. If Cooper Industries had the U.S. Marshall record the writ of execution before Sun Bank had filed its lien with the FAA on September 24, 1980, under federal law, Cooper Industries would have been the first to record its lien, and be entitled to priority.[131]

However, this is not always the case. Once the title instruments are recorded with the Federal Aviation Administration, the law of the state will determine priority. The Supreme Court concluded:

> Although state law determines priorities, all interest must be federally recorded before they can obtain whatever priority to which they are entitled under state law. As one commentator has explained: "The only situation in which priority appears to be determined by operation of the [federal] statute is where the security holder has failed to record his interest. Such failure invalidates the conveyance as to innocent third persons. But recordation itself merely validates; it does not grant priority." Scott, "Liens in Aircraft; Priorities," 25 J. Air L. & Commerce 193, 203 (1958) (footnote omitted).[132]

Also, if a judgment creditor records a judgment lien on the aircraft, but the aircraft was previously transferred by the judgment debtor, the judgment creditor may find that its lien will not reach the title of the equitable owner.[133] For example, in March 1982, Compass Insurance Company (Compass), a judgment creditor of Hollywood Flying Services, Inc. (Hollywood), obtained a lien on a Cessna aircraft. Compass recorded the lien on June 8, 1982, with the FAA register. The record title at the FAA reflected Hollywood as the record owner. However, in August 1979, Hollywood had sold the aircraft to Mid South. In May, 1981, Mid South sold the plane to Moore Flying, Inc.

---

129 *Id.* at 930.

130 *Id.* at 927; *cf.* South Shore Bank v. Tony Mat, Inc., 712 F.2d 896, 898 (3d Cir. 1983); Bank of Lexington v. Jack Adams Aircraft Sales, Inc., 570 F.2d 1220 (5th Cir. 1978).

131 United States v. City of New Britain, 347 U.S. 81 (1954).

132 Philko Aviation, Inc. v. Shackett, 462 U.S. 406, at 413 (1983); *See* Aircraft Trading and Services, Inc. v. Braniff, Inc., 819 F.2d 1227, 1231–32 (2d Cir. 1987); South Shore Bank v. Tony Mat, Inc., 712 F.2d 896, 899 (3d Cir. 1983).

133 Compass Insurance Co. v. H.P. Moore, 806 F.2d 796 (8th Cir. 1986).

The sales transactions were not recorded with the FAA until June 30, 1983, about one year after Compass recorded its judgment lien. The court held that the judgment lien of Compass could not attach to property which at the time was not longer owned by or in the possession of Hollywood. The court also found a judgment creditor was not the kind of innocent third party who engages in transactions in reliance on FAA records.[134]

§ 5.19 Execution Against State and Local Governments

It is often difficult to obtain a judgment against a state or local government, and collecting on the claim may be even more difficult.[135] If a creditor obtains a judgment against a state or local government in federal court, questions arise concerning the methods available to enforce the judgment. Actually, several methods of enforcement may be possible. The usual method of using a writ of execution under Federal Rule of Civil Procedure 69(a) may be an available remedy against a state or municipal government. If the state or municipality fails to appropriate the money, the court may issue mandamus for compliance with its order. If the state or municipality fails to pay, the court, under Federal Rule of Civil Procedure 70, may enforce a money judgment against a state or local government by ordering the defendant to pay it. A review of some of the reported cases illustrates several alternatives available in enforcing a judgment against a state or municipal government.

One method to collect on a federal judgment against a state or local government is by using a writ of execution under Federal Rule of Civil Procedure 69(a) to seize public funds or property.[136] For example, in *Bowman v. City of New Orleans,*[137] the plaintiffs were street musicians who attacked the constitutionality of a city ordinance that barred all music performances and other street entertainment during Mardi Gras, 1986. The district court

---

[134] Compass Insurance Co. v. H.P. Moore, 806 F.2d at 799; *cf.* Gacharna v. Air Operations International, Inc. (In Re Air Operational International, Inc.), 97 Bankr. 843, 848–49 (Bankr. W.D.N.C. 1989).

[135] *See* Blum, *It's Harder To Collect From Cities,* 13 The National Law Journal 1 (1991); Miller and Turner, *Enforcement Of Money Judgments Against The State,* 64 Fla. B. J. 29–33 (1990).

[136] Bowman v. City of New Orleans, 747 F. Supp. 344 (E.D. La. 1989), *aff'd,* 914 F.2d 711 (5th Cir. 1990); Collins v. Thomas, 649 F.2d 1203 (5th Cir. 1981), *cert. denied,* 456 U.S. 936 (1982); Gary W. v. State of Louisiana, 441 F. Supp. 1121 (E.D. La. 1977), *aff'd,* 622 F.2d 804 (5th Cir. 1980), *cert. denied,* 450 U.S. 994 (1981); Gates v. Collier, 616 F.2d 1268 (5th Cir. 1980); Hankins v. Finnel, 759 F. Supp. 569 (W.D. Mo. 1991); La Raza Unida v. Volpe, 545 F. Supp. 36 (N.D. Cal. 1982).

[137] 747 F. Supp. 334 (E.D. La. 1989), *aff'd,* 914 F.2d 711 (5th Cir. 1990).

entered a temporary restraining order, and then the parties entered into a consent judgment where the City admitted it violated the First and Fourteenth Amendments to the United States Constitution and 42 U.S.C. § 1983. Under the consent judgment the City agreed to pay $6,330.00 in attorney's fees and $500.05 in court costs. Interest on any unpaid fees and costs began to accrue on February 1, 1987. The plaintiffs received $6,830.05 on April 22, 1988, representing the entire principal due, but no interest. Subsequently on June 28, 1989, the plaintiffs filed a writ of execution to seize a New Orleans bank account, and served garnishment interrogatories on the bank. The City moved to quash the writ of execution. After the district court refused to quash the writ and denied the stay pending appeal, the City filed an appeal to the United States Court of Appeals for the Fifth Circuit.

The City relied on its interpretation of Federal Rule of Civil Procedure 69, which states that "proceedings on and in aid of execution shall be in accordance with the practice and procedure of the state in which the district court is held." The City of New Orleans argued that the substantive provisions of the Louisiana Constitution and Louisiana Revised Statutes both exempted public property from seizure and required that money judgments against the state or any of its political subdivisions be satisfied only from specially appropriated funds, and thus restricted the power of federal courts to order the seizure of public property to satisfy its judgments. The Fifth Circuit, affirming the district court, held that Federal Rule of Civil Procedure 69 (providing for execution of district court judgments) applies to states, their officials and municipalities, like New Orleans.

In *Gates v. Collier,*[138] plaintiffs sought damages under the Civil Rights Attorney's Fee Awards Act of 1976, 42 U.S.C. § 1988, based upon the conditions they faced at a Mississippi's Parchman Penitentiary. In earlier litigation, the district court found, and the Fifth Circuit affirmed, that various practices violated the constitutional rights of some of the prisoners. In *Gates v. Collier* the litigation primarily involved the issue of attorneys' fees. In enforcing the judgment in that case, the district court faced a similar situation as faced by the district court in the *Bowman* case. In *Gates,* a Mississippi law required legislative appropriation of funds to satisfy money judgments rendered against the state. To enforce the federal judgment, the district court ordered the Mississippi Auditor and Treasurer added as defendants, and ordered defendant John Collier, Superintendent of the Mississippi State Penitentiary, to submit a requisition to the Auditor for the issuance of a warrant upon the Treasurer to satisfy the judgment out of funds appropriated for the operation of Parchman Penitentiary or out of any other funds subject to the control of the treasurer.[139]

---

[138] 616 F.2d 1268 (5th Cir. 1980).

[139] Gates v. Collier, 616 F.2d 1268, at 1270.

In affirming the authority of the district court to make such a decision despite the absence of specific direction in the Civil Rights Attorneys' Fee Awards Act of 1976, the Fifth Circuit stated:

> In all likelihood, Congress assumed it was unnecessary to consider the subject because the Federal Rules of Civil Procedure contains a provision for the execution of district court judgments, Fed. R. Civ. P. 69, a provision authorizing the court to appoint an individual to do any act on behalf of a party who has refused to comply with the judgment himself, Fed. R. Civ. P. 70. . . . Here, the district court acted well within its authority to ensure compliance with its lawful orders. If statutory authority is needed for the court's actions, it may be found in Fed. R. Civ. P. 70.[140]

Another example of a procedure to use against a municipality is illustrated in *Transportation Cybernetics, Incorporated v. Forest Transit Commission, Forest County, Wisconsin.*[141] In this case, an arbitrator entered an award of $403,336.56 in favor of Transportation Cybernetics, Inc. (TCI) against Forest Transit Commission (FTC), a commission which was created by Forest County and the towns of Tipler and Long Lake, all Wisconsin municipalities. TCI then petitioned the district court for confirmation of the award pursuant to 9 U.S.C. § 9 (1988). Subsequently, TCI moved the district court under Federal Rule of Civil Procedure 69(a) for an order in the nature of mandamus to require the Clerk of Forest County to levy a tax for satisfaction of the judgment entered against the FTC. On appeal, the Seventh Circuit remanded the case to the district court to issue the appropriate writ of mandamus, ordering the Clerk of Forest County to satisfy the judgment against the FTC.[142] In its analysis, the Seventh Circuit explained:

> When requested in an appropriate motion, a district court may under Rule 69(a) issue a writ of mandamus as provided by the law of the state in which that court sits. [Cites omitted.] Wisconsin law clearly provides for a writ of mandamus as an action supplemental to and in aid of judgment [cites omitted], which can be applied against a nonparty to the original judgment as well as against a party.[143]

In summary, when considering collection alternatives against state and local governments, there are several methods of collection available, including, a writ of execution under Federal Rule of Civil Procedure 69, an order to pay under Federal Rule of Civil Procedure 70, a writ of mandamus, or, perhaps, an

---

140 *Id.*, at 1271.

141 950 F.2d 350 (7th Cir. 1991).

142 950 F.2d 350, 355; *See* Miller and Turner, *Enforcement Of Money Judgments Against The State,* 64 Fla. B.J. 29, at 30–1 (1990).

143 950 F.2d 350 at 353.

administrative action under state law. State law restrictions on executions against municipal or state governments should not prevent a federal district court from providing a remedy to collect the judgment it rendered.[144]

§ 5.20 Execution on Corporate Stock

Once considered as a chose in action under common law, corporate stock is now reached by execution as provided by various state statutes. The method of levy differs. Some states require a levy on the corporate secretary or other officer without the necessity of seizure of the stock certificate. Some states hold that delivery of a writ of execution to the levying officer gives the judgment creditor a lien on general intangibles, such as corporate stock. Other states require that the stock certificate, being a negotiable item, must be taken into custody by the seizing officer. Numerous articles discuss this topic in detail.[145]

A brief analysis of some state law will be helpful in comparing specific state requirements for executing against corporate stock. Reference must also be made to whether the particular state has adopted the Uniform Commercial Code, and if so, reference should be made to Article 8, § 8-317, entitled "Creditors' Rights" for consideration of whether the particular corporate stock is considered a security as defined in § 8-102(1), which may only be executed on by actual seizure.[146]

Practice Tips

1. If the state law permits execution against corporate stock it is always preferable to have the levying officer actually seize the corporate stock if it can be found.
2. If the stock cannot be immediately located it is always a safe practice to seek a restraining order preventing the judgment debtor from encumbering or transferring the stock, and requiring the judgment debtor to turnover or deliver the stock to the judgment creditor.

---

144 *See* Miller and Turner, *Enforcement Of Money Judgments Against The State*, 64 Fla. B.J. 29, at 31–2 (1990).

145 *See* Laurence, *Enforcing A Money Judgment Against The Defendant's Stocks And Bonds: A Brief Foray Into The Forbidding Realms Of Article Eight And The Fourth Amendment,* 38 Ark. L. Rev. 561 (1985); Gillette & Maher, *Revised Article 8: Issuers Beware,* 15 U.C.C. L.J. 146 (1982); Kennedy, *The Rights Of Levying Creditors Against Negotiable Property Under The Uniform Commercial Code,* 31 Bus. Law 1517 (1976); Louiseaux, *Liability Of Corporate Shares To Legal Process,* 1972 Duke L.J. 947 (1972); Annot., 21 A.L.R. 3d 964, 981 (1964).

146 *Id.*

3. If the stock is in the possession of a third party, ascertain if state law permits a writ of garnishment or other process to be served on the third party requiring that party to turnover or deliver to the judgment creditor any unencumbered or surplus shares.

California. In California, to levy upon a security, like corporate stock, the levying officer must comply with § 8-317 of the Commercial Code.[147] Under that section the sheriff or U.S. Marshal is required to personally serve the writ of execution and notice of levy on an officer of the corporation who is being served. No levy of execution upon corporate share is valid until the security is actually seized by the sheriff or U.S. Marshal.[148]

Illinois. The shares of stock in a corporation or a shareholder's interest in any corporation may be levied upon in the enforcement of a judgment and sold to satisfy the judgment.[149] To make the levy, the sheriff or U.S. Marshal must leave a copy of the judgment with the clerk, treasurer or cashier of the company, if there is such officer, and, if not, with the person who is in charge of the books and papers of the corporation.[150] The property of the corporation shall be considered seized when the copy is left with the corporate officer and shall be sold in the same manner as goods and chattels.[151]

Michigan. In Michigan, a sheriff, U.S. Marshal, or other levying officer can execute against corporate shares by actually seizing the certificates. Alternatively, the levying officer makes a valid levy when the shares are surrendered to the corporation which issued the shares, or their transfer is enjoined or restrained.[152] A responsible corporate officer or corporate custodian of records is obliged to give the levying officer a certificate of the number of shares or the amount of interest held by the judgment debtor once the corporate officer is shown the writ of execution.[153] The levying officer is required to leave a copy of the writ of execution which contains a certification with the corporate officer or custodian of records from whom the levying officer took the corporate shares.[154] The purchaser of corporate stock sold on execution is entitled to have the transfer of shares recorded on the corporate

[147] Cal. Com. Code § 8-317 (Deering 1984); Cal. Civ. Proc. § 680.345 (security includes an interest in property or in an enterprise).

[148] *Id.*

[149] Ill. Rev. Stat. ch. 110, § 12-171.

[150] *Id.*

[151] *Id.*

[152] Mich. Comp. Laws § 600.6037(1).

[153] Mich. Comp. Laws § 600.6037(2).

[154] Mich. Comp. Laws § 600.6037(3).

books and new stock certificates issued for those bought upon the execution sale.[155]

The court which issued the execution may upon motion, and without notice, restrain the transfer of any such shares of stock. The restraint is effective upon service of a certified copy of the order.[156] Upon sale of the corporate stock, the purchaser of the stock is entitled to stock dividends which accrue for the debtor after attachment or execution.[157]

Nevada. Corporate shares and interest in any corporation or company may be seized by a writ of execution and sold to satisfy a judgment against a debtor.[158]

New York. If corporate stock evidenced by a certificate is owned by the judgment debtor and the judgment debtor is in the possession of the stock, upon motion of the judgment creditor pursuant to New York Civil Practice Law and Rules § 5225(a), the court shall order turnover or delivery of the stock, or so much of it as needed to satisfy the judgment, to the judgment creditor.[159] If some other person holds the stock on behalf of the judgment debtor, that person shall be the garnishee and be required to deliver or turn over the stock, or so much of it as is required to satisfy the judgment, to the judgment creditor pursuant to New York Civil Practice Law and Rules § 5225(b).[160]

Ohio. If the judgment against the debtor cannot be satisfied by other personal property or real property subject to levy on execution, then the debtor's corporate stock or interests in a corporation shall be subject to the payment of the judgment pursuant to Ohio Revised Code Annotated § 2333.01.[161]

Texas. Pursuant to Texas Rules of Civil Procedure, Rule 641, a levy upon shares of stock of any corporation or joint stock company for which a certificate is outstanding is made by the levying officer seizing and taking possession of such certificate.[162]

---

155 Mich. Comp. Laws § 600.6037(4).

156 Mich. Comp. Laws § 600.6037(5).

157 Mich. Comp. Laws § 600.6037(6).

158 Nev. Rev. Stat. § 21.080; *cf.* Double O Mining Co. v. Simrak, 61 Nev. 431, 132 P.2d 605 (Nev. 1942).

159 *Cf.* Clarkson Co. Ltd. v. Shaheen, 533 F.2d 905, 922 (2d Cir. 1982).

160 *Cf.* Clarkson Co. Ltd. v. Shaheen, 533 F.2d 905, 910 (2d Cir. 1982).

161 Ball v. Towle Manufacturing Co., 67 Ohio St. 306, 65 N.E. 1015 (1902).

162 *See* Benson v. Greenville National Exchange Bank, 228 S.W.2d 272 (Tex. Civ. App. 1950).

Virginia. A writ of *fieri facias* shall be a lien on all the personal estate of the judgment debtor including intangible, unlivable property, such as corporate stock, from the time of the delivery of the writ of execution to the sheriff, U.S. Marshal, or other execution officer pursuant to Virginia Code § 8.01-501.[163]

§ 5.21 Body Execution

Body execution (*writ of capias ad satisfaciendum*) as a civil process is often perceived as an outmoded remedy for enforcing debts, but is still available today in most of the United States.[164] A body execution is

> [A] writ of execution . . . which commands the sheriff to take the party named, and keep him safely, so that he may have his body before the court on a certain day, to satisfy the damages or debt and damages in certain actions. It deprives the party taken of his liberty until he makes the satisfaction awarded.[165]

The United States Constitution contains no express provision against imprisonment for debt, but federal courts are required to follow the law of the state in which they sit.[166] Body execution statutes are not uniform, but most authorize a body execution whenever a defendant is found guilty of some kind of wrongdoing, such as committing a fraud, or a tort, or misconduct in public office or professional employment, or embezzlement or conversion of the plaintiff's property, or when the defendant is about to abscond.[167]

Section 2007 of Title 28 U.S.C. states:

> (a) A person shall not be imprisoned for debt on a writ of execution or other process issued from a court of the United States in any State wherein imprisonment for debt has been abolished. All modifications, conditions, and restrictions upon such imprisonment provided by State law shall apply to any writ of execution or process issued from a court of the United States in accordance with the procedure applicable in such State.
>
> (b) Any person arrested or imprisoned in any State on a writ of execution or other process issued from any court of the United States in a civil action shall have the same jail privileges and be governed by the same regulations as persons confined in like cases on process issued from the courts of such State. The

---

163 *In re* Lamm, 47 Bankr. 364 (E.D.Va. 1984).

164 *See* Note, *Body Attachment And Body Execution: Forgotten But Not Gone,* 17 Wm. & Mary L. Rev. 543, 550–51 n.45–52 (1976).

165 Black's Law Dictionary 262 (4th ed. 1968).

166 *See* 28 U.S.C. § 2007 (1982).

167 Kinsey v. Preeson, 746 P.2d 542, 546 (Colo. 1987).

> same requirements governing discharge as are applicable in such State shall apply. Any proceedings for discharge shall be conducted before a United States commissioner for the judicial district wherein the defendant is held.
>
> Procedures implemented to effect body attachment or body execution, however, must comport with the equal protection and the due process clauses of the fourteenth amendment. Due process requires that a defendant receive notice and an opportunity for a hearing prior to body attachment or body execution. With respect to body execution, the notice and hearing afforded in the suit on the merits does not satisfy due process requirements; consistent with the equal protection clause, a separate hearing to determine the defendant's ability to pay is necessary to avoid imprisonment by reason of indigency. . . . Thus, although body attachment and body execution are available to present day creditors, their operation is restricted by both the due process and equal protection clauses of the fourteenth amendment.[168]

Several cases are illustrative of the principal that body execution statutes most comport with the fourteenth amendment. In *Kinsey v. Preeson,*[169] the Supreme Court of Colorado struck down § 13-59-103 of the Colorado body execution statute as violative of the equal protection clause of the fourteenth amendment because it did not provide equal treatment between indigent and solvent debtors.

> The purpose of the body execution statute, to coerce a judgment debtor into paying the judgment, cannot be effected against an indigent debtor. The only real effect of the body execution against an indigent debtor is that of punishment. Such a punishment can be avoided by a solvent debtor but becomes mandatory against an indigent debtor. Thus, the body execution statute is invidiously discriminatory and unconstitutional under the fourteenth amendment.[170]

In *Landrigan v. McElroy,*[171] the Supreme Court of Rhode Island held that § 9-25-15 of the Rhode Island body execution statute contravened the equal protection and due process clauses of the fourteenth amendment on the basis that defendants were not granted a right to a meaningful adversary hearing, at a meaningful time, and after reasonable notice, to demonstrate that they were unable to pay the judgment against them. Likewise, in *Abbit v. Bernier,*[172] the court held the Connecticut's body execution statute violative of the fourteenth amendment right to equal protection when the statute did not give the debtor a preincarceration hearing concerning his ability to pay the debt.

---

168 *See* Note, *Body Attachment And Body Execution: Forgotten But Not Gone,* 17 Wm. & Mary L. Rev. 543, 570 (1976).

169 746 P.2d 542 (Colo. 1987).

170 *Id.* at 550.

171 457 A.2d 1056 (R.I. 1983).

172 387 F. Supp. 57 (D. Conn. 1974).

Five years later, in *Palumbo v. Manson,*[173] the court found the Connecticut body execution statute facially constitutional, but ruled that the imprisonment of the debtor in this particular case was unconstitutional because it was based solely on the defendant's lack of assets or funds to pay the judgment debt. In *Grimes v. Miller,*[174] found that the provisions of §§ 1-311 and 23-32 of the North Carolina General Statutes on body execution violated debtor's due process rights when they required the imprisoned debtor to give 20 days notice of the time and place at which his petition to be discharged by reason of insolvency and full disclosure will be filed. The court held that this provision postpones unconscionably and unconstitutionally the right of the imprisoned debtor to have his day in court, and ruled that the hearing must be held on debtor's petition within three days after it is filed.

§ 5.22 Search and Seizure Issues in Postjudgment Process

When attorneys send a sheriff or U.S. Marshall to enter into a judgment debtor's home or business to levy execution ont he debtor's property fourth amendment search and seizures issues should be considered.[175] The concern for the judgment creditor's lawyer is whether the sheriff or U.S. Marshall should have a search warrant or execution warrant, in addition to the usual writ of execution. In *G.M. Leasing Corp. v. United States,*[176] the Internal Revenue Service searched a taxpayer's place of business for the purpose of seizing the petitioner's assets to satisfy alleged income tax liability. The Supreme Court found that the entry into the petitioner's office with a search warrant violated the fourth amendment and did not satisfy the exigent circumstances exception to the warrant requirement.[177] The Supreme Court has recognized a number of exceptions which may justify a search without a warrant. Exceptions have been found in the following cases:

---

[173] 35 Conn. Sup. 130, 400 A.2d 288 (Conn. Super. Ct. 1979).

[174] 429 F. Supp. 1350 (M.D.N.C. 1977), *aff'd,* 434 U.S. 978 (1977).

[175] *See* G.M. Leasing Corp. v. United States, 429 U.S. 338 (1977); Hamrick v. Ashland Finance Co., 423 F. Supp. 1033 (S.D. W.Va. 1976); Mizoszewski v. Sears Roebuck Co., 346 F. Supp. 119 (W.D. Mich. 1972); Dorsey v. Community Stores, Inc., 346 F. Supp. 103 (E.D. Wis. 1972); Laprease v. Raymours Furniture Co., 315 F. Supp. 716 (N.D. N.Y. 1970); State v. Hinchey, 220 Neb. 825, 374 N.W.2d 14 (Neb. 1985); Note, *State v. Hinchey: The Validity Of A Sheriff's Warrantless Execution On Personal Property Within The Home Of The Judgment Debtor,* 39 Ark. L. Rev. 739 (1986); Laurence, *Enforcing A Money Judgment Against The Defendant's Stocks And Bonds: A Brief Foray Into The Forbidding Realms Of Article Eight And The Fourth Amendment,* 38 Ark. L. Rev. 561 (1985).

[176] 429 U.S. 338 (1977).

[177] 429 U.S. 338, at 359–60.

1. Consent[178]
2. Automobile searches[179]
3. Exigent circumstances[180]
4. Searches incident to arrest[181]
5. Inspections and regulatory searches[182]
6. Stop and frisk searches[183]
7. Plain view[184]

The Supreme Court in *G.M. Leasing Corp. v. United States* stated:

> It is one thing to seize without a warrant property resting in an open area or seizable by levy without an intrusion into privacy, and it is quite another thing to effect a warrantless seizure of property, even that owned by a corporation, situated on private premises to which access is not otherwise available for the seizing officer.
>
> Indeed, one of the primary evils intended to be eliminated by the Fourth Amendment was the massive intrusion on privacy undertaken in the collection of taxes pursuant to general warrants and writs of assistance.[185]

By analogy, the decision of the Supreme Court in *G.M. Leasing Corp.* extends the fourth amendment interest in the privacy of one's business into the area of judgment execution. Counsel who seek to execute on the business assets of a judgment debtor must consider the fourth amendment when sending a levying officer into the private business premise of the judgment debtor. Besides the writ of execution, the levying officer should also have an execution warrant when making the foray into the forbidding realm of the fourth amendment.

The Supreme Court of Nebraska in *State v. Hinchey,*[186] set new precedent in Nebraska when executions are made to levy on property in the debtor's home. In *Hinchey,* a deputy sheriff was directed to the apartment of Hinchey to attempt to serve a writ of execution to satisfy a small claims judgment of

---

178 Schnecklock v. Bustamonte, 412 U.S. 218 (1973).

179 New York v. Belton, 453 U.S. 454 (1981).

180 United States v. Jeffers, 342 U.S. 48 (1951).

181 Chimel v. California, 395 U.S. 752 (1969).

182 South Dakota v. Opperman, 428 U.S. 364 (1976).

183 Terry v. Ohio, 392 U.S. 1 (1968).

184 United States v. Lee, 274 U.S. 559 (1927); Coolidge v. New Hampshire, 403 U.S. 443 (1971); *See* Note, *State v. Hinchey: The Validity of a Sheriff's Warrantless Execution on Personal Property Within the Home of the Judgment Debtor*, 39 Ark. L. Rev. 739, 742–43 n.13–19 (1986).

185 429 U.S. 338, 354–55 (1977).

186 220 Neb. 825, 374 N.W.2d 14 (1985).

$208.40. The writ from the clerk of court directed the deputy sheriff to seek and take possession of property pursuant to Nebraska execution statutes. Under Nebraska Revised Statutes, § 25-1516 the sheriff must first seek to satisfy the judgment by levying against personal property, and then, if there is a deficiency, the sheriff may levy against real property. The specific facts of this event are important.

The Supreme Court of Nebraska summarized the facts as follows:

> Upon arriving at the Hinchey home Deputy Glesmann knocked on the door of the apartment, and after a brief delay Hinchey answered the door. The deputy identified himself to Hinchey, stated his purpose, and asked for permission to enter the Hinchey premises. Hinchey refused. The officer explained to Hinchey that arrangements had to be made for payment of the judgment. After a few minutes and four or five additional requests for admission by the deputy, to which Hinchey each time said "No," Hinchey finally agreed to let the deputy into his home. Before doing so, however, he said, "Wait a second, let me put something away." The deputy testified that he clearly understood that Hinchey wanted him to wait in the hall and did not want him to come into the apartment until Hinchey returned to the door. Hinchey walked back into the apartment. At this time the front door of the apartment was partially open, and the deputy proceeded to follow Hinchey into the apartment. Once inside the apartment the deputy observed a jar which appeared to contain marijuana. Hinchey was immediately instructed to sit on the couch and not to move and was subsequently arrested by the deputy for possession of drug paraphernalia in violation of Neb. Rev. Stat. § 29-441 (Cum. Supp. 1984) and possession of marijuana, less than one ounce, in violation of Neb. Rev. Stat. § 28-416(6) (Cum. Supp. 1984).[187]

The court in *Hinchey* ruled that he marijuana seized at Hinchey's apartment could not later be admitted into evidence at Hinchey's criminal trial because the deputy entered his home on a warrantless search and seizure. Even though the deputy had a valid writ of execution, the court determined that the warrantless seizure violated Hinchey's fourth amendment rights.

However, in addition to the fourth amendment issue in the criminal trial, the Supreme Court of Nebraska spelled out an entirely new procedure in dicta regarding civil execution practice. The court noted that whenever it becomes necessary for the sheriff or other levying officer to enter into a person's home for the purpose of levying on property, the sheriff or other levying officer should have an execution warrant. The court addressed this new procedure in specific detail by stating:

> We hold that the procedure to be followed to obtain an "execution warrant" should be similar to that prescribed by Neb. Rev. Stat. §§ 29-830 to 29-835 (Reissue 1979), which provide for the issuance of "inspection warrants." Such an execution warrant should be issued only by a judge of a court of record

[187] 374 N.W.2d at 16.

> upon reasonable cause supported by affidavit setting out that a writ of execution has been issued and returned unsatisfied in whole of in part and that the affiant has reason to believe that there is property subject to execution in the possession of the debtor kept and maintained within the debtor's residence, not otherwise available for execution, describing the property sought and the place and purpose of the execution. If the judge is satisfied that there is reasonable cause to believe that there is property of the debtor within the debtor's possession and that other property is not available for levy and execution, the judge may then issue an execution warrant authorizing the officer to enter the premises and levy upon the property subject to execution. In this manner the fourth amendment prohibition against unreasonable searches and seizures will be satisfied.[188]

The impact of the *Hinchey* decision is that it extends the fourth amendment interest in the privacy of one's home into an entirely new area of operation, namely, that of judgment execution.[189] The impact of the *G.M. Leasing* case is that it extends the fourth amendment interest in the privacy of one's business into the area of tax collection, and by analogy, judgment collection, as well. Certainly before sending a levying officer into the privacy of a debtor's home or business to make a levy and seizure of personal property careful scrutiny must be given to the impact of these cases on the debtor's fourth amendment rights.

---

188 *Id.* at 20.

189 *See* Note, *State v. Hinchey: The Validity Of A Sheriff's Warrantless Execution On Personal Property Within The Home Of The Judgment Debtor,* 39 Ark. L. Rev. 739, 757 (1986).

CHAPTER 6

NEW LITIGATION TO ENFORCE JUDGMENTS

§ 6.1 Introduction

This Chapter focuses on some of the major theories of recovery plaintiff's counsel should consider in postjudgment litigation to enforce a judgment. In this Chapter the discussion will include the following claims for relief:

1. Fraudulent transfer claim
2. Constructive trust fund claim
3. Piercing the corporate veil claim
4. Federal priority statute claim

If during postjudgment discovery, plaintiff's counsel uncovers fraudulent or other unlawful activity, he must make a preliminary determination whether to seek relief in supplementary proceedings (See **Chapter 4**); or to seek relief by execution against the property (See **Chapter 5**); or to seek relief by filing new litigation against third parties to recover damages or to recover fraudulently or otherwise unlawfully transferred property. A suit to recover on a judgment under one or more of these theories of recovery may be filed like any other lawsuit, and is initiated by the filing of a complaint. See Federal Rules of Civil Procedure 3, 8. Of course, plaintiff's counsel may join a complaint for fraudulent conveyances in a single action with a claim on the debt. Federal Rule 18(b) states: "In particular, a plaintiff may state a claim for money and a claim to have set aside a conveyance fraudulent as to that plaintiff, without first having obtained a judgment establishing the claim for money."

The Chapter includes a discussion of the basic elements needed in pleading each theory and examples of some cases discussing each theory.

FRAUDULENT TRANSFER CLAIM

§ 6.2 Basic Elements in Pleading a Uniform Fraudulent Transfer Claim

"The fraudulent conveyance, as known in our law, may be roughly defined as an infringement of the creditor's right to realize upon the available assets of the debtor."[1] The idea of setting aside fraudulent transfers began in England with The Statute of Fraudulent Conveyance, 13 Eliz., c.7 (1570) which was designed to prevent fraudulent transfers and to raise revenue for the Crown

[1] G. Glenn, The Law of Fraudulent Conveyances, § 1 (1931).

and punish offenders who sought to avoid forfeiture of property.[2] Anglo-American fraudulent transfer law originated with the Statute of 13 Elizabeth . . . which deemed void any conveyance "to delay, hinder or defraud creditors and others of their just and lawful actions, suits, debts." The Statute of Elizabeth is still part of common law or statutory law of every American jurisdiction.[3]

Following the principles established in the Statute of Elizabeth in the United States, 30 states have adopted the Uniform Fraudulent Transfer Act (UFTA), eight states have adopted the Uniform Fraudulent Conveyance Act (UFCA), and the remaining states and territories have adopted their own form of fraudulent transfer law.[4] The Federal Fraudulent Transfer Act (FFTA)[5] is based on UFTA, with a few minor changes. For purposes of this book, the discussion of the UFTA and its provisions will be of assistance in analyzing the provisions of FFTA. A fraudulent conveyance is a transfer in which the debtor tries to put some or all of his property beyond the reach of his creditors.[6] These laws make fraudulent transfers by debtors unlawful, and creditors may use the particular state or Federal law to have the transaction set aside or voided.

In *Boston Trading Group, Inc. v. Burnazos,*[7] the First Circuit Court of Appeals explained this process:

> Fraudulent conveyance law permits creditors to recover money that a debtor has disposed of in a manner similar to that described by the following examples:
>
> First (and most important), suppose that a debtor conveys property to a friend whom he expects will use the property in a way that benefits the debtor (suppose, for example, the friend lets the debtor retain possession of the property or secretly agrees to return the property after the debtor's creditors have given up). In such a case, the debtor in effect lies to his creditors, pretending he has no property left, when he really has some (in the hands of his friend). The law calls this untruthful kind of conveyance "fraudulent" and permits the creditor to void the transfer and attach the property in order to satisfy his debt.
>
> Second, suppose the debtor transfers his property to a family member or friend or someone else in a "special relationship," but does not himself expect

---

2 United States v. Neidorf, 522 F.2d 916, 920 (9th Cir. 1975), *cert. denied,* 423 U.S. 1087 (1976).

3 4 Collier, Bankruptcy ¶ 548.02[3], at 548-27 (15th rev. ed. 1984).

4 Unif. Fraud. Tranf. Act (1984 Act) §§ 1–13, 7A U.L.A. 170 (Supp. 1991); Unif. Fraud. Convey. Act (1918 Act) §§ 1–14, 7A U.L.A. 138 (Supp. 1991); Martindale-Hubbell Law. Dig. (1991).

5 FFTA is contained in the Federal Debt Collection Procedures Act of 1990, and codified in Title 28 U.S.C. §§ 3301–3308.

6 5 Am. Jur Proof of Facts 2d *Fraudulent Conveyances* 597.

7 835 F.2d 1504 (1st Cir. 1987).

to continue to benefit from the property. Rather he simply prefers that the property go to a friend rather than to an enemy or to a stranger. This type of transfer violates the principle, "be just before you are generous," and the creditor can recover from the friend.

Third, suppose the debtor exchanges assets a creditor might readily reach (say, shares of stock) for assets that are difficult for a creditor to seize (illiquid assets, or, say a homestead). Even though the conveyance is open, truthful, and not to a friend, it hinders creditors in their efforts to satisfy debts. The creditor will (in some circumstances but not when the transfer is merely to satisfy an antecedent debt) be able to void the transfer and seize the assets.[8]

§ 6.3 Basic Elements in Pleading a Fraudulent Transfer Claim under the Federal Fraudulent Transfer Act

In both UFTA and UFCA there are certain basic elements which are defined or explained in more detail in the particular statute. The elements are for simplicity summarized as follows:

1. **Existence of a creditor**[9]—to whom a debt or claim is owed by the debtor-transferor.
2. **Transfer or conveyance**[10] **of property**—the debtor or someone acting on his or its behalf makes a transfer or conveyance of property.
3. **Actual intent to defraud**—the debtor has the actual intent to defraud his creditors. [Naturally, actual fraud is difficult to prove since the

---

[8] *Id.* at 1508 (cites omitted).

[9] In UFCA § 1, *creditor* is "a person having any claim, whether matured or unmatured, liquidated or unliquated, absolute, fixed or contingent." In UFTA § 1(4) *creditor* means "a person who has a claim." UFTA § 1(3) also defines *claim* as "a right to payment, whether or not the right has been reduced to judgment, liquidated, unliquidated, fixed, contingent, matured, unmatured, disputed, undisputed, legal, equitable, secured, or unsecured." Additonally UFTA § 1(5) defines *debt* as "liability on a claim." In UFTA § 1(9) *person* is defined broadly as "an individual, partnership, corporation, association, organization, government or governmental subdivision or agency, business trust, estate, trust, or any other legal or commercial entity.

[10] UFCA § 1 "'Conveyance' includes every payment of money, assignment, release, transfer, lease, mortgage or pledge of tangible or intangible property, and also creation of any lien or encumbrance." UFTA § 1(12) defines *transfer* as "every mode, direct or indirect, absolute or conditional, voluntary or involuntary, of disposing of or parting with an asset or an interest in an asset, and includes payment of money, release, lease, and creation of a lien or other encumbrance."

debtor generally will not admit the fraud, and so the fraud is proved by circumstantial evidence called "badges of fraud."] In cases decided under the older UFCA the courts developed a series of factors to consider in proving actual fraud, and commonly labelled these "badges of fraud."[11] These "badges of fraud" have now been codified in the more recent fraudulent transfer law, UFTA, at § 4(b)(1)–(11). Under § 4(b) of UFTA, the court may consider one or more of these factors as determining actual fraud by the debtor.[12]

---

[11] At common law, federal courts have developed indicia of fraud, commonly referred to as "badges of fraud." Among the most common badges of fraud are included one or more of the following:

1. financial difficulties, insolvency or substantial indebtedness of the debtor
2. transfers made without consideration or inadequate consideration
3. the pendency or threat of litigation
4. secrecy or concealment of the transfers
5. debtor making the transfer continues to have the benefit, possession or control over the property
6. the disputed transfers were conducted in a manner different from usual business transactions
7. a close relationship between the transferror and the transferee.

United States v. John P. Bertie, 529 F.2d 506, 508 n.3 (9th Cir. 1976); Boston Trading Group, Inc. v. Burnazos, 835 F.2d 1504, 1509 (1st Cir. 1987); Kelly v. Thomas Solvent Company, 725 F. Supp. 1446, 1456–57 (W.D. Mich. 1988); United States v. Vertac Chemical Corporation, 671 F. Supp 595, 617–18, *vacated on other grounds,* 855 F.2d 856 (8th Cir. 1988).

[12] The factors are:

1. the transfer or obligation was to an insider
2. the debtor retained possession or control of the property
3. the transfer or the obligation was disclosed or concealed
4. before the transfer was made or the obligation was incurred, the debtor had been sued or threatened with suit
5. the transfer was of substantially all the debtor's assets
6. the debtor absconded
7. the debtor removed or concealed assets
8. the value of the consideration received by the debtor was reasonably equivalent to the value of the asset transferred or the amount of the obligation incurred
9. the debtor was insolvent or became insolvent shortly after the transfer was made or the obligation was incurred
10. the transfer occurred shortly before or shortly after a substantial debt was incurred
11. the debtor transferred the essential assets of the business to a lienor who transferred the assets to an insider of the debtor.

4. **Lack of Consideration or Reasonably Equivalent Value[13] for the transfer**—means that the issue of fair consideration or reasonable value for the transfer will likely be an element of proof in a fraudulent transfer case.
5. **Insolvency[14] of the Debtor**—the issue of whether the debtor was insolvent or rendered insolvent by the transfer will likely be an element of proof.
6. **Time of the Transfer**—a transfer of real estate under UFCA is deemed effective when the deed is recorded at the registry of deeds.[15] Under UFTA, § 6(1)(i) and (ii) give guidelines for determining when a transfer occurs.[16]

Several of these basic elements of proof, such as: (1) the existence of a debt or claim; (2) a transfer by the debtor; (3) insolvency of the debtor, and perhaps one or more of the other elements will be part of the proof plaintiff's counsel needs in proving any one of the creditor's rights theories discussed in this Chapter.

---

[13] UFTA § 3(a) defines *value* as being "given for a transfer or an obligation if, in exchange for the transfer or obligation, property is transferred or an antecedent debt is secured or satisfied, but value does not include an unperformed promise made otherwise than in the ordinary course of the promisor's business to furnish support to the debtor or another person." UFTA § 3(b) states: "a person gives a reasonably equivalent value if the person acquires an interest of the debtor in an asset pursuant to a regularly conducted, noncollusive foreclosure sale or execution of a power of sale for the acquisition or disposition of the interest of the debtor upon default under a mortgage, deed of trust, or security agreement.

[14] Under UFCA § 2(1) "A person is insolvent when the present fair salable value of his assets is less than the amount that will be required to pay his probable liability on his existing debts as they become absolute and matured." UFTA contains a new definition of insolvency in § 2, in the balance sheet test: "(a) A debtor is insolvent if the sum of the debtor's debts is greater than all of the debtor's assets at a fair valuation (with "fair valuation" being left undefined)." UFTA contains an additional insolvency presumption in § 2 with the equity test: "(b) A debtor who is generally not paying his [or her] debts as they become due is presumed to be insolvent." Thus UFTA's test of insolvency makes it easier than under the prior UFCA provisions for creditors to prove a fraudulent transfer when insolvency is one of the elements of proof, since satisfaction of either insolvency test under UFTA will prove insolvency.

[15] Lovett v. Shuster, 633 F.2d 98, 104 (8th Cir. 1980); Mitchell v. Travis, 473 F.2d 503, 506 (5th Cir. 1973).

[16] UFTA § 6(1) states: "a transfer is made: (i) with respect to an asset that is real property other than a fixture . . . when the transfer is so far perfected that a good-faith purchaser of the asset from the debtor . . . cannot acquire an interest in the asset that is superior to the interest of the transferee."

Under UFCA and UFTA certains sections are most frequently used by creditors to avoid fraudulent transfers by debtors. Section 4 of UFCA[17] makes fraudulent every conveyance or obligation incurred by a person who was insolvent at the time of the transfer, or was rendered insolvent by the transfer, if the transfer was made without fair consideration, regardless of the actual intent of the debtor. Section 6 of UFCA[18] makes fraudulent every conveyance or obligation incurred without fair consideration when the person entering into the transaction is about to incur debts beyond his ability to pay. Section 7[19] of UFCA makes fraudulent every conveyance made with actual intent to hinder, delay or defraud present or future creditors.

Section 5(a) of UFTA[20] is derived from UFCA and is limited to a creditor who extended credit before the transaction. Section 4(a)(1)[21] of UFTA is derived from Section 7 of UFCA. Section 4(a)(2)[22] of UFTA is derived from Sections 5 and 6 of UFCA.

Since the most common fraudulent transfer law today is UFTA, and since the FFTA is modelled after UFTA, an outline of the proof needed to prove fraudulent transfers is useful.

---

17 UFCA § 4: Every conveyance made and every obligation incurred by a person who is or will be thereby rendered insolvent is fraudulent as to creditors without regard to his actual intent if the conveyance is made or the obligation is incurred without a fair consideration.

18 UFCA § 6: Every conveyance made and every obligation incurred without fair consideration when the person making the conveyance or entering into the obligation intends or believes that he will incur debts beyond his ability to pay as they mature, is fraudulent as to both present and future creditors.

19 UFCA § 7: Every conveyance made and every obligation incurred with actual intent, as distinguished from intent presumed in law, to hinder, delay, or defraud either present or future creditors, is fraudulent as to both present and future creditors.

20 UFTA § 5(a): A transfer made or obligation incurred by a debtor is fraudulent as to a creditor whose claim arose before the transfer was made or the obligation was incurred if the debtor made the transfer or incurred the obligation without receiving a reasonably equivalent value in exchange for the transfer or obligation and the debtor was insolvent at that time or the debtor became insolvent as a result of the transfer or obligation.

21 UFTA § 4(a): (a) A transfer made or obligation incurred by a debtor is fraudulent as to a creditor, whether the creditor's claim arose before or after the transfer was made or the obligation was incurred, if the debtor made the transfer or incurred the obligation:

(1) with actual intent to hinder, delay, or defraud any creditor of the debtor; . . .

22 UFTA § 4(a)(2): (a)(2) without receiving a reasonably equivalent value in exchange for the transfer or obligation, and the debtor:

(i) was engaged or was about to engage in a business or transaction for which the remaining assets of the debtor were unreasonably small in relation to the business or transaction; or

(ii) intended to incur, or believed or reasonably should have believed that he [or she] would incur, debts beyond his [or her] ability to pay as they became due.

Fraudulent Transfers—Outline of Proof

1. Intent to hinder, delay or defraud creditors.
   UFTA § 4(a)(1); FFTA § 3304(b)(1)(A).
2. No equal value and
   (a) assets remaining too small or
   UFTA § 4(a)(2)(i); FFTA § 3304(b)(1)(B)(i)
   (b) unable to pay debts.
   UFTA § 4(a)(2)(ii); FFTA § 3304(b)(1)(B)(ii)
3. Debt before transfer and no equal value and an insolvent debtor.
   UFTA § 5(a); FFTA § 3304(a)(1)(A) and (B)
4. Debt before transfer and transfer to an insider and for an antecedent debt and debtor insolvent and the transferee had knowledge.
   UFTA § 5(b); FFTA § 3304(a)(2)(A) and (B).

§ 6.4 First Circuit Fraudulent Transfers

In reviewing the different requirements of Sections 4, 6 and 7 of UFCA, the First Circuit Court of Appeals, in *Boston Trading Group, Inc. v. Burnazos,*[23] had an opportunity to review the Massachusetts Uniform Fraudulent Conveyance Act. In this case the receiver of two companies that managed pools of money for commodity investors brought an action against Burnazos, the former owner of the companies to recover alleged fraudulent conveyances of money. In reviewing the law, the First Circuit explained that Massachusetts General Laws Chapter 109A, § 7 (1986) concerns "actual fraud", and § 4 concerns "constructive fraud." By way of explanation, the First Circuit states:

> It is also important to understand the basic difference between "actual fraud" and "constructive" fraud . . . The courts gradually developed a set of objective criteria, known as "badges of fraud," that they would use as a basis for inferring fraudulent intent. When "badges," such as insolvency and inadequate consideration were present, the courts would presume fraud and void the transaction. In § 3 and § 4, of the Uniform State Law, the "constructive" fraud provisions, the Commissioners codified some of those "badges."[24]

In the district court, the jury had returned a verdict against Burnazos on § 4 (constructive fraud). The First Circuit decided that the jury was not properly instructed on the law as to constructive fraud. The court found Burnazos

---

[23] 835 F.2d 1505 (1st Cir. 1987).

[24] *Id.* at 1509.

entitled to a new trial on the constructive fraud claim because the jury did not find that Shaw and Kepreos (the debtor/transferors on this theory) insolvent, as § 4 requires.[25]

In *Barrett v. Continental Illinois National Bank and Trust Company,*[26] Barrett and Crittenden, the two owners of a commodity trading house known as Eastern Capital Corporation (Eastern), sold their stock to Michael Maduff in December 1982. He purchased Eastern and promised to put additional capital into the company. As part of the deal, Barrett and Crittenden kept an option to repurchase the stock of Eastern for $51,000 plus the amount of any unrepaid capital contributions made by Maduff. In May 1984, Eastern, at the request of Maduff, transferred about $2 million to Continental Bank.

Barrett and Crittenden filed suit under § 5 of the Massachusetts UFCA, claiming that the transaction with Continental Bank left Eastern with an "unreasonably small capital" and was therefore a fraudulent conveyance. The district court concluded that the plaintiffs failed to prove a violation of § 5. The First Circuit agreed with the district court. The district court looked at the company's capital throughout a reasonable period of time surrounding the dates of the transfer. The First Circuit decided that the district court had properly weighed the raw financial data against the nature of the business and its need for capital at the time of the transfer, and found the transaction proper.[27]

§ 6.5 Second Circuit Fraudulent Transfers

A corporate receiver obtained a judgment against another corporation in *Orr v. Kinderhill Corporation.*[28] While the receiver's suit was pending against Kinderhill Corporation (Kinderhill), the corporation deeded some real property to its wholly-owned subsidiary, Kinderhill Investment Company (KIC), for nominal consideration. After the deeds were transferred, but before they were recorded, Kinderhill distributed the stock of KIC to Kinderhill stockholders. Later, Key Bank, with knowledge of the transactions, lent money to KIC and took back mortgages on the real estate as security. After obtaining a judgment against Kinderhill, Orr, the receiver, brought a fraudulent transfer suit for constructive fraud under the New York UFCA to set aside the transfers by Kinderhill to KIC and KIC's pledge of the real estate to Key Bank. The Second Circuit affirmed the decision that the transfer of property by Kinderhill to KIC did not have any corresponding benefit to Kinderhill. As a transaction not supported by fair consideration, the district court had properly set it aside as a fraudulent conveyance.

---

[25] *Id.* at 1510.

[26] 882 F.2d 1 (1st Cir. 1989), *cert. denied,* 494 U.S. 1028 (1990).

[27] *Id.* at 5.

[28] 991 F.2d 31 (2d Cir. 1993).

On May 5, 1990, the government in *United States v. Gelb*[29] filed a complaint to set aside some real estate conveyances by Gelb in 1978, in an attempt to collect a criminal fine and restitution from him. The original deed of Gelb to some commercial property was defective in its description, and the deed was corrected on November 10, 1986. The court examined the potential application of the Federal Debt Collection Procedures Act (FDCPA) of 1990 to this action. It decided that the effective date of the FDCPA was May 29, 1991, over one year after the complaint was filed. However, the court concluded that the FDCPA provisions applied retroactively under § 3631(b)(1) of the Act. As such, the six-year statute of limitations in § 3306(b)(1) applied to the government's complaint. Therefore, the statute of limitations began to run when Gelb delivered or recorded the corrective deed, rather than when he conveyed the property pursuant to the inaccurate deed, and, thus, the government's complaint was timely filed under the provisions of the FDCPA.

§ 6.6 Third Circuit Fraudulent Transfers

In recent years there have been a number of cases from the Third Circuit Court of Appeals involving the question of whether a leveraged buy-out constituted a fraudulent transfer under the facts of the particular case. In one of the leading cases analyzing the issues in a leveraged buy-out, *United States v. Tabor Court Realty Corp.*,[30] the Third Circuit examined a complex leveraged buy-out and decided whether mortgages given in the transaction were fraudulent conveyances within the meaning of the constructive and intentional fraud sections of the Pennsylvania UFCA, 39 Pennsylvania Statutes §§ 354–357, and if so, whether a later assignment of the mortgage was void as against creditors.[31]

The action was brought by the United States to reduce to judgment alleged delinquent federal income taxes, interest, and penalties against a corporation and its subsidiaries and to collect certain tax claims and set aside as fraudulent conveyances certain mortgages purporting to encumber lands of corporations and subsidiaries. By way of background the court stated:

---

[29] 783 F. Supp. 748 (E.D.N.Y. 1991).

[30] 803 F.2d 1288 (3d Cir. 1986), *cert. denied sub. nom.*, McCellan Realty Company v. United States, 483 U.S. 1288 (1987).

[31] The district court had made 481 findings of facts and issued three separate published opinions: United States v. Glenagles Investment Co., 565 F. Supp. 556 (M.D. Pa. 1983) (Gleneagles I); 571 F. Supp. 935 (1983) (Gleneagles II); and 584 F. Supp. 671 (1984) (Gleneagles III).

> A leveraged buy-out is not a legal term of art. It is shorthand expression describing a business practice wherein a company is sold to a small number of investors, typically including members of the company's management, under financial arrangements in which there is a minimum amount of equity and a maximum amount of debt. The financing typically provides for a substantial return of investment capital by means of mortgages or high risk bonds, popularly known as "junk bonds." The predicate transaction here fits the popular notion of a leveraged buy-out. Shareholders of the Raymond Group sold the corporation to a small group of investors headed by Raymond's president; these investors borrowed substantially all of the purchase price at an extremely high rate of interest secured by mortgages on the assets of the selling company and its subsidaries and those of additional entities that guaranteed repayment.
>
> To effectuate the buy-out, Great American obtained a loan commitment from Institute Investors Trust on July 24, 1973, in the amount of $8,530,000. The 1973 interrelationship among the many creditors of the Raymond Group, and the sale to Great American—a seemingly empty corporation which was able to perform the buy-out only on the strength of the massive loan from IIT—forms the backdrop for the relevancy of the Pennsylvania Uniform Fraudulent Conveyance Act, one of the critical legal questions presented for our decision.[32]

The Third Circuit analyzed the complex series of transactions, and affirmed the decision of the district court that the leveraged buyout was a fraudulent transfer under §§ 4 and 7 of the Pennsylvania UFCA, and remanded a small portion of the district court orders to declare void the assignment of the IIT mortgages and other security instruments of McClellan Realty Company.

In *Moody v. Security Pacific Business Credit, Inc.*,[33] a trustee in bankruptcy brought an action against participants in a leveraged buy-out of a corporate debtor under the Pennsylvania UFCA. The Third Circuit affirmed the district court decision that Jeannette Corporation, the Chapter 11 debtor, was not left with an unreasonably small capital merely because after the leveraged buy-out its sole source of operating capital was its line of credit with Security Pacific Business Credit, Inc.[34]

§ 6.7 Ninth Circuit Fraudulent Transfers

In *Hayes v. Palm Seedlings Partners-A (In Re Agricultural Research and Technology Group, Inc.)*,[35] a bankruptcy trustee for Agricultural Research

---

32 803 F. 2d 1288, 1292 (1986).

33 971 F.2d 1056 (3rd Cir. 1992).

34 *Id.* at 1072–73.

35 916 F.2d 528 (9th Cir. 1990).

and Technology Group, Inc. (Agretech) brought a fraudulent conveyance action under the Hawaii UFTA, seeking to recover funds from a partnership, Palm Seedlings Partners—A, its general partner, and its limited partners. The Ninth Circuit affirmed the district court findings that Agretech transferred monies in fraud of creditors to Palm Seddlings by means of a "Ponzi" scheme.

> A Ponzi scheme is an arrangement whereby an enterprise makes payments to investors from the proceeds of a later investment rather than from profits of the underlying business venture, as the investors expected. The fraud consists of transferring proceeds received from the new investors to previous investors, thereby giving other investors the impression that a legitimate profit making business opportunity exists, where in fact no such opportunity exists.[36]

The court held that the mere existence of a Ponzi scheme has been found to fulfill the requirement of actual intent to defraud.[37]

In *United States v. John P. Bertie,*[38] the United States brought suit on behalf of the U.S. Small Business Administration to enforce provisions of a loan guarantee agreement and to set aside certain conveyances by Mr. Bertie and his wife. The Berties had transferred two parcels of real estate they owned to Mr. Bertie as trustee for their minor children. The district court found the existence of several badges of fraud, including:

1. the transfers were made without consideration
2. the relationship between the transferors and the beneficiaries of the transferee trust was that of parents and children
3. the transferors were heavily indebted at the time of the transfers
4. lawsuits were imminent by creditors, and in particular by the plaintiff
5. Bertie, as trustee of the trust, continued in possession and control over the property and did not maintain separate books or records for the trust, and never made an accounting to the beneficiaries of the trust.[39]

§ 6.8 Tenth Circuit Fraudulent Transfers

In *United States v. Christensen,*[40] the United States brought a civil action to reduce federal tax assessments to judgment, to set aside the taxpayer's conveyances of two parcels of real estate, and to foreclose tax liens against the

---

[36] *Id.* at 531.

[37] *Id.* at 536.

[38] 529 F.2d 506 (9th Cir. 1976).

[39] *Id.* at 508.

[40] 751 F. Supp. 1532 (D. Utah 1990), *appeal dismissed,* 961 F.2d 221 (10th Cir. 1990).

taxpayer's interest in those parcels. Under the Utah UFTA, the court found the conveyances of real property by Christensen were fraudulent under several badges of fraud.[41]

§ 6.9 —Form of Fraudulent Transfer Complaint under the Federal Debt Collection Procedures Act

[Usual Headnote]

1. Allegation of Jurisdiction and Venue.

2. Parties.

3. Background Facts.

4. The Transfers Summarized.

Count One—Federal Debt Collection Procedures Act

5. The allegations of Paragraphs 1–4 above are incorporated herein by reference.

6. __________ [describe debt] is a debt as that term is used in the various sections of the Federal Debt Collection Procedures Act (FDCPA), 28 U.S.C. §§ 3001, *et seq.*

7. Such debts arose before the transfers described in Paragraphs ___–___ above.

8. The transactions described in Paragraphs ___–___ are transfers within the meaning of § 3301(6) of the FDCPA, 28 U.S.C. § 3301(6).

9. Defendant ______ made the transfers described in Paragraphs ___–___ above without receiving reasonably equivalent value for them.

10. On information and belief, Defendant _______ was either insolvent at the time he made the transfers or was rendered insolvent by them.

11. Pursuant to Section 3304(a) of the FDCPA, 28 U.S.C. § 3304(a), the transfers described in paragraphs ___–___ are fraudulent as to Defendant ______'s debts to the United States.

---

[41] *Id.* at 1537.

§ 6.10 Time for Filing Fraudulent Transfer Claims

Under the UFCA there are no statute of limitations provisions, but a creditor is subject to any applicable state statute of limitations inserted in the state version of the uniform act. UFTA § 9 contains a statute of limitations provisions which varies according to state law.[42] FFTA in 28 U.S.C. § 3306(b) contains either a six- or two-year limitation on fraudulent transfer actions depending on the section of the statute used to set aside the transfer.

CONSTRUCTIVE TRUST FUND CLAIM

§ 6.11 Constructive Trust Fund Claim

Mr. Justice Story first enunicated the trust fund doctrine in *Wood v. Dummer* in 1824.[43] "In its simplest form, the trust fund theory holds that under certain circumstances and conditions the property of the corporation will be deemed a trust fund for the benefit of the corporation's creditors, as well as its shareholders. When dissolution occurs, the assets distributed to the shareholders are conceived as constituting a trust fund available for the satisfaction of any unpaid corporate debts. Thus, the creditors have an equitable lien upon the property and a right to priority of payment over the stockholders."[44] Justice Story in *Wood v. Dummer* commented:

> It appears to me clear upon general principles, as well as legislative intention, that the capital stock of banks is to be deemed a pledge or trust fund for the payment of the debts contracted by the bank. The public, as well as the legislature, have always supposed this to be a fund appropriated for such purpose. The individual stockholders are not liable for the debts of the bank in their private capacities. The charter relieves them from personal responsibility, and substitutes the capital stock in its stead. Credit is universally given to this fund by the public as the only means of repayment.[45]

The principal issue in the *Wood* case concerned whether the capital stock in the shareholder's hands was liable to the payment of debts of the bank.

---

42 *See* Aberdeen Federal Savings & Loan Association, 794 P.2d 1322 (Wash. Ct. App. 1990) (three-year state statute on fraud applied to fraudulent conveyance action rather than ten-year statute based on judgments).

43 30 F. Cas. 435 (No. 17,944) (C.C.D. Me 1824).

44 Knepper, Liability of Corporate Officers for Debts of Financially Troubled Corporations, ___ Com. L. J. 389 (Oct. 1976).

45 30 F. Cas. 435, 437 (No. 17,944) (C.C.D. Me. 1824).

Justice Story decided that the paid-in-capital of the bank was a trust fund for the payment of the bank's debts to creditors.

The corporate trust fund theory has continued to develop.[46] In the leading case from the Supreme Court, *Pepper v. Litton* Justice Douglas in delivering the opinion for the Court described the duties of the dominant or controlling stockholder:

> He who is in such a fiduciary position cannot serve himself first and his cestuis second. He cannot manipulate the affairs of his corporation to their detriment and in disregard of the standards of common decency and honesty. He cannot by the intervention of a corporate entity violate the ancient precept against serving two masters. . . . He cannot utilize his inside information and his strategic position for his own preferment.[47]

Where the corporate fiduciary has distributed the assets of an insolvent corporation to its stockholders while leaving its creditors unpaid, the creditors can seek to hold the corporate fiduciary personally liable, and seek to satisfy their claims from the asset in the hands of the stockholders.[48]

§ 6.12 Basic Elements in Pleading a Constructive Trust Fund Claim

The basic elements in pleading a constructive trust fund claim can be summarized as follows:

1. **Existence of a Creditor**—to whom a debt or claim is owed by the corporation, and the date of the creditor's judgment against the corporation.
2. **Dissolution or Substantial Liquidation of the Corporation**—the corporation is dissolved or a substantial amount of its assets are transferred, distributed, loaned or liquidated.
3. **Transfer of Corporate Assets to Shareholder**—the corporate assets are distributed by a fiduciary to the shareholders, a relative of the shareholders, or to a new corporation in which the fiduciary has a substantial interest, leaving the corporate creditors unpaid.

---

46 Norton, *Relationship of Shareholders to Corporate Creditors upon Dissolution; Nature and Implications of the "Trust Fund" Doctrine of Corporate Assets,* 30 Bus. Law 1061 (1975).

47 308 U.S. 295, 311 (1939). *Cf.* Pierce v. United States, 255 U.S. 398, 402 (1920).

48 255 U.S. 398, 402 (1920). Justice Brandeis states: "The corporation cannot disable itself from responding by distributing its property among its stockholders and leaving remediless those who have valid claims. In such a case the claims after being reduced to judgments may be satisfied out of the assets in the hands of stockholders." *See* 16 Am. Jur. Proof of Facts 3d *Fiduciary Duty* § 8 (1992).

4. **Insolvency of the Corporation**—the corporation is insolvent at the time of the distribution, or the distribution itself leaves the corporation without sufficient assets to satisfy outstanding creditors.

§ 6.13 Second Circuit Constructive Trust Fund Cases

In *Clarkson Company Limited v. Shaheen,*[49] Newfoundland Refinery Company Limited (NRC) in 1974 and 1975 advanced or loaned money to its controlling director, John Shaheen, and companies controlled by him when NRC was insolvent.

The Second Circuit, in affirming the decision against Shaheen, quoted from *New York Credit Men's Adjustment Bureau, Inc. v. Weiss*[50] as follows: "If the corporation was insolvent at that time it is clear that defendants, as officers and directors thereof, were to be considered as though trustees of the property for the corporate-beneficiaries."[51]

In *Plastic Contact Lens Company v. Frontier Of Northeast, Inc.,*[52] Frontier, on January 5, 1966, filed a certificate of dissolution with the State of New York and distributed all of its assets to the stockholders of the corporation. The district court found the individual defendants liable jointly and severally to the creditors of the corporation under the corporate trust fund doctrine.

§ 6.14 Fourth Circuit Constructive Trust Fund Cases

In the situation where a corporation becomes insolvent, the Fourth Circuit in *Federal Deposit Insurance Corp. v. Sea Pines Company,*[53] applied the constructive trust fund doctrine and piercing the corporate veil doctrines in reversing the district court and holding a parent company liable for the debt of its subsidiary.

---

[49] 660 F.2d 506 (2d Cir. 1981), *cert. denied,* 455 U.S. 990 (1982).

[50] 305 N.Y. 1, 110 N.E.2d 397 (1953).

[51] *Id.* at 7.

[52] 324 F. Supp. 213, 220 (W.D. N.Y. 1969), *aff'd* 441 F.2d 67 (2d Cir. 1971), *cert. denied,* 404 U.S. 881 (1971).

[53] 692 F.2d 973, 977 (4th Cir. 1982), *cert. denied,* 461 U.S. 928 (1982); *Cf.* Davis v. Woolf, 147 F.2d 629, 633 (4th Cir. 1945).

§ 6.15 Fifth Circuit Constructive Trust Fund Cases

The Fifth Circuit Court of Appeals also recognizes the constructive trust fund principal. In *American National Bank Of Austin v. Mortgageamerica Corporation (In Re Mortgageamerica Corporation),*[54] Long, who controlled Mortgageamerica, stripped the company of its assets, leaving it insolvent and unable to pay American National Bank of Austin. The bankruptcy trustee prosecuted a suit against Long under both the Texas Fraudulent Transfer Act and the corporate trust fund theory. The Fifth Circuit affirmed the district court decision on appeal that the bankruptcy trustee had the right to bring the action for constructive trust fund violations and fraudulent transfers on behalf of all creditors and shareholders of Mortgageamerica.[55]

§ 6.16 —Form of Constructive Trust Fund Complaint

[Usual Headnote]

1. Allegation of Jurisdiction and Venue.

2. Parties.

3. Background facts, including the date and kind of debt owed the creditor-plaintiff, and the date of its judgment against the corporation.

4. Describe the position of the fiduciary in the corporation.

5. Describe the facts which indicate that the corporation is insolvent.

6. Summarize the transfers made from the corporation at the time of the insolvency, or how the transfers rendered the corporation insolvent. Indicate who received the transfers, and his relationship to the fiduciary.

7. Prayer for Relief—Plaintiff prays that its judgment against the __________ corporation be established as a lien against the assets of (describe the assets of the shareholders, or describe the new corporation to which the assets of the judgment-debtor corporation were transferred upon liquidation or winding up

---

[54] 714 F.2d 1266 (5th Cir. 1983).

[55] 714 F.2d 1266, 1276–77. *Cf.* Neill v. Phinney, 245 F.2d 645, 651–52 (5th Cir. 1957); United States v. Thomas, 515 F. Supp 1351, 1356 (W.D. Tex. 1981); Whisenhunt v. Park Lane Corporation, 418 F. Supp. 1096, 1098 (N.D. Tex. 1976).

of the judgment-debtor corporation) ________________ under the constructive trust fund doctrine for a sum equal to the amount of plaintiff's judgment, plus interest to date, and that the assets be sold and the proceeds applied to satisfy plaintiff's judgment.

PIERCING THE CORPORATE VEIL

§ 6.17 Piercing the Corporate Veil Claim

The general rule in corporate law is that shareholders, officers and directors maintain a separate identity from their corporation, and corporate liabilities remain liabilities of the corporation, not liabilities of the shareholder, officer or director.[56] However, limited corporate liability is subject to "the judicially imposed exception to this principle by which courts disregard the separateness of the corporation and hold a shareholder responsible for the corporation's action as if it were the shareholder's own."[57] Courts exercise the power to pierce the corporate veil reluctantly and cautiously, and the burden of proof is always on the party asserting the claim.[58]

In one variety of piercing case, the court determines the issue of whether a dominant officer, director and/or shareholder is actually the alter ego of the corporation, and thus, whether the corporate veil should be pierced to hold the individual personally liable. In another variety of piercing case, the court determines whether a controlling parent corporation should be liable for the debts of its subsidiary. In each variety of piercing case the courts look at a number of factors in determining liability.

§ 6.18 Basic Factors in Piercing the Corporate Veil

There are a variety of factors that courts review in determining individual liability in piercing the corporate veil or "alter ego" cases. Among the factors[59] for determination are:

---

[56] Thompson, *Piercing The Corporate Veil: An Empirical Study,* 76 Cornell L. Rev. 1036 (1991). This article is an excellent article on the study of this doctrine and contains statistics on this topic from over 2,000 cases.

[57] *Id.,* 1036. *See also* Note, *Piercing The Corporate Veil: The Alter Ego Doctrine Under Federal Common Law,* 95 Harv. L. Rev. 853 (1982); *Hartman, Piercing the Corporate Veil in Federal Courts: Is Circumvention of a Statute Enough?,* 13 Pac. L. J. 1245 (1982).

[58] DeWitt Truck Brokers v. W. Ray Flemming Fruit Co., 540 F.2d 681 (4th Cir. 1976).

[59] *See Id.,* 540 F.2d, at 685–87; United States v. WRW Corporation, 986 F.2d 138, 143 (6th Cir. 1993); Michigan Carpenters Council, Health and Welfare Fund, 933 F.2d 376, 384–85 (6th Cir. 1991), *cert. denied,* 112 S. Ct. 585 (1991); United States v. Fidelity

1. Undercapitalization of the corporation
2. Failure to observe corporate formalities
3. Nonpayments of dividends
4. The insolvency of the debtor corporation at the time
5. Siphoning of funds of the corporation (by excessive salary or otherwise) by the dominant stockholder
6. Nonfunctioning of other officers and directors
7. Absence of corporate records
8. The fact that the corporation is merely a facade for the operations of the dominant stockholder or stockholders
9. Factors leading to a picture of basic fairness

Factors in determining[60] a parent corporation's liability for subsidiary's debts include the following:

1. Parent owns all stock of the subsidiary
2. Common directors and officers
3. Parent finances subsidiary
4. Parent causes subsidiary's incorporation
5. Subsidiary has grossly inadequate capital
6. Parent pays salaries or expenses of subsidiary
7. Subsidiary has no business except with its parent or subsidiary or has no assets except those transferred by its parent or subsidiary
8. Directors and officers do not act independently in interests of subsidiary
9. Formal legal requirements of the subsidiary such as keeping corporate minutes are not observed

---

Capital Corp., 920 F.2d 827, 837–38 (11th Cir. 1991); Wesco Manufacturing, Inc. v. Tropical Attractions of Palm Beach, Inc., 833 F.2d 1484, 1486 (11th Cir. 1987); Kashi v. Gratsos, 790 F.2d 1050, 1056–57 (2d Cir. 1986); Van Dorn Company v. Future Chemical and Oil Corp., 753 F.2d 565, 569–70 (7th Cir. 1985); Labadie Coal Co. v. Black, 672 F.2d 92, 97–98 (D.C. Cir. 1982); Jefferson Pilot Broadcasting v. Hilary & Hogan, 617 F.2d 133 (5th Cir. 1980); Bruhn's Freezer Meats v. United States Department of Agriculture, 439 F.2d 681 (4th Cir. 1976); G.M. Leasing Corp. v. United States, 514 F.2d 935, 939–40 (10th Cir. 1975), *aff'd in part, rev'd in part* 429 U.S. 338 (1977); Towe Antique Ford Foundation v. Internal Revenue Service, 791 F. Supp. 1450 (D. Mont. 1992); Ramaria Familienstiftung v. United States, 643 F. Supp. 139, 146 (S.D. Fla. 1986).

60 Rea v. An-Son Corporation, 79 F.R.D. 25, 30–31 (W.D. Okla. 1978); *Cf.* Ministry of Defense v. Gould, Inc. 969 F.2d 764, 769–70 (9th Cir. 1992); Krivo Industrial Supply Company v. National Distillers and Chemical Corporation, 483 F.2d 1098, 1102–03 (5th Cir. 1973); H.H. Robertson Company v. V.S. Dicarlo General Contractors, Inc., 789 F. Supp. 998, 1000 (E.D. Mo. 1992), *aff'd* 994 F.2d 476 (8th Cir. 1993).

10. Distinctions between parent and subsidiary are disregarded or confused
11. Subsidiary does not have full board of directors

§ 6.19 Example Cases in Piercing the Corporate Veil

The leading case in applying the alter ego or instrumentality doctrine to an individual is *Dewitt Truck Brokers v. W. Ray Flemming Fruit Company*,[61] In that case, Dewitt Truck Brokers (Dewitt), a creditor of the W. Ray Flemming Fruit Company (Company), brought an action to impose individual liability against W. Ray Flemming (Flemming) for the company's debt to Dewitt for transportation charges. The company was in the business of a commission agent, selling fruit produce for the farm growers in the Edgefield, South Carolina area.

The Fourth Circuit Court of Appeals affirmed the district court findings after looking at all the factors in analyzing alter ego liability.[62] Significant facts established at trial included that:

1. Flemming owned about 90 percent of the Company's stock.
2. The other director of the Company, Bernstein, was not active in company affairs, and was a mere figurehead.
3. There were no records of company board meetings.
4. The company never had stockholders' meetings.
5. No stockholder other than Flemming ever received any salary, dividend, or fee from the company.
6. The company never showed any profits, and Flemming's salary was never voted on by the Board.
7. The company was undercapitalized in that any risk capital had been reduced to about $3,000.00.
8. The company never paid any dividends.
9. Flemming advised Dewitt that he personally would take care of the hauling charges if the company failed to do so.
10. Flemming's salary per year was at about the same rate as the company owed Dewitt in hauling charges.

Based upon the analysis of these factors, the Fourth Circuit affirmed the district court's "disregard of the corporate entity in furtherance of basic and fundamental fairness."[63]

---

[61] 540 F.2d 681 (4th Cir. 1976).

[62] 540 F.2d 681, 685–89 (4th Cir. 1976).

[63] 540 F.2d, at 689.

In *United States v. WRW Corporation,*[64] the Sixth Circuit Court of Appeals affirmed the district court's piercing the corporate veil of WRW Corporation on the following facts:

1. WRW was undercapitalized because its initial capital of $3,000.00 was insufficient to pay normal operating expenses.
2. WRW failed to observe corporate formalities and proper corporate authorizations.
3. The individual officers commingled funds with WRW.
4. WRW never distributed any dividends.
5. There was *no* evidence of siphoning off funds.

In *Rea v. An-Son Corporation,*[65] the district court made an exhaustive inquiry into the factors in parent-subsidiary veil piercing. The court also commented on the policy for veil piercing in such situations: On the other hand, the notion of a separate corporate existence of parent and subsidiary or affiliated corporations will not be recognized where one corporation is so organized and controlled and its business conducted in such a manner as to make it merely an agency, instrumentality, adjunct, or alter ego of another corporation and the separate identity of two corporations will not be extended to permit one of the corporations to evade its just obligations or to promote fraud or illegality or injustice. Upon disregard of the corporate entity, the parent corporation may be held liable for the acts of the subsidiary.[66]

FEDERAL PRIORITY STATUTE CLAIM

§ 6.20 Federal Priority Claim

When the United States is a creditor it enjoys the protection of the Federal Priority Statute, 31 U.S.C. § 3713.[67] In *United States v. Moore,*[68] Chief Justice Warren explained the history of this statute.

---

[64] 986 F.2d 138, 143 (6th Cir. 1993); *cf.* H.H. Robertson Co. v. United States Dicarlo General Contractors, Inc., 789 F. Supp. 998 (E.D. Mo. 1992), *aff'd* 994 F.2d 476 (8th Cir. 1993).

[65] 79 F.R.D. 25, 30–31 (W.D. Okla. 1978).

[66] *Id.* at 29.

[67] 31 U.S.C. § 3713(a)(1) A claim of the United States Government shall be paid first when—

(A) a person indebted to the Government is insolvent and—

(i) the debtor without enough property to pay all debts makes a voluntary assignment of property;

> The Statute at issue is almost as old as the constitution, and its roots reach back even further into the English common law. . . . The earliest priority statute enacted in the Act of July 31, 1789, 1 Stat. 29, which dealt with bonds posted by importers in lieu of payment of duties for release of imported goods. It provided that the "debt due to the United States" for such duties shall be discharged first "in all cases of insolvency, or where any estate in the hands of executors, administrators shall be insufficient to pay all the debt due from the deceased."[69]

The law developed as a way of ensuring that debts owed the federal government were given priority over debts to other creditors, and has remained basically unchanged now for over two hundred years. The policy of paying first the debts due the federal government was a vestige of English common law. The first part of the statutory scheme (31 U.S.C. § 3713(a)(1)) establishes that the federal government has a priority claim in a situation where a debtor's property is being distributed among his creditors and it is insufficient to satisfy all of them. In such a case, the United States has priority over general unsecured claims and over secured claims which arise after the priority statute has been triggered in some way. "Since the Government's priority is fixed when the triggering event occurs, subsequent transfer by the debtor, including subsequently created security interests should not prevail against the Government."[70]

The second part of the statute (31 U.S.C. § 3713(b)) places the burden on the person who controls the debtor's assets to see that the government is paid first.[71] Thus, some person acting on behalf of the debtor, such as an executor, assignee, receiver, or officer, director, or shareholder of a corporate debtor, has a responsibility under the statute to apply the assets controlled to payment of the government's claim as a priority. If the law is not followed, the individual becomes answerable out of personal funds.

(iii) property of the debtor, if absent, is attached; or

(iiii) an act of bankruptcy is committed; or

(B) the estate of a deceased debtor, in the custody of the executor or administrator, is not enough to pay all debts of the debtor.

(2) This subsection does not apply to a case under title 11.

(b) A representative of a person or an estate (except a trustee acting under title 11) paying any part of a debt of the person or estate before paying a claim of the Government is liable to the extent of the payment for unpaid claims of the Government. (Pub. L. 97-258, Sept. 13, 1982, 96 Stat. 972)

68 423 U.S. 77 (1975).

69 *Id.* at 80 (1975).

70 Lurey, *The Federal Priority Statute—Secured Creditor Versus The United States,* 52 Los Angeles Bar J. 525 (April 1977).

71 King v. United States, 379 U.S. 329 (1964).

§ 6.21 Basic Elements in Pleading a Federal Priority Statute Claim

To prove a prima facie case under the Federal Priority Statute, the following basic elements are necessary:

1. There is a debt due to the United States.
2. The debtor is insolvent.
3. An event occurs which triggers the priority statute:
   (a) The debtor without enough property to pay all debts makes a voluntary assignment of property;
   (b) property of the debtor, if absent, is attached; or
   (c) an act of bankruptcy is committed; or (acts of bankruptcy include preferential transfers, fraudulent transfers, failure to discharge liens, and receivership/assignment for the benefit of creditors.)
   (d) the estate of a deceased debtor, in the custody of the executor or administrator is not enough to pay all debts of the debtor.
4. Property of debtor is distributed by someone (except a bankruptcy trustee) acting on behalf of the debtor.

For Step 1, the debt (or claim of the United States) is defined very broadly in cases involving the statute. It includes:

1. Unemployment compensation taxes
2. Gasoline tax
3. Income tax
4. Buoy damage by insolvent
5. Civil penalties, environmental claims, and tax penalties
6. Criminal fines
7. Custom duties
8. Excess profits tax
9. Capital stock taxes
10. Surety on bail bonds
11. Emergency loans by federal agencies
12. Sum due on notes from federal agencies
13. Indian funds deposited in bank
14. Losses where contractor defaulted
15. Misappropriated army paymaster funds
16. Funds held by navy disbursing agents
17. Claim against endorser of protested bill of exchange

18. Judgments
19. Debts due any other government agencies
20. Any other U.S. tax claims
21. Tort claims
22. Forfeitures[72]

Regarding Step 2, the government must allege insolvency, and prove it. Insolvency in the statute is used in the bankruptcy sense that all of assets held by the debtor are insufficient to pay all liabilities then due. Step 3 concerns some triggering event, that is the assets are held by an assignee, receiver, or creditor of the debtor, as a result of a voluntary transfer by the debtor, or application of some type of legal process, such as, an attachment, or perhaps, one of the acts of bankruptcy is committed. Step 4 is that property of the debtor is distributed by someone acting on behalf of the debtor. That person can be someone having control of the debtor's assets (such as an executor, assignee, receiver, officer, director, or shareholder of a corporation) who makes a distribution or transfer of the debtor's assets without paying the government's claim. The transferor must know or have notice of the debt due the United States at the time of the wrongful transfer.

§ 6.22 Example Federal Priority Statute Cases

There are basically two types of cases which arise under the Federal Priority Statute. In the first type of case, the government seeks priority to the debtor's assets held by a fiduciary (that is, an assignee, receiver, conservator, liquidator, administrator, or executor) before distribution. In the second type of case, the government seeks liability under the Federal Priority Statute against the person who controlled the distribution of the debtor' assets without paying the claim of the United States.

In *Bramwell v. U.S. Fidelity Co.,*[73] a deposit of an Indian reservation of the United States was made in an Oregon bank. The bank became insolvent, and Bramwell, the Oregon superintendent of banks, took control of the bank's affairs. The United States collected from Fidelity, the bonding company, and Fidelity, as assignee of the United States, under the priority statute, brought suit against Bramwell to require him to pay it first, out of the assets of the insolvent bank. The state of Oregon argued that title to the assets remained in

[72] *See generally*, Brown, *The Federal Priority Statute: An Overview From The Current Government Propective,* 21 The Trial Lawyer's Guide 121 (1978). (Since this article was written there have been changes in the statute, and trustees in bankruptcy are no longer liable under the statute.)

[73] 269 U.S. 483 (1926); *cf.* Gordon v. United States Dept. of Treasury, 846 F.2d 272 (4th Cir. 1988).

the bank until transferred to purchasers at sales authorized by the Court in the liquidation proceedings. Justice Butler said that the bank did not have to be "divested" of its property or Bramwell have to be "invested" with the property. The fact was that Bramwell's role in liquidating the bank was "in substance the same as those of a trustee having legal title of property for the purpose of converting it into to be paid over to specific [creditors]."[74] As such, it was a transfer, and Fidelity, as assignee of the United States had to be paid first.

In *United States v. Gotwals,*[75] Gotwals was an attorney who represented an insolvent debtor in an action which resulted in a judgment against the debtor by the United States. Eleven days before the judgment, the debtor, also an attorney, assigned Gotwals his rights to payment of legal fees in another case, amounting to $13,000. The assignment to Gotwals was for services "which had been rendered or which were to be rendered." The court allowed the government to enforce its right of priority against the property [money] in the possession of Gotwals, since the transfer by the debtor was clearly done with the intent to prefer Gotwals over the other creditors of the debtor, namely, the United States.

In *Lakeshore Apartments, Inc. v. United States,*[76] Lakeshore borrowed $3,000,000 from National Life Insurance Company in 1947 to build and operate a large apartment complex in the state of Washington. The loan was insured under the provisions of the Federal Housing Administration (FHA). After a business decline in 1960, Lakeshore defaulted on the loan, and under its agreement, National assigned Lakeshore's note and mortgage to the Federal Housing Administration. [This was Step 1, a debt became due the United States.]

Then, in 1962, the stock of the corporation was transferred to new owners, Behar and Brown and their wives. Behar and Brown, and the former Lakeshore shareholders, set up a partnership known as ABC Management Company (ABC) to manage the apartment complex and receive a fee for their services. Later, in June 1963, Brown and Behar, as officers and directors of Lakeshore, had the corporation issue several checks for over $30,000 to ABC for management services rendered. The checks were held by ABC for several months, some were cashed on August 23rd and some on September 13, 1963. [This was Step 4, property of the debtor distributed by someone acting on behalf of the debtor.] At the same time, Lakeshore was experiencing financial problems and was in default on its FHA loan, and the United States had filed a complaint to foreclose and have a receiver appointed for the corporation. [Appointment of the receiver was Step 3 of the process, the triggering event.] It was established later, that Lakeshore's liabilities

---

[74] *Id.* at 491.

[75] 156 F.2d 692 (10th Cir. 1946), *cert. denied,* 329 U.S. 781 (1946).

[76] 351 F.2d 349 (9th Cir. 1965).

exceeded its assets during the period of April 1963 through September of that year. [This was Step 2, the corporation was insolvent.] Once the receiver was appointed, on September 13th, he quickly determined that the management fees had been paid by check and cashed shortly before, and on the day, of his appointment.

Thereafter, the United States filed a civil complaint seeking to establish personal liability against Behar and Brown, Lakeshore's shareholder-managers, for disbursing Lakeshore's funds in violation of the Federal Priority Statute. The court found that Behar and Brown were controlling shareholders and managers of Lakeshore.[77] They also knew of the debt due the United States when they authorized the checks for payment to ABC. The court found the priority statute was violated when Lakeshore, an insolvent debtor of the United States, committed an act of bankruptcy by making a "preferential transfer" to ABC, that is Behar and Brown gave ABC's debt preference over the claim of the United States, and thus Behar and Brown subjected themselves to transferee liability.

In *United States v. Gottheiner (In re Peter Gottheiner)*[78] Gottheiner was the president and principal shareholder of a medicare provider, California Coordinated Health Care Services, Inc. (CCHCS). When CCHCS was terminated from the Medicare program, it owed the United States $812,351.66. The United States obtained a judgment against CCHCS on October 6, 1978. During the time that CCHCS was insolvent Gottheiner caused the corporation to make transfers of CCHCS funds to himself in repayment of loans and direct payments of funds coming into CCHCS accounts. The bankruptcy court held that Gottheiner was personally liable for $89,487.00 under the priority statute for these payments, and since these acts were "defalcations" within Bankruptcy Act § 17(a)(4), the debt was nondischargeable.

---

[77] *Cf.* United States v. Lutz, 295 F.2d 736 (5th Cir. 1961); United States v. Golden Acres, Inc., 684 F. Supp. 96 (D. Del. 1988); United States v. Vertac Chemical Corporation, 671 F. Supp. 595 (E.D. Ark. 1987), *vacated on other grounds,* 855 F.2d 856 (8th Cir. 1988); United States v. Excellair, Inc., 637 F. Supp. 1377 (D. Colo. 1986); United States v. 58th Street Plaza Theatre, Inc., 287 F. Supp. 475 (S.D.N.Y. 1968); United States v. Sullivan, 214 F. Supp. 701 (W.D. Pa. 1963).

[78] 3 Bankr. 404 (Bankr. N.D. Cal. 1980), *aff'd,* 703 F.2d 1136 (9th Cir. 1983).

CHAPTER 7

RECEIVERSHIP AS A COLLECTION DEVICE

Eric S. Benderson

§ 7.1 Introduction

Geared to the practitioner, this chapter provides an overview of federal equity receiverships, the grounds for their appointment, the role of counsel, the administration of the estate, including applicable statutory requirements under federal law, the handling of assets and claims, and compensation of the receiver and attorneys involved with the estate. It also provides a description of some specialized receiverships found in federal law, particularly receiverships provided for by the Federal Debt Collection Procedures Act of 1990, 28 U.S.C. § 3001 *et seq.*

A federal equity receivership is one of the most powerful weapons in the lawyer's debt collection arsenal. By its nature, it affords a flexible and effective approach to both the preservation of a debtor's assets and the liquidation of those assets for maximum value. For the creditor, a federal equity receivership is, in many instances, preferable to bankruptcy, particularly reorganization under Chapter 11 of the Bankruptcy Code, which has a much more elaborate statutory scheme and procedural structure. In the hands of experienced counsel, a federal equity receivership may afford the best means of preventing the dissipation of assets and the mismanagement of a business or, worse, fraud.

Except where a statute may provide otherwise, the appointment of a receiver is looked upon as an extraordinary equitable remedy, to be granted only as a last resort in order to prevent irreparable harm to a property interest held by a party to litigation. In most instances the remedy will be sought to prevent gross mismanagement, fraud, or other situations which lead to the loss, dissipation, or waste of assets.[1] The receivership remedy is by its nature auxiliary to the primary relief requested in the litigation.[2] This is because the

1 *See e.g.* Burnrite Coal Briquette Co. v. Riggs, 274 U.S. 208 (1927); and Cowin v. Bresler, 741 F.2d 410 (D.C. Cir. 1984).

2 Pusey & Jones Co. v. Hanssen, 261 U.S. 491 (1922).

power to appoint a receiver with control over the affairs of an entity, in order to preserve a legally recognized property interest held by a party, is considered inherent in and incidental to the court's jurisdiction over the basic cause of action.[3] As noted by the Illinois Supreme Court:

> The appointment of a receiver is a branch of equity jurisdiction not dependent upon any statute, and rests largely in the discretion of the appointing court. It had its origin in the English Court of Chancery at an early date, and it was incidental to and in aid of the jurisdiction of equity to enable it to accomplish, as far as practicable, complete justice among the parties before it.[4]

Since the remedy is an extraordinary one that is usually granted by federal courts only when absolutely necessary to prevent irreparable injury and to accomplish a specific purpose for which no other remedy is adequate, the grounds for appointment should be considered carefully by counsel before seeking such relief. Courts have appointed receivers to manage all sorts of entities, including a State Board of Agriculture, prisons, and school districts.[5] A receiver has even been appointed to take over management of a company in order to insure compliance with the antitrust laws.[6] These diverse situations to which this equitable remedy has been applied illustrate its flexibility as a tool covering a wide variety of situations. Those availing themselves of this remedy are as diverse as the circumstances to which it has been applied, including creditors, shareholders, partners, governmental agencies and departments, and even the entity itself. For our purposes we shall concern ourselves mainly with cases where a receiver acts as a caretaker of a company during litigation in order to preserve some recognized property interest of the litigants, or liquidates a company and distributes the proceeds.

It is imperative that in deciding whether to seek a receiver to control, operate, or liquidate a business entity, counsel undertakes a cost benefit analysis in the first instance. This is because the receiver, who is an extension of the

---

[3] Kennedy v. I.C. & L.R. Co., 3 F. 97 (C.C. S.D. Ohio 1880).

[4] Chicago Title & Trust Co. v. Mack, 180 N.E. 412, 413 (1932). Receivership, as an equitable remedy, has had a long history, tracing its origin back to the reign of Edward VI in England in the Sixteenth Century. 16 W. Fletcher, Cyclopedia of the Law of Private Corporations, "Receivers" § 7668 (rev.perm.ed. 1989).

[5] *See* Lewis v. Kugler, 446 F.2d 1343, 1351 n. 18 (3d Cir. 1971) (In this civil rights case complaining about unreasonable searches and seizures by New Jersey State Police, receivership was among the possible remedies the Court found applicable); Hellebust v. Brownback, 824 F.Supp. 1524 (D. Kan. 1993) (Governor appointed as receiver to run Kansas State Board of Agriculture until such time as the state devised a constitutional method for the selection of board members); Newman v. State of Alabama, 466 F. Supp. 628 (M.D. Ala. 1979); (receiver appointed to run Alabama prison system); Morgan v. McDonough, 540 F.2d 527 (1st Cir. 1976); and Turner v. Goolsby, 255 F. Supp. 724 (S.D. Ga. 1966) (receivers appointed in these civil rights cases to run schools).

[6] United States v. American Tobacco Co., 221 U.S. 106 (1911).

court, must seek court approval for all significant actions and this can add significantly to the cost of running a business. Thus, the receivership's expense may outweigh its value. In addition to a cost benefit analysis, counsel should carefully consider whether the particular circumstances of the debtor justify the court employing this extraordinary remedy. Another consideration is the qualifications and experience of the person or entity who will be proposed to act as receiver and the likelihood the court will accept such proposal or select its own appointee.[7]

§ 7.2 A Receivership Is an Extraordinary Remedy Sought in Conjunction with Other Relief Such as a Money Judgment

A receivership is considered an extraordinary remedy that is available to a litigant only upon a showing that other relief is not adequate to protect the litigant's rights.[8]

The party seeking a receivership must show that it has some legally recognized right in the property that is the subject of the litigation, and that this right amounts to more than a mere claim against the defendant involved.[9] In *Piambino v. Bailey,* the Eleventh Circuit found, in the context of a class action seeking the appointment of a receiver over a fund that had been created to compensate purchasers of distributorships in a nationwide pyramid marketing scheme, that Florida plaintiffs, who were "merely prosecuting a tort action for the recovery of unliquidated money damages" and had "not reduced their claims to judgment" were not entitled to the appointment of a receiver.[10] On the other hand, the court in *McDermott v. Russell*[11] allowed the possibility of appointing a receiver in a case involving the claim to ownership

---

7 18 U.S.C. § 1910 makes it a crime for a federal judge to appoint a relative as a receiver:

> Whoever, being a judge of any court of the United States, appoints as receiver, or trustee, any person related to such judge by consanguinity, or affinity, within the fourth degree—shall be fined not more than $10,000 or imprisoned not more than five years, or both.

8 Cowin v. Bresler, 741 F.2d at 417–418 (D.C. Cir. 1984); Chambers v.Blickle Ford Sales. Inc., 313 F.2d 252 (2d Cir. 1963); Mintzer v.Arthur L. Wright Co., 263 F.2d 823 (3d Cir. 1959); Maxwell v.Enterprise Wallpaper Mfg. Co., 131 F.2d 400 (3d Cir. 1942); Cutler v. 65 Sec. Plan, 831 F. Supp. 1008 (E.D.N.Y. 1993); Levin v. Garfinkle, 514 F. Supp. 1160 (E.D. Pa. 1981); and Haase v.Chapman, 308 F. Supp. 399 (W.D. Mo. 1969).

9 Piambino v. Bailey, 757 F.2d 1112 (11th Cir. 1985); Leone Industries v. Associated Packaging, Inc., 795 F.Supp. 117, 120 (D. N.J. 1992); Mintzer v. Arthur L. Wright Co., 263 F. Supp. 823, 825; McDermott v. Russell, 523 F. Supp. 347, 352 (E.D. Pa. 1981); and Securities & Exchange Comm'n v. Republic Nat. Life Ins. Co., 378 F. Supp. 430, 437 (S.D. N.Y. 1975).

10 Piambino v. Bailey, 757 F.2d 1112, 1131–1132.

11 McDermott v. Russell, 523 F. Supp. 347.

of fifty percent of a corporation, based upon plaintiff's assertion that in return for helping to bring about the reorganization of the company, he was promised that ownership interest.

As previously mentioned, the request for receivership relief must be auxiliary to a request for some primary relief, such as a money judgment or an injunction. As Justice Douglas stated:

> This Court has frequently admonished that a federal court of equity should not appoint a receiver where the appointment is not a remedy auxiliary to some primary relief which is sought and which equity may appropriately grant.[12]

Thus, in seeking the equitable remedy of a federal receivership, a party must seek it in aid of some primary relief, such as a money judgment, and demonstrate that such extraordinary relief is the only relief that is adequate to protect the party's rights in the property which is the subject of the litigation.

§ 7.3 Grounds for the Appointment of a Receiver Generally

Although the federal courts have the inherent equitable power to appoint a receiver,[13] we have seen that in the absence of a statute providing otherwise, that this extraordinary remedy will be employed only in the most compelling circumstances.[14] As the Third Circuit has stated: ". . .where there is no fraud or imminent danger of the property being lost, injured, diminished in value, or squandered and where legal remedies do not appear to be inadequate the appointment of a receiver should not be granted."[15] The converse is equally true, that where other remedies are inadequate and where fraud, mismanagement, concealment or dissipation of assets is or is likely to be present, the

---

[12] Kelleam v. Maryland Casualty Company of Baltimore, Md., 312 U.S. 377, 388 (1940); and Gordon v. Washington 295 U.S. 30, 38 (1935). *See also,* Pusey & Jones Co. v. Hanssen, 261 U.S. 491 (1922); Britton v. Green, 325 F.2d 377, 382 (10th Cir. 1963); Guy v. Citizens Fidelity Bank and Trust Company, 429 F.2d 828, 833-834 (6th Cir. 1970); and Resolution Trust v. Fountain Circle Associates, 199 F. Supp. 48, 49 (N.D. Ohio 1992).

[13] Burnrite Coal Briquette Co. v. Riggs, 274 U.S. at 212; U.S. v. Vertac Chemical Corp., 671 F. Supp. 595, 623 (E.D. Ark. 1987) vacated 855 F.2d 856 (8th Cir. 1988); Bracco v. Lackner, 462 F. Supp. 436, 456 (N.D. Calif. 1978).

[14] Republic of Philippines v. New York Land Co., 852 F.2d 33, 36 (2d Cir. 1988); Chambers v. Blickle Ford Sales, Inc., 313 F.2d 252, 260 (2d Cir. 1963); Bracco v. Lackner. 462 F. Supp. at 456; and GA Enterprises, Inc. v. Leisure Living Communities, Inc., 355 F. Supp. 947.

[15] Mintzer v. Arthur L. Wright, Co., 263 F.2d at 826. For a similar expression of this viewpoint, *see* GA Enterprises, Inc. v. Leisure Living Communities, Inc., 335 F. Supp. at 949.

court may appoint a receiver to preserve the assets, at least temporarily.[16] The grounds used by federal courts to justify the appointment of a receiver may apply to both a temporary receiver appointed pending the outcome of litigation, i.e., pendente lite, or a permanent receiver, seeking liquidation of the company. Thus, for example, in relation to the appointment of a receiver pendente lite, a court stated:

> Similarly, the various transfers and financial manipulations in this case, although not direct evidence of fraud, raise a sufficient inference of fraud to indicate to this court that if affirmative protective measures are not implemented immediately, the collateral in question may be further transferred or dissipated to the irreparable detriment of plaintiff herein and thousands of innocent bystanders plaintiff represents. The appointment of a receiver in such circumstances is not a final disposition of this matter by any means. Such appointment only serves to preserve the immediate status quo and protect the interests of all the parties who may be involved. . .[17]

The grounds traditionally considered by courts in determining whether a receivership is an appropriate remedy include: (1) the possible existence of fraudulent conduct; (2) the danger of property being concealed, lost, or diminished in value; (3) the adequacy of other remedies; and (4) the harm to the movant if appointment is denied versus the harm to the parties opposing the receivership if appointment is granted.[18]

The court may also consider the size of the receivership estate and its ability to bear the expenses of a receivership.

In *Commodity Futures Trading Comm. v. Comvest Trading Corp.,*[19] the Commodities Futures Trading Commission (CFTC) sought the appointment of a receiver for a commodities broker, after the defendants had consented to a protective order and a permanent injunction which prohibited the dissipation of assets and the destruction of records and prevented the company from soliciting or accepting funds from clients during such time as the company continued to be undercapitalized and its customer accounts improperly segregated in violation of CFTC Rules and Regulations. In reviewing the grounds for the appointment of a receiver, the court noted the following factors:

---

16 Haase v. Chapman. 308 F. Supp. 399 (W.D. Mo. 1969). *See also* Cowin v. Bresler, 741 F.2d 410.

17 Bookout v. Atlas Financial Corp., 395 F. Supp. 1338 (N.D. Ga. 1974).

18 U.S. v. Vertac Chemical Corp., 671 F. Supp. at 623. *See also* Aviation Supply Corp. v. R.S.B.I. Aerospace, Inc., 999 F.2d 314, 316–317 (8th Cir. 1993); Consolidated Rail Corp. v. Fore River Ry. Co., 861 F.2d 322, 326–327, (lst Cir. 1988); Select Creations, Inc. v. Paliafito American, Inc., 828 F. Supp. 1301, 1367 (E.D. Wis. 1992); Brill & Harrington Investments v. Vernon S. & L., 787 F. Supp. 250, 253–254, (D. D.C. 1992); and New York Life Ins. Co. v. Watt Inv. Corp., 755 F. Supp. 287, 292 (E.D. Calif. 1992).

19 Commodity Futures Trading v. Comvest Trading Corp., 481 F. Supp. 438 (D. Mass. 1979).

> Factors weighed by courts in determining whether a receiver should be appointed have included fraudulent conduct on the part of the defendant; imminent danger their property would be lost, concealed, injured, diminished in value, or squandered; the inadequacy of the available legal remedies; the probability that harm to plaintiff by denial of the appointment would be greater than the injury to the parties opposing appointment; and the plaintiff's probable success in the action and the possibility of irreparable injury to his interest in the property.
>
> Another set of relevant factors—or what might be described as another perspective for evaluation of factors relevant to appointment of a receiver concerns the degree of probability that the interests of the plaintiff and others sought to be protected would in fact be well served by receivership. What is the probability that assets subject to the proposed receivership have a value sufficient to outweigh the added costs likely to result from receivership? What are the dimensions of those probable costs, and what practical provisions can be made for bearing them?
>
> One more relevant set of factors—or another perspective—concerns the nature of the assignment the court will be presenting to the person or other legal entity appointed as receiver, if the motion for receivership is allowed. Can the court assure the person or entity appointed that the undertaking is a useful one and one that will serve the public interest? Can provision be made for assurance of reasonable compensation to the receiver and for the availability of reasonable resources to pay for services of others whose assistance the receiver will need to discharge effectively the assigned responsibility, or instead is it probable that the receiver will in effect be acting without compensation and without resources for engaging essential supporting services of others?[20]

In denying the CFTC's motion for the appointment of a receiver, the court noted that it was being asked to appoint a receiver to protect less than $11,000 in assets, as a way of protecting the interests of investors with claims of over $600,000. Moreover, the court noted that the protective and injunctive orders already in place provided an adequate remedy against the dissipation of assets with regard to any illegal activity. Finally, the court noted that the CFTC had provided no viable plan to assure that if a receiver would be appointed, he would be adequately compensated and have available the necessary resources.[21]

In *Mintzer v. Arthur L. Wright Co.,*[22] the customers of a securities brokerage house sought the appointment of a receiver in conjunction with their suit against the brokerage house seeking compensation for their losses as the result of the improper dealings of one of the defendant's sales representatives. In reversing the district court, which had ordered the appointment of a receiver, the Third Circuit noted that, although the sales representative had

---

20 *Id.* at 441.

21 *Id.* at 442.

22 263 F.2d 823.

grossly abused the trust placed in him by the company, the evidence did not show that the defendant's business was "operated fraudulently or that its own assets were mishandled so as to present the possibility of their dissipation" should the company be permitted to continue management of its own affairs.[23] The court also noted that the mere threat of insolvency posed by the aggregate of the claims against the defendant was not sufficient reason for the appointment of a receiver, since a receiver could not increase the assets of defendant which would be available to satisfy any judgment.[24]

Similarly, in *Meineke Discount Muffler Shops, Inc. v. Noto,*[25] a franchisor was denied the appointment of a receiver pendente lite with respect to its suit seeking damages and the termination of the franchise with one of its franchise muffler shops upon the basis of breach of contract and fraud. The suit stemmed from allegations that the franchisee had been collecting money for work performed on customers' cars without issuing "Meineke receipts" to the customers, and without accounting for such sales to Meineke. In denying the plaintiff's request for the appointment of a receiver, the court noted that although plaintiff had demonstrated a likelihood of success on the merits, the fraudulent activities cited by the plaintiff were attributable to an employee who had since been fired, and there was no showing that the fraudulent activity had continued since that time.

In *Leighton v. One William Street Fund, Inc.,*[26] the Second Circuit upheld the lower court's denial of the appointment of a receiver in a shareholder's derivative suit against a mutual fund, and in which waste of the Fund's assets and a conflict of interest with respect to the Fund's manager were alleged, upon the grounds that plaintiff had an adequate remedy at law through compensatory damages, and there was no showing that the defendant would be unable to pay any damage award.

In *Chambers v. Blickle Ford Sales, Inc.,*[27] the Second Circuit upheld the district court's denial of the appointment of a receiver upon the grounds that plaintiff had adequate remedies at law, specifically garnishment and attachment, so that the extraordinary remedy of the appointment of a receiver was not necessary.

In *Republic of Philippines v. New York Land Co.,*[28] the Second Circuit upheld the district court which had issued an injunction and appointed a special property adviser to oversee the management of several real estate projects that were subject to claims by the Philippine Government, rather than

---

[23] *Id.* at 826.

[24] *Id.*

[25] 603 F. Supp. 443 (E.D.N.Y. 1985).

[26] 343 F.2d 565 (2d Cir. 1965).

[27] 313 F.2d 252.

[28] 852 F.2d 33. In Leone Industries v. Associated Packaging, Inc., 795 F. Supp. 117, "a special fiscal agent" was appointed instead of a receiver.

appoint a receiver. The request for a receiver was based upon allegations that the money for the projects was wrongfully extracted from the Philippine Government by its former rulers, Ferdinand and Imelda Marcos. The court found that the injunction and the special property adviser adequately protected the plaintiff and were far less intrusive than a receiver.

Similarly, in *Beckerman v. Sands,*[29] the court denied the appointment of a receiver in a diversity action by two participants in a real estate syndicate, who had alleged breach of trust and diversion of syndicate funds. The court based its decision upon its view that the allegations of the complaint, as supplemented by affidavits, were not "sufficient to prove, as they stand, a level of conduct on the part of the defendants which would justify the appointment of a receiver," thus imposing a burdensome and unnecessary expense upon the syndicate.[30]

Finally, *Bracco v. Lackner,*[31] involved residents of a convalescent home who as a class, sought to prevent the cut-off of federal and state Medicaid benefits to the convalescent center. The court denied the request for the appointment of a receiver upon the grounds that there was no evidence that injunctive relief would not adequately protect the plaintiffs' rights, since state officials had scrupulously obeyed the court's previous orders.

On the other hand, the federal courts have not hesitated to grant a request for the appointment of a receiver in situations where property or legal rights are in danger of being lost or injured, and no other adequate remedy is available. For example, as previously noted, a receiver was appointed to oversee the management of the Alabama prison system.[32] In *Morgan v. McDonough,*[33] the court appointed a receiver for a South Boston high school, because of the inadequacies of other remedies to protect black students who attended the school. In *Marshall v. Snyder,*[34] the Second Circuit upheld the appointment of a receiver under the Employee Retirement Income Security Act of 1974 (ERISA), 29 U.S.C. §§ 1001 *et seq.,* at the request of the Secretary of Labor in order to take charge of three employee benefit plans under the control of local Teamster Union officials. As a basis for its decision, the Second Circuit cited the district court's finding that there were inherent conflicts of interest and the potential for self-dealing on the part of these union officials. The court also cited the actual conduct of these officials since a prior consent order, and the seriousness of the charges of misappropriation of trust fund monies.[35]

---

29 364 F. Supp. 1197, 1201 (S.D.N.Y. 1973).

30 *Id.* at 1201.

31 462 F. Supp. 436.

32 Newman v. State of Ala., 466 F. Supp. 628.

33 540 F.2d 527.

34 572 F.2d 894 (2d Cir. 1978).

35 *Id.* at 897. But, see Donovan v. Robbins. 558 F. Supp. 319, 329 (N.D. Ill. 1983) where such relief was not deemed to be required.

In *Securities & Exchange Comm'n v. Keller Corp.,*[36] the Seventh Circuit upheld the appointment of a receiver of an investment company in order to prevent fraud and mismanagement:

> The district court was vested with inherent equitable power to appoint a trustee-receiver under the facts of this case. The prima facie showing of fraud and mismanagement, absent insolvency, is enough to call into play the equitable powers of the court. It is hardly conceivable that the trial court should have permitted those who were enjoined from fraudulent misconduct to continue in control of Kellco's affairs for the benefit of those shown to have been defrauded. In such cases the appointment of a trustee-receiver becomes a necessary implementation of injunctive relief.[37]

In *United States v. American Tobacco Co.,*[38] as noted earlier, the Supreme Court held that a receiver could be appointed to manage the affairs of a tobacco company in order to prevent further violation of the antitrust laws. It then remanded the case back to the lower court for a finding to see if such relief was necessary.

In what must be one of the most unique situations on record utilizing the appointment of a receiver, a New York Appellate Court upheld the appointment of a receiver to enforce a money judgment held by a wife against her husband, who had confessed judgment in favor of his mother and brother after failing to pay his wife's judgment.[39]

Finally, in *U.S. v. Vertac Chemical Corp.,*[40] a federal court appointed a receiver to manage the affairs of the manufacturer of agricultural chemical products to insure compliance with federal environmental laws:

> The appointment of a receiver is a necessary remedy in this case. The evidence is overwhelming that Vertac engaged in the Inter-AG transaction for the purpose of freeing its remaining, viable operations from the environmental liabilities associated with its Jacksonville site. The present management of Vertac has demonstrated its willingness to manipulate numbers and corporate assets to facilitate nonperformance of *Vertac's* environmental responsibility under various orders previously entered by the Court.[41]

The issue of a company's solvency in many instances is not a determinative factor with respect to either a court's appointment or termination of a federal equity receiver. In *Bailey v. Proctor,*[42] the First Circuit refused to terminate the

---

[36] 323 F.2d 397, 403 (7th Cir. 1963).

[37] *Id.* at 403.

[38] 221 U.S. 106 (1911).

[39] Melluzzo v. Melluzzo. 404 N.Y.S.2d 147 (N.Y. App. Div. 1978).

[40] 671 F. Supp. 595.

[41] *Id.* at 623.

[42] 160 F.2d 78 (1st Cir. 1947).

receivership of an investment company, which had been appointed because of management's "gross abuse of trust," even though the company under the receiver was now solvent:

> Since the receivership may be inaugurated for a solvent corporation, solvency, especially where it may be of a transient nature, does not terminate jurisdiction to continue a receivership created on grounds other than insolvency.[43]

Similarly, in *Adelman v. CGS Scientific Corp.,*[44] a case involving allegations of securities fraud, the court stated "solvency is not a bar to the appointment of a custodian or receiver." The court, however, refused to appoint a receiver in Adelman, because the harm to the company by the appointment of a receiver was greater than the harm to the plaintiff.[45]

§ 7.4 Grounds for the Appointment of a Receiver for a Particular Purpose

We will concern ourselves here with the grounds for the appointment of a receiver in aid of judgment enforcement and in aid of foreclosure.

§ 7.5 —Judgment Enforcement

The rule with respect to judgment enforcement is that "[o]rdinarily a creditor who seeks the appointment of receivers must reduce his claim to judgment and exhaust his remedy at law" first.[46] More recently, the Eleventh Circuit adopted this rule in *Piambino v. Bailey.*[47] As discussed previously, the court rejected an attempt by a group of allegedly defrauded plaintiffs, who had purchased distributorships in a nationwide pyramid marketing scheme, to obtain the appointment of a receiver as a means of freezing the company's assets, upon the grounds that plaintiffs' claims were mere unliquidated tort claims that had not been reduced to judgment:

> This precedent holds that the receivership remedy [plaintiffs] sought is available only to plaintiffs with an equitable interest in the property to be seized or

---

43 *Id.* at 82.

44 332 F. Supp. 137, 147 (E.D. Pa. 1971).

45 *See also* Maxwell v. Enterprise Wallpaper Mfg., Co., 131 F.2d 400, 404 (3d Cir. 1942); and Cowin v. Bresler, 741 F.2d at 417.

46 Shapiro v. Wilgus. 287 U.S. 348, 355 (1932). See also, Harkin v. Brundage, 276 U.S. 36, 52 (1928).

47 757 F.2d 1112.

> with judgments that cannot otherwise be satisfied. Such a receivership is not available to plaintiffs . . . who are merely prosecuting a tort action for the recovery of unliquidated money damages and have not reduced their claims to judgment.[48]

It should be noted, however, that this rule is not followed in all situations. For example, in *Kingsport Press v. Brief English Systems,*[49] the Second Circuit upheld the appointment of a receiver to carry on defendant's correspondence school business, because it offered the possibility that all creditors would be paid in full even though the creditor seeking the receivership had not reduced its claim to judgment. After noting the general rule that ordinarily a receiver will not be appointed where the creditor seeking that appointment has not reduced its claim to judgment, the court found that the circumstances in the instant case dictated a different result:

> The [district court] judge on the facts presented, adopted the only course that seemed to give the creditors of the defendant a chance to be paid in full or, even if they should not be paid in full, to be treated equally. Upon the bill of complaint filed in the District Court showing that the creditors could be paid in full if the business of the defendant was properly managed, it was for the court to determine as a matter of discretion whether a receiver ought to be appointed. We should not interfere with the exercise of that discretion in the absence of proof of abuse.[50]

More recently, a federal district court appointed a receiver prior to judgment to preserve and protect the assets of defendant game manufacturers and their owners, which had been ordered attached pursuant to Wisconsin's prejudgment attachment law.[51] In doing so, the court noted that the case met "all of the required factors for appointment of a receiver," including evidence of fraud and an imminent danger that the assets would be lost or taken from the court's reach.[52]

Nevertheless, *Levin v. Garfinkle*[53] is a recent example of the more typical situation where the appointment of a receiver is necessary to enforce a judgment. Plaintiff, after obtaining an award of compensatory and punitive damages for fraud, misrepresentation, and breach of fiduciary duty in connection with a series of complex real estate transactions, was thwarted in his efforts to obtain satisfaction of his judgment. As noted by the district court, the

---

48 *Id.* at 1131–1132.

49 54 F.2d 497 (2d Cir. 1931).

50 *Id.* at 500.

51 Select Creations, Inc. v. Paliafito America, Inc., 828 F. Supp. at 1367.

52 *Id.*

53 514 F. Supp. 1160 (E.D. Pa. 1981).

record was "replete with evidence of fraud, and since the entry of judgment the Garfinkle interests have not only done everything in their power to frustrate Levin's attempts lawfully to discover assets and to execute, they have also attempted to obstruct the orders of this court."[54] Since plaintiff had reduced his claim to judgment, and because of the actions of defendant there was no adequate remedy at law, the court granted the request to appoint a receiver.

Similarly, in *Aviation Supply Corp. v. R.S.B.I. Aerospace, Inc.*,[55] the Eighth Circuit upheld the appointment of a receiver to acquire and liquidate the assets of a judgment debtor, where the judgment debtor invoked his Fifth Amendment privilege against self-incrimination to avoid producing documents and answering questions about his assets. The Eighth Circuit also noted, as grounds for the appointment of the receiver, the judgment debtor's attempt to defeat the interests of the judgment creditor, by granting a family-owned business a prior security interest in his assets. The family had moved to quash the judgment creditor's garnishment under Missouri law. With respect to the invocation of the privilege against self-incrimination, the court stated:

> However, the remedies of a judgment creditor include the ability to question the judgment debtor about the nature and location of assets that might satisfy the judgment. That remedy has proved unavailing to ASC. Whenever it questioned [the judgment debtor] about his assets, he invoked his constitutional privilege against self-incrimination. Such a refusal to cooperate, even if grounded in a constitutional right, may be considered in determining whether to appoint a receiver.[56]

Thus, "[a] receiver may be appointed . . . to protect a judgment creditor's interest in a debtor's property when the debtor has shown an intention to frustrate attempts to collect the judgment," but it must also be shown that the judgment "cannot otherwise be satisfied."[57]

§ 7.6 —Foreclosure

In the absence of a provision in the mortgage providing for the appointment of a receiver in the event of default, a mortgagee seeking the appointment of a receiver during foreclosure to preserve and protect mortgaged property and

---

[54] *Id.* at 1163.

[55] 999 F.2d 314.

[56] *Id.* at 317. For a similar result see U.S. v. Ianniello, 824 F.2d 203, 208 (2d Cir. 1987).

[57] Leone Industries v. Associated Packaging, Inc., 795 F. Supp. at 120, citing Piambino v. Bailey, 757 F.2d at 1131. *See also* Citronelle-Mobile Gathering, Inc. v. Watkins, 934 F.2d 1180 (11th Cir. 1991).

collect rent must make a showing that the mortgaged property is inadequate security for the debt and that the mortgagor is insolvent or without assets sufficient to cover the creditor's debt, and that there is cause to believe that the property is being wasted or deteriorated in the hands of the mortgagor:

> Courts of equity always have the power, where the debtor is insolvent, the mortgaged property is an insufficient security for the debt, and there is good cause to believe that it will be wasted or deteriorated in the hands of the mortgagor, as like cutting up timber, suffering dilapidation, etc., to take charge of the property by means of a receiver and preserve not only the corpus but the rents and profits to the satisfaction of the debt.[58]

Something more than "the mere inadequacy of the security and insolvency of the debtor" are required by the courts "to bestow upon the receiver the power to manage the property in addition to the collection of rent."[59] Usually this additional showing can be met by evidence that the property is in danger of being wasted or diminished in value.[60]

In *United States v. Sylacauga Properties, Inc.*[61] the Fifth Circuit overturned the appointment of a resident property manager of a project as receiver, as well as the lower court's staying of the government's foreclosure action, upon the grounds that the appointment of the resident manager of the project as receiver posed a conflict of interest, and the stay of the foreclosure was in violation of the government's contractual right to promptly foreclose upon default. This opinion relied upon the Supreme Court's decision in *Duparquett Huot Co. v. Evans,* which defined the limited nature of a foreclosure receivership:

> A receivership in a foreclosure suit is limited and special. The rents and profits are impounded for the benefit of a particular mortgagee, to be applied upon the debt in the event of a deficiency. [citations omitted]. *** There is neither winding up of the business nor attempt to reorganize it and send it going anew.[62]

While the request for the appointment of a receiver during a mortgage foreclosure will be denied in the absence of a showing of appropriate

---

58 Garden Homes v. United States, 200 F.2d 299, 301 (1st Cir. 1953) quoting the Supreme Court's holding in Kountze v. Omaha Hotel Co., 107 U.S. 378, 395 (1882) regarding these requirements. *See also,* Grant v. Phoenix Life Ins. Co., 121 U.S. 105 (1887). For recent expositions of these grounds, see New York Life Ins. Co. v. Watt West Inv. Corp., 755 F. Supp. 287; and Midwest Sav. Association v. Riversbend Associates 724 F. Supp. 661 (D. Minn. 1989).

59 Resolution Trust v. Fountain Circle Associates, 799 F.Supp. at 51.

60 *Id.* at 52.

61 323 F.2d 487 (5th Cir. 1963).

62 297 U.S. 216, 221 (1936).

grounds for such an appointment,[63] the courts will enforce a provision in a mortgage that provides for the appointment of a receiver upon default.[64]

Relief in the form of the appointment of a receiver to collect rents and protect property from waste has also been granted ex parte in foreclosure actions if appropriate circumstances exist:

> [w]here the defendants could not be located, rents are about to come due and their disposition is unknown, and plaintiffs offer proof that they are entitled to receive rents and that the defendants have failed to make monthly payments of principal, interest and escrow due . . . despite repeated requests. . .[65]

§ 7.7 —Receiverships under the Federal Debt Collection Procedures Act of 1990, 28 U.S.C. § 3001 et seq.

Congress enacted the Federal Debt Collection Procedures Act of 1990 (FDCPA) as part of the Crime Control Act of 1990, Public Law 101-647.[66] Effective May 29, 1991, the FDCPA gives the federal government a number of important pre-and post-judgment remedies under the FDCPA, as part of its efforts to improve governmental debt collection. Receivership is among the prejudgment remedies provided.[67] As with other prejudgment remedies under the FDCPA, such as prejudgment garnishment and attachment, the statutory prerequisites for prejudgment remedies must be met.[68]

---

63 Midwest Sav. Ass'n. v. Riversbend Associates, 724 F. Supp. 661.

64 United States v. Mountain Village Co., 424 F. Supp. 822 (D. Mass. 1976); and United States v. American Nat. Bank & Trust Co., 573 F. Supp. 1319 (N.D. Ill. 1983). In Citibank, N.A. v. Nyland (CFG Ltd.), 839 F. 2d, 97(2d Cir. 1988), the Second Circuit stated that "[I]t is entirely appropriate for a mortgage holder to seek the appointment of a receiver where the mortgage authorizes such appointment, and the mortgagee has repeatedly defaulted on conditions of the mortgage which constitute one or more events of default." Although the court in New York Life Ins. Co. v. Watt West Inv. Corp., 755 F. Supp. at 292 found no "principle" under Federal law (such as exists under California law) relieving a creditor from the necessity of showing that the property is insufficient to secure a loan, where a provision in the mortgage provides for the appointment of a receiver upon default, the fact that the parties "agreed to the appointment of a receiver in the deed of trust is entitled to great weight." *See also* Western Federal Savings Loan Association v. Heflin Corp., 797 F. Supp. 790 (N.D. Cal. 1992).

65 Federal Home Loan Mortgage v. Spark Tarrytown, 813 F. Supp. 234, 236–237 (S.D.N.Y. 1993). *See also* Arkansas Louisiana Gas Co. v. Kroeger, 303 F.2d 129, 132 (5th Cir. 1962) allowing appointment of a receiver ex parte where there is some urgent necessity.

66 104 Stat. 4933.

67 28 U.S.C. § 3103.

68 28 U.S.C. § 3101.

Like the other prejudgment remedies in the FDCPA, the prejudgment receivership remedy can be obtained by the United States without prior notice of the application. Nevertheless, pursuant to 28 U.S.C. 3004(c), service may be made "[a]t such time as counsel for the United States considers appropriate," but must be completed prior to the time that the receivership is put into effect.

The statutory prerequisites for the attainment of a prejudgment remedy by the United States such as appointment of a receiver are contained in 28 U.S.C. § 3101. The application of the United States, must be supported by an affidavit,[69] showing "the probable validity of the claim for a debt and the right of the United States to recover what is demanded in the application,"[70] as well as the grounds for such a prejudgment remedy.[71] These grounds include that the debtor with the effect of "hindering, delaying or defrauding the United States," (A) is about to leave the jurisdiction of the United States; (B) has or is about to assign, dispose, remove, conceal, ill-treat, waste, or destroy property; (C) has or is about to convert the debtor's property into money, securities, or evidence of debt in a manner prejudicial to the United States; or (D) has evaded service of process by concealing himself or has temporarily withdrawn from the jurisdiction of the United States.[72]

Upon the filing of an application by the United States setting forth one of the aforementioned grounds for a prejudgment receivership, counsel for the United States must then prepare for issuance by the Clerk, a Notice for service on the debtor, and "on any other person whom the United States reasonably believes, after exercising due diligence, has possession, custody, or control of property affected by such remedy."[73] Three copies of the Notice must be served on each such person.[74]

The Notice will be in the form approved by the chief judges of the federal districts in the state in which the court entertaining the action is located.[75] The Notice must provide the name of the debtor, the amount of the debt, the reason for the debt, and that a lawsuit has been filed to collect the debt. The Notice must also set forth the major exemptions which apply in the state where property that will be the subject of the receivership is located, and that the debtor may request a hearing by notifying the clerk of the court in writing and sending a copy of the request to counsel for the United States. The Notice must also provide that the debtor may request a hearing within five days after the clerk receives the request. The Notice must explain that the

---

69 28 U.S.C. § 3101(c).

70 28 U.S.C. § 3101(c)(1).

71 The grounds are enumerated in 28 U.S.C. § 3101(b).

72 28 U.S.C. § 3101(b)(1)(A)–(D).

73 28 U.S.C. § 3101(d).

74 28 U.S.C. § 3101(d).

75 28 U.S.C. § 3101(d).

debtor will be given an opportunity to state why the debt may not be owing, why the property that is the subject of the receivership request should not be taken at that time, or why the property to be taken is exempt or belongs to someone else. The Notice will also inform the debtor that if the debtor wishes to assert that it lives outside the federal judicial district in which the court entertaining the action is located, it must make a written request for transfer to the debtor's district within twenty days of service.[76]

A debtor may move to quash the Order granting the prejudgment receivership remedy, at a hearing requested by the debtor at any time before judgment on the claim for the debt.[77] The court should hold the hearing "as soon as practical" or, upon the debtor's request, within five days after receiving the request for a hearing, or "as soon thereafter as possible."[78]

The hearing on the debtor's or property holder's motion to quash will be limited to four issues: (1) the probable validity of the government's claim for the underlying debt, and the validity of any defenses or claim of exemption asserted by the debtor or property holder; (2) compliance with the statutory requirements for the issuance of the prejudgment receivership remedy; (3) the existence of one of the grounds for prejudgment remedies set forth in 28 U.S.C § 3101(b) mentioned above; and (4) the inadequacy of alternative remedies to protect the interests of the United States.[79]

If the requirements of § 3101 are satisfied, and the United States shows "reasonable cause to believe that there is a substantial danger that the property will be removed from the jurisdiction of the court, lost, concealed, materially injured or damaged or mismanaged," the court may appoint a receiver "for property in which the debtor has a substantial non-exempt interest."[80]

The receiver may then be authorized to take possession of the debtor's real and personal property, and "sue for, collect and sell obligations upon such conditions and for such purposes as the court shall direct."[81] The receiver is also empowered "to administer, collect, lease, repair or sell" as the court directs.[82]

The statute requires that a receiver appointed to manage residential or commercial property "shall have demonstrable expertise in the management of [those] types of property."[83]

The FDCPA prohibits a receiver appointed under the Act from employing attorneys, accountants, appraisers, auctioneers, or other professional persons

---

[76] 28 U.S.C. § 3101(d)(1), Notice.

[77] 28 U.S.C. § 3101(d)(2).

[78] 28 U.S.C. § 3101(d)(2).

[79] 28 U.S.C. § 3101(d)(2).

[80] 28 U.S.C. § 3103(a).

[81] 28 U.S.C. § 3103(b)(A).

[82] 28 U.S.C. § 3103(b)(1)(A) & (B).

[83] 28 U.S.C. § 3103(b)(1)(B).

without a court order authorizing such employment.[84] The receiver is also required to keep "written accounts," itemizing receipts and expenditures, describing the property of the estate, and naming the depositor of receivership funds. These accounts are required to be open for inspection by any person having an interest in the property of the estate. The receiver is also required to file reports at regular intervals, as directed by the court, and serve the debtor and the United States with copies of such reports.[85]

At the termination of the receivership, the receiver shall file a final accounting of all the receipts and disbursements,[86] and apply for compensation, setting forth the amounts sought and the services rendered.[87] In this regard, the statute provides that the receiver's compensation cannot exceed five percent of the sums received and disbursed by the receiver, unless the court directs otherwise.[88]

Finally, § 3103(c) provides that the receivership shall not continue past the entry of judgment, or the conclusion of an appeal of such judgment, unless the court directs its continuation under 28 U.S.C. § 3203(e) or otherwise.

Section 3203(e), dealing with postjudgment collection remedies, provides that the court may appoint a receiver, or in the case of a prejudgment receiver appointed under 28 U.S.C. § 3103, continue the receivership pending "levy of execution," if there is "a substantial danger that the property will be removed from the jurisdiction of the court, lost, materially injured or damaged or mismanaged."[89] Thus, the court may direct that the receivership continue past the point of judgment either in aid of levy of execution or otherwise.

§ 7.8 Specific Federal Agency Receiverships

A number of Federal agencies and departments make use of federal equity receiverships for their enforcement activity.[90] Those departments and agencies

---

[84] 28 U.S.C. § 3103(b)(B)(2).

[85] 28 U.S.C. § 3103(d).

[86] 28 U.S.C. § 3103(g)(3).

[87] 28 U.S.C. § 3103(g).

[88] 28 U.S.C. § 3103(g)(1). If there are no funds remaining in the estate to compensate a receiver, the court may fix the receiver's compensation, and direct payment from the party that sought the receiver's appointment. 28 U.S.C. § 3103(g)(2).

[89] 28 U.S.C. § 3203(e).

[90] While receiverships over failed banks and savings and loan institutions of the Federal Deposit Insurance Corporation (FDIC) and the Resolution Trust Corporation (RTC) are of some notoriety today, these receiverships are not of federal equity derivation. In reality, FDIC and RTC receiverships, as contemplated by the Federal Deposit Insurance Act, 12 U.S.C. § 1821, and the Financial Institutions Reform and Enforcement Act of 1989, 12 U.S.C. § 1464 are generically different from traditional court supervised federal equity receiverships. By statute, FDIC or RTC are appointed receiver over a bank or savings

that have used federal equity receiverships for regulatory enforcement purposes include the Securities and Exchange Commission, the Commodity Futures Trading Commission, the Small Business Administration, the Labor Department and the Department of Housing and Urban Development.

Although the courts have held that liquidation of a company is not a penalty prescribed by the securities laws, and that liquidation of a company is more properly the subject of a bankruptcy proceeding,[91] nevertheless, the courts have not been reluctant to appoint a receiver for a company that has been involved in securities violations,[92] and where appropriate to allow liquidation of the company.[93]

Similarly, although the Commodity Exchange Act, as amended, 7 U.S.C. § 1 *et seq.,* does not specifically provide for the appointment of receivers for violation of the Act and regulations, a federal district court may fashion such a remedy under its equitable powers.[94] Furthermore, in appropriate circumstances the court exercising its equitable powers will appoint a permanent receiver to liquidate the company.[95]

A receiver can also be an appropriate remedy under the Employee Retirement Income Security Act of 1974 (ERISA), as amended, 29 U.S.C. §§ 1001-1461, where serious fiduciary violations have occurred.[96]

The Small Business Investment Act of 1958, as amended, 15 U.S.C. § 681 et seq. empowers the SBA to seek the appointment of a receiver for a Small Business Investment Company (SBIC) that has violated the Act and regulations in an action in United States district court, in addition to an

---

and loan institution administratively, rather than by a federal court, 12 U.S.C. §§ 1821(c)(2) and (4) and 1464(d)(2)(H)(ii), although a court may review such appointment within thirty days, 12 U.S.C. §§ 1821(c)(7) and 1464(d)(2)(B). Although this statutory framework is not contemplated by traditional federal equity receiverships discussed in this chapter, some of the case law relating to these receiverships serves as useful precedent.

91 Esbitt v. Dutch-American Mercantile Corp., 335 F.2d 141 (2d Cir. 1964) and Los Angeles Trust Deed & Mortgage Exchange v. Securities & Exch. Corp., 285 F.2d 162 (9th Cir. 1960), cert. den. 366 U.S. 919 (1961).

92 Securities & Exch. Com'n. v. Lincoln Thrift Ass'n., 577 F.2d 600 (9th Cir. 1978); SEC v. United Financial Group, 576 F.2d 217 (9th Cir. 1978); Securities & Exch. Com'n. v. Keller Corp., 323 F.2d 397 (7th Cir. 1963).

93 Securities & Exch. Com'n. v. Lincoln Thrift Ass'n., 577 F.2d 600, Esbitt v. Dutch-American Mercantile Corp., 335 F.2d 141 (2d Cir. 1964) and Securities & Exch. Com'n. v. Bartlett, 422 F.2d 475 (8th Cir. 1970).

94 Commodity Futures Trading v. Comvest Trading Corp., 481 F. Supp. 438 (D. Mass. 1979).

95 Commodity Futures Trading Com. v. FITC. Inc., 52 B.R. 935 (N.D. Calif. 1985).

96 Marshall v. Robbins, 624 F.2d 1106 (7th Cir. 1980); Marshall v. Snyder, 572 F.2d 894 (2d Cir. 1978); and Donovan v. Robbins, 558 F. Supp. 319 (N.D. Ill. 1983).

injunction and a money judgment for such violations.[97] The Act is somewhat unique in regard to federal equity receiverships in that it allows the federal district court the discretion to appoint the SBA as receiver of the company.[98] Under the statutory scheme, SBA may apply to the appropriate United States district court for SBA's appointment as receiver.[99] The traditional requirements for appointment of a receiver and the granting of injunctive relief are not required. In this regard the Fifth Circuit stated in *First Louisiana Investment Corp. v. United States:*

> The appellant would have us test the exercise of the court's discretion in the appointment of a receiver for it by conventional standards. The appellant would have us hold that the statutory provision for a receivership, 15 U.S.C.A. § 687c(b), supra is only a jurisdictional provision and does not affect the usual requirements for invoking this extraordinary remedy. We do not so read the statute. It is our opinion that where a licensee has engaged in violations of the Act or of rules, regulations, or orders issued pursuant to the Act, the court has the power, under the statute, to appoint a receiver as well as to grant injunctive relief.[100]

Thus, all that need be shown by the Small Business Administration for the appointment of itself as receiver over an SBIC is violations of the Act or regulations.[101] The receivership court is authorized by the Act to take exclusive jurisdiction over the Licensee and all of its assets.[102] Once the court has taken exclusive jurisdiction over the company by means of a receivership, it functions as a federal equity receiver.[103] Finally, as previously mentioned, the Act provides that SBA may be appointed receiver of an SBIC in the court's discretion.[104] An

---

97 *See* United States v. Vanguard Investment Co., Inc., 667 F. Supp. 257 (M.D.N.C. 1987), 694 F. Supp. 1219 (M.D.N.C. 1988), *aff'd,* 907 F.2d 439 (4th Cir. 1990); United States v. Coleman Capital Corp., 387 F.2d 916 (7th Cir. 1969); United States v. Cape Fear Capital Corp., 286 F. Supp. 135 (N.D. Pa. 1968); United States v. Boca Raton Capital Corp., 285 F. Supp. 504 (S.D. Fla. 1968) and United States v. Norwood Capital Corp., 273 F. Supp. 236 (D.S.C. 1967).

98 15 U.S.C. § 687c(c).

99 *Id.*

100 351 F.2d 495, 497–498 (5th Cir. 1965).

101 15 U.S.C. 681 *et seq.* and 13 C.F.R. 107.1 *et seq.*

102 15 U.S.C. 687c, United States v. Royal Business Funds Corp., 29 Bank. Rpt. 777 (S.D.N.Y. 1983), aff'd. 727 F.2d 12, 14 (2d Cir. 1983); U.S. v. Vanguard Inv. Co., Inc., 694 F. Supp. 1219, 1229.

103 United States v. Franklin National Bank, 512 F.2d 245, 251 (2d Cir. 1975), United States v. Royal Business Funds Corp., 724 F.2d at 16; and United States v. Norwood Capital Corp., 273 F. Supp. 236 (D. S.C. 1967).

104 15 U.S.C. 687c(c).

analysis of this statutory provision under which SBA may be appointed receiver is found in *United States v. Norwood Capital Corp.*[105] In summary, these factors include the Agency's expertise in liquidating SBICs, and the need for personnel that are familiar with the operations and regulatory problems associated with these companies, as well as the fact that SBA is usually the primary creditor.

We have also seen that courts will appoint a receiver to collect rents and profits and to manage property where a federally insured mortgage provides for such appointment upon default,[106] or even in the absence of such a provision in the mortgage, if circumstances justify it.[107]

§ 7.9 Blanket Receivership Stay Orders

The initial court order approving and setting up the receivership should contain a provision for a blanket receivership injunction restraining the initiation or continuation of all legal proceedings involving the receiver and the property of the receivership estate.[108]

In *Jordan v. Independent Energy Corp.,* the Court had appointed a temporary receiver, and "stayed all persons, firms or corporations from 'commencing, prosecuting, continuing or enforcing any suit or proceeding, or from executing or issuing or causing the execution or issuance of any court attachment . . . or other proceedings for the purpose of impounding or . . . interfering with any property owned by or in the possession of defendant . . .' "[109]

Such a blanket stay provision is not only sanctioned by the courts, but in fact is widely recognized as necessary in order to prevent interference with the orderly administration of the receivership estate and dissipation of the

---

105 273 F. Supp. 236.

106 *See e.g.* United States v. Chappell Livestock Auction, Inc. 523 F.2d 840, 842 n.2 (8th Cir. 1975); United States v. Oueen's Court Apartments, Inc. 296 F.2d 534 (9th Cir. 1961); Garden House, Inc. v. United States, 200 F.2d 299 (lst Cir. 1953) and 207 F.2d 459 (1st Cir. 1953); and United States v. Mountain Village Co., 424 F. Supp. 822.

107 *See e.g.* View Crest Garden Apartments, Inc. v. United States, 281 F.2d 844, 849 (9th Cir. 1960).

108 Jordan v. Independent Energy Corp., 446 F. Supp. 516, 519 n. 2 (N.D. Tex. 1978). "The term 'blanket receivership injunction' refers to the broad injunctive language restraining all persons from instituting any action which would interfere with the receiver's possession of the receivership property."

109 *Id.* at 520. For cases approving similar court orders, see United States v. Royal Business Funds Corp., 724 F.2d 12, 14 (2d Cir. 1983); Securities & Exch. Com'n. v. AnCar Oil Co., 604 F.2d 114 (1st Cir. 1979); Securities & Exch. Com'n. v. United Fin. Group, Inc., 576 F.2d 217, 221 n. 8 (9th Cir. 1978); and SEC v. Lincoln Thrift Ass'n, 557 F.2d 1274, 1277 n.1 (9th Cir. 1977).

estate's assets.[110] As stated by the Ninth Circuit in *Sec. & Exch. Com'n v. United Fin. Group, Inc.:*

> The receivership court has broad equitable powers to prevent interference with the administration of the estate by blanket stay orders as well as injunctions against particular actions . . . [111]

For suggested language to place in a proposed order regarding a blanket receivership injunction see the form section of this chapter.[112]

There is some question as to whether such a receivership stay can prevent the receivership entity or creditors of the receivership entity from placing the entity in bankruptcy, particularly with regard to Chapter 11 of the Bankruptcy Code. This will be discussed shortly.

A normal injunctive order entered pursuant to Federal Rule of Civil Procedure 65(d) "is binding only upon the parties to the action, their officers, agents, servants, employees, and attorneys, and upon those persons in active concert or participation with them who receive actual notice of the order by personal service or otherwise." Despite the language of Rule 65(d), however, a blanket receivership injunction is binding against non-parties as well as parties if they have notice of the order.[113] The rationale for affirming the effectiveness of a blanket receivership injunction against parties and non-parties alike was given by the Ninth Circuit in *Wencke:*

> The power of the district court to issue a stay, effective against all persons, of all proceedings against the receivership entities rests as much on its control over the property placed in receivership as on its jurisdiction over the parties to the securities fraud action. The district court took control over the properties in question when it imposed the receivership and appointed Gould as receiver to manage those properties. The blanket stay was found by the district court necessary to achieve the purposes of the receivership. We conclude the district court had the power to enter the order.[114]

---

[110] *See* Sec. & Exch. Com'n. v. United Fin. Group, Inc., 576 F.2d at 220 and Diners Club, Inc. v. Bumb, 421 F.2d 396 (9th Cir. 1970).

[111] 576 F.2d at 221, n. 8.

[112] The need for a stay similar to a blanket receivership injunction, as discussed above, has been recognized in the bankruptcy context by the imposition statutorily of an automatic stay. Bankruptcy Code, Section 362, 11 U.S.C. § 362.

[113] Sec. & Exch. Com'n. v. Wencke, 622 F.2d at 1369.

[114] *Id. See also* S.E.C. v. Universal Financial, 760 F.2d 1034, 1038, (9th Cir. 1985). In Diners Club, Inc. v. Bumb, 421 F.2d at 398, the Ninth Circuit used a similar rationale for affirming the use of a restraining order against further proceedings in another court by a non-party against a bankruptcy reorganization trustee.

This principle regarding injunctive relief is not limited to receivership and bankruptcy proceedings. There are cases upholding the effectiveness of an injunction against nonparties in other contexts which counsel may find helpful.[115]

§ 7.10 Prevention of Bankruptcy Filings

Not infrequently, the principals of a company in receivership, or, on occasion, disaffected creditors unhappy with a receiver's actions, will seek to wrest control of the company from the receiver by a subsequent bankruptcy filing, usually under Chapter 11. This is because Chapter 11 will likely allow the debtor to remain in control of the business during the reorganization as debtor in possession.

The traditional view of the federal courts has been that such a filing is permissible without the prior approval of the receivership court and despite any blanket stay order that it has issued.[116] For example, in *In Re Yaryan Naval Stores Co.,*[117] three unsecured creditors filed a petition in the United States District Court for the Northern District of Ohio praying that the company be adjudged a bankrupt. This was subsequently approved by a resolution of the board of directors of the company. The filing occurred a little over six months after a federal receiver had been appointed for the company in United States District Court for the Southern District of Georgia as a result of a creditor's suit. It was contended by the receivers appointed in the Georgia suit that the bankruptcy filing was in violation of the stay order entered in the receivership proceeding. In upholding the bankruptcy adjudication, the Sixth Circuit stated:

> In the present case, the Naval Stores Company had the undeniable right to go into voluntary bankruptcy, and to take any legitimate steps to bring about that result, and to obtain for itself and its creditors the benefits of the Bankruptcy Act.
>
> * * *

---

115 An early civil rights case which involved the desegregation of the Little Rock, Arkansas schools, Cooper v. Aaron, 358 U.S. 1 (1958), is useful Supreme Court precedent in this regard. In United States v. Crookshanks, 441 F. Supp. 268 (D. Ore. 1977), the district court refused to dismiss criminal contempt proceedings against non-parties to a suit for violating a temporary restraining order protecting the fishing rights of certain Indian tribes under a treaty involving fishing in the Columbia River. The court based its holding, in part, upon the view that "a court can enjoin non-parties whose actions threaten to interfere with compliance with prior orders of the court."

Id. at 270. U.S. v. Hall, 472 F.2d 261, 265–266; and Puget Sound Gillnetters, Ass'n. v. U.S. Dist. Court, 573 F.2d 1123, 1132–1133 (9th Cir. 1978).

116 In Re Yaryan Naval Stores Co., 214 F. 563 (6th Cir. 1914); and Struthers Furnace Co. v. Grant, 30 F.2d 576 (6th Cir. 1929).

117 214 F. 563.

> . . . To deny the right of the debtor, when such insolvency is found to exist, to take the benefit of the act and thereby secure a discharge from its debts, is to deny the ultimate paramountcy of the act, which is designed, not merely for the benefit of creditors, but for that of the debtor as well.[118]

Moreover, there is a preference expressed by the courts for bankruptcy when the object of the receivership is to liquidate the company.[119] Nevertheless, in *Esbitt v. Dutch-American Mercantile Corp.*,[120] the Court allowed the liquidation to continue in the receivership because it was almost completed.

More recent precedent, however, has held that "[a] debtor subject to a federal receivership has no absolute right to file a bankruptcy petition," and accordingly needs the permission of the court overseeing the receivership to file in bankruptcy.[121] In *United States v. Royal Business Funds Corp.,* the district court had enjoined a Chapter 11 filing by the principals of the corporation without its leave upon the grounds that the District court, through the receivership, had taken exclusive jurisdiction over the company pursuant to the Small Business Investment Act of 1958, as amended,[122] which provides that the receivership court "may, to such extent as it deems necessary, take exclusive jurisdiction of the licensee or licensees and the assets thereof."[123] In affirming the district court, the Second Circuit rationalized its holding upon the basis that the principals of the company had consented to the receivership, and that the receiver had injected over three million dollars into the company. In addition, the Small Business Administration, which was acting as receiver, was by far the largest creditor of the company, and it appeared to be the only source of financing for the company's operations. In view of these factors the court held that it was necessary to obtain the approval of the district court for the bankruptcy filing.

In another case involving an SBA receivership, it was held that where SBA had previously been appointed as temporary receiver, a subsequent bankruptcy filing by the officers of the corporation was "a nullity" because the officers and directors of the company no longer had any corporate authority to accomplish the filing.[124] Indeed, the District Court noted that:

---

118 *Id.* at 565–566.

119 *See e.g.* Los Angeles Trust Deed & Mortgage Exchange v. Securities and Exchange Commission, 285 F.2d 162, 182 (9th Cir. 1960), cert. den., 366 U.S. 919 (1961); and Esbitt v. Dutch-American Mercantile Corp., 335 F.2d 141, 143 (2d Cir. 1964).

120 335 F.2d 141.

121 United States v. Royal Business Funds Corp., 724 F.2d 12, 16 (2d Cir. 1983). The Second Circuit reaffirmed this holding in United States v. Vulpis, 961 F.2d 368 (2d Cir. 1992).

122 15 U.S.C. § 687c(b).

123 United States v. Royal Business Funds Corp., 29 B.R. 777 (S.D.N.Y. 1983).

124 United States v. Vanguard Inv. Co., Inc., 667 F. Supp. 257 (M.D.N.C. 1987), 694 F. Supp. 1219 (M.D.N.C. 1988), *aff'd* 907 F.2d 439 (4th Cir. 1990).

> Vanguard has not pointed to any specific reasons why under the facts of this case, a proceeding in bankruptcy would be fairer or more efficient either to itself or to creditors, than a receivership. Indeed, the timing of the filing of the petition is consistent with a motive to undermine this Court's jurisdiction . . . Vanguard is not entitled as a matter of right to file a bankruptcy petition and therefore . . . the petition filed by Vanguard is of no force and effect.[125]

A similar result was reached in a commodities fraud case involving a receivership established by the Commodities Futures Trading Commission.[126]

Decisions by the Eighth and Ninth Circuits, respectively, involving receiverships established by the Securities and Exchange Commission as a result of securities law violations are also noteworthy.[127]

A thorough treatment of both sides of this issue can be found in *Jordan v. Independent Energy Corp.*[128]

From a review of these cases it is evident that courts deciding this issue look to the circumstances under which the bankruptcy petition was filed, or is requested to be filed, and consider the following factors: (1) whether the debtor consented to the receivership; (2) the amount of funds invested in the receivership by the receiver; (3) to what stage the receivership has progressed; (4) the reasons given for the proposed bankruptcy filing; (5) the number of creditors; (6) whether under the circumstances of the case the company can be better liquidated in a bankruptcy proceeding or in a liquidating receivership; (7) and whether the bankruptcy filing is deemed a bad faith evasion of the receivership court's jurisdiction. All these factors should be carefully weighed and considered by counsel opposing the bankruptcy filing on behalf of the receiver. In addition, counsel for the receiver should be aware of *United States v. Kras,*[129] which, while not involving a receivership, determined that a debtor has no constitutional right to a discharge in bankruptcy.

The forms section of this Chapter provides an example of a standard receivership order with a blanket stay provision, including a specific prohibition against the filing of a bankruptcy petition without the consent of the court overseeing the receivership.

---

125 U.S. v. Vanguard Inv. Co., Inc., 667 F. Supp. at 261.

126 Commodities Futures Trading Com. v. FITC, Inc., 52 B.R. 935 (N.D. Calif. 1985).

127 Securities & Exch. Com'n. v, Hardy, 803 F.2d 1034 (9th Cir. 1986); Securities & Exch. Com'n. v. Lincoln Thrift Ass'n., 577 F.2d 600 (9th Cir. 1978); and Securities & Exch. Com'n. v. Bartlett, 422 F.2d 475 (8th Cir. 1970).

128 446 F. Supp. 516.

129 409 U.S. 434 (1973).

§ 7.11 Relief from the Blanket Receivership Stay

When a particular claimant is not within the purview of 28 U.S.C. § 959(a), as discussed next the federal courts employ other criteria in determining whether to lift a blanket receivership stay. This was clearly articulated in *Securities & Exch. Com'n. v. Wencke*:[130]

> The district court should consider whether refusing to lift the stay genuinely preserves the status quo or whether the moving party will suffer substantial injury if it is not permitted to proceed. The merit of the moving party's claim is also a relevant consideration. Where the claim is unlikely to succeed (and the receiver therefore likely to prevail), there may be less reason to require the receiver to defend the action now rather than defer its resolution. On the other hand, where the likelihood that the receiver will prevail is small, when the receiver's position is considered realistically and not in the abstract, there is less reason to permit the receiver to avoid resolving the claim; a blanket stay should not be used to prejudice the rights which innocent and legitimate creditors may have against receivership entities. [citation omitted].
>
> The time at which the motion for relief from the stay is made also bears on the exercise of the district court's discretion. Where the motion for relief from the stay is made soon after the receiver has assumed control over the estate, the receiver's need to organize and understand the entities under his control may weigh more heavily than the merits of the party's claim. As the receivership progresses, however, it may become less plausible for the receiver to contend that he needs more time to explore the affairs of the entities. The merits of the moving party's claim may then loom larger in the balance.[131]

The Ninth Circuit remanded the case back to the district court for a determination of whether it was appropriate for that court to lift the stay.

In a later decision *S.E.C. v. Universal Financial,*[132] the Ninth Circuit applied the criteria for determining whether to lift the stay articulated in *Wencke*[133] and in affirming the district court's ruling, concluded that the stay should not be lifted in order to enable defrauded investors to pursue their claims in litigation brought outside of the receivership proceedings. The court reasoned that such relief from the stay would result in a multiplicity of actions in different forums with an attendant increase in litigation costs for all parties, thus diminishing the size of the receivership estate. In explaining its prior holding in *Wencke*[134] the court stated:

---

130 622 F.2d at 1373–1374 (Wencke I). *See also* S.E.C. v. Wencke, 742 F.2d 1230, 1231 (9th Cir. 1984) (Wencke II).

131 622 F.2d at 1373-1374.

132 760 F.2d 1034.

133 Securities & Exch. Com'n. v. Wencke, 622 F.2d 1363.

134 *Id.*

> This test differs in emphasis from the traditional equitable criteria employed by courts to decide whether to grant, deny, or continue a preliminary injunction. The traditional preliminary injunction test would require the Receiver to show a probability of success on the merits and the possibility of irreparable harm to the receivership if the stay is not continued. [citation omitted]. The Wencke test simply requires the district court to balance the interests of the Receiver and the moving party.[135]

In a related series of decisions by a district court in Maryland overseeing the receivership of an SBIC, the stay was lifted at the request of a divorcee in order to allow her to initiate a foreclosure action which would enable her to obtain funds for her support and that of her minor child.[136] The court found that refusal to lift the stay would have caused the greater injury, and that she had demonstrated a likelihood of success on the merits. In a companion case the Court denied relief from the blanket stay to another party because of the failure to show a likelihood of success in pursuing its claim.[137] The court also refused to lift the stay in another situation because there was no showing that that party was injured by continuation of the stay.[138]

§ 7.12 28 U.S.C. § 959(a) Allows Some Suits to Be Filed Without Permission of the Court Overseeing the Receivership

Section 959(a),[139] creates a limited exception to the need to obtain court relief from a blanket receivership stay for the commencement of litigation against the receiver. This exception is limited expressly by the language of Section 959(a) to suits involving the receiver's "acts or transactions in carrying on business connected with" receivership property.[140] Furthermore, as discussed below, even this limited exception is not absolute.[141]

---

135 S.E.C. v. Universal Financial, 760 F.2d at 1038.

136 U.S. v. ESIC Capital, Inc., 685 F. Supp. 483 (D. Md. 1988).

137 U.S. v. ESIC Capital, Inc., 675 F. Supp. 1462 (D. Md. 1987).

138 U.S. v. ESIC Capital, Inc., 675 F. Supp. 1464 (D. Md. 1987).

139 28 U.S.C. § 959(a).

140 28 U.S.C. § 959(a) provides:

> Trustees, receivers, or managers of any property, including debtors in possession, may be sued, without leave of the court appointing them, with respect to any of their acts or transactions in carrying on business connected with such property. Such actions shall be subject to the general equity power of such court so far as the same may be necessary to the ends of justice, but this shall not deprive a litigant of his right to trial by jury.

141 Diners Club, Inc. v. Bumb, 421 F.2d 396.

Section 959(a) both currently and in prior versions, applies not only to federal equity receiverships, but to bankruptcy stays as well.

This statutory exception to the need to obtain relief from the blanket stay order was enacted after the Supreme Court's ruling in *Barton v. Barbour,*[142] which held that a tort claimant could not sue a receiver in a court other than that overseeing the receivership without the latter's permission. Seen in this light, § 959(a) was originally "intended to permit actions redressing torts committed in furtherance of the bankrupt's business operations, and is not cast to foster interference '[with] the use, control, maintenance and operation of the bankrupt's property.'"[143] In its current version, however, it should be seen as having a broader meaning than that, particularly as providing a means of enforcement of subsection 959(b) "which requires businesses to operate in accordance with all applicable state laws while under the control of a trustee in bankruptcy or receiver.[144]

As indicated above, tort suits involving the acts of the receiver or trustee in bankruptcy after the commencement of a bankruptcy or receivership proceeding are one of the most common category of suits that may be commenced without obtaining the prior consent of the bankruptcy or receivership court. Thus, in *McNulta v. Lochridge,*[145] the Supreme Court affirmed an Illinois state court holding that a wrongful death suit in state court against a successor receiver of a railroad was properly brought without the permission of the federal court overseeing the receivership of the railroad company. Similarly, a wrongful death suit arising out of the operation of a railroad, after the railroad filed for bankruptcy protection under Chapter X of the former Bankruptcy Act,[146] was held to be proper even though the consent of the bankruptcy court was not obtained prior to its filing in *Valdes v. Feliciano.*[147] This was because the suit arose out of the operation of the railroad after the filing of the bankruptcy petition, even though a reorganization trustee had not yet been appointed.

In a contract case[148] the Supreme Court held that under an earlier version of § 959(a) it was not necessary to obtain the permission of the bankruptcy

---

[142] 104 U.S. 126 (1881). *See* discussion in Diners Club, Inc. v. Bumb, 421 F.2d at 399.

[143] In re American Associated Systems, Inc., 373 F. Supp. 977, 979 (E.D. Ky. 1974). Section 959(a) would also seem to have the benefit of encouraging third parties to do business with the receiver or trustee in bankruptcy by putting them on the same footing as any other business, as far as litigation involving their business operations is concerned.

[144] Matter of Creative Cuisine, Inc., 96 B.R. 144, 146 (Bankr. N.D. Ill. 1989) citing H.R. Rep. No. 95-595, 95th Cong., 1st Sess. 443 (1977), U.S. Code Cong. & Admin. News, 1978, p. 5787.

[145] 141 U.S. 327 (1891).

[146] 11 U.S.C. § 501 *et seq.*

[147] 267 F.2d 91, (1st Cir. 1959).

[148] Thompson v. Texas Mexican R. Co., 328 U.S. 134 (1946).

court for the maintenance of a suit in state court seeking compensation from a bankrupt railroad for the continued use of plaintiff's trackage rights and terminal facilities after plaintiff had terminated the contract for such use, despite stay orders entered by a bankruptcy court. The basis for this holding was that the suit involved "only a money claim against the estate for acts of the trustee in operating trains over respondent's tracks."[149] Thus, the suit would not interfere with the trustee's control over the property of the estate.

A similar result was reached in a patent infringement suit wherein it was alleged that the reorganization trustee had violated plaintiff's patent rights.[150]

While the purpose of § 959(a) is to make federal receivers and bankruptcy trustees subject to suit without the permission of the bankruptcy or receivership court for causes of action arising out of their operation of the business,[151] § 959(a) does not apply to suits involving acts or transactions occurring before the bankruptcy or receivership.[152]

A claim for attorney fees incurred in the defense of a suit against a company in receivership, as well as its former officers, for past wrongful acts was also considered outside the scope of § 959(a) by the Ninth Circuit.[153] This was because the suit for attorney fees, "was not brought with respect to any acts or transactions by the [receiver] in carrying on business connected with receivership property."[154]

The attempt to collect and liquidate the assets of a debtor in bankruptcy or in receivership is not an "act or transaction in carrying on business" connected with the property of the estate.[155] Thus, any suit against a receiver for such activity would not come within the purview of § 959(a). For example, a tort suit brought against a trustee in bankruptcy for alleged wrongful actions taken in collecting a debt owed to the debtor was not sanctioned by § 959(a), because the trustee's actions did not involve "carrying on business" within the meaning of § 959(a).[156] Similarly, a landlord's suit seeking possession of

---

149 *Id.* at 138.

150 Anderson v. Scandrett, 19 F. Supp. 681 (D. Minn. 1937).

151 Eddy v. LaFayette, 163 U.S. 456 (1896).

152 Riehle v. Margolies, 279 U.S. 218 (1929). *See also* Ex parte Baldwin, 291 U.S. 610 (1934) involving the alleged nonfeasance of a bankrupt railroad in failing to maintain passenger service. Since the service had been terminated months before the commencement of the bankruptcy proceeding, the court found that such nonfeasance was not an "act or transaction" within the meaning of 28 U.S.C. § 959(a).

153 SEC. & Exchange Com'n v. United Fin. Group, Inc., 576 F.2d at 220.

154 *Id.* at n.7. Nevertheless, the Court concluded that since a California state court had already allowed the suit under Section 959(a), the issue was thus res judicata in the federal courts.

155 Austrian v. Williams, 216 F.2d 278, 285 (2d Cir. 1954) cert. denied 348 U.S. 953 (1955).

156 In re American Associated Systems, Inc., 373 F. Supp. 977.

property held by a debtor under a defaulted lease could not be brought without leave of court pursuant to § 959(a) once a receiver had been appointed.[157] This is because "[a] suit for possession [of property] clearly falls outside the scope of § 959(a)."[158]

Even those suits coming within the purview of § 959(a) may be enjoined by the bankruptcy or receivership court if they threaten to interfere with the administration of the estate or the bankruptcy trustee's or receiver's control over the property of the estate. This is in keeping with that part of § 959(a) which provides that "[s]uch actions shall be subject to the general equity power of such court so far as the same may be necessary to the ends of justice."[159] In *Diners Club, Inc. v. Bumb,*[160] the court upheld a bankruptcy court's stay of a suit against a debtor that manufactured credit cards under contract with a major credit card company for causing the misuse of the credit card company's secret list of customer names and numbers, even though the suit was clearly within the purview of § 959(a):

> We believe that in the exercise of a sound discretion, the judge of the reorganization court has the power in a proper case to enjoin the continuation of a suit in another court—even a suit within the purview of the first sentence of § 959(a).[161]

§ 7.13 The Receiver's Compliance with State Law under 28 U.S.C. § 959(b)

As discussed below, 28 U.S.C. § 959(b) requires a federal equity receiver to comply with state law in manag[ing] and operat[ing] the property in his possession."[162] Of particular significance, recently, has been compliance with

---

157 Securities & Exchange Com'n v. Lincoln Thrift Ass'n., 557 F.2d 1274, 1277 n.1 (9th Cir. 1977).

158 *Id.*

159 Kennison v. Philadelphia & Reading Coal & Iron Co., 38 F. Supp. 980, 983 (D. Minn. 1940), interpreted the last sentence of 28 U.S.C. § 959(a) as "merely reserv[ing] to the [bankruptcy or receivership] court the sole power over the matter of satisfaction of the rights determined by such other courts."

160 421 F.2d 396; Accord Matter of Investors Funding Corp. of N.Y., Etc., 547 F.2d 13 (2d Cir. 1978); and In re Baptist Medical Center of New York, 80 B.R. 637 (Bankr. E.D.N.Y. 1987).

161 *Id.* at 401. *See also,* Matter of Creative Cuisine, Inc., 96 B.R. at 147.

162 28 U.S.C. § 959(b), states: "Except as provided in section 1166 of title 11, a trustee, receiver or manager appointed in any cause pending in any court of the United States, including a debtor in possession, shall manage and operate the property in his possession as such trustee, receiver or manager according to the requirements of the valid

state environmental laws.[163] Section 959(b), however, is not limited to compliance with state environmental laws. On the contrary, § 959(b) would seem to mandate compliance with all state laws wherever the receiver is operating or managing property in his possession.

In upholding an earlier version of § 959, the Supreme Court determined that a receiver of an oil refining company that was attempting to reorganize must comply with a California law requiring that the company obtain a license and a bond in order to continue its operations, even though the receiver had stated that the company could not afford to do this and would have to go out of business.[164] Another early decision noted that "a federal receiver or trustee could [not] ignore the rules of law of the state of operation affecting the conduct of the business committed to his charge."[165] Section

---

laws of the State in which such property is situated, in the same manner that the owner or possessor thereof would be bound to do if in possession thereof."

This subsection applies to both receivers and bankruptcy trustees. As a result, it was amended effective October 1, 1979 to take into account 11 U.S.C. § 1166 of the new Bankruptcy Code, which, subject to certain exceptions, makes the trustee or debtor in a railroad reorganization subject to the provisions of the Interstate Commerce Act and "orders of any Federal, State or local regulatory body" to the same extent as if the debtor had not filed in bankruptcy.

Although departing from the express language of Section 959(b), one court at least, has stated that it requires compliance not only with state law, but federal law as well, In re St. Mary Hosp., 86 B.R. 393, 398 (Bankr. E.D. Pa. 1988): "We believe that it is inescapable . . . that 28 U.S.C. § 959(b) requires a debtor to conform with applicable federal, state, and local law in conducting its business." Moreover, as noted previously, 28 U.S.C. § 959(a) would seem to facilitate compliance with state law under 28 U.S.C. § 959(b) in the operation of a business by a receiver or trustee in bankruptcy by excepting suits seeking to enforce compliance with state law from a blanket receivership stay order or automatic stay in bankruptcy. Matter of Creative Cuisine, Inc., 96 B.R. at 146. *See also* a similar reference in Gillis v. California, 293 U.S. 62, 66 (1934): "The same statute which required receivers to observe the laws of the State, gave permission to sue them in State courts under stated circumstances."

Criminal penalties may attach to a receiver's wilful failure to manage the property of the estate in accordance with state law, since 18 U.S.C. § 1911 provides:

"Whoever, being a receiver, trustee, or manager in possession of any property in any cause pending in any court of the United States, willfully fails to manage and operate such property according to the requirements of the valid laws of the State in which such property shall be situated, in the same manner that the owner or possessor thereof would be bound to do if in possession thereof, shall be fined not more than $3000 or imprisoned not more than one year, or both."

163 *See e.g.* Midlantic Nat. Bank v. New Jersey D.E.P., 474 U.S. 494 (1986); and In re Wall Tube & Metal Products Co., 831 F.2d 118 (6th Cir. 1987).

164 Gillis v. California, 293 U.S. at 66: [T]here seems no ground whatever for saying that Congress cannot withhold or withdraw from courts of equity the right to empower receivers in conservation proceedings to disregard local statutes."

165 Palmer v. Webster and Atlas National Bank of Boston, 312 U.S. 156, 166 (1941). *See also* Erb v. Morasch, 177 U.S. 584 (1900).

959(b) would encompass "state tort and agency law."[166] It would also encompass rent control laws,[167] as well as local regulations regarding building maintenance, fire protection, lighting, heating, and similar matters governing the provision of rental housing.[168] In *Saravia v. 1736 18th St., N.W., Ltd., Partnership,*[169] the court found that an apartment building operator that had filed under Chapter 11 of the Bankruptcy Code was not relieved of the duty to comply with local regulations governing rental housing under § 959(b), even though the tenant leases were rejected under the Bankruptcy Code,[170] thus relieving the landlord of his private contractual obligations.

While there is some authority that construes § 959(b) as being only applicable to operating businesses,[171] or not mandating compliance with state regulation in all situations,[172] the courts seem always to require the receiver's adherence to state and local law and regulation whenever the public health and safety is at issue.

Nowhere is this more clearly stated than in cases dealing with environmental cleanup. In *Midlantic Nat. Bank v. New Jersey D.E.P.*[173] the Supreme Court used § 959(b) as a rationale for its holding that a trustee cannot abandon

---

166 Reading Co. v. Brown, 391 U.S. 471, 477 n.7 (1968).

167 Cullen v. Bowles, 148 F.2d 621 (2d Cir. 1945); Finn v. 415 Fifth Ave. Co., 153 F.2d 501 (2d Cir.), cert denied sub nom, Meighan v. Finn, 328 U.S. 839 (1946); and In re Friarton Estates Corp., 65 B.R. 586 (Bankr. S.D.N.Y. 1986).

168 Saravia v. 1736 18th St. N.W., Ltd. Partnership, 844 F.2d 823 (D.C. Cir. 1988).

169 *Id.*

170 11 U.S.C. § 365(h).

171 This was implied in Midlantic Nat. Bank v. New Jersey D.E.P., 474 U.S. 494, as interpreted by the Court of Appeals in Saravia v. 1736 18th St., N.W. Ltd. Partnership, 844 F.2d at 827. *See also,* In re Security Gas & Oil, Inc., 70 B.R. 786, 796 (Bankr. N.D.Cal. 1987) holding that 28 U.S.C. 959(b) is not applicable to a business that has ceased all operations. That case dealt with the question of whether state authorities in West Virginia could be enjoined from enforcing state law requiring the debtor to "plug" abandoned oil and gas wells and restore the original contours of the property. The court found that on the facts of the particular case there was no imminent danger to the public health or safety and that the state's enforcement action would unduly interfere with the adjudication of the bankruptcy case. Therefore, the state's enforcement action was subject to the stay order issued in the bankruptcy proceeding. The court also noted that the result might have been different under Section 959(b) if the enforcement action involved the debtor's operations after the bankruptcy petition had been filed. *Id.* at 795 ns. 5 and 6.

172 The court in Crawford v. Duluth St. Ry. Co., 60 F.2d 212, 216 (7th Cir. 1932), while acknowledging that an earlier version of Section 959(b) required receivers to manage and operate property in accordance with the valid laws of the state where the property was located, found the Superior, Wisconsin City Council's refusal to allow a trolley car company to abandon portions of its rail lines under a local ordinance requiring such approval "unreasonable, and the enforcement of the regulatory statute in the circumstances . . . a deprivation of rights protected by the constitution."

173 474 U.S. at 505.

property in a bankruptcy proceeding in contravention of a state statute or regulation designed to protect the public health or safety from identified hazards. The Sixth Circuit[174] went even further in this regard, concluding that Section 959(b) applied in liquidating bankruptcy cases when it came to compliance with state environmental laws:

> Nor are we convinced that Section 959(b) is inapplicable to liquidating trustees, as respondents argue. The *Midlantic* Court found that Section 959(b) *supported* its conclusion that the Bankruptcy Code does 'not preempt all state laws that otherwise constrain the excuse of a trustee's powers.' [citation omitted]. Furthermore, the court noted Congress' intentions that the trustee's efforts 'to marshall and distribute the assets of the estate' give way to the governmental interests in public health and safety. [citation omitted]. We believe that whether a trustee is liquidating, managing or reorganizing the debtor's estate, his efforts under the Code remain the same—the consolidation and distribution of the estate's assets to the benefit of its creditors. As such, that the trustee in this case is liquidating the estate rather than reorganizing it is inconsequential, especially in the critical context of the public's welfare. In either case, an environmental hazard on the estate's property is within the control of the trustee.[175]

From the foregoing it is clear that a receiver is well advised to comply with the requirements of state law with regard to all its activities, especially those activities that affect the health and safety of the public. As *Gillis v. California*[176] makes clear, § 959(b) was intended by Congress to prevent receivers from "transact[ing] local business, contrary to State statutes obligatory upon all others." This makes good sense since any other rule would threaten the public's health, safety, and welfare.

---

[174] In re Wall Tube & Metal Products. Co., 831 F.2d 118 (6th Cir. 1987).

[175] *Id.* at 122. *See also* In re Charles George Land Reclamation Trust, 30 B.R. 918 (Bankr. D. Mass. 1983) (interpreting 28 U.S.C. 959(b) as requiring the trustee to comply with environmental regulations or suffer daily penalties of $25,000); In re Kish, 41 B.R. 620, 625 (Bankr. E.D. Mich. 1984) (in refusing to stay a state court suit seeking to enjoin continued operation of a landfill in alleged violation of state law, the court stated "[t]rustees who operate the business of a debtor are bound to abide by all state laws and regulations respecting the operation and use of the assets of such business"); In re Kaiser Steel Corp., 87 B.R. 662, 665 (Bankr. D. Colo. 1988) (in a suit brought by state authorities in Utah seeking to compel a debtor to post a bond or cease mining and initiate reclamation activity, the court stated "[i]t is clear that, as to its ongoing post-petition mining activities, the Debtor must comply with the laws of Utah, and the State has a legitimate interest in enforcing those laws, particularly where the failure to do so would have an adverse impact on the environment"); and In re Stevens, 68 B.R. 774 (D. Me. 1987) (trustee in bankruptcy could not abandon drums of PCB-contaminated waste oil, as this would contravene state laws designed to protect the public health, citing 28 U.S.C. § 959(b)).

[176] 293 U.S. at 66.

§ 7.14 Receiver's Liability for Taxes under 28 U.S.C. § 960

Section 960[177] imposes a duty on federal equity receivers to comply with all federal, state, and local tax obligations. The receiver's tax obligations under Section 960 extend to all applicable nondiscriminatory taxes, whether they involve liquidations or normal business operations.[178]

The tax liability covered by § 960 is thus all inclusive, covering such tax liabilities as: (1) federal and state income taxes,[179] (2) local real estate taxes,[180] (3) state sales taxes,[181] (4) state unemployment insurance taxes,[182] (5) real estate transfer taxes stemming from the sale of real estate,[183] (6) state usage taxes,[184] as well as (7) any interest and penalties with regard to these taxes.[185] There is some question whether a receiver is liable under § 960 for state corporate franchise taxes.[186]

---

177 28 U.S.C. § 960 provides:

> Any officers and agents conducting any business under authority of a United States court shall be subject to all federal, state and local taxes applicable to such business to the same extent as if it were conducted by an individual or corporation.

As seen from its language, Section 960 is also applicable to bankruptcy proceedings. The tax liabilities allowed under Section 960 "must be deemed expenses of administration and therefore charges to be satisfied in preference to the claims of general creditors." Michigan v. Michigan Trust Co., 286 U.S. 334, 344 (1932).

178 Cal. Equalization Bd. v. Sierra Summit, 490 U.S. 844 (1989). This case resolved the conflict that had developed between the circuits as to whether a liquidation sale in a receivership or bankruptcy proceeding was within the meaning of the express language "conducting any business" of 28 U.S.C. § 960. Prior to this decision by the Supreme Court, the Second and Fifth Circuits had held that the relevant state sales tax was applicable to liquidation sales under 28 U.S.C. § 960. See In re Leavy, 85 F.2d 25 (2d Cir. 1936); and In re Hatfield Construction Co., 494 F.2d 1179 (5th Cir. 1974), respectively. The Ninth and Eleventh Circuits, on the other hand, had held that the relevant state sales tax was not applicable because the trustee in bankruptcy was not "conducting any business" within the contemplation of 28 U.S.C. § 960. *See* California State Board of Equalization v. Goggin, 245 F.2d 44 (9th Cir. 1957), cert denied, 353 U.S. 961 (1957); and Matter of Cusato Bros. Intern., Inc., 750 F.2d 887 (11th Cir. 1985), respectively.

179 Richardson v. United States., 386 F. Supp. 424, 427 n.1 (C.D. Cal. 1974).

180 Borock v. City of New York, 268 F.2d 412 (2d Cir. 1959).

181 In re Hatfield Construction Company, 494 F.2d 1179 (5th Cir. 1974).

182 The Southern Cross, 120 F.2d 466 (2d Cir. 1941).

183 Matter of Woodland Builders, Inc., 87 B.R. 774 (Bankr. D. Conn. 1988).

184 Cal. Equalization Bd. v. Sierra Summit, 490 U.S. 844.

185 In Boteler v. Ingels, 308 U.S. 57 (1939), the Supreme Court held that a bankrupt's estate is not only liable for automobile license fees, imposed while the bankruptcy trustee is conducting the business of the debtor, but the penalty imposed thereon. *See also* Mayer v. Gros, 116 F.2d 733 (5th Cir. 1940); and In re Chicago & N. W. Ry. Co., 119 F.2d 971 (7th Cir. 1941).

186 This would seem to depend on whether the tax is for the right to be a corporation, in which case it is not applicable to a receiver, or for the right to transact business, in

Section 960's imposition of these taxes on receivership or bankruptcy estates is intended to put them on an equal footing with all other businesses. As the Supreme Court noted after reviewing the legislative history of an earlier version of 28 U.S.C. § 960 in *Palmer v. Webster & Atlas Nat. Bank:*

> What Congress intended was that a business in receivership, or conducted under court order, should be subject to the same tax liability as the owner would have been if in possession and operating the enterprise.[187]

§ 7.15 Receiver's Duty to Report to the Court

As noted earlier, a receiver is viewed as an arm of the court acting in a fiduciary capacity for the benefit of all those who have an interest in the receivership estate.[188] Therefore, a receiver must act openly at all times, share all material information with the court overseeing the receivership, and ultimately get court approval for the receiver's actions.[189]

In addition to getting prior court approval for all significant actions such as the sale of assets, the receiver should report all past activity with regard to the receivership estate by filing periodic reports with the court overseeing the receivership. These reports are usually denoted ad seriatim, such as the "Receiver's First Report." They relate the activities of the receiver and those of the receiver's agents during the relevant time period. The report should include a listing of all receipts and disbursements, the disposal of assets, the retention of agents and professionals, legal developments, and any other matters of significance during the reporting period. While most federal court jurisdictions do not prescribe by local rule the time and frequency for filing such reports,[190] it is recommended that receiver's reports be filed on a quarterly basis or where appropriate, monthly. This not only assures the court that

---

which case it is taxable to the receiver. 7B J. Moore, M. Waxner, H. Fink, D. Epstein, G. Grother Moore's Federal Practice ¶ 66.04[4], 1914–1915 (2d ed. 1989) citing Michigan v. Michigan Trust Co., 286 U.S. at 341–342.

[187] 312 U.S. 156, 163 (1941).

[188] Crites, Inc., v. Prudential Ins. Co., 322 U.S. 408, 414 (1944); and Phelan v. Middle States Oil Corp., 154 F.2d 978, 991 (2d Cir. 1946).

[189] Crites, Inc. v. Prudential Ins. Co., 322 U.S. at 414–415.

[190] Some Local Rules do require the filing of periodic reports by receivers. These jurisdictions include the Central District of California, Local Rule 25.6.1 (every six months); Eastern District of California, Local Rule 232(e) (once a year for permanent receivers, and a day before the hearing to continue a temporary receiver); Northern District of California, Local Rule 225.5; and Southern District of California, Local Rule 66.1(e) (initial report for permanent receiver within 30 days of appointment and as the court directs thereafter); District of Hawaii, Local Rule 221(1)(b) (within one month of filing the inventory," and quarterly thereafter); Western District of Pennsylvania, Local Rule 18(b) (within three months after filing "the inventory," and quarterly thereafter);

the receiver is acting appropriately and timely, but also prevents complaints from interested parties that information as to the receiver's activities are not being reported in a timely fashion, or worse, are being kept from the court.

Two jurisdictions that do have local rules regarding reporting by receivers that are representative of this reporting requirement are the Central and Northern Districts of California. In the Central District of California, Local Rule 25 requires the filing of a receiver's report within six months of appointment and semi-annually thereafter, showing: (a) receipts and expenditures; and (b) all acts and transactions of the receiver.[191]

In the Northern District of California, Local Rule 225.5 requires the filing of an initial receiver's report within 30 days of a permanent receiver's appointment:

> Within 30 days of appointment, a permanent receiver shall file with the court a verified report and petition for instructions, which shall be heard on ten days notice to all known creditors and parties. The report shall contain a summary of the operations of the receiver, an inventory of the assets and their appraised value, a schedule of all receipts and disbursements, and a list of all creditors, their addresses and the amounts of their claims. The petition shall contain the receiver's recommendation as to the continuance of the receivership and reasons therefor. At the hearing, the judge shall determine whether the receivership shall be continued and, if so, shall fix the time for future reports of the receiver.

Although commonly receivers merely file their reports with the court overseeing the receivership, it may be more advantegous to seek formal court approval of the receiver's report by way of notice, motion, and hearing.[192]

It is quite risky, however, to use the report as a means of sanctioning past receivership actions for which prior court approval has not been obtained, such as the borrowing of money. Thus, for example in *Chicago Deposit Vault Co. v. McNulta,*[193] the lessor of premises leased by a receiver of a railroad attempted to enforce the remaining term of the lease in the receivership proceeding, even though the receivership was about to be terminated. The court overseeing the receivership had never specifically approved the receiver's

---

Western District of Washington (within six months after filing of "the inventory," and biannually thereafter).

The "inventory" required to be filed by the receiver in the jurisdictions requiring it, such as the Western District of Pennsylvania, Local Rule 18(a), usually consists of a listing "of all property and assets in his possession or in the possession of others who hold possession as his agent, and in a separate schedule an inventory of the property and assets of the estate not reduced to possession by him but claimed and held by others."

191 Local Rule 25.6.1 (C.D. Cal.)

192 Local Rule 232(e)(2), Eastern District of California requires a hearing on the report and the court's approval or disapproval of it.

193 153 U.S. 554 (1893).

execution of the lease. The lessor, however, argued that the order appointing the receiver gave the receiver sufficiently broad powers to enter into such a lease, and the court's approval of a number of receivership reports which listed the lease payments was sufficient court approval. In rejecting these arguments the Supreme Court stated with respect to the lower court's approval of the receiver's reports, which listed the disbursements under the lease:

> The receiver's reports which were approved by the court did not disclose the fact of the existence of the lease, or its terms and provisions, in such manner as to make the court's approval of the reports a confirmation of the lease.[194]

§ 7.16 The Receiver's Jurisdiction and Control over Property of the Receivership Estate

Once the statutory prerequisites of § 754[195] have been met, namely that a copy of the complaint and order of appointment of the receiver have been filed in each federal judicial district in which property of the receivership estate is located, the federal district court that appointed the receiver assumes exclusive jurisdiction and control over the property of the receivership estate, even though it is in different federal judicial districts.[196] Thus, a receiver upon appointment in one federal judicial district should, within 10 days of the entry of his appointment, file a copy of that order, as well as a copy of the complaint initiating the action in each federal judicial district where property is thought to be located. If this is done, then the receiver's jurisdiction and control over the property of the estate in other federal judicial districts is retained as part of the exclusive jurisdiction of the federal district court that originally appointed the receiver. Therefore, it cannot be emphasized enough

---

[194] 153 U.S. at 560.

[195] 28 U.S.C. § 754 provides:

> A receiver appointed in any civil action or proceeding involving property, real, personal or mixed, situated in different districts shall, upon giving bond as required by the court, be vested with complete jurisdiction and control of all such property with the right to take possession thereof.
>
> He shall have capacity to sue in any district without ancillary appointment, and may be sued with respect thereto as provided in section 959 of this title.
>
> Such receiver shall, within ten days after the entry of his order of appointment, file copies of the complaint and such order of appointment in the district court for each district in which property is located. The failure to file such copies in any district shall divest the receiver of jurisdiction and control over all such property in that district.

[196] United States v. Arizona Fuels Corp., 739 F. 2d 455 (9th Cir. 1984); Haile v. Henderson Nat. Bank, 657 F.2d 816 (6th Cir. 1981); United States v. Franklin National Bank, 512 F.2d 245, (2d Cir. 1975); Tcherepnin v. Franz, 439 F. Supp. 1340 (N.D. Ill. 1977).

that the ministerial act of filing copies of the complaint and order of appointment in every federal judicial district where property of the receivership estate is thought to be located should be accomplished in accordance with the ten day statutory period of § 754. Moreover, this exclusive jurisdiction and control over the property covers all property of the receivership estate whether "real, personal or mixed."[197]

Once the filing of the copies of the complaint and order have been accomplished under § 754, the assets of the receivership estate are protected from levy and execution in other jurisdictions by creditors who have not obtained the permission of the court overseeing the receivership for such action.[198]

Section 754 also gives the receiver the capacity to sue, and provided 28 U.S.C. § 959 is complied with as well as any stay order, be sued, in any other district without the need for ancillary appointment.[199]

If a receiver for one reason or another fails to file a copy of the complaint and order of his appointment in one or several jurisdictions where property of the receivership estate is located, current case precedent allows a liberal construction of § 754, thereby making effective late compliance. Thus, in *Securities & Exchange Com. v. Equity Service Corp.*,[200] The Third Circuit interpreted § 754 as allowing a receiver who has failed to file a copy of the complaint and order of his appointment within the 10-day period to reassert jurisdiction and control in that judicial district by a later filing, as long as the rights of others have not been prejudiced during the intervening period.[201] The Court noted that even though compliance with § 754 was months late, the receiver had filed copies of both the complaint and order of his appointment

---

197 28 U.S.C. § 754.

198 Lee v. Freeman, 79 F.2d 868 (5th Cir. 1935); and Link v. Powell, 57 F.2d 591 (W.D. S.C. 1932).

199 As noted in Mentink v. World Time Corp. of America, 131 F.R.D. 210, 211 (S.D. Fla. 1990):

> Before 1948, federal courts did not recognize the capacity of foreign receivers to institute an action, even if they could sue or be sued in the forum state's court. The underlying rationale for this practice was stated in Great Western Mining & Mfg. Co. v. Harris, 198 U.S. 561, 576, 25 S.Ct. 770, 774, 49 L. Ed. 1163, 1168 (1905) to the effect that every jurisdiction 'has the right and power to determine for itself who the receiver shall be.' . . .
>
> . . . The view expressed in that decision was sharply criticized for causing great hardship and delay in the judicial process, because it required the appointment of ancillary receivers in every district in which debtors had to be sued. [citation omitted] As a result of the enactment and subsequent 1948 amendment of Rule 17(b), the capacity of federal receivers is to be determined in accordance with section 754 of the Judicial Code, which provides that an appointed receiver 'shall have the capacity to sue in any district without ancillary appointment.' [statutory citation omitted]

200 632 F.2d 1092 (3rd Cir. 1980).

201 *Id.* at 1095.

nearly a year before the plaintiffs had brought the state court action, and so they could not "assert prejudice from lack of notice because the receiver was not in strict compliance with § 754."[202] The Ninth Circuit in *United States v. Arizona Fuels Corp.*,[203] also used the rationale of actual notice as one of the bases for its holding that compliance with § 754 was unnecessary.

In *Kilsheimer v. Rose & Moskowitz*,[204] the Second Court gave effect to a late filing of the complaint and order of appointment upon the grounds that there was no property to which the receiver could have obtained either possession or title at the time of his appointment. This was because all of the property that was the subject of the receivership estate was vested in a reorganization trustee, and such possession or title could not be obtained by the receiver until the dismissal of the reorganization proceedings.

In *Tcherpnin v. Franz*,[205] compliance with § 754 was deemed unnecessary in a suit brought by a receiver as an ancillary action in the court that had appointed him to set aside a fraudulent conveyance, even though it affected property in another federal judicial district where a copy of the complaint and order of appointment had not been filed. This was because of the ancillary nature of the action, and the fact that the court overseeing the receivership had in personam jurisdiction over the parties:

> Here, however, as will be discussed in relation to venue, jurisdiction over Count IX is in personam so that jurisdiction over property that may be subject to an in personam decree need not be shown for this court to exercise its proper ancillary jurisdiction. Accordingly, section 754 is not applicable here.[206]

The Ninth Circuit in *United States v. Arizona Fuels Corp.*[207] also used personal jurisdiction of the receivership court over a creditor as one of the bases for finding that compliance with § 754 was not necessary:

> But where the property is essentially in the form of a monetary credit, held by a party over whom the Court already has jurisdiction, who has actual notice of the receivership and has previously appeared in the receivership court, there is no purpose served in requiring the Receiver to trace the funds to Houston and make a § 754 filing there.[208]

While § 754 if complied with provides the federal district court that appointed the receiver with exclusive jurisdiction and control over the property

---

[202] *Id.*

[203] 739 F.2d at 460.

[204] 257 F.2d 242 (2d Cir. 1958).

[205] 439 F. Supp. 1340 (N.D. Ill. 1977).

[206] *Id.* at 1344.

[207] 739 F.2d at 460.

[208] *Id.* at 460–461.

of the receivership estate in other federal judicial districts, it does not afford an independent basis for subject matter jurisdiction for actions brought by the receiver in judicial districts other than the appointing one.[209] In *United States v. Franklin National Bank,*[210] a receiver of a small business investment company appointed in the United States District Court for the Southern District of New York, filed suit in the Eastern District of New York,[211] seeking to recover monies paid by the Franklin National Bank to the looters of the corporation. After noting that no independent jurisdictional basis was needed if the suit could have been brought in the Southern District of New York because it would have had ancillary subject matter jurisdiction,[212] the Second Circuit held that it was necessary for there to be an independent subject matter jurisdictional basis for the receiver to maintain the suit in the Eastern District of New York, which the court found lacking.

But it would appear that § 754 does not afford any basis for in personam jurisdiction in the ancillary action pending in the court that appointed the receiver. Such in personam jurisdiction would have to come from the traditional sources of such jurisdiction. Thus, the First Circuit affirmed the dismissal by the district court overseeing the receivership in Massachusetts on traditional in personam jurisdictional grounds of a suit brought by the receiver of a charitable corporation against the corporation's former officers and directors, who resided out of state.[213] The suit alleged that these officers and directors had breached their fiduciary duties owed to the corporation, which resulted in an adverse antitrust judgment:

> It is well established that a federal district court has subject matter jurisdiction in ancillary actions brought in the court where the receiver is appointed 'to accomplish the ends sought and directed by the suit in which the appointment was made.' [citations omitted]. As stated above, the receiver in this case requested and was granted authority by the appointing court to commence an action against the defendants for breach of their fiduciary duties which caused the AFTF to violate the antitrust laws and to incur the adverse judgment in the district court in Washington.

---

209 United States v. Franklin National Bank, 512 F.2d 245 (2d Cir. 1975).

210 *Id.*

211 Suit had originally been filed in the Southern District of New York, but was dismissed because of improper venue in that district. *Id.* at 247, n.6.

212 An ancillary suit may be brought in the federal judicial district of the receiver's appointment without any independent basis for subject matter jurisdiction. Haile v. Henderson Nat. Bank, 657 F.2d at 822; United States v. Franklin National Bank, 512 F.2d at 249; Bryan v. Bartlett, 435 F.2d 28, 30 n.2 (8th Cir. 1970); Glusband v. Euro-Swiss Intern. Corp., 85 F.R.D. 597, 598 (S.D. N.Y. 1979); and Tcherepnin v. Franz, 439 F. Supp. at 1344.

213 American Freedom Train Found. v. Spurney, 747 F.2d 1069 (1st Cir. 1984).

> We find nothing in the language of section 754 or in the decisional law which precludes the district court from exercising its in personam equitable jurisdiction in ancillary actions brought by the receiver. If there is in personam jurisdiction, it need not be shown that the court has jurisdiction over property under section 754. [citation omitted]. Instead, the limits of the district court's jurisdiction should comport with the general standards applicable to suits brought under the court's in personam equity jurisdiction, barring any special statutory exceptions. Since we have concluded that the jurisdictional limitations of section 754 are inapplicable in plaintiff's in personam action, we find it necessary to . . . determine whether the court had jurisdiction over defendants under the Massachusetts long-arm statute and the 'minimum contacts' standard of *International Shoe Company v. Washington,* 326 U.S. 310, 66 S. Ct. 154, 90 L.Ed. 95 (1945).[214]

Section 1692[215] complements § 754 by providing for nationwide service of process in those actions involving the property of the estate. By the terms of § 1692, once an order has been entered in such an action, it should be filed in the district where the affected property is located.

§ 7.17 Summary Proceedings to Determine the Receiver's Right to Possession of Property

Whether denoted "summary jurisdiction" or "summary proceedings" a court overseeing a federal equity receivership can adjudicate the receiver's right to possession of tangible or intangible property by summary means.[216] This power

---

[214] *Id.* at 1073–1074. This holding would appear to conflict with the Sixth Circuit's decision in Haile v. Henderson Nat. Bank, 657 F.2d 816, although the First Circuit in Spurney looked upon that aspect of the Haile decision as dicta, American Freedom Train Found. v. Spurney, 747 F.2d at 1073. As discussed in the next footnote, the Sixth Circuit in Haile based its rationale on 28 U.S.C. § 1692.

[215] 28 U.S.C. Section 1692 provides: "In proceedings in a district court where a receiver is appointed for property, real, personal or mixed, situated in different districts, process may issue and be executed in any such district as if the property lay wholly within one district, but orders affecting the property shall be entered of record in each of such districts."

At least one court has construed Section 1692 as also affording a basis for personal jurisdiction over persons outside the judicial district overseeing the receivership in the context of an ancillary action brought in that district. Haile v. Henderson National Bank, 657 F.2d at 825. Such personal jurisdiction could also arise from a claimant's filing of a claim in the receivership proceeding. *See* J. Moore, M. Waxner, H. Fink, D. Epstein, G. Grother, Moore's Federal Practice, 66.08 (2d Ed. 1989) and cases cited therein, Alexander v. Hillman, 296 U.S. 222 (1935); and Taylor v. Producers Pipe & Supply Co., 114 F.2d 785 (10th Cir. 1940). *See also* Legate v. Maloney, 334 F.2d 704, 708–709 (1st Cir. 1964).

[216] *See e.g.,* S.E.C. v. Wencke, 783 F.2d 829 19th Cir. 1986); S.E.C. v. Universal Financial, 760 F.2d 1034 (9th Cir. 1985); United States v. Arizona Fuels Corp., 739 F.2d 455 (9th Cir. 1984); and F.T.C. v. Crittenden, 823 F. Supp. 699, 702 (C.D. Calif. 1993).

of summary adjudication is similar to that found in bankruptcy practice.[217] In *Bien v. Robinson*[218] the Supreme Court sanctioned the use of summary proceedings to order the return of monies improperly obtained by the debtor's counsel shortly after the appointment of a receiver. The attorney, who had received the check prior to the receivership, had cashed it after the receiver's appointment and the issuance of an injunction preventing the payment or transfer of property or funds to anyone other than the receiver. The Supreme Court left no doubt that the receivership court had the power to recover the money thus paid by summary proceedings:

> Reduced to its last analysis, the contention of this branch of the case is that a court of equity, which, in the due exercise of jurisdiction, had appointed receivers of the assets and property of a corporation, and enjoined interference by others with such property, was without power, by summary process, after due notice and opportunity to be heard, to compel a repayment by one who, with knowledge of the order of injunction, and in violation of its terms, took in satisfaction of an indebtedness from a debtor to the corporation, property forming part of the assets of such corporation. We think the contention in the assignments of error based thereon are so manifestly frivolous as to be utterly insufficient to serve as the foundation for a writ of error.[219]

Similarly, an early Eighth Circuit case[220] upheld the use of summary procedures to compel the return of gas pipe owned by an oil company in receivership, after an evidentiary hearing determined that it was wrongfully taken from the company's storage yards.

> Constructively the pipe was in the possession of the receivers when it was removed by appellant's servants and agents. The power of the court to protect the possession of its receivers is too well-settled to require discussion. [citations omitted].
>
> . . .
>
> The purpose of the order entered by the court below was to vindicate the right of the receivers to the possession of the property, and not for the purpose of definitely and finally determining title. Thus construed, appellant has no cause to complain of the order made by the court below, and the same is affirmed.[221]

---

217 *See e.g.* Katchen v. Landy, 382 U.S. 323 (1966); and Matter of Reading Co., 711 F.2d 509, 515–517 (3rd Cir. 1983).

218 208 U.S. 423 (1908).

219 *Id.* at 428.

220 McMullen v. Hurley, 291 F. 374 (8th Cir. 1923).

221 *Id.* at 376.

Moreover, where the property in question is of a nature such as oil that can be co-mingled and lose its separate identity or where the property has been disposed of the court may by summary means order that money be substituted and paid to the court.[222]

More recently, several Ninth Circuit cases have upheld the use of summary proceedings to determine a receiver's right to possession of property.[223] In *United States v. Arizona Fuels Corp.*,[224] the district court overseeing the receivership had ordered Tenneco Oil Company to return to the possession of the receiver funds that the oil company had attempted to setoff against an indebtedness arising from oil deliveries before the receivership. In affirming this use of summary procedures, the Ninth Circuit stated:

> Tenneco argues that the funds in its possession were presumptively Tenneco's. But possession is not determinative; summary proceedings are appropriate to determine rights to possession, although not ultimate rights to title or ownership. [citations omitted]. Tenneco's argument would universally preclude summary proceedings to protect the receivership assets from illegitimate but minimally articulate possessors . . . The district court's order determined the Receiver's right to possession of the funds, based on adjudication of the right to setoff, without determining the validity of Tenneco's claims as a creditor of Arizona Fuels. We hold that summary proceedings were appropriate and proper for this purpose.[225]

Although the use of summary proceedings has been approved for use in determining the receiver's right to possession of property, it should be borne in mind that the procedural protections afforded third parties coming before the receivership court in such proceedings are not very different from the procedural protections found in plenary proceedings. As noted by the Ninth Circuit in *S.E.C. v. Wencke:*

> We indicated that to determine the adequacy of a summary proceeding in a given case, courts must focus not on the form of the proceedings, but on their

---

222 Burnham v. Todd, 139 F.2d 338 (5th Cir. 1943).

223 S.E.C. v. Wencke, 783 F.2d 829; S.E.C. v. Universal Financial, 760 F.2d 1034; and United States v. Arizona Fuels Corp., 739 F.2d 455.

224 739 F.2d at 458–459.

225 *Id.* at 459. In American Brakeshoe & Foundry Co. v. New York RYS. Co., 10 F.2d 920 (2d Cir. 1926), the use of summary proceedings to recover funds held by third party fiduciaries, which were claimed by the receiver, was upheld even though normally such claims against third parties not otherwise involved in the receivership would be plenary in nature. This was because the third parties had filed petitions in the receivership proceeding seeking the return of their property. On the other hand, the Third Circuit eschewed the use of summary proceedings in a railroad reorganization under the former Bankruptcy Act with respect to a determination of the bankrupt's ownership rights in a company that provided it with rolling stock. Nevertheless, it upheld the district court upon the basis of diversity jurisdiction, since no essential characteristic of a plenary hearing was lacking, Matter of Reading Co. 711 F.2d 509.

> substance: in Universal Financial, for example, 'the distinction between summary and plenary proceedings was of no consequence . . . because the district court afforded [the non-parties challenging its jurisdiction] virtually all of the procedural protections which would have been available in plenary proceedings.' [citation omitted]. We did not accept the contention that the lack of a formal complaint and answer prevented the district court from exercising its jurisdiction and resolving the dispute, because the parties challenging jurisdiction had notice concerning the nature of the proceedings, were permitted extensive discovery, including the taking of depositions, and were permitted to file briefs and exhibits with the district court, and because, except for dispensing with the filing of a complaint and answer, the district court applied the Federal Rules of Evidence and Civil Procedure.[226]

Similarly, in *S.E.C. v. Universal Financial,*[227] the court upheld the use of summary procedures in determining the ownership interest of various investors in mortgage notes. In rejecting the argument that summary proceedings were unconstitutional where the third-party claimant could make out a substantial claim to ownership of the notes held by the receiver, the Ninth Circuit held that the distinction between summary and plenary proceedings was of no consequence:

> We agree with the Receiver, however, that the distinction between summary and plenary proceedings was of no consequence here because the district court afforded Investors virtually all of the procedural protections which would have been available in plenary proceedings. [citations omitted]. Investors were allowed extensive discovery, including the right to take depositions, and were permitted to file numerous briefs and exhibits in connection with the test cases. The court applied the Federal Rules of Evidence and the Federal Rules of Civil Procedure. Although there was no formal complaint or answer, Investors cannot seriously claim that they lacked notice of the nature of the proceedings. Because Investors cannot explain how the summary proceedings differed from the process they would have received in a plenary suit, their challenge to the district court's exercise of summary jurisdiction must fail.[228]

§ 7.18 The Power of the Receiver to Enter into Contracts

Since a receiver derives all power from the court, it is essential for a receiver prior to entering into contracts or expending funds to obtain a court order specifically authorizing the contract or expenditure. The rationale for this

---

226 *Id.* at 836–837.

227 760 F. 2d at 1037 (9th Cir. 1985).

228 *Id.* at 1037.

rule was very well expressed by the Supreme Court in a case noted earlier, *Chicago Deposit Vault Co. v. McNulta:*[229]

> The receiver being an officer of the court, and acting under the court's direction and instructions, his powers are derived from and defined by the court under which he acts. He is not such a general agent as to have any implied power, and his authority to make expenditures and incur liabilities—like the one in question—must be either found in the order of his appointment, or be approved by the court, before they acquire validity, and have any binding force upon the trust.

In that case, as we have seen, the Supreme Court refused to enforce the remaining term of a lease entered into by a receiver without previous court approval. The court rejected the argument that the order appointing the receiver was sufficient authority for the receiver's execution of the lease even though that order provided that "[s]aid receiver shall also have authority, subject to the supervision of the court, . . . to make all contracts that may be necessary in carrying on the business of said railroad, subject to the supervision of this court . . . ."[230] Neither this language in the order appointing the receiver, nor the fact that the court overseeing the receivership had approved periodic reports listing expenditures for the lease was sufficient in the Supreme Court's eyes to constitute court approval of the lease. Accordingly, the receiver must seek prior court approval for expenditures and contractual obligations.

§ 7.19 Obtaining Credit for Receiverships

While it is true as noted by the Eighth Circuit that "[o]rdinarily the main purpose of the appointment of a receiver of a private business corporation or company is to prevent not to promote, the borrowing of money upon its assets and the increase of the indebtedness secured thereon,"[231] sometimes it will be necessary for a receiver to borrow money or get an extension of credit in order to care for and preserve assets or enhance their value. If it is necessary for a receiver to obtain funds through borrowing, the receiver should always obtain prior court authorization. If prior court authorization is not obtained, the borrowing is not binding against the receivership estate.[232]

---

229 153 U.S. at 561.

230 *Id.* at 555.

231 Byrnes v. Missouri National Bank, 7 F.2d 978, (8th Cir. 1925).

232 Amick v. Hotz, 101 F.2d 311, 312 (8th Cir. 1939). *See also* Cake v. Mohun, 164 U.S. 311, 816 (1896); and Cowdrey v. Galveston, Etc., R.R. Co., 93 U.S. 352 (1877).

Such a request to the court overseeing the receivership should be as specific as possible, including the amount of money to be borrowed and whether the receiver is to be given the authority to pledge the assets of the receivership estate as collateral. The receiver should also explain why such borrowing is necessary and how it will benefit the assets of the estate. For example, is such borrowing necessary for the care and preservation of the assets or will it enhance their value, such as by keeping them as a going business. The lien position of the creditor supplying these funds should be specified. Interested parties should receive notice of the proposed financing and an opportunity for a hearing.

Lack of notice and a hearing is not per se fatal to the transaction, but in *Amick v. Hotz,* the court stated "[t]hat the entry of such an order without notice might constitute a serious abuse of discretion, . . . but it is our opinion . . . that the lack of notice does not render such an order a nullity."[233] It is not advisable to seek subsequent court ratification after the financing takes place, since as stated by the Second Circuit in *In re American Cooler Co. Inc.:*

> We think that the judge should not retroactively validate the loan unless he is confident that he would have authorized it if a timely application had been made, and unless, in addition, he is reasonably persuaded that the creditors have not been harmed by a continuation of the business made possible by the loan. He should also take into account, as bearing on the good faith of the debtor and lender, whether they have honestly believed that they had the authority to enter into the transaction. . . . We should emphasize that this equitable power must be cautiously exercised, and that only a foolhardy lender will attempt to make it serve as a substitute for proper authorization.[234]

If the court approves the financing, the receiver should issue a certificate (receiver's certificate) promising to pay a sum certain. Frequently, the creditor providing such financing will be given a priority lien.[235] The receiver should present the request to the court by way of motion supported by a detailed affidavit specifying the money needed and why. If a priority lien is requested, then the other creditors should have notice of the request and an opportunity for a hearing. A sample motion and receiver's certificate are set forth later in this chapter.

---

233 101 F.2d at 313.

234 125 F.2d 496, 497 (2d Cir. 1942).

235 It should be noted, however, that "[a]s a rule, receiver's certificates issued by the receiver of a merely private corporation neither public nor a quasi-public corporation, are not a charge against the assets of the corporation in preference to existing liens as against lienors who have not consented to their issue." Koursey v. International Harvester Co., 109 F.2d 774, 779 (10th Cir. 1940).

§ 7.20 Disposition and Sale of Property by the Receiver

Since a federal equity receivership is under court supervision, all sales of real and personal property, whether tangible or intangible, should be by way of application to the court for an order authorizing the sale. In addition, the requirements of 28 U.S.C. § 2001(a), must be met with respect to the procedures to be followed for such sales, whether public or private.[236] Although § 2001 by its express terms applies only to the sale of real estate, 28 U.S.C. § 2004 requires that the procedures prescribed by § 2001 must be used for sales of personalty also, unless the "court orders otherwise."[237]

Even though § 2001 has been construed as not applying to execution sales,[238] since all property sales by the receiver will be authorized by court order, the requirements of § 2001 must be followed.

---

236 28 U.S.C. § 2001(a) provides in pertinent part:

a) * * *

Property in the possession of a receiver or receivers appointed by one or more district courts shall be sold at public sale in the district wherein any such receiver was first appointed, at the courthouse of the county, parish, or city situated therein in which the greater part of the property in such district is located, or on the premises or some parcel thereof located in such county, parish, or city, as such court directs, unless the court orders the sale of the property or one or more parcels thereof in one or more ancillary districts.

(b) After a hearing, of which notice to all interested parties shall be given by publication or otherwise as the court directs, the court may order the sale of such realty or interest or any part thereof at private sale for cash or other consideration and upon such terms and conditions as the court approves, if it finds that the best interests of the estate will be conserved thereby. Before confirmation of any private sale, the court shall appoint three disinterested persons to appraise such property or different groups of three appraisers each to appraise properties of different classes or situated in different localities. No private sale shall be confirmed at a price less than two-thirds of the appraised value. Before confirmation of any private sale, the terms thereof shall be published in such newspaper or newspapers of general circulation as the court directs at least ten days before confirmation. The private sale shall not be confirmed if a bona fide offer is made, under the conditions prescribed by the court, which guarantees at least a ten per centum increase over the price offered in the private sale.

237 28 U.S.C. 2004 provides in pertinent part: "Any personalty sold under any order or decree of any court of the United States shall be sold in accordance with section 2001 of this title, unless the court orders otherwise."

238 Weir v. U.S., 339 F.2d 82 (8th Cir. 1964). This case discusses the difference between an execution sale which does not fall within the purview of Section 2001, and a judicial sale which does: "The Supreme Court in [Yazoo & M.V.R. Co. v. Clarksdale, 257 U.S. 10 (1921)] noted the distinction between judicial sales '*** made under order or decree of the court and requiring confirmation by the court for their validity ***' and executions (which issue by mere praecipe of the judgment creditor *** and only come under

Publication of notice of a public sale must be in accordance with the requirements of 28 U.S.C. § 2002, namely publication of a notice of sale containing a court approved description of the property, appearing in a regularly issued publication of general circulation in the "county, state or judicial district of the United States wherein the realty is situated."[239]

In the event that a private sale of receivership property is contemplated special care should be taken to adhere to the requirements of § 2001(b). These requirements were set forth in *United States v. Garcia:*

> As required by Section 2000(b), the court appointed three disinterested persons to appraise the property and file their valuations with the court. . . . The district court further adhered to the requirements of Section 2000(b) by causing the terms of the proposed private sale to be published in a newspaper of general circulation for ten days along with the conditions for making offers higher than at least ten per cent (10%) over the minimum two-thirds value of the property as determined by the three court-appointed appraisers. A hearing on confirmation of the private sale was held on May 4, 1972, where, in the absence of higher offers, the court confirmed the private sale.[240]

Although § 2001(b) only requires appraisals for the private sale of real property and not for public sales,[241] an appraisal is helpful and may be necessary, even though a public sale is being conducted, in order to satisfy the court and interested parties when seeking confirmation of the sale that the price obtained was adequate.

---

judicial supervision on complaint of either party' [citation omitted] as being different things." *Id.* at 85. *See also* United States v. Branch Coal Corporation, 390 F.2d 7, 9–10 (8th Cir. 1964).

239 28 U.S.C. 2002 provides:

> A public sale of reality or interest therein under any order, judgment or decree of any court of the United States shall not be made without notice published once a week for at least four weeks prior to the sale in at least one newspaper regularly issued and of general circulation in the county, state, or judicial district of the United States wherein the realty is situated.
>
> If such realty is situated in more than one county, state, district or circuit, such notice shall be published in one or more of the counties, states, or districts wherein it is situated, as the court directs. The notice shall be substantially in such form and contain such description of the property by reference or otherwise as the court approves. The court may direct that the publication be made in other newspapers.
>
> This section shall not apply to sales and proceedings under Title 11 or by receivers or conservators of banks appointed by the Comptroller of the Currency.

240 474 F.2d 1202, 1204 (5th Cir. 1973).

241 J. Ray McDermott & Co. Inc. v. Vessel Morning Star, 457 F.2d 815, 818 (5th Cir. 1972), cert. den. 409 U.S. 948 (1972); Breeding Motor Freight Lines, Inc. v. Reconstruction Finance Corp., 172 F.2d 416 (10th Cir. 1949), cert. den. 338 U.S. 814 (1949).

§ 7.21 Establishing a Bar Date for Claims in a Liquidating Receivership

Sometime during the pendency of a liquidating receivership, it is advisable to petition the court for permission to give notice to all claimants, of the last day for filing claims in the receivership proceeding in order to share in the distribution of the estate. The date so fixed by the court is denoted a Bar Date, and claims filed after that date will be barred from receiving any distribution from the estate.[242] Notice of this Bar Date should be given by mail to individual claimants whose identity and address are known to the receiver[243] and by publication in an appropriate newspaper or journal to reach any claimants whose identity and address are not known to the receiver. Usually, the petition for and notice of a Bar Date is accomplished after the receiver has made substantial progress in liquidating the assets of the receivership estate."

In *S.E.C. v. Hardy,*[244] the court found that the notice and claims deadlines approved by the district court were fair and reasonable. In upholding the Bar Date, the Ninth Circuit noted:

> Reasonable administrative procedures, crafted to deal with the complex circumstances of each case, will be upheld. A district judge simply cannot effectively and successfully supervise a receivership and protect the interests of its beneficiaries absent broad discretionary power. We would be remiss were we to interfere with a district court's supervision of an equity receivership absent a clear abuse of discretion.[245]

Courts have, at times, however, shown some flexibility in allowing the late filing of claims where circumstances justify it.[246]

In petitioning the court for a Bar Date, counsel should also seek approval for the form and manner of notice to be given to claimants. The notice itself should appear in an appropriate publication. The appropriateness of the publication

---

242 S.E.C. v. Hardy, 803 F.2d 1034 (9th Cir. 1986).

243 Notice by First Class Mail is usually sufficient.

244 *Id.* at 1038.

245 *Id.* For additional authority upholding the use of a Bar Date, *see* Krause v. Featherstone, 376 F.2d 832 (1st Cir. 1967).

246 S.E.C. v. Hardy, 803 F.2d at 1039 and St. Louis & S.F.R. Co. v. Spiller, 274 U.S. 304 (1927). In Spiller, the Supreme Court decided the issue of whether a claimant, whose claim was based upon overcharges by a railroad that had gone into receivership, could recover his claim from the assets of the receivership estate that had been transferred to a new company. In allowing the claim against these assets now held by the new company, Justice Brandeis noted that the receiver had knowledge of the claim because of the receiver's involvement in the claim's lengthy litigative history; and that based on that history, it was also clear that neither the receiver nor the new company considered the failure to file a claim in the receivership proceeding as barring the relief. St. Louis & S.F.R. Co. v. Spiller, 274 U.S. at 314.

depends upon the scope of the receivership and the estimated number of claimants. Obviously, a receivership involving a public company with thousands of shareholders will require notice in a publication with much wider readership than a smaller closely held company with relatively few claimants.[247]

§ 7.22 Priority of Claims

A receivership court has no general authority to displace valid contractual liens.[248] The doctrine of equitable priority is recognized, however, in some circumstances such as for reimbursement of expenses related to the preservation of property in the receivership estate.[249]

In *Gaskill v. Gordon,*[250] the court held that the receiver was entitled to a first priority lien on an apartment building that was in receivership to cover the receiver's costs for repairs and improvements. This first priority lien was superior to a valid pre-existing first contractual lien. The court further held that the receiver did not have to show that each dollar expended led to a corresponding increase in the value of the property.

Where the receivership involves an insolvency, and the United States is a general unsecured creditor, the United States may claim priority under 31 U.S.C. § 3713(a) (formerly 31 U.S.C. § 191) if a voluntary assignment attachment, or an act of bankruptcy occurred.[251]

---

247 *See* the forms section of this chapter for the form and content of a motion seeking an order approving a Bar Date and the manner and method of notice of the Bar Date. The forms section of this chapter also provides a suggested order approving the manner and method of notice, as well as the claims Bar Date.

248 Thomas v. Western Car Co., 149 U.S. 95 (1893).

249 *Id.* at 111; and Gaskill v. Gordon, 831 F. Supp. 631 (N.D. Ill. 1993). *See also* New York Dock Co. v. Steamship Pozman, 274 U.S. 117 (1927) (a similar result in the context of an admiralty case); S.E.C. v. Alpine Mut. Fund Trust, 824 F. Supp. 987, 995–996 (D. Colo. 1993) (a case allocating the cost of the receivership among the various claimants); U.S. v. Ianniello, 824 F.2d at 209 (a case assessing the cost of the receivership against the United States, where it was the major beneficiary of the receivership, since the receiver was appointed to prevent the defendants from skimming the profits of a restaurant operation and thereby avoiding legitimate tax obligations). The power to determine the priority of claims stems from the federal court's "'broad powers and wide discretion to determine the appropriate relief in an equity receivership'" even to the point of denying remedies that would otherwise be applicable under principles of contract law. U.S. v. Vanguard Inv. Co., 6 F.3d 222, 226 (4th Cir. 1993), quoting with approval S.E.C. v. Elliott, 953 F.2d 1560, 1569–70 (11th Cir. 1992).

250 831 F. Supp. 631.

251 Section 3713(a) provides:

(a)(1) A claim of the United States Government shall be paid first when—

(A) a person indebted to the Government is insolvent and—

For example, in *F.T.C. v. Crittenden,* the district court held that the Internal Revenue Service could claim priority for back taxes under 31 U.S.C. § 3317(a) with respect to a receivership of a copier supply business, based upon the insolvency of the business and the proposed distribution of the receivership funds, which constituted an act of bankruptcy.[252]

A receiver who ignores this statute does so at his peril, since to ignore it is to risk personal liability under 31 U.S.C. § 3713(b) (formerly 31 U.S.C. § 192).[253]

§ 7.23 Post Appointment Interest

As a general rule, once a receiver is appointed to take possession of the debtor's estate, interest ceases to run on the indebtedness of creditors.[254] This parallels the general rule in bankruptcy proceedings that interest ceases to run after the filing of the petition in bankruptcy.[255] The rationale for this rule is that an insolvency proceeding such as a receivership or bankruptcy by its nature causes delay. It would be inequitable, therefore, for anyone to gain an advantage or suffer a loss because of such delay, which is attributable to the law. As stated in *Thomas v. Western Car Co.:*

> We cannot agree that a penalty in the name of interest should be inflicted upon the owners of the mortgage lien for resisting claims which we have disallowed. As a general rule, after the property of an insolvent passes into the hands of a receiver or of an assignee in [in]solvency (sic), interest is not allowed on the claims against the funds. The delay in distribution is the act of the law; it is a necessary incident to the settlement of the estate.[256]

(i) the debtor without enough property to pay all debts makes a voluntary assignment of property;

(ii) property of the debtor, if absent, is attached; or

(iii) an act of bankruptcy is committed.

252 F.T.C. v. Crittenden, 823 F. Supp. 705, 707–708 (C.D. Cal. 1993).

253 31 U.S.C. § 3713(b) provides in pertinent part:

"A representative of a person or an estate . . . paying any part of a debt of the person or estate before paying a claim of the Government is liable to the extent of the payment for unpaid claims of the Government." *See* United States v. Butterworth-Judson, Co., 269 U.S. 504 (1926); United States v. Whitney, 654 F.2d 607, 609 (9th Cir. 1981); United States v. Clover Spinning Mills Co., 373 F.2d 274 (4th Cir. 1966) and U.S. v. Crocker, 313 F.2d 946 (9th Cir. 1963).

254 Vanston Bondholders Protect. Comm. v. Greene, 329 U.S. 156 163 (1946); and Thomas v. Western Car Co., 149 U.S. 95.

255 Sexton v. Dreyfus, 219 U.S. 339 (1911); In re Black Ranches, Inc., 362 F.2d 8, 15 (8th Cir. 1966); and In re Industrial Machine & Supply Co., 112 F. Supp. 261 (W.D. Pa. 1953).

256 149 U.S. at 116–117.

Thus, interest on the claims of unsecured creditors is normally not allowed after the receiver is appointed to take possession of the debtor's property, where the estate has insufficient assets to pay the claims of unsecured creditors. On the other hand, where the estate has sufficient assets to pay unsecured creditors, or a secured creditor's collateral is sufficient to provide for the payment of interest accruing after the appointment of a receiver or the filing of a bankruptcy petition, interest may be allowed.[257] The rationale for this rule is the same, only in this situation not to pay interest accruing after the appointment of a receiver or the filing of a bankruptcy petition would be to the prejudice of the creditor and provide a windfall for the debtor. As Justice Holmes stated:

> Interest and dividends accrued upon some of the securities after the date of the petition . . . There is no more reason for allowing the bankrupt estate to profit by the delay beyond the day of settlement than there is for letting the creditors do so. Therefore, to apply the subsequent dividends, etc., to subsequent interest, seems just.[258]

§ 7.24 Compensation for Receivers and Attorneys in Receivership Proceedings

At some stage in a receivership proceeding, both the receiver and attorneys involved in the proceeding must seek court approval for their compensation if it is to be paid out of the receivership estate. For a receivership of some duration, this should be done periodically. While the determination of allowable compensation is committed to the court's discretion,[259] and "a reasonable fee is based on all circumstances surrounding the receivership,"[260] the courts have evolved some standards for the review of receivers' and attorneys' fees in the absence of a statutory provision, such as that provided by the Bankruptcy Code for the trustee's fees.

---

257 Vanston Bondholders Protect. Com. v. Green, 329 U.S. at 164; and S.E.C. v. Alpine Mut. Fund, 824 F. Supp. at 994 (where the court allowed interest on the claims of unsecured creditors after appointment of a receiver).

258 Sexton v. Dreyfus, 219 U.S. at 346.

259 Stuart v. Boulware, 133 U.S. 78 (1890); Taylor v. Sternberg, 293 U.S. 470 (1935); and United States v. Code Products Corp., 362 F.2d 669 (3d Cir. 1966). The court's exercise of its discretion in determining just compensation for both receivers and receivers' attorneys is reviewable on appeal and "when the court has fallen into error which amounts to an abuse of discretion, relief will be granted." United States v. Code Products Corp., 362 F.2d at 673.

260 Donovan v.Robbins, 588 F. Supp. 1268, 1272 (N.D. Ill. 1984); and Securities & Exchange Com'n v. W. L. Moody & Co., Bank (Uninc.) 374 F. Supp. 465, 480 (S.D. Tex. 1974).

§ 7.25 —Receiver's Compensation

Even a cursory review of the cases in this area reveals that courts are bound to take a conservative approach to fee awards, adhering to the Supreme Court's admonition in *In re Gilbert*[261] that "the judges of the courts in fixing allowances for services . . . should be most careful . . . that vicarious generosity in such a matter . . . receive no countenance." Thus, in *United States v. Larchwood Gardens, Inc.*, the court forced two co-receivers to split one fee award, since "[u]nnecessary appointments of two persons to do work that obviously requires only one should not be made. Where they occur this court will not authorize double compensation."[262] With respect to an attorney fee request in *Southwestern Media, Inc. v. Rau*, the Ninth Circuit refused to allow counsel to charge a higher rate than his "comparable private rate," even though the claimed fee was based on the success of the attorney's work: In this case we must reiterate our holding that '[e]xcellent work is . . . not a basis for an enhanced award in excess of normal charges.' [citation omitted]. Jacobowitz's award, which concededly consisted partly of a 'bonus' element was improper and excessive.[263]

Given the court's conservative approach to fee awards both the receiver and counsel should keep accurate, contemporaneous time records.[264] In the *Larchwood Gardens* case, however, the court awarded compensation to the receiver in the form of "a reasonable percentage of the income produced" by the receiver although critical of the failure to keep accurate time records.[265]

The traditional standards for the review of receivers' fees include: (1) the results achieved by the receiver; (2) the ability, reputation and other professional qualities of the receiver necessary for the job; (3) the size of the estate and its ability to afford the expenses and fees; and (4) the time required to

[261] 276 U.S. 294, 296 (1928). *See also* United States v. Larchwood Gardens, Inc., 404 F.2d 1108, 1110 (3d Cir. 1968); United States v. Code Products Corp., 362 F.2d at 673; and Securities & Exch. Com'n v. W. L. Moody & Co., Bank (Uninc.), 374 F. Supp. at 483.

[262] 404 F.2d at 1112. *See also* United States v. Code Products Corp., 362 F.2d at 674 where the court refused to allow receiver's and attorney fees that were duplicative of work others performed.

[263] 709 F.2d 419, 428 (9th Cir. 1983). Although this was a bankruptcy case, the principle is the same. It should be noted that "[c]ompensation to equitable receivers is analogous to compensation to receivers in bankruptcy," Securities and Exch. Com'n v. W. L. Moody & Co., Bank (Uninc.) 374 F. Supp. at 481.

[264] United States v. Larchwood Gardens, Inc., 404 F.2d at 1111. ("Court appointed officers should keep contemporary time records of their work and report such information in any petitions for fees."); Southwestern Media, Inc. v. Rau, 708 F.2d at 426 ("for purposes of reviewing the reasonableness of his fee, we assume in light of [the receiver's] failure to keep proper time records that he actually worked the lowest number of hours consistent with his estimates.")

[265] 404 F.2d at 1111.

conclude the receivership.[266] With respect to the time required to conclude the receivership, quick action is desirable and should be rewarded, since to do otherwise would be to "reward slowness in decision and action." Thus, some courts give greater importance to "results" than time spent. [267]

§ 7.26 —Attorney's Compensation

The standards employed by the courts in reviewing attorney fee requests of counsel for the receiver are very similar to the standards used to review the receiver's request for compensation. They include: (1) the nature and complexity of the legal problems confronted and the skill necessary to resolve them; (2) the time and effort expended in advising the receiver; (3) the results achieved; and (4) the amount of money involved.[268]

Some courts rightly view the difficulty of the job, the expertise necessary to accomplish it, and the results achieved as more important than the time spent by the attorney.[269]

Finally, attorneys other than those representing the receiver may seek to claim attorney fees in the receivership estate for work related to the estate or a claim involving the estate. Such fees are normally not allowed and must be charged to the attorney's client, unless it can be shown that the attorney's work benefitted and enhanced the receivership estate.[270] The rationale for this rule was best expressed in *In re Gillaspie:*

> The only proper cases that can arise where courts of equity and bankruptcy as well can award compensation to an attorney out of funds due others than his clients, is where, as I have heretofore indicated, such an attorney for one of a class has 'created' or secured a fund and brought it into the custody of the court, which fund is to inure, not alone to the benefit of his client, but to that of all those belonging to this class. In such cases the courts award compensation

---

266 Securities & Exch. Com'n v. W. L. Moody & Co., Bank (Uninc.), 374 F. Supp. at 480–483. *See also* United States v. Code Products Corp., 362 F.2d at 673. ("In allowing fees 'the considerations are the time, labor and skill required, but not necessarily that actually expended, in the proper performance of the duties imposed by the court upon the receivers, the fair value of such time, labor and skill measured by conservative business standards, the degree of activity, integrity and dispatch with which the work is conducted and the result obtained,'" citing the Third Circuit's previous decision in Coskery v. Roberts & Mander Corp., 200 F.2d 150, 154 (3d Cir. 1952).

267 Securities and Exch. Com'n v. W. L. Moody & Co., Bank (Uninc.), 374 F. Supp. at 483.

268 *Id.* at 485–486.

269 *Id.* at 486.

270 Trustees v. Greenough, 105 U.S. 527 (1882); American Engineer Co. v. Metropolitan By-Products Co., 275 F.40 (2d Cir. 1921); Jefferson Hotel Co. v. Brumbaugh, 168 F. 867 (4th Cir. 1909); and In re Gillaspie, 190 F. 88 (N.D. W. Va. 1911).

to the attorney out of the fund due to all, not on the theory of his having an attorney's lien, but on the broader theory that all interested in the fund should contribute ratably to the cost of 'creating' or securing it.[271]

§ 7.27 Checklist for Receivers

____ A. In Cooperation with Counsel—

____ 1. Review complaint underlying action that led to receivership and order appointing receiver to determine scope of receivership and powers of the receiver.

____ 2. Determine the geographical location of all significant assets of the entity in receivership (entity) and within 10 days of the receiver's appointment file copies of the complaint initiating the action and the receiver's order of appointment in all federal judicial districts where assets are thought to be located pursuant to 28 U.S.C. § 754. (It is better to be overly broad than to take a chance on missing some jurisdictions where assets are located).

____ 3. Identify officers, directors, employees (especially accounting staff), accountants, attorneys, and agents for entity and prepare and send notice of receiver's appointment to them. (In the case of the entity's management officials and other key employees it is advisable to meet with them personally to inform them of their duties and responsibilities under the receiver's management and control).

____ 4. Take steps to insure immediate possession by the receiver of all books and records, particularly collateral documents, presently in the possession of others.

____ 5. Review the status of all litigation pending by and against the entity. Give notice to all parties in litigation with entity of any stay order entered by the court overseeing the receivership, and if necessary employ counsel to stay any such litigation.

____ 6. Review status of all federal, state, and local regulatory matters involving the entity, particularly health and environmental matters, as well as any S.E.C. matters.

---

271 190 F. at 91.

____ B. In Cooperation with Accountant—

____ 1. Review the status of all federal, state, and local tax filings and payments, especially status of employee withholding tax trust accounts.

____ 2. Review financial status of company.

____ 3. Review all existing financial and accounting systems and determine if improvements as to record keeping or safeguards are needed. This is a critical area, since many entities in receivership have great deficiencies in this regard.

____ 4. Give notice to all account debtors of receiver's appointment and where to send future payments.

____ 5. Determine all accounts payable, and give notice of the receivership and any stay orders.

____ C. Physical Site of Entity—

____ 1. Secure premises if receiver is to take over existing work site of entity, by changing locks, securing computer equipment and phones.

____ 2. Lease new premises and transfer office equipment, if court approval has been obtained for this.

____ 3. Review records and obtain, if necessary or appropriate, comprehensive hazard insurance, automotive equipment insurance, and any other type of insurance normally used in the trade or business of the entity.

____ D. Employees and Personnel—

____ 1. Determine employees and managers to be retained and those to be terminated.

____ 2. Determine funding needs for retained and terminated personnel.

____ 3. Determine what safeguards are needed to protect customer lists, trade secrets, and confidential financial information in possession of employees or agents of the entity.

____ E. Asset Identification and Protection—

____ 1. Cash accounts

____ a) Identify existing bank accounts—checking, savings, certificates of deposit, safety deposit or lock boxes

____ b) Determine if any deposits or withdrawals have been made since date of receiver's appointment.

____ 2. Provide notice of the appointment of the receiver to all banks and other financial institutions in which the entity maintains any type of account, including but not limited to checking, savings, certificates of deposit, money market funds, and safety deposit boxes. Arrange for the transfer of any funds or valuables in such accounts to receivership accounts as provided for in paragraph 3 below.

____ 3. Arrange with persons or institutions designated by the Receiver for the establishment of checking and savings accounts on behalf of the receiver, for the maintenance of records with respect to said accounts, and for the provision to the receiver of reports concerning said accounts.

____ 4. Take immediate possession of all negotiable instruments, marketable securities, bonds, etc., and secure them.

____ 5. Obtain keys to safety deposit box, make arrangements for inventory and removal of contents.

____ 6. Equipment, furniture, and vehicles:

____ a) Identify and obtain keys, title, registration, insurance certificates for all vehicles

____ b) Identify and compile inventory of all furniture and equipment and determine whether to retain or sell.

____ 7. Recover from authorized personnel all credit cards in use, and if necessary restrict use or cancel them.

____ F. File Identification and Transfer—

____ 1. Loans and investments

____ a) Original loan documents, collateral documents, mortgages, deeds, stock certificates, warrants, etc.—specifically inventory these documents and make arrangements to take immediate possession

____ b) Related operating files—correspondence, memoranda, financial information

____ c) Review each asset with responsible official of current staff of entity to determine status and any other information relevant to dealing with the asset

____ 2. General corporate books, records—

- ____ a) Articles of Incorporation, bylaws, minute books, corporate seal, stock certificates, and books
- ____ b) All business licenses or certificates
- ____ c) Corporate agreements: leases, equipment rentals, utility accounts (phone, electric, gas, etc.), contracts
- ____ d) Employment records and/or retainer agreements—to include names, addresses, telephone numbers, nature of tasks performed by employees, consultants, contractors, accountants, attorneys and others
- ____ e) List of all current creditors, including judgment creditors
- ____ f) Correspondence files—general corporate and of each officer, director, and employee
- ____ g) Any files related to creditors, e.g., participation agreements, promissory notes
- ____ h) Any computer programs, disks

____ 3. Financial records

- ____ a) General ledgers
- ____ b) Tax returns, federal, state, city, employer
- ____ c) Cash disbursements and receipts files
- ____ d) Paid invoices
- ____ e) Check books, bank statements, cancelled checks
- ____ f) Payroll records
- ____ g) Financial statements
- ____ h) Computer programs, disks, system configurations for processing general ledgers and generating financial information

§ 7.28 Checklist for Counsel's Initial Representation of the Receiver

____ 1. Review the order authorizing the appointment of the receiver and setting forth the powers and duties of the receiver.

____ 2. Review the order authorizing the receiver to retain counsel and other professionals and the terms and conditions of employment and compensation. (This should have already been carefully discussed with the receiver and embodied in a written agreement that has been authorized by the court).

____ 3. Learn the location of all property over which the receiver seeks jurisdiction and control.

____ 4. Insure the filing of the receiver's order of appointment together with the complaint initiating the action within ten days of the receiver's appointment pursuant to 28 U.S.C. § 754.

____ 5. Make a listing of all suits and administrative proceedings involving the receivership estate and determine their status.

____ 6. Review the effect of any stay order or stay provision in any order entered in the receivership proceeding and under 28 U.S.C. § 959.

____ 7. Determine whether the corporation in receivership is in good standing in its state of incorporation. In this regard, obtain and review the corporate charter, by-laws, and minutes of the board of directors meetings that bear on future operations.

____ 8. Determine the state of incorporation and good standing status of any subsidiary corporation, as well as whether it is qualified to do business in the states in which it is operating.

____ 9. Determine the status of all state and federal tax returns, required to have been filed by the corporation or entity in receivership, as well as any subsidiaries. This is a duty under 28 U.S.C. § 960.

____ 10. Determine if any SEC filings are required, and whether they have been made.

____ 11. Determine whether the business is in compliance with all federal and state health, safety and environmental requirements and orders.

____ 12. Determine whether the receiver has taken possession of all books and records formerly in the possession and control of the business entity in receivership, its officers, directors or third-parties, and if not, whether arrangements have been made to accomplish this.

____ 13. Obtain a listing of all current officers and directors, shareholders, and general or limited partners of the business entity.

____ 14. Determine whether the shareholders have retained, or had appointed for them by the court, counsel or other representatives to act on their behalf. Inform shareholders' counsel of your representation of the receiver.

____ 15. Prepare notice for the receiver to be sent to all interested parties informing them of the receiver's appointment, including officers, directors, claimants and account debtors. Account debtors should be informed in the notice where to make future payments.

____ 16. Determine whether sales of realty are contemplated in order to comply with 28 U.S.C. § 2001.

____ 17. Determine all accounts payable, and give notice of the receivership and any stay orders.

____ 18. Determine what documents and court orders are needed for the receiver to take control of all bank accounts and other assets, such as motor vehicles.

§ 7.29 Complaint Seeking Foreclosure of Real and Personal Property and the Appointment of a Receiver in Order to Manage and Sell a Going Business

[Caption]

COMPLAINT

I.

Jurisdiction

1. This is a civil action brought by [name of plaintiff]. Jurisdiction is conferred upon this court by virtue of [28 U.S.C. § 1331, and, (cite any other statute giving rise to federal jurisdiction); or 28 U.S.C. § 1332(a) since this case is between citizens of different states and involves an amount in controversy in excess of $50,000 exclusive of interest and costs].

II.

Parties

2. Plaintiff, [creditor's name] is a [state] corporation, [name of business] with its principal place of business in [city, state]. It is in the business of [nature of business].

3. Defendant [name of defendant-debtor] is a corporation organized under the laws of the State of [name] with its principal place of business located in [city, state].

4. Defendant [name of defendant-debtor] owns and operates a radio broadcasting business in [city, state] and broadcasts under the call signs _______ and ______.

5. Certain defendants are necessary parties only to the extent they have security or mortgage interests in the collateral securing the loans hereinafter described [name of plaintiff-creditor]. They include, viz:

[List in separate paragraphs each defendant by name, place of incorporation (if any), place of business, and the nature of its business, e.g. a national banking association, such as the following examples:]

a. Defendant [name] is an agency and instrumentality of the United States of America with authority to make and guarantee business loans;

b. Defendant [name] is a state chartered banking association with its principal place of business in the State of [name]; and

c. Defendant [name] is a [state] corporation with its principal place of business located in [city, state] and carries on a commercial lending business.

III.

General Allegations

Paragraphs 6-23:

[Set forth in summary form the transactional facts giving rise to the claims for relief including the instruments in default, the date of default(s), the amounts in default, and cite the provisions in the various loan documents entitling plaintiff-creditor to foreclose and to a deficiency judgment. In addition, if there are any, describe any provisions in the loan documents entitling the plaintiff-creditor to the appointment of a receiver].

COUNT I

(Action for Appointment of a Receiver)

24. This is an action for the appointment of a Receiver in connection with the foreclosure of real and personal property collateral securing the aforesaid [note].

25. [Name of plaintiff-creditor] realleges the allegations of paragraphs 1 through 23 of this Complaint.

26. The appointment of a Receiver is necessary in this action to protect [name of plaintiff-creditor]'s interest by ensuring continued operation of [name

of defendant-debtor]'s radio stations and to ensure that rents, revenues, and profits collected by [name of defendant-debtor] are applied to reduction of the outstanding debt under the [note].

27. [Name of plaintiff-creditor]'s collateral used in the broadcasting business of [name of defendant-debtor] is of minimal value without the necessary authorizations (hereinafter "Licenses") issued by the Federal Communications Commission ("FCC") to operate the radio stations. An interruption in the operation of these stations may result in the revocation of the [name of defendant-debtor]'s Licenses to operate their stations. At a minimum, such an interruption of service will prevent a sale of [name of defendant-debtor]'s broadcasting businesses as going concerns and potential buyers will take into account the diminished value of the stations due to the service interruption and risk that their Licenses may be lost. Therefore, any interruption in service during the pendency of this lawsuit will substantially diminish the proceeds that can be realized at a foreclosure sale and will result in a substantially greater deficiency judgment being entered against defendants.

28. [Name of plaintiff-creditor] is without an adequate legal remedy to prevent [name of defendant-debtor] from interrupting broadcasting service by its radio stations or otherwise operating the stations in a detrimental manner, thereby destroying the value of the stations and impairing [name of plaintiff-creditor]'s ability to enforce a judgment. [Name of plaintiff-creditor] is likewise without an adequate legal remedy to protect its rights to the rents, revenues, and profits collected by [name of defendant-debtor] even if it continued good faith operations of its station during the pendency of this lawsuit.

29. The Court appointed Receiver cannot operate the radio stations without the [name of defendant-debtor] Licenses being issued to it. The FCC recognizes its inability to fashion remedies for breaches of contractual agreements and its inability to make victimized parties whole. The FCC further recognizes that stations' licenses usually must accompany their physical assets. Thus, it is the FCC's policy to accommodate court decrees adjudicating disputes over contract and property rights by, for example, allowing involuntary assignments of broadcast licenses to effectuate such court orders.

30. Section ____ of the [security agreements] and Section ____ of the [loan agreement] provide that the defendant(s) will use its best efforts to assist in the preparation, execution, and filing with the FCC of any portions of any applications necessary to obtain FCC approval to assign the stations' Licenses. An application must be filed with the FCC to assign the stations' Licenses from [defendant-debtor] to such Receiver as is appointed by this Court to protect the stations' assets and value as described in paragraphs ____ above, prior to a private court-approved foreclosure sale.

WHEREFORE, [name of plaintiff-creditor] requests entry of an order appointing a Receiver: (a) to continue operation of [name of defendant-debtor]'s radio stations; (b) to collect all rents, revenues, and profits of the stations in accordance with the directions of this Court as to the management, operation, and control of the stations; (d) to solicit offers and bids from potential purchasers of the stations as ongoing businesses for further consideration and approval by further order of the Court; (e) to apply for and obtain a transfer of the FCC licenses and other governmental authorities necessary to manage, operate, and control the stations; and (f) requiring [name of defendant-debtor]'s expeditious cooperation with the Receiver in transferring the assets and stations' licenses to the Receiver.

[Add additional counts as appropriate for foreclosure of real and personal property mortgages and for a deficiency judgment, such as the following]:

COUNT II

(Foreclosure of Security Interest)

31. This is an action to foreclose a security interest in personal property located in [city], [county], [state].

32. [Name of plaintiff-creditor] realleges the allegations of paragraphs 1 through 23 of this Complaint.

33. The following defendants may claim some interest in the collateral because of Uniform Commercial Code Financing Statements (UCC-1's) filed with the Secretary of State, State of [name], to wit:

[List defendants as in the following example]

a. [Name of defendant-creditor] is named as secured party in a UCC-1 from [name of defendant-debtor] bearing file no. ____.

Accordingly, said defendants are joined as parties to the extent they have a security interest in the collateral.

WHEREFORE, [name of plaintiff-creditor] requests that this Court order that the property subject to its [security agreement] be sold and that the liens described above be determined subordinate to plaintiff's security interest, and that the proceeds applied to [name of plaintiff-creditor]'s claim, including principal, interest, costs and attorney fees.

COUNT III

(Foreclosure of Mortgage)

34. This is an action to foreclose a mortgage described in paragraph ____ above with respect to real property located in [city, county, and state].

35. [Name of plaintiff-creditor] realleges the allegations of paragraphs 1 through 23 of this complaint.

36. The following defendant-creditors may claim some interest in the aforesaid real property:

[list defendants as in the following example].

a. [Name of defendant-creditor] may claim an interest in said property by virtue of a mortgage described in [Liber _____ Folio _____] and recorded on [date] in [city, county, and state].

WHEREFORE, [name of plaintiff-creditor] requests that this Court order that the property subject to its mortgage be sold and that the liens described above be determined subordinate to the plaintiff's mortgage and the proceeds applied to [name of plaintiff-creditor]'s claim, including principal, interest, costs and attorney fees.

COUNT IV

(Action for Deficiency Judgment)

39. This is an action for a deficiency judgment arising in connection with a foreclosure of the plaintiff's collateral described above.

40. [Name of plaintiff-creditor] realleges the allegations of paragraphs 1 through 23 of the Complaint.

WHEREFORE, [name of plaintiff-creditor] requests that if the proceeds of the sales of the properties subject to plaintiff's [security agreement(s) and mortgage(s)] are not sufficient to satisfy [name of defendant-debtor]'s indebtedness to plaintiff under the [note], a deficiency judgment against [name of defendant-debtor] be entered for the sum remaining unpaid, together with reasonable attorney fees and costs.

§ 7.30 Motion for the Appointment of a Receiver Pendente Lite

Plaintiff [name], by its undersigned attorneys, hereby moves this Court for an order appointing a receiver pendente lite. The grounds for this Motion are Rule 66, Federal Rules of Civil Procedure, and Local Rule [if any], in that plaintiff is threatened with immediate and irreparable injury, loss and damage more fully described in the verified complaint initiating this action and of the nature meriting the appointment of a receiver as contemplated by said Rules. This Motion is based on the verified complaint filed in this action, the Affidavit of [name] including the Exhibits thereto, and the Memorandum of Points and Authorities filed herewith. A proposed Order is attached.[272]

§ 7.31 Plaintiff's Motion for Appointment of a Receiver to Collect a Money Judgment

Plaintiff, [name], by its undersigned attorneys hereby moves this Court pursuant to Rules 66 and 69(a) of the Federal Rules of Civil Procedure [and federal or state statute regarding appointment of a receiver] for the appointment of a Receiver for [name of entity] to take any and all actions necessary to collect the judgment owed to plaintiff [name of plaintiff].

Plaintiff specifically requests that [name] be appointed Receiver by the Court. This Motion is based upon the Affidavit of [name] including the Exhibits attached thereto, and the Memorandum of Points and Authorities filed herewith. A proposed Order is attached.

§ 7.32 Memorandum of Points and Authorities in Support of Plaintiff's Motion for Appointment of a Receiver

I.

Introduction

[Summarize procedural history of case and why there is a need for the appointment of a receiver to aid enforcement of judgment.]

II.

Factual Background Since Judgment

On [date], this Court entered judgment in favor of plaintiff [name] and against defendant [name] for the sum of [amount]. [Summarize facts requiring appointment of receiver].

---

[272] The complaint initiating the action should request, in part, relief in the form of the appointment of a receiver and contain allegations of fact showing the necessity for the appointment of a receiver. *See e.g.* New York Life Ins. Co. v. Watt West Inv. Corp., 755 F. Supp. at 289, and Cowin v. Bresler, 741 F.2d at 417.

III.

Necessity For a Receivership

As shown above, defendant [name] is insolvent. Defendant [name] has substantial and conflicting claims to its assets, including, among others this plaintiff, [names of other known creditors]. If [name]'s operations are shutdown by creditors, substantial harm and injury will follow. The going concern value of the business will be jeopardized, present suppliers and customers lost, equipment damaged by the shutdown, and eventually there will be substantial costs incurred to resume operations. Accordingly, continued operation of the business is vital to preserving its value.

The best alternative at present is for a receiver to be appointed to preserve and protect the going concern value of [name], by continued operation of the business.

Additionally, the record in this case is replete with evidence of [current management's] mishandling of corporate records and finances, and it is imperative that [current management] be removed and replaced by a receiver. As this Court has found in awarding judgment to plaintiff:

> "The record shows the financial records of [name] omitted some transactions, misrepresented others, and concealed the diversion of corporate funds to [name] for personal use. These records have been generally unreliable." [Record p.]

To allow [current management] to continue operating the business now that plaintiff's judgment is final would only allow [current management] further opportunity to misrepresent other transactions, conceal assets, and divert funds for their own use.

IV.

Applicable Law

Rule 69(a) of the Federal Rules of Civil Procedure provides in pertinent part:

> The procedure on execution, in proceedings supplementary to and in aid of a judgment, and in proceedings on and in aid of execution shall be in accordance with the practice and procedure of the state in which the district court is held * * *.

Thus, Section . . . of [state statute] dealing with the appointment of receivers, is applicable. That statute provides:

[Quote State Statute]

The appointment of a receiver is a matter which lies in the sound discretion of the Court. *Edmonston v. Sisk,* 156 F.2d 300 (10th Cir. 1946); *Kingsport Press v. Brief English Systems,* 54 F.2d 497 (2d Cir. 1937).

Even where there is a specific state statute governing the appointment of a receiver, the Court retains the full panoply of its equity powers and may appoint a receiver where statutory requirements are not met. For "[t]he appointment of such a receiver is a branch of equity jurisdiction not dependent upon any statute." *Pittsburgh Equitable Meter Co. v. Paul C. Loeber & Co.,* 160 F.2d 721 (7th Cir. 1947). See also, *New York Life Ins. Co. v. Watt West Inv. Corp.,* 755 F. Supp. 287, 290-291 (E. D. Calif. 1992).

In *In Re Metropolitan Railway Receivership,* 208 U.S. 90 (1908), the Supreme Court upheld the appointment of a receiver to administer the management of Metropolitan Railway Corporation finding that:

> A refusal to appoint a receiver would have led in this instance almost inevitably to a very large and useless sacrifice in value of a great property, operated as one system through the various streets of a populous city . . ., and to very great inconvenience to the many thousands of people who necessarily use the road every day of their lives. The orders appointing the receivers and giving them instructions are most conservative and well calculated to bring about the earliest possible resumption of normal conditions when those who may be the owners of the property shall be in possession of and operate it.

In *Pittsburgh Equitable Meter Co. v. Paul C. Loeber & Co.,* 160 F.2d 721, the Court upheld the appointment of receiver to manage the corporation despite the fact that the debtor had no assets. The Court found that the appointment of the receiver was justified because the judgment debtor may have diverted assets of the corporation. *Id.* at 727.

In *Edmonston v. Sisk,* 156 F.2d 300, the Court upheld the appointment of a receiver by a lower court despite the fact that adequate remedies at law existed. The Court found that the appointment of a receiver under the circumstances was within the Court's discretion. *Id.* at 303. Similarly, the Court in *Kingsport Press, Inc. v. Brief English Systems, Inc.,* 54 F.2d 497, upheld the appointment of a receiver because it was the only method of insuring that the business would be properly managed and creditors would be paid. *Id.* at 500.

The foregoing review demonstrates that the appointment of a receiver lies within the discretion of the Court. The analysis under Rule 69(a) is made on a case by case basis looking to the law of the forum state and the particular facts of the case. Here, the defendant's past behavior demonstrates that the plaintiff will be damaged if a receiver is not appointed; assets may disappear or be damaged. Furthermore, a receiver is needed to manage the affairs of the business in this state, and to protect the value of these properties as before stated.

Although the defendant has property in several states, this does not prevent the Court from appointing one receiver to manage the defendant's assets. Federal law provides for the appointment of a receiver where property is located in several districts.[273] Plaintiff therefore respectfully requests that a receiver be appointed over defendant's properties listed below in Section V.

V.

Property Covered By Receivership

The properties owned by [name], over which the Receiver will have control, are as follows:

[List Property]

VI.

Qualifications of Receiver

Plaintiff recommends to this Court the appointment of [name], as Receiver herein. [name of proposed receiver] has extensive experience in the operation and management of [type of business], and has substantial other business experience.

[Describe business experience and attach resume as exhibit].

At our request, [name of proposed receiver] made an inspection of the [name and address of business facility] on [date], and is willing to serve as receiver of [name of entity in receivership]. The terms and conditions of his proposed employment are attached as Exhibits ____ and ____ to the Affidavit of [name] filed herewith.

---

[273] 28 U.S.C. § 754 provides:

> A receiver appointed in any civil action or proceeding involving property, real, personal or mixed, situated in different districts shall, upon giving bond as required by the court, be vested with complete jurisdiction and control of all such property with the right to take possession thereof.
>
> He shall have capacity to sue in any district without ancillary appointment, and may be sued with respect thereto as provided in section 959 of this title.
>
> Such receiver shall, within ten days after the entry of his order of appointment, file copies of the complaint and such order of appointment in the district court for each district in which property is located. The failure to file such copies in any district shall divest the receiver of jurisdiction and control over all such property in that district.

§ 7.33 Order Initiating Federal Equity Receivership with Provision for Blanket Receivership Stay and Prohibiting Bankruptcy Filing Without Prior Approval of Federal District Court

[CAPTION]

ORDER

IT IS HEREBY ORDERED, ADJUDGED AND DECREED THAT:

1. Pursuant to the provisions of 28 U.S.C. § 754 and Federal Rule of Civil Procedure 66 [other provisions of Federal law may also apply],[274] this Court shall take exclusive jurisdiction of [name of entity in receivership], and all of its assets, wherever located, and [name of receiver] (Receiver) is hereby appointed receiver of [name of entity in receivership] to serve without bond until further Order of this Court. [The Receiver is appointed for the purpose of liquidating all of {name of entity in receivership}'s assets and satisfying the claims of creditors therefrom in the order of priority as determined by this Court.][275]

2. The Receiver shall have all the powers, authorities, rights and privileges heretofore possessed by the officers and directors of [name of entity in receivership] under applicable state and federal law, by the Articles of Incorporation, and By-Laws of said corporation,[276] in addition to all the powers and authority

---

[274] Assuming that the requirements of 28 U.S.C. § 754 are met and a copy of the order of appointment of the receiver and the complaint initiating the action are filed in every federal judicial district in which property of the receivership estate is located, the court may assume jurisdiction over the complete estate. Other provisions of federal law may also provide a basis for exclusive jurisdiction, such as the Small Business Investment Act of 1958, as amended, 15 U.S.C. § 687c.

Federal Rule of Civil Procedure 66 prohibits the dismissal of the action without permission of the court overseeing the receivership once a receiver has been appointed. Thus, a party is unable to thwart the court-approved objectives of the receivership or prejudice the rights of other interested persons. Rule 66 also incorporates historical federal equity practice into the "administration" of the receivership estate. The scope of the receiver's "administration" of the estate under Rule 66 was explained in Phelan v. Middle States Oil Corp., 210 F.2d 360, 363 (2d Cir. 1954): "In our opinion 'administration' means the receiver's dealings with the property, and the 'practice' in such administration refers to orders he must get to allow him to dispose of the property, to spend money to protect it, to distribute it among the creditors or lienors, and the like. In short, the 'practice' means the procedure by which he gets the power to do those things which an owner of the property would have without court authorization."

[275] This sentence is to be used only in the case of a liquidating receivership.

[276] *See* United States v. Myers, 308 F. Supp. 859, 860 (D. Md. 1970) for affirmation of receiver's assumption of the powers and authority of the corporation's former officers and directors.

of a receiver at equity, and all powers and authority conferred upon the Receiver by the provisions of 28 U.S.C. § 754 and [any other appropriate provision of law]. [The directors, officers, employees and agents of {name of entity in receivership} are hereby dismissed, except, {names of officers and employees that will be retained}. Those persons, formerly employed by the Receiver who are retained, shall have no authority with respect to {name of entity in receivership's} operations or assets, except to the extent as may hereafter be expressly granted by the Receiver][277] The Receiver shall assume and control the operations of [name of entity in receivership] and shall pursue and preserve all of its claims.

3. The past and/or present officers, directors, agents, partners and employees of [name of entity in receivership], as well as all those acting in their place, are hereby ordered and directed to turn over to the Receiver forthwith all books, records, documents, accounts and all other instruments and papers of [name of entity in receivership], and all other assets and property of the corporation, whether real, personal, or mixed. [Name of appropriate official of entity in receivership], formerly [official title] of [name of entity in receivership], shall furnish a written statement within ____ days after the entry of this Order, listing the identity and location of all assets of [name of entity in receivership] as well as the names, addresses and amounts of claims of all known creditors of [name of entity in receivership]. Within ____ days following the entry of this order, [name of appropriate official of entity in receivership] shall also furnish a written report describing all assets of [name of entity in receivership], including the estimated value of said assets. All persons having control, custody or possession of any assets or property of [name of entity in receivership] are hereby directed to turn over such property to the Receiver.

4. The Receiver shall promptly give notice of its appointment to all known officers, directors, agents, employees, shareholders, creditors, debtors, and partners of [entity in receivership] as the Receiver deems necessary or advisable to effectuate the operation of the receivership. All persons and entities owing any obligation, debt, dividend, or a distribution with respect to a partnership interest, to [name of entity in receivership] shall, until further ordered by this Court, pay all such obligations in accordance with the terms thereof to the Receiver at [name and address] and its receipt for such payments shall have the same force and effect as if [name of entity in receivership] had received such payments.

5. The Receiver is hereby authorized to open such Receiver's accounts at banking or other financial institutions, on behalf of [name of entity in receivership], [to utilize its personnel], and [subject to Court approval] to employ such other agents as it may deem necessary to effectuate the operation of the receivership including, but not limited to, attorneys, accountants, and appraisers, and is further authorized [subject to Court approval], to expend receivership funds to

[277] Frequently, certain key officers and employees necessary for the company's operations must be retained. Accordingly, this sentence may be omitted or modified according to the receiver's needs.

compensate such agents [in such amounts and upon such terms as the Receiver shall deem reasonable in light of the usual fees and billing practices and procedures of such agents. The Receiver is not required to obtain Court approval prior to the disbursement of receivership funds for payments to agents employed by the Receiver or payments for expenses that the Receiver deems advantageous to the orderly administration and operation of the Receivership].[278]

6. [Name of entity in receivership]'s past and/or present officers, directors, agents, shareholders, employees, debtors, creditors, and partners and other appropriate persons shall answer under oath to the Receiver all questions which the Receiver may put to them and produce any documents as required by the Receiver regarding the business of said corporation, or any other matter relevant to the operation or administration of the receivership or the collection of funds due to [name of entity in receivership]. In the event that the Receiver deems it necessary to require the appearance of the aforementioned persons, it shall direct notice for any such appearance by certified mail including documents requested, if any, and said persons shall appear with the documents requested, if any, and give answer to the Receiver within ____ days of service of said notice at the time and place designated therein.

7. The Receiver may [with prior Court approval] form subsidiary corporations of [name of entity in receivership] for any lawful purpose connected with the responsibilities and duties of the Receiver.[279]

---

278 It is usually advisable for the Receiver to move the Court upon notice to interested persons for approval of each agent's retention and the agent's compensation, as well as the payment of all but de minimis expenses. (If it is a recurring expense such as rent, an initial blanket order covering future payments will be sufficient). Nevertheless, depending upon the size and scope of the receiver's operations, limited blanket approval, as indicated above, may be appropriate. This will reduce the burden on the court overseeing the receiver's operations, as well as reduce the legal expense associated with repeated motions seeking court approval. If limited blanket court approval is sought by the Receiver and obtained, then all retention of agents, the terms of their retention and compensation, and all amounts paid by the Receiver for the relevant period should be reported in the Receiver's periodic reports to the court as described in this Chapter.

It should also be noted that receivers who are appointed under the Federal Debt Collection Procedures Act of 1990 are required to seek specific court authorization for the retention of "attorneys, accountants, appraisers, auctioneers, or other professional persons." *See* 28 U.S.C. § 3103(b)(2). Some local rules of the federal courts also require a court order for the retention of professionals, such as lawyers and accountants, and for the setting of their compensation. *See e.g.* Local Rule 232(g), Eastern District of California; Local Rule 225-2, Northern District of California; and Local Rule 66.1b, Southern District of California.

279 As with any business operation, it may be necessary or advantageous to form a subsidiary corporation for a purpose connected with the receivership operations, such as sale-lease back arrangements, or for the formation of a corporate subsidiary needed for the operation of a restaurant, hotel or similar enterprise, or to protect assets from liability. Accordingly, while the power to form subsidiary corporations may be assumed from paragraph 2 of this Order, counsel may wish to make such power explicit. Although

8. [The Receiver may convene a meeting or meetings of the shareholders of any wholly-owned subsidiary of {name of entity in receivership} without further notice and may vote all shares of {name of entity in receivership} at any such meeting or meetings.]

9. [The Receiver may convene the meeting of any other subsidiary upon ___ days notice to the shareholders, and may vote all shares of {name of entity in receivership} at any such meeting or meetings.][280]

10. The parties to any and all civil legal proceedings of any nature, including arbitration proceedings, involving [name of entity in receivership] or any assets of [name of entity in receivership], including subsidiaries and partnerships, wherever located, and excluding the instant proceeding, involving [name of entity in receivership], the Receiver, or any of [name of entity in receivership]'s past or present officers or directors sued for, or in connection with, any action taken by them while acting in such capacity of any nature, whether as plaintiff, defendant, third-party plaintiff, third-party defendant, or otherwise, are enjoined from commencing or continuing any such legal proceeding, or from taking any action, in connection with any such proceeding.

11. [All civil legal proceedings of any nature, including but not limited to arbitration proceedings involving {name of entity in receivership} or any assets of {name of entity in receivership}, including subsidiaries and partnerships, wherever located, and excluding the instant proceeding, involving {name of entity in receivership}, the Receiver, or any of {name of entity in receivership}'s past or present officers or directors sued for, or in connection with, any action taken by them while acting in such capacity of any nature, whether as plaintiff, defendant, third-party plaintiff, third-party defendant, or otherwise, are stayed in their entirety until further Order of this Court.][281]

---

there is scant authority, the power of a federal equity receiver to form a subsidiary corporation was recognized in dicta in In re Prudence, 14 F. Supp. 249, 251 (E.D.N.Y. 1936).

280 Paragraphs 8 and 9 of this Order should be used where the entity in receivership has subsidiaries.

281 Although the bracketed language of paragraph 11 enjoining legal proceedings of any nature is sometimes used in orders such as this, especially by government agencies, care should be exercised in the use of this language. This is because of the Anti-injunction Act, 28 U.S.C. § 2283, which prohibits the federal courts from issuing injunctions to stay state court proceedings unless "expressly authorized by Act of Congress, or where necessary in aid of its jurisdiction, or to protect or effectuate its judgments." Therefore, unless specific circumstances merit this injunctive language, it is best to omit it, especially since other language in the order prohibits the parties to such litigation from continuing the litigation. As the Seventh Circuit noted in Federal S.& L. Ins. Corp. v. PSL Rlty. Co., 630 F.2d 515, 522 (7th Cir. 1980):

> The circumstances precipitating the injunction must also be appropriate for injunctive relief. In this case the district court found itself compelled to invoke its injunctive powers to protect its jurisdiction under the established principle that

12. No person or entity shall be allowed without the express authorization of this Court to file a petition on behalf of or against [name of entity in receivership] under the Bankruptcy Code, 11 U.S.C. §§ 101 et seq. until further order of this Court.[282]

13. [Name of entity in receivership] and its past and/or present directors, officers, agents, employees and other persons acting in concert or participation therewith be, and they hereby are, enjoined from either directly or indirectly taking any actions or causing any such action to be taken which would dissipate the assets and property of [name of entity in receivership] to the detriment of the Receiver appointed in this cause, including but not limited to destruction of records.

§ 7.34 Motion for an Order Approving and Confirming the Receiver's First Report

[CAPTION]

[Title of Motion]

[Name of receiver], as Receiver for [name of entity in receivership], by undersigned counsel, hereby moves this Court for an Order approving and confirming the First Receiver's Report for the Period from [date] through[date], which is submitted herewith, and further requests that the Order authorize the Receiver to charge-off and abandon those claims which the Receiver has determined are uncollectible, and to continue to pursue those claims for which there is a likelihood of recovery.

---

when a court of competent jurisdiction has obtained possession, custody, or control of property, that possession may not be disturbed by any other court.

For other cases upholding the use of an injunction against a state court proceeding, *see* Chicago Title & Trust Co. v. Fox Theaters Corporation, 69 F.2d 60 (2d Cir. 1934) and Cayuga Indian Nation of New York v. Fox, 544 F. Supp. 542 (N.D.N.Y. 1982). Cases where an injunction against a state court proceeding were not found appropriate include Hemmick v. Chrysler Corp., 769 F. Supp. 525, 531 (S.D.N.Y. 1991) and Dey v. Brenack Stevedoring Co., Inc., 272 F. 127 (E.D.N.Y. 1921).

Agencies and departments of the United States may more readily use such language since it has been held that 28 U.S.C. § 2283 "does not apply to injunctions issued at the request of the United States." Securities and Exch. Com'n v. Wencke, 577 F.2d at 623 (Wencke I); and 622 F.2d at 1368 (Wencke II), relying on Leiter Minerals. Inc. v. United States, 352 U.S. 220 (1957).

282 See the discussion in this chapter as to the legal efficacy of this provision of the receivership stay order.

§ 7.35 Receiver's First Report

[CAPTION]

[Title]

This Receiver's First Report ("First Report"), which covers the period from [date] through [date], is being filed with this Court by [name of receiver], who was appointed Receiver for[name of entity in receivership] pursuant to an Order of this Court dated _______.

I. OPERATION OF THE RECEIVERSHIP

A. Personnel

Pursuant to orders of this Court dated respectively [list by date], the Receiver retained the following lawyers, accountants, and other professionals to assist the Receiver in the operation of the receivership. Specifically, the Receiver retained [name of individual] to act as an agent of the Receiver in the administration of the assets and accounts of [name of entity in receivership] to liquidate its assets in an orderly manner, and to pursue claims. The Receiver has also retained [name of firm], an accounting service, to assist in the maintenance of the books and records of [name of entity in receivership]; to prepare various filings; to prepare interim financial statements; and, generally to assist in administration of the financial affairs of [name of entity in receivership].

In addition, pursuant to an order of this court dated ______, the Receiver retained the law firm of [name of law firm] to represent the Receiver in the following cases: [name of case, docket number, and court] as discussed below.

B. Bank Accounts

The Receiver maintains the following accounts: [List all accounts maintained by the receiver by bank and type of account, noting whether account is insured.].

C. Tax, Accounting and Corporate Compliance Matters

[State status of all tax matters, whether current or delinquent, and what action the receiver has taken during the reporting period with regard to reporting and paying tax liabilities.]

D. Office Space and Expenses

[Name of entity in receivership] rents office space pursuant to a lease approved by Order of this Court dated __________. The lease is for a term of ____________ at [amount] per month. [In many instances, the receiver will merely take over the existing offices of the entity in receivership. This should not only be approved by the court overseeing the receivership at an early stage in the receivership, but reported here.]

II. STATUS OF LIABILITIES OF [ENTITY IN RECEIVERSHIP]

A. Receiver's Certificates

[List status of all monies borrowed by receiver, if any, during reporting period, which are usually evidenced by receiver's certificates.]

B. Judgments

[List and describe the status of all judgments against the entity in receivership].

C. Claims Bar Date Procedure

[It may be appropriate or helpful to the court to describe the proposed method of handling claims. For example, it might be stated: The Receiver intends to file a petition with this Court within the next three months, requesting an order approving procedures for notifying all potential claimants against the receivership estate of the time for filing claims and setting an absolute deadline for receipt of all such claims against [name of entity in receivership.]

III. STATUS OF RECEIVERSHIP ASSETS

Under this Court's supervision, the Receiver and its agents are marshalling [name of entity in receivership]'s assets, and will liquidate, close out, or recommend the abandonment of collection efforts with respect to some assets and account debts. The status of these assets and the recommendations with respect to some of them are set forth below.

A. Assets at Time of Receiver's Appointment

[List and describe, including, if appropriate, a valuation or estimate. But be careful with regard to any valuation or estimate because it may be used against the receiver by adverse parties when the receiver proposes to sell the asset for less than its estimated value.]

B. Assets Fully Liquidated During this Reporting Period

[List and describe, including amounts realized.]

C. Assets for Which Write-off is Recommended

[List and describe reason for recommendation.]

IV. LITIGATION

[List and describe status].

V. RECEIPTS AND DISBURSEMENTS

Schedule A, annexed hereto, sets forth receipts and disbursements for the period from the inception of the receivership through [date].

Date:

Respectfully submitted,
[Name of entity in receivership]

By: ______________________________
[Name of receiver]

Statement of Cash Receipts and Disbursements for the Period from [date] to [date]

	CURRENT PERIOD From [date]	CUMULATIVE PERIOD From [date]
CASH IN BANK BEGINNING OF PERIOD	$	$
RECEIPTS		
[List receipts]	[amount]	[amount]
Total Receipts		
DISBURSEMENTS		
[List all disbursements]	[amount]	[amount]
Total Disbursements		
CASH IN BANK END OF PERIOD		

Schedule A

§ 7.36 Order Approving and Confirming the First Receiver's Report

[CAPTION]

[Title]

Upon the motion of [name of receiver], as Receiver for [name of entity in receivership], and the First Receiver's Report for the Period from [date] through [date], filed therewith, and this Court being duly advised as to the merits,

HEREBY ORDERS THAT the First Receiver's Report is approved and confirmed, and hereby authorizes the Receiver to charge-off and abandon pursuit of the claims the Receiver has determined are uncollectible, as set forth in the First Receiver's Report, and continue to pursue those claims for which there is likelihood of recovery.

§ 7.37 Motion for Order to Show Cause and Turnover Order

[CAPTION]

[Title]

This motion is filed by [name of receiver], Receiver for [name of entity in receivership], by undersigned counsel for the Receiver, to request the issuance by the Court of an Order to Show Cause to [name of entity in possession of property sought by the Receiver], ordering [name of entity in possession of property sought by the Receiver] to Show Cause why it should not turn over to said Receiver, possession of all [describe property sought, such as certificates of title on all trucks, trailers and other vehicles], now held by [entity in possession of property sought by the receiver] [under its security agreement with (name of entity in receivership), and why its security agreements with {name of entity in receivership} should not be voided by the Court.][283]

In support of this motion, a Memorandum of Points and Authorities, the Affidavit of [name], a proposed Order to Show Cause, and a Proposed Turnover Order are attached.[284]

---

283 The bracketed language is illustrative of the description of property and third party's claim to possession which is to be voided by the Court.

284 Although omitted here, a memorandum of law and an affidavit should accompany this motion detailing both the factual and legal bases for the Receiver's claim to possession of the property in question. *See e.g.* Haile v. Henderson Nat. Bank, 657 F.2d at 821.

§ 7.38 Order to Show Cause Seeking Turnover Order

[CAPTION]

ORDER TO SHOW CAUSE

Having considered the Receiver's motion to have [name of entity in possession of property sought by the Receiver] turn over all [describe property which is the subject of the turnover order and any other relief requested such as the voiding of the third party's security interest] for good cause shown,

It is on this _________ day of __________, 199__

ORDERED that [name of entity in possession of property sought by the receiver], show cause before this Court on the ________ day of ___________, 199__, at [time] in Courtroom number _______, why it should not turn over all [describe property which is the subject of the turnover order], [and further why it should not have this Court void the security agreements it holds from {name of entity in receivership}].

It is further,

ORDERED that the Clerk of Court shall send a copy of this Order to all counsel of record for the plaintiff, defendant(s), and [name of entity in possession of property sought by the Receiver} within _____ days hereof.

____
United States District Judge

F.2d at 821.

§ 7.39 Turnover Order

[CAPTION]

ORDER

Having considered the Receiver's motion to have [name of third party in possession of property sought by the Receiver] turn over [describe property in dispute and any other relief sought such as the voiding of security agreements or liens on the property], as well as the response of [name of third party in possession of property sought by the Receiver] to the Order to Show Cause entered by this Court on [date];

IT IS HEREBY ORDERED that [name of entity in possession of property sought by the Receiver] turn over said property [listed on the schedule attached hereto as Exhibit "A"] [immediately/or by (date)] to the Receiver appointed in this Cause at [location property is to be delivered].

It is further,

ORDERED that [state any further relief that is to be granted].

____
United States District Judge

§ 7.40 Motion for Court Approval of Borrowing by the Receiver and Issuance of a Receiver's Certificate

[CAPTION]

[Title of Motion]

[Name of receiver], Receiver for [name of entity in receivership], by undersigned counsel, hereby moves this Court for authority of [name of entity in receivership] to borrow [amount] for [use of proceeds of borrowing, such as to fund business operations].

The Receiver further moves this Court for authority to disburse the [amount of borrowing], or some part of it, for the following purposes:

[Describe or list use of funds.]

WHEREFORE, your Receiver respectfully requests that the Court enter an order authorizing the Receiver to fund the aforementioned transactions by borrowing from [lender], the sum of [amount], to issue a Receiver's Certificate for a period of ____ years[s] bearing interest at the rate of ____ % per annum for this purpose, which will have priority over all other debts and obligations of [name of entity in receivership].

A Memorandum of Points and Authorities, the Affidavit of [name],[285] a proposed Order, and a proposed Receiver's Certificate are attached to this motion.

---

[285] An affidavit, usually by the Receiver, outlining the reasons for the borrowing, including the benefit to accrue to the receivership estate, and the use of proceeds should accompany the motion, as well as a memorandum of points and authorities.

§ 7.41 Order Approving Borrowing by the Receiver and the Issuance of a Receiver's Certificate

[CAPTION]

[ORDER]

THIS CAUSE COMING ON TO BE HEARD on the motion of the [name of receiver], Receiver for [name of entity in receivership], due notice having been given to all interested parties,[286] and the Court being duly advised as to the merits,

IT IS ORDERED that the Receiver be and hereby is authorized to borrow [amount] from [name of lender] to fund [purpose of borrowing, such as the operational expenses of the receivership] through the issuance of a Receiver's Certificate of Indebtedness for said amount, for a period of ___, with interest at ___% per annum. Said certificate of indebtedness shall have priority over all debts, obligations and claims of stockholders of [name of entity in receivership].

IT IS FURTHER ORDERED that the Receiver is authorized to pay [list use of funds, such as current operating costs of the receivership].

____
UNITED STATES DISTRICT COURT JUDGE

§ 7.42 Receiver's Certificate of Indebtedness

[CAPTION]

Receiver's Certificate of Indebtedness

On or before ____ months after the date of this Certificate, the undersigned, Receiver for [name of entity in receivership], appointed in the above-captioned proceedings, and in no other capacity, promises to pay to the order of [name of lender], the sum of [amount] with interest thereon at the rate of ____ percent per annum.

This Certificate of Indebtedness is issued pursuant to an Order of this Court entered in the above-captioned proceeding on [date]. Pursuant to said Order,

---

286 Notice of the receiver's request to borrow funds should be given to all creditors that will be affected by the borrowing and to the representative of the shareholders.

this Certificate is given priority in payment over all other debts and obligations[287] of [name of entity in receivership], whether presently existing or hereinafter incurred, including without any limitation any claims of stockholders of [name of entity in receivership].

This Certificate of Indebtedness is executed by the undersigned solely as Receiver in the above-captioned proceedings.

IN WITNESS WHEREOF, the undersigned Receiver has caused this document to be executed this _____ day of _____, 199__.

____
Receiver for [name of entity in receivership]

§ 7.43 Receiver's Motion for Leave to Proceed with Private Sale of Real Property

[CAPTION]

[Title of Motion]

[Name of receiver], Receiver for [name of entity in receivership], by undersigned counsel, hereby moves this Court for leave to proceed with a private sale of real property pursuant to 28 U.S.C. 2001(b), including the appointment of three appraisers, publication of notice of the sale, and the scheduling of a confirmation hearing.

In support of this motion, the Receiver files herewith the Affidavit of [name], a Memorandum of Points and Authorities, and a proposed Order.[288]

---

287 The extent of priority as provided in the Court Order authorizing the Receiver's Certificate will vary with the circumstances of each case and the purpose for which the money will be used. Thus, if the secured creditors have benefited by having the property subject to their lien preserved or improved, the Receiver's Certificate will be given priority over their secured claims. *See e.g.* Gaskill v. Gordon, 831 F.Supp. 631.

288 The affidavit has been omitted from these forms because it is so fact specific, but it should, at a minimum, give the description of the property to be sold, the reason why a private sale is necessary, the terms of sale, and the names and qualifications of the three persons or groups of persons who will be making an evaluation of the property.

§ 7.44 Memorandum of Points and Authorities in Support of Motion for Leave to Proceed with the Private Sale of Real Property

[CAPTION]

[Title of Motion]

I

Preliminary Statement

On [date], [name of receiver] was appointed receiver of [name of entity in receivership] by Order of this Court for the purpose of holding and managing the assets of [name of entity in receivership] in order to prevent fraud and waste and to liquidate said assets. Among the assets to be liquidated is real property located at [street address]. The receiver proposes to sell said real property by private sale in compliance with the requirements of 28 U.S.C. 2001(b), which governs the sale of real property by receivers. Section 2001(b) requires that before confirmation of such sale, that the Court appoint three disinterested persons to appraise such property; that the sale price be at least two thirds (2/3) of the appraised value; and that the terms of the sale be published in a publication of general circulation at least ten days before confirmation. The private sale may not be confirmed unless, after publication of the aforesaid notice, there are no bona fide offers of at least 10 percent more than the price offered by the offeror of the private sale.

II

Terms of Sale

The property consists of [describe property such as office building]. The Receiver has received a [cash] offer of [amount] for the property. The legal description of the property, and the terms and conditions of the sale, are set forth in the [contract for sale] attached as Exhibit ___ to the Affidavit of [name].

The Receiver has determined that the sale of the property upon the terms and conditions set forth in the aforesaid contract for sale is in the best interest of the receivership estate. The attached Affidavit of [name] sets forth in detail the reasons why such private sale is in the best interest of the receivership estate. Briefly stated, these reasons are [state reasons].

III

Appointment of Appraisers

Pursuant to 28 U.S.C. 2001(b), the Court must appoint three disinterested persons to appraise the real property in question for the purpose of insuring that the private sale price is at least two thirds of the appraised value. If these appraisals differ in value, the average value of the three appraisals is the appraised value. See *United States v. Garcia,* 474 F.2d 1202, 1204 (5th Cir. 1973). As set forth in the Affidavit of [name], the Receiver has selected three highly qualified individuals to appraise the real property. [Name and describe briefly the qualifications of the three persons who will appraise the real property in question].

IV

Notice of Sale

In compliance with the requirements of Section 2001(b), the Receiver proposes to publish notice of the sale and confirmation hearing, substantially in the form annexed to the Affidavit of [name] filed with this memorandum, for ten consecutive days prior to the confirmation hearing, in [name and location of publication]. Actual notice of the confirmation hearing will be sent to the purchaser by certified mail.

V

Conclusion

Based on the foregoing reasons, the Receiver hereby requests this Court to grant its motion by approving the proposed Order submitted herewith:

(1) appointing [name of three appraisers] as appraisers pursuant to 28 U.S.C. Section 2001(b);

(2) approving publication of the notice of the sale in the form attached as Exhibit ___ to the Affidavit of [name] for ten consecutive days prior to the confirmation hearing in [name of publication]; and

(3) scheduling a confirmation hearing for the purchase of the real property located at [street address].

§ 7.45 Notice to Confirm Private Sale of Real Property by Receiver[289]

Pursuant to 28 U.S.C. Section 2001, [name of receiver], Receiver for [name of entity in receivership], hereby gives notice of a hearing on [date] at [time] before the United States District Court for the District of ________, [address, including location of courtroom], to confirm the sale of real property located at [address], for a contract price of [amount]. The terms and conditions of the contract of sale are available for review at the Clerk's Office, United States District Court (at the above address), or by contacting [name of the receiver], Receiver for [name of entity in receivership] at [address and phone number].

Interested parties may submit bids, before confirmation, of at least [amount] (10% in excess of the current contract price), pursuant to 28 U.S.C. 2001(b). Written bids must be received by the Receiver at the aforesaid address by [time] prior to [date].

TERMS OF SALE: [ALL CASH]. A deposit of ten percent (10%) of the sales price is required at the time the bid is submitted, which if the high bid will be nonrefundable; the balance must be paid at closing. Failure to remit full payment will allow the Receiver to cancel the sale, retain the deposit and otherwise dispose of the property, at the risk and expense of the defaulting purchaser. The deposit and balance must be in the form of cash or a certified check. All terms and conditions that are described in the contract of sale on file with the Receiver at the aforesaid address, and the Clerk's Office, United States District Court for the District of ________ apply to any sale of this property.

§ 7.46 Order Approving Leave to Proceed with Private Sale of Real Property

[CAPTION]

[Order]

This cause coming on to be heard on the motion of [name of receiver], Receiver for [name of entity in receivership], due notice having been given to all interested parties, and the court being duly advised as to the merits. IT IS HEREBY ORDERED THAT,

1. The Receiver is hereby authorized to sell the real property of [name of entity in receivership] located at [address] in accordance with the requirements of 28 U.S.C. 2001(b).

---

289 This notice should be attached to the affidavit as an exhibit.

2. The property to be sold consists of [describe property, such as "a two-story office building of concrete construction comprising ____ square feet"], more fully described in a contract of sale, attached as Exhibit _____ to the Affidavit of [name].

3. [Names of three persons or entities appointed to appraise property] are hereby [approved or][290] appointed to appraise the aforesaid property pursuant to 28 U.S.C. 2001(b). Said appraisals shall be completed by [date].

4. The Receiver shall publish notice of the offer received from [name of purchaser making offer], in the form attached as Exhibit ____ to the Affidavit of [name], for ten consecutive days prior to the confirmation hearing in [name and location of the publication].

5. The confirmation hearing is scheduled on [date] at [time] in Courtroom [identify].[291]

6. If the sale price received from [name of purchaser making offer] is at least two-thirds (2/3) of the appraised value,[292] and no bona fide offer received after publication of the aforesaid notice in [name of publication] exceeds this offer, the offer received from [name of purchaser making offer] as embodied in the contract of sale attached to the Affidavit of [name] as Exhibit ____ shall be confirmed.

§ 7.47 Motion Seeking an Order Establishing the Bar Date for Claims and Approving the Form and Manner of Notice to Claimants of the Claims Bar Date

[CAPTION]

[TITLE OF MOTION]

The [name of receiver], as Receiver for [name of entity in receivership], hereby moves this Court for an Order: (1) establishing a Bar Date, by which any claims against [name of entity in receivership] or the receivership estate must be filed, in writing, with the Receiver, or be forever barred and discharged and

290 Sometimes the Receiver may have available one or more recent appraisals of the property and these may be used and/or supplemented in order to save time and expense. If this is the case, the court should be asked to approve use of these appraisals or merely to supplement them.

291 The confirmation hearing must be scheduled a sufficient time after completion of the appraisals, and at least ten days after first publication of the notice.

292 If the three appraisals vary in amount, they will be averaged to determine the appraised value. United States v. Garcia, 474 F.2d at 1204.

(2) approving the form and manner of the notice to be given to claimants of a claims Bar Date; and A Memorandum of Points and Authorities and the Affidavit[293] of [name] and accompanying Exhibits in support of this Motion are attached.

§ 7.48 Memorandum of Points and Authorities in Support of Order Establishing a Claims Bar Date and Approving the Form and Manner of Notice to Claimants

[CAPTION]

[TITLE OF MEMORANDUM]

This matter is before the Court upon the Motion of [name of receiver], Receiver for [name of entity in receivership], for an Order approving procedures for notifying all persons and entities having claims against the receivership estate and setting a deadline for receipt of all such claims.

The Receiver asks this Court to approve the following manner of giving notice to potential creditors and claimants of [name of entity in receivership]:

(1) Within thirty (30) days of entry of an Order in connection with this Motion, the Receiver will send notice, in the form of Exhibit "A" attached to the proposed Order which is annexed, via first-class mail to each of the persons or entities, believed by the Receiver and its counsel to be an actual or potential claimant of [name of entity in receivership] whether as creditor, agent, shareholder, director, officer, employee, partner, participant investor or lender, including any other persons or entities who have, during the term of the Receivership, asserted a claim of whatever kind or nature against the Receivership; and

(2) Notice, substantially in the form of Exhibit "A," attached to the proposed Order, which is annexed, will be published once each calendar week for four weeks, in the [name of publication], with the first notice appearing within thirty (30) days of entry of the Order in connection with this Motion.

In addition, the Receiver asks the Court to set a Bar Date for claims thirty (30) days from the last date of notice by publication, and to enjoin all persons or entities, other than the Receiver, from asserting, pursuing or prosecuting any

293 An affidavit is not required, but may be needed or helpful in setting forth the relevant history of the receivership and any discussion of the anticipated number and nature of outstanding claims. It is omitted here.

claims not submitted to the Receiver, in the required form, on or before that date. Thus, the Receiver asks that any claims not submitted to the Receiver at the address appearing in the proposed Order, which is annexed, in writing on or before the Bar Date for claims, be thereafter permanently barred and discharged.

The reasons for this Motion concerning the recommended form, manner, and timing of notice to claimants and the proposed Bar Date for claims are as follows. By Order dated ___________, this Court appointed [name of receiver] as Receiver for [name of entity in receivership]. Pursuant to Rule 66 of the Federal Rules of Civil Procedure and the Court's general equity powers, this Court is authorized to prescribe the form and manner of notice to claimants and to establish a Bar Date for claims in order to begin the process of winding up this receivership. *S.E.C. v. Hardy,* 803 F.2d 10334 (9th Cir. 1986).

After reviewing the files and records of [name of entity in receivership] over the course of this receivership, which has now lasted for [duration of receivership], the Receiver is reasonably confident that it has identified many of the potential claimants who may have claims against [name of entity in receivership] or the receivership estate. It is to those persons or entities that Notice, substantially in the form of Exhibit "A," attached to the proposed Order which is annexed, will be mailed.

As an additional safeguard, and in an effort to provide notice to potential claimants now unknown to the Receiver, the receiver also proposes publishing notice, in the form of Exhibit "A" attached to the proposed Order which is annexed. The Receiver proposes to publish this notice once each week for four calendar weeks in the [name of publication]. The Receiver believes that this publication is most likely to reach and to be read by persons or entities who might assert claims against [name of entity in receivership] or the receivership estate.

If the Court approves these procedures and enters the proposed Order, the proposed Bar Date for claims will afford all potential claimants at least thirty (30) days from the time notice is given during which to submit their claims to the Receiver.

The receiver proposes to inform the Court of any and all claims it has received before that date. The receiver also proposes to review all claims it receives, negotiate with the claimants, and attempt to settle all claims, subject to the Court's approval. In the event that a claimant and the Receiver are unable to resolve a dispute over a claim, the Receiver proposes to move for summary disposition of the dispute. Such procedures will afford any claimants with a fair process for resolving their claims, while enabling the Receiver to wind up their receivership proceeding as quickly as possible.

The imposition of a Bar Date for claims is necessary so that the Receiver can recommend, subject to the Court's approval, a plan to distribute [name of entity in receivership]'s assets to all claimants who have rendered timely claims without fear that other claimants might later appear to assert claims against [name of entity in receivership] or the receivership estate. The Receiver is, therefore, asking this Court to impose a permanent injunction as part of the Bar Date for claims in order to prevent persons or entities from asserting tardy claims.

For the reasons set forth above, the Receiver asks that its Motion be granted and that the proposed Order which is attached, be entered establishing an absolute Bar Date for claims and setting forth procedures for notifying claimants against the receivership estate.

§ 7.49 Order Establishing a Bar Date and Approving the Form and Manner of Notice to Claimants

[CAPTION]

[ORDER]

Upon full consideration of the Receiver's Motion for an Order Establishing a Bar Date For Claims and Approving the Form and Manner of Notice to Claimants filed by [name of receiver] ("Receiver,") Receiver for [name of entity in receivership], and this Court being duly advised as to the merits,

IT IS HEREBY ORDERED THAT:

1. The Receiver's Motion for an Order Establishing a Bar Date For Claims and Approving the Form and Manner of Notice to Claimants is GRANTED;

2. Within thirty (30) days of entry of this Order, the Receiver shall send notice, in the form set forth as Exhibit "A" hereto, via first class mail, to those persons or entities, which the Receiver has reason to believe are or have been creditors, agents, shareholders, directors, officers, employees, partners, participant investors or lenders with [name of entity in receivership], and to persons or entities who have, during the term of the receivership, asserted a claim (of whatever kind or merit) against [name of entity in receivership], the receivership estate, or assets or funds in the possession of the Receiver;

3. The Receiver shall also publish notice, substantially in the form set forth in Exhibit "A" hereto, once each week for four weeks in the [name of publication], with the first notice appearing within thirty (30) days of the date of entry of this Order;

4. This Court hereby finds that the notice provided in the form and manner described in Paragraphs 2 and 3 above is reasonable notice, under the circumstances, to persons or entities who may have claims against [name of entity in

receivership], the receivership estate, or assets or funds in the possession of the Receiver;

5. All persons or entities having claims against [name of entity in receivership], the receivership estate, or assets or funds in the possession of the Receiver shall file all such claims in writing and in the form prescribed in paragraph 6 of this Order, with the Receiver, c/o [receiver's name and mailing address], within thirty (30) days of the last day of notice by publication, which date will be stated in the mailed and published notices;

6. In setting forth a claim against [name of entity in receivership], the receivership estate or assets or funds in the possession of the Receiver, all persons and entities shall state in writing: (1) the full name and address and telephone number of the claimant; (2) the amount of the claim; (3) the specific grounds for each claim; and (4) the date on which the obligation was allegedly incurred by [name of entity in receivership] or the receivership estate, and provide at the time of filing such written claims any documents or other materials which the claimant believes supports the claim or might assist the Receiver to evaluate the claim;

7. In the event that the Receiver recommends denial of any claims, it is hereby authorized and directed to move for summary disposition of said claim(s) and to furnish a copy of the moving papers to the claimant(s); in such case the claimant may respond within 30 days, and the Court will resolve said claim(s) expeditiously through a summary procedure that the Court will determine at that time; and

8. To permit the final winding-up of this receivership proceeding, and to give effect to the Bar Date for claims established in Paragraph 5 above by which claims must be filed or forever barred, any persons or entities, which fail to file a claim against [name of entity in receivership], the receivership estate, or assets or funds in the possession of the Receiver, in the form and by the time and date required by this Order shall be forever barred and permanently enjoined from asserting, pursuing or prosecuting any such claims, of any kind or nature, whether now known or unknown, against [name of entity in receivership], its Receiver, their successors or assigns, or against assets or funds in the possession of the Receiver.

IT IS SO ORDERED.

DATED:

____

UNITED STATES DISTRICT JUDGE

NOTICE TO ALL CREDITORS OR CLAIMANTS
OF [NAME OF ENTITY IN RECEIVERSHIP]

By Order of the United States District Court for the ________ District of __________, dated ____________, persons or entities who wish to assert a claim against [name of entity in receivership] must do so by filing a written claim with the Receiver on or before [date thirty (30) days after last date of notice by publication]. All previously submitted claims against [name of entity in receivership] or its Receiver must be resubmitted in accordance with this Notice.

[name of entity in receivership] has been in receivership since ______________, by Order of the Court identified above, entered in Civil Action No. _______________. [name of receiver] is the court-appointed Receiver.

Present your claims against [name of entity in receivership], the receivership estate, or assets or funds in the hands of the Receiver, in writing, to:

[name and address of receiver]

Claims must be received no later than 5:00 p.m. [.S.T., [date] thirty (30) days after last date of notice by publication].

Your claim must state; (1) the full name, address and telephone number of the claimant; (2) the amount of the claim; (3) the specific grounds for each claim; and (4) the date on which the obligation was allegedly incurred by [name of entity in receivership] or the Receiver. Attach all other documents or materials which support the claim, or which the Receiver might require in evaluating the claim. If you fail to provide any of the specified information, your claim will be deemed incomplete and untimely.

Failure to present a complete and timely claim to the Receiver on or before [date] will result in your claim being forever barred, and you will not thereafter be able to make a claim against [name of entity in receivership], the receivership estate, or any other assets or funds in the possession of the Receiver.

____

EXHIBIT "A"

§ 7.50 Receiver's Motion for an Order Approving the Disposition of Claims, Distribution of Proceeds from the Liquidation of the Receivership Estate, and the Termination of the Receivership

[CAPTION]

[Title]

[Name of receiver], as Receiver for [name of entity in receivership], hereby moves this Court for an Order approving the disposition of claims, the proposed distribution of the proceeds from the liquidation of the assets of the receivership estate, and the termination of the receivership of [name of entity in receivership].

A Receiver's Report and a proposed Order are attached.

§ 7.51 Receiver's Report Recommending the Allowance and Denial of Claims Filed in the Receivership, Distribution of the Receivership Estate in the Order of Priority, and the Termination of the Receivership

[CAPTION]

[Title]

[Name of receiver], Receiver for [name of entity in receivership], files this report recommending the confirmation and denial of claims filed in the receivership, the distribution of the receivership estate, and the termination of the receivership.

Pursuant to previous order of this Court dated [date], the Receiver sent notice to those persons or entities which the Receiver had reason to believe were creditors or claimants of [name of the entity in receivership].

In addition, the Receiver published notice once each week for four weeks in [publication] as directed by this Court. All persons or entities having claims against [name of entity in receivership] were directed to file such claims with the Receiver, in writing, by [time], [date].

The Receiver received [number] claims by the [date] bar date [and no claims have been received subsequent to the bar date].

The Receiver hereby recommends disposition of these claims as follows:

I. Claims

A. Allowed Claims

[List and describe each claim and the reason for allowance.]

B. Disallowed Claims

[List and describe each claim and the reason for disallowance.]

II. Assets to be Distributed

[List and describe each asset and manner of distribution.]

III. Expenses to be Paid

[List and describe nature and amount of expense.]

IV. Priority of Distribution

[List in order of priority and amount of each claim to be paid, such as (1) taxes; (2) expenses of administration.]

V Dissolution of Entity

[Describe steps to be taken to dissolve entity in receivership or to wind up receivership estate.]

§ 7.52 Order Approving the Disposition of Claims, the Distribution of the Proceeds from the Liquidation of the Receivership Estate, and the Termination of the Receivership

[CAPTION]

[ORDER]

The Receiver, having submitted a Motion for an Order Approving the Disposition of Claims, the Distribution of Assets, and the Termination of the Receivership, and a Report recommending that certain claims be allowed and paid, others denied, the distribution of the proceeds from the liquidation of the receivership estate,and the receivership terminated, notice having been given to all interested parties, and this court being duly advised as to the merits;

IT IS ORDERED as follows:

1. The following claims are allowed in the amounts set forth below and paid in the following order of priority in the amounts shown:

a. [identify and describe each claim briefly in the order of priority, and state the amount allowed and paid.]

2. The following claims are disallowed:

a. [identify and describe each claim briefly and the reason for denial, such as the failure of the claimant to file a claim by the claims bar date.]

3. All claims not specifically granted herein are hereby denied; and all persons who did not file a claim by the claims bar date, are hereby permanently enjoined from asserting, pursuing, or prosecuting any such claims, whether now known or unknown, against [name of entity in receivership], the Receiver, the Receiver's agents, representatives or employees, their successors or assigns, or the receivership assets.

4. [Name of entity in receivership] is hereby ordered dissolved and the receivership of [name of entity in receivership] terminated upon dissolution of [name of entity in receivership].

§ 7.53 Form of Letter of Engagement of Attorney by the Receiver

[date]
[address]

Re: [Caption of Litigation Involving Receivership]

Dear ______:

This letter embodies the complete terms of engagement whereby the law firm of [name] has been retained by [name of receiver] as Receiver of [name of entity in receivership] to undertake the following legal matters involving the receivership [insert purpose for which firm has been retained, such as the preparation of an opinion of counsel or the initiation of litigation against a debtor, officer, or director]. The firm will represent the Receiver in these legal matters as authorized by an Order of the receivership court dated _________.

It is agreed that the legal services will be performed by [name of lead attorney] at the rate of [amount] per hour. [Services may also be performed by other attorneys, paralegals, and secretaries of the firm at rates per hour set forth below: list each category of counsel, paralegal, and secretary and their hourly rate as well as charges for copying, word processing and travel].

Monthly statements should include a description of the specific activities undertaken in the matter itemizing all charges, legal and administrative, by time spent. Statements for services should be submitted to the receiver at [address].

All legal fees and expenses will be paid only out of the [name of entity in receivership]'s receivership estate, subject to the review and approval of the receivership court. All legal costs and expenses are the sole responsibility of the receivership estate of [name of entity in receivership] and not of the receiver or his agents personally.

It is expected that counsel will consult with [the receiver] prior to undertaking any significant action, e.g., settlement proposals, motions for summary judgment, etc. Counsel is not authorized to act for the Receiver in these matters without obtaining prior approval of the Receiver based upon counsel's estimate of its cost. In some instances, actions also may require prior approval of the receivership court.

Sincerely,

[name]

Receiver for [name of entity in receivership]

Agreed and Approved:

____

[name of counsel]
for [name of law firm]

APPENDIX A

COMPARISON CHART ON DRIVER'S LICENSE INFORMATION

Alabama

—Motor vehicle reports (MVRs) of drivers licensed in Alabama are available from Alabama Department of Public Safety Headquarters, 500 Dexter Avenue, Montgomery. There is a charge of $5.75 for each report. Personal checks are not accepted. MVRs may also be requested by writing Alabama Department of Public Safety, Driver License Division, Administrative Unit, P.O. Box 1471, Montgomery, Alabama 36102-1471, or by calling the Accident Records Unit (205) 242-4241. In requesting the report a driver's license number or social security number in addition to the report, will be of assistance in retrieving the report.

Arkansas

—Driver's residence addresses are considered confidential.

California

—Many records are now open to public inspection under Government Code § 6253. However, under Government Code § 6254 residence address is now considered confidential, unless an attorney is trying to obtain the information for a particular case directly involving a motor vehicle or motorcycle. Service of process also authorizes release of residence addresses. The address is State of California, Department of Motor Vehicles, P.O. Box 942890, Sacramento, CA 94290-0001.

Colorado

—Driver's records and current address are searched by: (a) Full name and date of birth; (b) Colorado driver license or identification card number;

(c) Full name and address. The charge is $2.00 for each item searched, and $2.50 for each item searched and certified. Mail requests to: State of Colorado, Department of Revenue, Traffic Records Section, 140 W 6th Avenue, Room 103, Denver, CO 80204–5195.

Connecticut

—Driver's records and current address are public information. However, to obtain the information, you have to have the name and date of birth of the driver for license number and address information to be identified. Mail request forms to the State of Connecticut, Department of Motor Vehicles, Copy Record Unit, 60 State Street, Wethersfield, CT 06109–1896.

Delaware

—All vehicle registration, license and driver's performance records for the past three years are public records and available to the public, for a fee of $4.00 each. Title 21, Del. Laws, Section 305(a) and (e). The address is: State of Delaware, Department of Public Safety, Division of Motor Vehicles, P.O. Box 698, Dover, Delaware 19903.

Florida

—Driver's records, including a current address, are available to the public. If you furnish the name and date of birth of the driver, or the driver's license number, along with a $3.00 fee made payable to the Division of Driver Licenses, you can obtain the driver's address and driving record. Mail the request to: State of Florida, Department of Highway Safety & Motor Vehicles, Division of Driver Licenses, Neil Kirkman Building, Tallahassee, Florida 32399–0575.

Maryland

—Driver's records, including a current address, are available to the public for a $2.00 fee made payable to the Motor Vehicle Administration. Mail the request to: State of Maryland, Motor Vehicle Administration, 6601 Ritchie Highway, N.E., Glen Burnie, MD 21062.

Mississippi

—A driver's current address check is available for the fee of $5.00. The request should include the name, driver's license number, if available, the correct fee and a self-addressed, stamped envelope. Mail the request to: State of Mississippi, Department of Public Safety, Driver Records, Post Office Box 958, Jackson, Mississippi 39205–0958.

Oregon

—Driver's license information, including a current address, is available to the public for $1.50. Mail the request to: State of Oregon, Department of Transportation, Motor Vehicles Division, 1905 Lana Ave., N.E., Salem, OR 97314–1624.

Utah

—Driver's license information, including a current address, is available to the public for $3.00. The request should include the full name of the licensee, including a middle initial, a date of birth, and a Utah license number, if available. On a driver's recent move to the State of Utah, allow about a month before requesting new driver's license information. Mail the request to: State of Utah, Department of Public Safety, Driver License Division, Attn: MVR Section, 4501 South 2700 West—3rd Floor, P.O. Box 30560, Salt Lake City, UT 84130–0560.

INDEX